CHEROKEE DESCENDANTS

WEST

AN INDEX TO THE
GUION MILLER APPLICATIONS

VOLUME II (A-M)

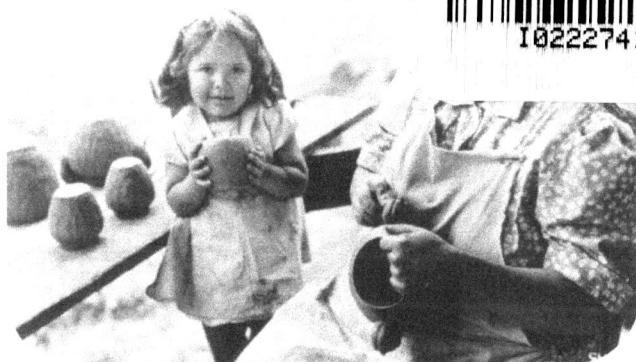

Cherokee Potter Maude French Welch and her
granddaughter "Koodaloo" Joyce Welch Tranter

TRANSCRIBED BY

JEFF BOWEN

NATIVE STUDY
Gallipolis, Ohio
USA

Originally published:
Baltimore, Maryland
2011

Reprinted by:

Native Study LLC
Gallipolis, OH
www.nativestudy.com

Library of Congress Control Number: 2020915858

ISBN: 978-1-64968-036-5

Made in the United States of America.

Other Books and Series by Jeff Bowen

1901-1907 Native American Census Seneca, Eastern Shawnee, Miami, Modoc, Ottawa, Peoria, Quapaw, and Wyandotte Indians (Under Seneca School, Indian Territory)

1932 Census of The Standing Rock Sioux Reservation with Births And Deaths 1924-1932

Census of The Blackfeet, Montana, 1897- 1901 Expanded Edition

Eastern Cherokee by Blood, 1906-1910, Volumes I thru XIII

Choctaw of Mississippi Indian Census 1929-1932 with Births and Deaths 1924-1931   Volume I

Choctaw of Mississippi Indian Census 1933, 1934 & 1937, Supplemental Rolls to 1934 & 1935 with Births and Deaths 1932-1938, and Marriages 1936-1938 Volume II

Eastern Cherokee Census Cherokee, North Carolina 1930-1939 Census 1930-1931 with Births And Deaths 1924-1931 Taken By Agent L. W. Page Volume I

Eastern Cherokee Census Cherokee, North Carolina 1930-1939 Census 1932-1933 with Births And Deaths 1930-1932 Taken By Agent R. L. Spalsbury   Volume II

Eastern Cherokee Census Cherokee, North Carolina 1930-1939 Census 1934-1937 with Births and Deaths 1925-1938 and Marriages 1936 & 1938 Taken by Agents R. L. Spalsbury And Harold W. Foght Volume III

Seminole of Florida Indian Census, 1930-1940 with Birth and Death Records, 1930-1938

Texas Cherokees 1820-1839 A Document For Litigation 1921

Choctaw By Blood Enrollment Cards 1898-1914 Volumes I thru XVII

Starr Roll 1894 (Cherokee Payment Rolls) Districts: Canadian, Cooweescoowee, and Delaware Volume One

Starr Roll 1894 (Cherokee Payment Rolls) Districts: Flint, Going Snake, and Illinois   Volume Two

Starr Roll 1894 (Cherokee Payment Rolls) Districts: Saline, Sequoyah, and Tahlequah; Including Orphan Roll Volume Three

Other Books and Series by Jeff Bowen

Cherokee Intruder Cases Dockets of Hearings 1901-1909 Volumes I & II

Indian Wills, 1911-1921 Records of the Bureau of Indian Affairs
Books One thru Seven;

Native American Wills & Probate Records 1911-1921

Turtle Mountain Reservation Chippewa Indians 1932 Census with Births & Deaths, 1924-1932

Chickasaw By Blood Enrollment Cards 1898-1914 Volume I thru V

Cherokee Descendants East An Index to the Guion Miller Applications Volume I

Visit our website at **www.nativestudy.com** to learn more about these
and other books and series by Jeff Bowen

This book is dedicated to Joyce Welch Tranter (Koo da loo). A very special and dear true-blood Cherokee without whose inspiration and friendship this work would not be so meaningful.

Love you and God bless.

INTRODUCTION

On the 348 rolls of this microfilm publication are reproduced the applications submitted for shares of the money that was appropriated for the Eastern Cherokee Indians by the Congress on June 30, 1906. The Eastern Cherokee applications, August 29, 1906 - May 26, 1909, are part of the Guion Miller Enrollment Records that are among the records of the U.S. Court of Claims. This publication also includes a general index to Eastern Cherokee applications (two vols.).

History

Before the U.S. Court of Claims was established in 1855 there was no procedure by which claims arising against the U.S. Government could be enforced by suit. Consideration of claims was provided for when the Treasury Department was established in 1789; later acts of the Congress authorized the Department to settle all claims by or against the Government. If a claim was rejected by the Treasury Department, the claimant's only course of action was to appeal directly to the Congress. Petitions to that body for relief had become so numerous by the middle of the 19th century that the Congress was beginning to find it impossible to make the proper and necessary investigations for actions on the claims.

The U.S. Court of Claims was established by an act of February 24, 1855, to hear claims against the United States including those referred to the court by the Congress, based on any law of the Congress, any regulation of an executive department, or any contract with the Government, whether explicit or implied. Under this act the court served only as a fact finding agency, and its conclusions were submitted to the Congress for approval and for the granting of awards. In 1863 the Congress enlarged the court's jurisdiction and gave it authority to render judgments against the Government, with the right of appeal to the Supreme Court. An act of 1925 abolished appeals from the Court of Claims to the Supreme Court and substituted writs of certiorari.

An act approved July 1, 1902 (32 Stat. 726), gave the Court of Claims jurisdiction over any claim arising under treaty stipulations that the Cherokee Tribe, or any band thereof, might have against the United States and over any claims that the United States might have against any Cherokee Tribe or band. Suit for such a claim was to be instituted within 2 years after the act was approved. As a result, three suits were brought before the court concerning grievances arising out of the treaties:

(1) *The Cherokee Nation* v. *The United States*, General-Jurisdiction Case No. 23199; (2) *The Eastern and Emigrant Cherokees* v. *The United States*, General-Jurisdiction Case No. 23212; and (3) *The Eastern Cherokees* v. *The United States*, General-Jurisdiction Case No. 23214.

On May 18, 1905, the court decided in favor of the Eastern Cherokees and instructed the Secretary of the Interior to identify the persons entitled to participate in the distribution of funds for payment of the claims. On June 30, 1906, the Congress appropriated more than $1 million for this purpose. The task of compiling a roll of eligible persons was begun by Guion Miller, special agent of the Interior Department. In a decree of April 29, 1908, the court (1) vacated that part of its earlier decision that had given the Secretary of the Interior responsibility for determing[sic] the eligbility[sic] of claimants and (2) appointed Miller as a special commissioner of the Court of Claims.

The same decree also provided that the fund was to be distributed to all Eastern and Western Cherokee Indians who were alive on May 28, 1906, who could establish the fact that at the time of the treaties they were members of the Eastern Cherokee Tribe or were descendants of such persons, and that they had not been affiliated with any tribe of Indians other than the Eastern Cherokee or the Cherokee Nation. The decree further provided that claimants should already have applications on file with the Commissioner of Indian Affairs, or should file such applications with the special commissioner of the Court of Claims on or before August 31, 1907. Additionally, applications for minors and persons of unsound mind were to be filed by their parents or persons having their care and custody, and applications for persons who had died after May 28, 1906, were to be filed by their children or legal representatives.

In his report of May 28, 1909, Miller stated that 45,847 separate applications had been filed, representing a total of about 90,000 individual claimants, 30,254 of whom were enrolled as entitled to share in the fund – 3,203 residing east and 27,051 residing west of the Mississippi River. On June 10, 1909, the court confirmed and approved the roll, submitted by Miller in his report, of Eastern Cherokees who were entitled to a share of the fund except "so much as shall be expected [excepted] to on or before August 30, 1909." After the exceptions had been filed and investigated, Miller submitted a supplemental report and roll to the court on January 5, 1910. In this report he stated that about 11,750 exceptions had been made, that the names of 610 persons [238 east and 372 west if the Mississippi] had been added to the roll, and that the names of 44 persons [5 east and 39 west of the Mississippi] had be stricken from the roll because clerical errors in enrollment had been discovered. Thus the final figure on the total number of persons entitled to share in the fund was 30, 820, of which 3,436 persons resided east and 27,384 resided west of the Mississippi River. On March 15, 1910, the court finally decreed that the rolls be approved and that, after certain deductions for expenditures, payments were to be made equally among the Eastern Cherokees who enrolled. The court also authorized the Secretary of the Treasury to issue a warrant in favor of each person.

In certifying the eligibility of the Cherokees, Miller used earlier census lists and rolls that had been made of the Cherokees by Hester, Chapman, Drennen and others between 1835 and 1884. Copies of some of these rolls and the indexes to them are filed with the Miller records [filmed as M685]. Other enrollment records used by Miller are among the classified subject files of the Bureau and are designated as "33931-11-053 Cherokee Nation."

Records

The applications contain sworn evidences of identity and were filed with the Interior Department's Office of Indian Affairs until April 29, 1907 [the last application was No. 22268], after which the applications were filed directly with the court. The application required each claimant to state fully his or her English and Indian names, residence, age, place of birth, name of husband or wife, name of tribe, and names of children. It further required the English and Indian names of the claimant's parents and grandparents, place of their birth, place of their residence in 1851 if they were living at that time, dates of their death, and a statement as to whether any of them had ever before been enrolled as Indians for annuities or other benefits and, if so, with what tribe. Each claimant was also to furnish the names of all brothers and sisters, with their ages and residences, and the names and residences of all uncles and aunts. Applications were required to be made under oath and to be supported by affidavits of two witnesses who were well acquainted with the applicant. With each application is a card showing final action taken and the reasons therefore. Filed with many of the applications are inquiries concerning the status of the cases, requests for further evidence, protests about unfavorable actions, form letters that had been sent by the special commissioner to the applicants as notices of rejection of their applications and returned by the Post Office Department as unclaimed, affidavits and statements of witnesses, powers of attorney, and last wills and testaments. The applications are arranged by the number assigned at the time the application was received. There are some gaps in the application numbers; these are explained on insert sheets at the appropriate places on the film. The index is arranged alphabetically by name [either English or Indian] of claimant.

Many of the files contain a cross-reference card to other applications. This cross-reference card often refers to the EX file, the report on exceptions filed by Miller on January 5, 1910.

Related Records

The records reproduced in this microfilm publication are part of the records in the custody of the National Archives and Records Service [NARS] designated as Records of the U.S. Court of Claims, Record Group [RG] 123. Among related records in this record group are additional records relating to Miller's enrollment of the Eastern Cherokees. These include receipts for Treasury warrants and miscellaneous correspondence, 1906 - 11. The original of these records is in RG 123; a copy is in RG 75.

Some related records in Records of the Bureau of Indian Affairs, RG 75, have been reproduced as NARS Microfilm Publication T496, *Census Roll, 1835, of the Cherokee Indians East of the Mississippi and Index to the Roll.* Also in RG 75 are the classified subject files of the Bureau.

Records Relating to Enrollment of Eastern Cherokees by Guion Miller, 1908-10, M685, contains the general index to Eastern Cherokee applications, 2 volumes; the report submitted by Guion Miller, May 28, 1909, 10 volumes; the roll of Eastern Cherokees, May 28, 1909; the report on exceptions filed, January 5, 1910; the supplemental roll of Eastern Cherokees, January 5, 1910; transcripts of testimony, February, 1908 - March, 1909, 10 volumes; various indexes and rolls of Eastern Cherokee Indians, 1851, 1854, and 1884; and miscellaneous notes and drafts.

Additional records relating to the enrollment of Eastern Cherokee Indians are in Records of the Office of the Secretary of the Interior, Record Group 48.

These records were prepared for filming by Jestine Turner and William D. Grover, who also prepared these introductory remarks.

THE EASTERN CHEROKEES

v.

No. 23,214

THE UNITED STATES

ORDER.

Ordered this 10th day of June, 1909, that the report of Special Commissioner Guion Miller, bearing date the 28th day of May, 1909, together with the exhibits therewith, including the roll of the individual Eastern Cherokees reported by the said Special Commissioner as entitled to participate in the fund arising from Item 2 of the judgment filed in this cause, be received and filed in this cause.

2. It is further ordered that the said Special Commissioner cause the said roll of individual Eastern Cherokees found by him to be entitled to share in said fund, to be printed and distributed.

3. It is further ordered hat the said roll of individual Eastern Cherokees entitled to share in the fund arising from the judgment in this cause, as reported by Special Commissioner Guion Miller on the 28th day of May, 1909, be and the same is hereby approved, ratified and confirmed, except as to so much of the same as shall be specially excepted to on or before the 30th day of August, 1909. All such exceptions shall be forwarded to the Clerk of the Court of Claims, Washington, D.C., and shall be in writing, and shall state fully the grounds upon which such exceptions are based, and shall be supported by an affidavit of a person having knowledge of the facts and shall contain the name, age and post office address of each individual claimed

to have been omitted from said roll, or to have been improperly placed thereon. Said exceptions and affidavits shall be filed in duplicate in each case, but only the originals must be sworn to. In case an exception is filed on behalf of an individual whose name has been omitted from said roll the said exception shall set forth fully the English and Indian name, the ancestor through whom claim is made, who was living in 1835 or 1851, and shall give the age of said ancestor in 1835 or 1851. Such exceptions must further state the number of the claimant's application. All such exceptions shall be set down for hearing on the third Monday in October, 1909.

Sample Application

The following information obtained from Microfilm M1104- Roll # *86* ,
Cherokee (Eastern & Western) Applications of the U.S. Court of Claims.

Application No. *8421*	**Action:** *Reject*
Name: *William L. French* and *X* children.	
Residence: *Trough, SC*	
Reasons: *It does not appear that any ancestor was ever enrolled or that any ancestor was party to the treaties of 1835-6 & 1846. Applicant says his mother was an Old Settler.*	

Commissioner of Indian Affairs,   Washington, D.C.

Sir:

I hereby make application for such share as may be due me of the fund appropriated by the Act of Congress, approved June 30, 1906, in accordance with the Decrees of the Court of Claims of May 18, 1905, and May 28, 1906, in favor of the Eastern Cherokees. The evidence of identity is herewith subjoined.

1. State full name:

    English name: *William L. French*

    Indian name: *"Co-dos-ki"*

2. Residence: *Trough, SC*

3. Town and post office:

4. County: *Swain Co.*   5. State: *NC*

xi

Sample Application

6. Date and place of birth: *near Tahlequah, Ind. Ter. Age 40 yrs*

7. By what right do you claim to share? If you claim through more than one relative living in 1851, set forth each claim separately: *I claim in my own right. I am a full blood Cherokee. My father Frank French, or French Hawk, a full blood and my mother Annie French also a full blood.*

8. Are you married? *yes*

9. Name and age of wife or husband: *Awee French, age 30 years, a full blood Cherokee*

10. Give names of your father and mother, and your mother's name before marriage:

Father - English name: *French Hawk - Frank French*

Indian name: *Col-lun-see   Gar-lun-chi*

Mother - English name: *Annie French*

Indian name: *do*

Maiden name: *Annie Grease*

11. Where were they born?

Father: *North Carolina*

Mother: *Georgia*

Sample Application

12. Where did they reside in 1851, if living at that time

Father: *near Tahlequah, IT*   Mother: *near Tahlequah, IT*

13. Date of death of your father and mother:

Father: *died in 1874*   Mother: *died in 1873*

14. Were they ever enrolled for annuities, land or other benefits? If so, state when and where:

Yes, in Indian Territory in 1878[sic]

15. Name all your brothers and sisters, giving ages, and if not living, the date of death:

1) *George French   age 37   lives at Whittier, NC*

2)

3)

16. State English and Indian names of your grandparents on both father's and mother's side, if possible:

Father's side: *Don't know*

Mother's side: *Don't know*

17. Where were they born? *Don't know*

18. Where did they reside in 1851, if living at that time? *Dead*

Sample Application

19. Give names of all their children, and residence, if living, if not living, give dates of death:

1) _____

2) _____

3) _____

20. Have you ever been enrolled for annuities, land or other benefits? If so, state when and where

Near Tahlequah, Ind. Terr. On Roll in Cherokee Nation in 1883. I am now Secretary of the Council of the Eastern Band of Cherokee Indians.

21. To expedite identification, claimants should given the full English and Indians names, if possible, of their paternal and maternal ancestors back to 1835:

Mother, Annie French, on Old Settler and drew money as an Old Settler. Father, French Hawk, was an Eastern Emigrant Cherokee

REMARKS
(Under this head the applicant may give any additional information that he believes will assist in proving his claim.)

I hereby appoint Belva A. Lockwood, of Washington, D.C. my true and lawful attorney for me, and in my name, place and stead, and agree to allow her a commission of ten (10/0) percent.

_____

Sample Application

I solemnly swear that the foregoing statements made by me re true to the best of my knowledge and belief.

(Signature)   *William L. French*

Subscribed and sworn to before me this *26th* day of   *Dec.*

#8421

Trough, South Carolina
March 24th, 1908

Hon. Guion Miller, Spec. Com.
Washington, D.C.

Sir,

After some delay, received your letter in difference to my application for participation in fund in favor of the Eastern Cherokees, which No. is 8421. Having moved from my former post office to the above named office.

My father's Indian name was Gar-lun-chi. But do not know by what name he was known in English. But best of my recollection, he was called Frank French sometimes or French Hawk. I was quiet small when my parents died. My mother's name is Annie - Eng. Annie Greasy Fat. You will find her name on the Old Settler Roll, as my brother George and myself drew her part of the Old Settler payment. We received pay direct from the Commissioner of Indian Affairs. But I am not able to tell you my grand parents name on either side; neither do I know their births, only that my mother was an Old Settler.

But I have been told that my father was an Emigrant Cherokee. I do not know that I was enrolled in any roll in 1883 - if so, it was not from any fund from the government. I may have been enrolled in the west, made by order of the National Council, of the Cherokee Nation, in the distribution arising from what was known as the lease funds. I was enrolled with the western Cherokees, in their distribution of funds while I was there.

I am a full blood Cherokee, raised at Cherokee Orphan Asylum in Cherokee Nation West. And as for reference you can see Hon. Robt. L. Owen, U.S. Senator from Oklahoma, as he was my teacher at the school in the year of 1882 or 3, if I mistake not.

If further information is wanted, let me know, and will try to get it. But it is almost impossible as I do not know where to get it as I moved from the Cherokee Nation West about 19 years ago.

Hoping to hear from you again as to my claim.

Sample Application

Yours Respectfully.

Wm. L. French
Present Post Office   Trough, SC

The above letter was communication that accompanied the above party's application. It appears he was able to prove himself as a Western Cherokee but didn't have the documentation to show his father as an Eastern or Emigrant Cherokee, which was the main requirement for acceptance to the Guion Miller Roll.

INTRODUCTION

Between May, 1905, and April, 1907, the U.S. Supreme Court authorized the Secretary of the Interior to identify the descendants of Eastern Cherokees entitled to participate in the distribution of more than $1 million in outstanding claims against the U.S. government based upon the Treaties of 1835-36 and 1845. On May 28, 1909, Commissioner Guion Miller, representing the Interior Department, submitted to Congress his findings with respect to 45,857 separate applications for compensation (totaling about 90,000 individual Native American claimants). Miller qualified about 30,000 persons inhabiting approx. 39 states and 3 countries to share in the fund. Ninety percent of the eligible were living west of the Mississippi River.

Among the records created by the Guion Miller Commission are (1) an Index to the 45,000 Eastern and Western Cherokee Applications (National Archives Record Group 123) and (2) a collection of Abstracts of the Commission's findings, arranged by application number (Record Group M685). The Index—the subject of this series—and the Abstracts contain complimentary information and together provide a detailed accounting of the Cherokee applicants and their family members.

The work at hand, *Cherokee Descendants East: An Index to the Guion Miller Applications*, is a verbatim transcription of the first portion of the index found on National Archives Record Group 123. It refers to the Cherokee applicants living East of the Mississippi River in 1909 (about 3,200 applicants, or 10% of the total). For each head of household named in the application we are given the following additional information: Guion Miller roll number, city and state of residence, and the names of other householders with their ages and relationship to the head. A history of the Guion Miller Commission and several sample applications precede the index of applicants, while an addendum and comprehensive name index conclude the work. Two additional, larger volumes will cover Cherokee applicants residing West of the Mississippi.

As alluded to above, persons interested in Cherokee genealogy should also consult the Abstracts of the Guion Miller Commission applications. This information has been published in the 12-volume series, *Eastern Cherokee by Blood, 1906-1910*, by this author. These abstracts name the applicant, the number of persons in the household, an abstract of each enrollee's case, and the disposition (admitted or rejected), including cross-references to other applications and connections to other families.

NB The contents of this book was originally published in 1996.

Jeff Bowen
Gallipolis, Ohio
www.NativesStudy.com

Roll
of
Eastern Cherokees

**ENTITLED TO PARTICIPATE IN THE FUND
ARISING FROM THE JUDGMENT OF THE
COURT OF CLAIMS OF MAY 28, 1906**

AS REPORTED BY

GUION MILLER, SPECIAL COMMISSIONER

May twenty-eight, nineteen hundred and nine

Key: Guion Miller Application Number; Name; Address, Relation (to Head); Age in 1906

3301 ABBOTT, Anna Choteau, OK, 19; Angeline D, 1/3

12391 ABBOTT, Annie L, Pryor Creek, OK, 21; Louisa J, D, 3; Leona M D, 1

16435 ABBOTT, Butler, Kinnison, OK, 17

12591 ABBOTT, Eugene M, Tahlequah, OK, 28; 12635 Netty M, W, 25; Mary E, D, 3; Gertrude, D, 1/12

22758 ABBOTT, John W, Tahlequah, OK, 26

16735 ABERCROMBIE, Ruth A Collinsville, OK, 33; Sidney G, S, 11; Cora L, D, 9; David M, S, 6; John B, S, 3

30536 ABNEY, Birdie A Afton, OK, 37; William Fred, S, 8; Jessie C D, 6

32002 ABSTON, Elizabeth R, Grove, OK, 35

5026 ACKLEY, Mary, Muskogee, OK, 38; Oliver F, S, 19; Madge E D, 17; Letta D, 14; Edna E, D, 10

4631 ACORN, Caty, Stilwell, OK, 80

12698 ACORN, Charley, Stilwell, OK, 22

4633 ACORN, Dick, Evansville AR, 50; 13390 Katie, W, 31; Feather, Margaret D, 14; Otay, S, 12; Henry, S, 9; Lacy D, 1

4625 ACORN, Ezekiel, Stilwell, OK, 40; 13639 Sarah, W, 27; Celie, D, 5; French, D, 3

35537 ACORN, Johanna, Stilwell, OK, 17; Duncan Annie D, 1/12

4591 ACORN, John, Stilwell, OK, 32; 4629 Nannie, W, 36; Annie, D, 9; Lizzie, D, 9

4630 ACORN, Liza, Stilwell, OK, 50

22942 ADAIR, Albert, Stilwell, OK, 22

5385 ADAIR, Anna Choteau, OK, 82

22761 ADAIR, Arthur A Adair, OK, 25

7000 ADAIR, Arthur F, Tahlequah, OK, 48; 10316 Mollie E, W, 48; Arthur L, S, 15; Owen L, S, 13

7449 ADAIR, Candy, Stilwell, OK, 54

4946 ADAIR, Charles L, Fairland, OK, 31; Cora M, D, 5; Lou A D, 3; Hazel B, D, 1

26070 ADAIR, Cherokee, Sallisaw, OK, 23

[ADAIR, Clauda. See #6255] ⎤   *(Note: entries separate*
[ADAIR, Cleo. See #6255] ⎦   *from other family groups)*

38501 ADAIR, Dora, Sallisaw, OK, 24; Charles L, S, 4; Ren D, 1

6295 ADAIR, Edward E, Sallisaw, OK, 53; 24825 Rachel L, W, 48

22778 ADAIR, Edward H, Stilwell, OK, 36; William W, S, 12; Hugh M, Jr, S, 10; Walter S, S, 8; Mary L D, 5; John W, S, 2

5586 ADAIR, Edward S Choteau, OK, 55; Clemice D, 16; Robert P, S, 13

23546 ADAIR, Enoch M Choteau, OK, 55; Arthur D, S, 2; Porter Rogers, S, 1/3

26111 ADAIR, Ezekiel E Dutch Mills AR, 29; 6598 Ida L, W, 27

7452 ADAIR, Florence W, Evansville AR, 21

[ADAIR, Floyd. See #27435]   *(Note: entry separate from other family groups)*

Key: Guion Miller Application Number; Name; Address, Relation (to Head); Age in 1906

24793 ADAIR, Frank C, Westville, OK, 34; Ezekiel S, S, 7; Talitha J, F, 5; John Edgar, S, 3; Eudora A D, 1

[ADAIR, Frankie M. See #16863]   *(Note: entry separate from other family groups)*

9426 ADAIR, George W, Stilwell, OK, 34; Yula D D, 12; Pearl E D, 10; Verda M, D, 5; Velma M D, 2

6682 ADAIR, Henry G, Nowata, OK, 41; 6789 Caroline, W, 46; George, S, 19; Ute, S, 11; Katie D, 10; Levi, S, 6

2273 ADAIR, Hugh M, Stilwell, OK, 68

4231 ADAIR, James F Braggs, OK, 35; Monica D, 13;   Edith D, 9; John L, S, 7; James F, Jr, S, 5

23174 ADAIR, James W, Stilwell, OK, 34

24794 ADAIR, Jesse E; Dutch Mills AR, 38; Madison B, S, 12; Annie E D, 8; Daisy D, 6; Virgil C, S, 2

5956 ADAIR, John II, Sallisaw, OK, 51

5957 ADAIR, Samuel H, Evansville AR, 47; Louvenia F, D, 18; John R. T, S, 11; Watie M, S, 11; Juanita A, D, 9; Carlotta R, D, 6

6583 ADAIR, Samuel T, Stilwell, OK, 40; Mary E, D, 17; George W, S, 15; Samuel W, S, 13; Lull E, D, 11; Lillie E, D, 8

22874 ADAIR, Sarah L, Centralia, OK, 21

27553 ADAIR, Sarah R, Sallisaw, OK, 25

22941 ADAIR, Thomas, Stilwell, OK, 33; Isaac, S, 6

16876 ADAIR, Thomas C, Sallisaw, OK, 9; James L, Bro, 6; Luzenia, Sis, 4; By Wm H. Brackett, Gdn.

6574 ADAIR, Thomas J, Tahlequah, OK, 50; 6575 Lena, W, 37; Emily, D, 13

27835 ADAIR, Timothy, Stilwell, OK, 24; 9378 Mattie, W, 20

4709 ADAIR, Virgil B Dutch Mills AR, 66

3716 ADAIR, Virgil H Adair, OK, 37; Viola D, 13; Mildred H D, 8; Winnie D, 5; Virgil J, S, 3; Velma D, 2

5021 ADAIR, Walter Thompson, Tahlequah, OK, 22

4064 ADAIR, William C, Ft Gibson, OK, 15;   By Lova Adair, Gdn

34195 ADAIR, William D Chelsea, OK, 21

5539 ADAIR, William P Adair, OK, 45; 19644 Maggie, W, 31; DeWitt, J, S, 14; Walter T, S, 12; Mary E D, 8; William C, S, 1

27551 ADAIR, William P. Sallisaw, OK, 26

 356 ADAIR, William Pendelton, Adair, OK, 48

27682 ADAIR, William T Choteau, OK, 21

[ADAM, Maud. See #16784] *(Note: entry separate from other family groups)*

[ADAM, Richard. See #1268] *(Note: entry separate from other family groups)*

Key: Guion Miller Application Number; Name; Address, Relation (to Head); Age in 1906

23221 ADAMS Charlotte M, Stilwell, OK, 10; Norma E, Sis 8; Maud E, Sis 5; Grace L, Sis, 3; By Myrtle Adams, Gdn.

16879 ADAMS, John, Grove, OK, 19

32042 ADAMS, Lula Como CO, 25

4015 ADAMS, Mary, Park Hill, OK, 25; Myers Andrew, S, 10; Adams, Grover C, S, 3; Johny[sic], Mc, S, 1

13437 ADAMS, Mary L, Ochelata, OK, 18; Roy L, S, 2; William O, S, 1

3543 ADAMS, Maudie, Sallisaw, OK, 17

8668 ADAMSON, Nancy, Tulsa, OK, 25; Gaylor, Elizabeth D, 4; Adamson, Benjamin F, S, 1

12499 ADDINGTON Cicero W, Stilwell, OK, 31; 27772 Mollie E, W, 31; Clarence G, S, 5; Frederick E, S, 4

16734 ADDINGTON, Joel C Collinsville, OK, 17; William J Bro, 15; Oscar P Bro, 13; Addison B Bro, 8; Delora P, Sis, 7;   By William A. Addington, Gdn.

17700 ADDINGTON, Margaret A, Vera, OK, 33; Truman C, S, 15; Alice D D, 13; Jesse J, S, 11; Ida B D, 9; Henry E, S, 7; Laura C D, 4; Lena D, 1

22468 ADKINS, Josephine Collinsville, OK, 16

8754 ADKINS, Tillie Collinsville, OK, 36; 24618 Brown, Minnie D, 19; Emma D, 10; Amy D, 5; Edward, S, 3; Carl, S, 1/12

11705 ADKISSON, Jasper N, Tahlequah, OK, 38; 29238 Susie [Died 12-(19)06], 34; Clarence M, S, 14; Thomas E, S, 11; Kittie D, 9; Paralee D, 7; Callice M D, 5; Susie D, D, 3

9616 ADKISSON, Samuel A, Eureka, OK, 35; Sam, S, 11; John W, S, 9; Milow, S, 6; Jennie M, D, 5; Chester, S, 2

1584 ADLER, Mary Olive Adair, OK, 19

4929 AGENT Dick, Moody, OK, 45; 4930 Polly, W, 37; Arch, S, 15; Watuck, S, 13; Ella, D, 8

28300 AGNEW, Ellen, Keefeton, OK, 35

2909 AGNEW, Mary E, Keefeton, OK, 57; Sephus E, S, 19

28299 AGNEW, Robert M, Keefeton, OK, 27

28630 AGNEW, Walter L, Keefeton, OK, 22

[AH-NE-CHE, Levi. See #3694] ⎤   *(Note: entries separate*
[AH-NE-CHE Bud. See #3694] ⎦   *from other family groups)*

12649 AH-QUAH-TAKY, Tahlequah, OK, 20

3288 AH-TUR-YO-LAR or Tom Chuculuck, Locust Grove, OK, 60; 22006 Nancy, W, 64

22804 AIKINS Anne, Stilwell, OK, 40

[AIMES Anna. See #10286] ⎤   *(Note: entries separate*
[AIMES, Myrtle. See #10286] ⎦   *from other family groups)*

Key: Guion Miller Application Number; Name; Address, Relation (to Head); Age in 1906

774 AKIN Andrew T, Oolagah, OK, 55; 773 Jennie, S[sic], 17; Watie T, S, 17; William O, S, 15; Thomas Frank, S, 13; Mabel T D, 11; Jennie L D, 8; Maggie B, D, 3

1498 AKIN Carrie, Wagoner, OK, 29; Charlie F, S, 7; Arch P, S, 5; Eliza M D, 3; Oscar F, S, 1

24863 AKIN Don P Dutch Mills AR, 26

26021 AKIN, Ellis A, Westville, OK, 23; 26022 Emma J, W, 27

29042 AKIN, Eudorah A Dutch Mills AR, 40; 3247 Francis R, Hus, 51; Jesse O, S, 20; Robert L, S, 17

3520 AKIN, Fannie C, Vinita, OK, 48; Raymond P, S, 12

[AKIN, Francis R. See #3247]   *(Note: entry separate from other family groups)*

32440 AKIN, Strange W, Tulsa, OK, 22

3248 AKIN, Tennessee Dutch Mills AR, 57

11299 ALBERTY, Albert C, Westville, OK, 29; Julianna D, 7/12

5208 ALBERTY, Andrew J, Stilwell, OK, 61; Bishop M, S, 18; Samuel J, S, 16

240 ALBERTY, Anna, Pryor Creek, OK, 52; William, S, 19; Arthur, S, 15; John [invalid], S, 3

27527 ALBERTY Bertha, Stilwell, OK, 21

9479 ALBERTY Clara, Westville, OK, 17

[ALBERTY Cornelius. See #2181]   *(Note: entry separate from other family groups)*

6918 ALBERTY, David R, Rose, OK, 22

6939 ALBERTY, Edward Baron, OK, 36; 1918 Nancy, W, 26

5228 ALBERTY, Eliza M, Tahlequah, OK, 67

26242 ALBERTY, Ellis C, Westville, OK, 22

11300 ALBERTY, Ellis R, Tahlequah, OK, 34; 25715 Callie W, 31; 11300 Robert G, S, 14; James H, S, 11; Lora May D, 9; Albert B, S, 4

6744 ALBERTY, Ellridge, Westville, OK, 21; 24201 Emma, W, 19

5709 ALBERTY, John, Stilwell, OK, 57; 5599 Emily C, W, 61

22782 ALBERTY, John G, Stilwell, OK, 33; Grover L, S, 13; Emmett A, S, 11; Daily, S, 7, George G, S, 4

27526 ALBERTY, Joseph R, Stilwell, OK, 24

27683 ALBERTY, Joshua Choteau, OK, 28; Gladys D, 1

23932 ALBERTY, Lafayette, Stilwell, OK, 24

23930 ALBERTY, Mattie, Stilwell, OK, 28

23931 ALBERTY, Mollie, Stilwell, OK, 21

11782 ALBERTY, Sue M Claremore, OK, 44; Cecil E, S, 18; Nannie W D, 14; Maggie M , D, 11; Bernice L D, 6; James R, S, 1

13115 ALBERTY, William, Stilwell, OK, 18; Jesse M Bro, 12; Lucy C, Sis, 10; John B Bro, 7;   By Julie Alberty, Gdn.

CHEROKEE DESCENDANTS RESIDING WEST OF MISSISSIPPI RIVER.
VOLUME II   (A – M)

Key: Guion Miller Application Number; Name; Address, Relation (to Head); Age in 1906

23543 ALBERTY, William L, Stilwell, OK, 22

6619 ALBERTY, William P, Westville, OK, 31; Beula,D, 6; Minnie Bell D, 5; Olie M, D, 2

735 ALCORN, Mary E Braggs, OK, 66; Katie, GD, 4; Viola, GD, 2

[ALBERTY, William W. See #26241] ⎤   *(Note: entries separate*
[ALBERTY, Mose. See #26241]   ⎬   *from other family groups)*
[ALBERTY, Pete. See #26241]   ⎦

25495 ALDRIDGE, Ruth A, Wann, OK, 27
13097 ALECK, Aquilla, South West City, MO, 24

[ALECK Coon. See #26064] *(Note: entry separate from other family groups)*

1698 ALEX Arle, Eucha, OK, 57 [Deceased]
1724 ALEXANDER Aggie, Porum, OK, 51
5965 ALEXANDER Charles A Centralia, OK, 21
31298 ALEXANDER, Elmer H, Grove, OK, 37; Stephen D, S, 5; Simpson M, S, 3; William T, S, 2; Jessie A D, 1/12
2225 ALEXANDER, Job, Westville, OK, 54; 10605 Caroline, W, 40; Jessie D, 17; Carrie D, 14; Weston, S, 11; Jennie D, 5; Solomon, S, 1 [Died 7-(19)06]
27436 ALEXANDER, John, Porum, OK, 21
12142 ALEXANDER, Joseph, Ft. Smith AR, Box 27, 34
24694 ALEXANDER, Ludia, Keefeton, OK, 20
40028 ALEXANDER, Maud, Ft. Smith AR, 21
9695 ALEXANDER, Nannie, Porum, OK, 45; Andy, S, 17; John, S, 15
16704 ALEXANDER, Nora Ahniwake, OK, 18
7910 ALEXANDER, Paralie J, Ft. Gibson, OK, 49; Samuel D, S, 13
40029 ALEXANDER, Sophronia, Ft. Smith, AR, 41; Faye D, 17; Kate D, 12
12143 ALEXANDER, Thompson Chaffee, MO, 37
3212 ALEXANDER, William H, Grove, OK, 7;   By Florence M. Dilley, Gdn.
17605 ALFORD, Maggie, Fawn, OK, 40; Sue D, 15; Famin D, 13; Bob, S, 11; Nannie D, 8; Willie, S, 5; John, S, 4; Fred, S, 1
11185 ALFORD, Sallie M, Hanson, OK, 20; William D, S, 2
11482 ALLEN, Annie Braggs, OK, 18
22844 ALLEN, Annie E, Grove, OK, 25; Rosa D, 7; Grace D, 5; Oma D, 3; Luvina D, 7/12
28009 ALLEN, Charles W Collinsville, OK, 44; Estella M D, 13
27790 ALLEN, Clero C, Miami, OK, 26; Cyril L, S, 1
22654 ALLEN, Edwin W, Stilwell, OK, 22
32391 ALLEN, Henry Claremore, OK, 32; Joseph H, S, 10; Edna C D, 7; Susie M D, 2
27974 ALLEN, Henry F, Newport, WA, 45

CHEROKEE DESCENDANTS RESIDING WEST OF MISSISSIPPI RIVER.
VOLUME II (A – M)

Key: Guion Miller Application Number; Name; Address, Relation (to Head); Age in 1906

22822 ALLEN, Hugh M, Stilwell, OK, 20

7486 ALLEN, Irena Cherokee City AR, 17

14146 ALLEN, Jefferson, Spavinaw, OK, 52; 10643 Ce-nee, W, 45; Sarah D, 19; Aaron, S, 17

32394 ALLEN, John Claremore, OK, 27

28008 ALLEN, Lewis R Collinsville, OK, 35? Ethel V D, 10; Anna M D, 8; Olla J D, 5; Hazel D, 3

26337 ALLEN, Lucie N, Vinita, OK, 20

1069 ALLEN, Mary J Catoosa, OK, 61

32897 ALLEN, Michel U, Siloam Springs AR, 35; 32896 Lela A, W, 21; George Henry, S, 2

5108 ALLEN, Nancy A, Siloam Springs AR, 67

27833 ALLEN, Oscar R, Kansas City, MO, 27; Charles Berry, S, 2; Cora E D, 1

11822 ALLEN, Osceola, Foyil, OK, 29; 28841 Georgia, W, 21; Velma D, 3

9220 ALLEN, Ruth A Catale, OK, 45; Gretchen D, 5; Edna P D, 3

570 ALLEN, Susan, Sleeper, OK, 27; Morcellar, S, 9; Isam M, S, 7; Cicero, S, 2; Georgia D, 1/12

[ALLEN, Susie. See #8098]   *(Note: entry separate from other family groups)*

13372 ALLEN, Susie Centralia, OK, 34; Willie R, S, 16; Clarence V, S, 12; Elvie E D, 10; Joanna D, 8; Audry V D, 1

10909 ALLEN, Walter A, Stilwell, OK, 47; Mary L D, 14; Cephas, S, 12

16408 ALLISON Annie L Afton, OK, 25; Marguerite D, D, 1

28176 ALLISON, Edgar G Adair, OK, 25; Clara M D, 2

32245 ALLISON, Elmer C, Portland, OR, 21;   Care H. Anderson, Union Station

27204 ALLISON, Elmie R, Talala, OK, 22

6613 ALLISON, George A Choteau, OK, 26

29996 ALLISON, Ida B, Muskogee, OK, 22

8898 ALLISON, James T Beckville, TX, 61

747 ALLISON, Jasper P Choteau, OK, 32; Johnnie S, S, 7; Frankie P, S, 6

24385 ALLISON, Jimmie, Talala, OK, 20

25295 ALLISON, John L, Stilwell, OK, 40; Amos L, S, 16; Mildred M D, 14; John M, S, 3

314 ALLISON, John R, Talala, OK, 55; John, Jr, S, 18; Mary E D, 16; Una D, 13; Sabra D, 10; Edgar H, S, 7; Pina D, 3

[ALLISON, Laura Bell. See #9209]
[ALLISON, Paten. See #9209]   *(Note: entries separate*
[ALLISON Clara. See #9209]   *from other family groups)*
[ALLISON, Edith. See #9209]

14224 ALLISON, Mildred T Adair, OK, 66

CHEROKEE DESCENDANTS RESIDING WEST OF MISSISSIPPI RIVER.
VOLUME II   (A – M)

Key: Guion Miller Application Number; Name; Address, Relation (to Head); Age in 1906

30665 ALLISON, Robert Lee, Portland, OR, 36 1045 Williams Ave.

38771 ALLISON, Samuel M, Joplin, MO, 27   402 N. Amanda St.

31730 ALLISON, Thomas M, Grangeville, ID, 38; Clyde O, S, 14;   Willie H, S, 10

29143 ALLISON, Willie, Foyil, OK, 25

7499 ALLOWAY Clara I Catoosa, OK, 19

24870 ALSTON, Sarah C, Wagoner, OK, 39; Carleton, William, S, 3; Barnwell, Rutledge, S, 6

26183 ALSTON, Wilhelmina I, Tahlequah, OK, 51; 26185 Susan E D, 18; 26184 Elizabeth B, D, 14

25226 ALVIS, Fannie H, Mark, OK, 48; Oneita E D, 5; 4916 Ross, Lugie J, D, 14; Ora I, D, 12

24855 AMES, Julia A, Flint, OK, 51; George, S, 13; David L, S, 12; Sallie D, 10; Luster (Hiram), S, 9

23290 AMIS Amanda A, Ramona, OK, 40; William A, S, 20; James E, S, 17; Edwin R, S, 14, Margaret E D, 14

6984 AMONS, Mary, Stilwell, OK, 40; Norwood, S, 6;   Jack, S, 1

7962 AMOS, Margaret N. Sallisaw, OK, 23; Cleon, S, 2; Lester, S, 1

[AMOS, Pansy Madeline. See #24956] *(Note: entry separate from other family groups)*

28467 ANDERSON Amanda, Oglesby, OK, 25; Nevin T, S, 5; Lucile D, D, 1

9962 ANDERSON Austin, Pryor Creek, OK, 27; Lloyd, S, 2

4105 ANDERSON Cynthia C, Ft. Gibson, OK, 10;   By Amos Anderson, Gdn.

26731 ANDERSON Delilah, Vian, OK, 31; Lorenzo, S, 11; John W, S, 9; Emma D, 7; Ella M D, 5; Richard, S, 3; Lida D, 1

21638 ANDERSON, George, Porum, OK, 21

17561 ANDERSON, James, Porum, OK, 65; 21989 Sarah, W, 51; Sam, S, 7

9956 ANDERSON, Jesse, Pryor Creek, OK, 9;   By R. Anderson, Gdn.

26297 ANDERSON, John D, Ft. Gibson, OK, 22

4112 ANDERSON, Louisa, Ft. Gibson, OK, 44; William M, S, 19; Joe E, S, 17; Mark, S, 14; Fannie D, 12; Ida Lee D, 10; Amos M, S, 3

8780½ ANDERSON, Mabel, Mayes, OK, 43; Gladys M D, 14; Hellen R D, 13; Preston R, S, 10

35034 ANDERSON, Mary H, Kansas, OK, 22

8150 ANDERSON, Nancy M, Eureka, OK, 47; Theodora D, 15; Henry M, S, 12; Jesse M, S, 10; William C, S, 7

11014 ANDERSON, William B Chance, OK, 37; 22976 Lizzie, W, 28; Willie May D, 5

4923 ANDOES, Nancy, Grove, OK, 52; Que-la-ter, John, S, 18; Houston, S, 14

10606 ANDRE, Eliza, Ft. Gibson, OK, 59

25304 ANDRE, Paul P, Ft. Gibson, OK, 21

5281 ANDREWS, Mary Dutch Mills AR, 64

8346 ANDREWS, Polly, Vian, OK, 50

Key: Guion Miller Application Number; Name; Address, Relation (to Head); Age in 1906

4639 ANDREWS, Sarah C, Miles, OK, 30; Mary A D, 13; Alvin F, S, 10; Clyde E, S, 6; Bethel, S, 4; Mabel C D, 2

10667 ANDREWS, Susie C, Tulsa, OK, 27; Howard B, S, 1

1727 ANGEL, Rebecca Theodosia, Ogeechee, OK, 49; Jesse, S, 18; Laura A D, 15;

24424 ANGEL, William I, Fairland, OK, 20; Thomas A, S, 1

30195 ANGLIN, Georgia A. O, Flint, OK, 31; Lona M D, 10; Dessie P, D, 7; Maud V D, 5, Maggie V D, 3; William W, S, 1/3

16749 ANIBLE Caldonia E, Van Buren AR, 34; Tweedle, Florence M D, 15

23099 ANTOINE, James W, Tahlequah, OK, 34; Joseph M, S, 13; William C, S, 10; George K, S, 4; Lolitta M D, 1

124 ANTOINE, Sarah E, Ft. Gibson, OK, 60

32330 ARCH, E-yan-ne Braggs, OK, 38; 32331 Polly D, 18; Sally D, 12; Sam, S, 9

9943 ARCH, I. Ann, Kansas, OK, 54

14780 ARCH, Willie Campbell, OK, 39 [or Arch, Phillip.]; Wilson, S, 19; John, S, 17; Jimmie, S, 14; Ahama, S, 11; Lucy D, 9; Aggie D, 7; George, S, 4; Sinda D, 2; Olie D, ¼ [Died June 7 '08]

31433 ARCH, Richard Braggs, OK, 23

1930 ARCH, Sallie, Evansville AR, 84

14781 ARCH, Steve Campbell, OK, 38

17449 ARCH, Susie, Welling, OK, 26

[ARCH, Willie and children. See #14780]

(Note: entry separate from other family groups)

23122 ARCHER, James Sigel, Pueblo CO, 44 1118 Routt Ave; Annie M D, 17

26963 ARCHER, John R Adair, OK, 42

36681 ARCHER, Seth B, Montrose CO, 25; Thelma D, 1

23571 ARCHER, William Perry, Montrose, CO, 49; Don C, S, 16; William L, S, 12; Jaunita D, 10

26295 ARCHIBALD Delen R Afton, OK, 32; Donohoo, Madalene D, 9; Paul Langley, S, 6

17438 ARCHILLA, Jennie, Locust Grove, OK, 76

1265 ARLEDGE, John A Catoosa, OK, 23; Ada D, 1; William, S, 1/6

1266 ARLEDGE, Maud Catoosa, OK, 15; By Ada Henderson, Gdn.

1937 ARMERTEASKY, Runabout, Peggs, OK, 28

25763 ARMOR Cynthia A Centralia, OK, 42; Mrytle P D, 16; James O, S, 10

26910 ARMSTRONG Annah M, Tahlequah, OK, 19; Lilly M D, 1/3

24662 ARMSTRONG, Mary E Adair, OK, 35; Harold S, S, 9

8359 ARNECHER, John, Oaks, OK, 49; Jacob, S, 10

4430 ARNHART, Maria J, Seattle, WA, 28; Oowala C, S, 4; Aronda M, S, 1

22798 ARNING, Susan, Ruby, OK, 30 Hill, Hattie D, 9

7587 ARNOLD, Victoria Chelsea, OK, 48; I. Cecil, S, 20; George W, S, 18; Mary D, 16; Herbert, S, 14; Halbert, S, 14; Joseph, S, 13; Sallie L D, 9

Key: Guion Miller Application Number; Name; Address, Relation (to Head); Age in 1906

3913 ARNOLD, William, Hulbert, OK, 45

24263 ARROWOOD, Mertie P, Owasso, OK, 20; Goldie R D, 4; Roy, S, 14

7455 ARROWKEEPER, William, Spavinaw, OK, 53

280 ARTERBERRY, Mary A Choteau, OK, 34; P. W, S, 5; Ruth D, 3; Florence L D, 1

9966 ARTERBERRY, Oma W Choteau, OK, 20

23984 ARWOOD, John A Chelsea, OK, 22; James A, S, 4; Mary P D, 2

22011 AR-YU-S-DAH, Oaks, OK, 18

13885 ASHES, Sarah, Porum, OK, 32; Martha D, 11; Joe, S, 10; Buck, S, 6

29924 ASHLEY, Ora B Checotah, OK, 27; Amey M D, 5; Elsie L D, 2; Osker L, S, 1/6

29923 ASHLEY, Texas R Checotah, OK, 32

13082 ASKWATER, William, Hulbert, OK, 52

22936 ATHEY, Lizzie K, Vinita, OK, 37

24719 ATKINS, Margaret A, Siloam Springs, AR, 20; Mabel M D, 3; Jack H, S, 1

6580 AUGERHOLE Betsy, Stilwell, OK, 54

[AUGERHOLE, Eli. See #11487]   *(Note: entry separate from other family groups)*

25160 AUGERHOLE, Ludia Braggs, OK, 4; By J.W. Sumter, Gdn.

25161 AUGERHOLE, William Braggs, OK, 6; By J.W. Sumter, Gdn.

16517 AUSTIN Charles, Nowata, OK, 23

[AUSTIN, Lizzie. See #1996]
[AUSTIN, Minnie. See #1996]   *(Note: entries separate*
[AUSTIN, Josie. See #1996]   *from other family groups)*
[AUSTIN, Willie. See #1996]

12456 AUSTIN, Sarah R, Pryor, OK, 25; Lucinda D, 3

21753 AUSTIN, Sevolia, Nowata, OK, 18; By Walter H. Austin, Gdn.

16518 AUSTIN, Walter H, Nowata, OK, 21

21752 AUSTIN, Zerilda, Nowata, OK, 15; By Walter H. Austin, Gdn.

18865 AUTEN, Lenora M, Oolagah, OK, 23

6703 AUTREY, Mary C, Warner, OK, 23

31186½ AVANT, Troy, Tahlequah, OK, 8; By Thomas Blair, Gdn.

5219 AYERS, Nannie May Braggs, OK, 25; Wicks, Joseph, S, 10; Benjamin, S, 8

1572 BACHTEL, Mary J, Hudson, OK, 58; Daniel D, S, 18; Otis, S, 17; Elzy D, 15

464 BACKBONE Daniel Choteau, OK, 46

33145 BACKBONE, Polly Choteau, OK, 22; Rose, Nelson, S, 2

14182 BACKWARD Ada, Locust Grove, OK, 16

5607 BACKWARD Daniel, Locust Grove, OK, 51; 5781 Nellie, W, 33

6545 BACKWARD, Evans, Rose, OK, 24; 5118 Jennie, W, 20

Key: Guion Miller Application Number; Name; Address, Relation (to Head); Age in 1906

3846 BACKWARD, Sampson, Rose, OK, 24

460 BACKWARD Betsy, Spavinaw, OK, 58

13391 BACKWATER, Emma, Stilwell, OK, 22

8363 BACKWATER, Joe, Oaks, OK, 54; 8780, Lizzie, W, 50; Round, S, 13; Oo-wah-hu-ern-ske, S, 11

8777 BACKWATER, John, Eucha, OK, 34; 8778 Lizzie, W, 34; Nancy, S, 13; Willie, S, 13; Watee, S, 11; Katie D, 9; Sallie D, 7; Eliza D, 4; Pollie D, 1

43324 BACKWATER, Lyla, Locust Grove, OK, 32

26849 BACKWATER, Susie, Leach, OK, 18

16514 BACON Chas. B, Verdigris, OK, 18; By Chas. H. Bacon, Gdn.

16513 BACON Dana B, Verdigris, OK, 25

31569 BACON, John H Chelsea, OK, 40; Tressie P D, 6

29407 BACON, Harnage W, Overton, TX, 21

29408 BACON, Jimmie, Overton, TX, 19; Bina, Sis, 16; By Joe D. Bacon, Gdn.

16515 BACON, John L, Verdigris, OK, 21

12227 BACON, Kate, Verdigris, OK, 48; Gant, William, S, 17; Mattie D, 16; Chas Fount, S, 12

27168 BACON, Thomas S, Nowata, OK, 36

7689 BADGER, Lillie, Flint, OK, 26; Emaline D, 6; Joseph, S, 4; Hattie D, 2; Alice D, 1/6

12593 BADGET, Wm. Ross, Vinita, OK, 16; Mary, Sis, 15; George Bro, 10; By William R. Badget, Gdn.

24010 BAGGETTE,. Pearl E, Westville, OK, 38; Julia A D, 15; Pearl Elaine D, 13; Gracie D, 11; Daisy D, 9

16101 BAILEY, George Christie, OK, 35; 6678 Nannie, W, 37; Chicken, Nancie D, 13

1817 BAILEY, Jennie Christie, OK, 47

3285 BAILEY, Sarah E, Peggs, OK, 36; Elizabeth D D, 16; George Alfred, S, 14; Jennie L, D, 12; Sam M, S, 10; Josephine E D, 6; Sallie E D, 3; Theodore R, S, 2

17047 BAILEY, Steve Christie, OK, 22

9958 BAIN, Arch, Pryor Creek, OK, 25

23509 BAIRD, Susie, Catale, OK, 24; Neva L D, 8; Jettie I D, 6; Lessie M D, 2

27538 BAKER Bertha H Afton, OK, 25; Hattie L D, 7; Oliver R, S, 3

971 BAKER, Eliza J Bartlesville, OK, 34; Freddie Earl, S, 14; Etta May D, 12

12555 BAKER, Elizabeth Collinsville, OK, 51; Webster C, S, 17

28670 BAKER, Ina M, Foyil, OK, 18

23462 BAKER, Lee M, Ketchum, OK, 10; William, L Bro, 8; Calvin Bro, 5; Ray Bro, 3; By Jas L. Baker, Gdn

13992 BAKER, Luella Claremore, OK, 35

24519 BAKER, Mary J, Ketchum, OK, 22; Sarah E D, 4; Oliver C, S, 1

37271 BAKER, Maud, Narcissa, OK, 23; Goldie M D, 6; Arphie Ray, S, 1

38321 BAKER, Ruth, Texanna, OK, 29

CHEROKEE DESCENDANTS RESIDING WEST OF MISSISSIPPI RIVER.
VOLUME II   (A – M)

Key: Guion Miller Application Number; Name; Address, Relation (to Head); Age in 1906

28330 BAKER, Sarah M, Spavinaw, OK, 37; Mable M D, 13; Pearl E D, 11; Mary E D, 8; Opal F D, 2

31110 BAKEWELL, Bertha McE, Santa Barbara, CA, 28 1416 Bath St.

1933 BALDRIDGE, Archilla, Locust Grove, OK, 48; Swimmer, S, 9; Inis D, 7; Jackson, S, 4; Rosa E D, 3

13262 BALDRIDGE, Betsey, Marble, OK, 19

10707 BALDRIDGE, Caroline, Hanson, OK, 22

32839 BALDRIDGE, Charles, Wagoner, OK, 13; Johnson Bro, 8; By Maud Sly, Gdn.

43193 BALDRIDGE, Dick Brushy, OK, 53; 1449 Nakey, W, 60; Arlecher or Ahleach, S, 17; Sequoyah, S, 14

10706 BALDRIDGE, Eliza, Hanson, OK, 26

8884 BALDRIDGE, Elizajane, Maple, OK, 20

8335 BALDRIDGE, George, Sallisaw, OK, 58; 6981 Alcy, W, 38; Albert, S, 10; James, S, 7; John, S, ¾

8886 BALDRIDGE, George, Maple, OK, 56

8885 BALDRIDGE, George, Maple, OK, 54; 10740 Nannie, W, 34; 25605 Lucy D, 18; 8885 Rosie D, 17; Ada D, 16; Willie, S, 15; Floid, S, 9; Mary D, 6; David R, S, 2; Millard K, S, 1

8883 BALDRIDGE, Georgie, Maple, OK, 22

8280 BALDRIDGE, Jack, Hanson, OK, 23

12576 BALDRIDGE, James, Porum, OK, 41; William, S, 9; Charles, S, 7

14168 BALDRIDGE, James, Long, OK, 28; 34565 Allie, W, 36

3191 BALDRIDGE, Johnson, Melvin, OK, 52; Colston, S, 19; Lelia D, 14

3166 BALDRIDGE, Lottie, Ray, OK, 6; By John A. Cannon, OK

17878 BALDRIDGE, Okla.[sic], Hanson, OK, 18

31192 BALDRIDGE, Mayes, Ray, OK, 19

32838 BALDRIDGE, Mike, Melvin, OK, 6; Lucy, Sis, 4; Elizabeth, Sis, 2; Olive Cou, 1; By Johnson Baldridge, Gdn.

16765 BALDRIDGE, Nellie, Long, OK, 41; Emma D, 11

10705 BALDRIDGE, Richard, Sallisaw, OK, 52; 7459 Jennie, W, 68

[BALDRIDGE, Susie. See #11199]   *(Note: entry separate from other family groups)*

16661 BALDRIDGE, William, Hanson, OK, 21; 10707 Caroline, W, 22

10185 BALENTINE Annie M, Tahlequah, OK, 21

271 BALENTINE, Mary E, Vinita, OK, 50; Mary E, D, 17; Ellen S D, 14

11680 BALENTINE, Perry B, Tahlequah, OK, 20

10186 BALENTINE, William H, Tahlequah, OK, 24; 41008 Ollie B, W, 21

16109 BALENTINE, William H, Tahlequah, OK, 52; 7473 Mary D, W, 49

[BALEW, Jennie. See #2143]   *(Note: entry separate from other family groups)*

5881 BALLARD Ada B, Welch, OK, 29; Harlin E, S, 6; Forest A D, 4; Lucian K, S, 2

Key: Guion Miller Application Number; Name; Address, Relation (to Head); Age in 1906

32080 BALLARD Arch, Vian, OK, 35; William R, S, 6; Saphronia D, 4; Jack, S, 2

27256 BALLARD Archibald L Copan, OK, 28; 31051 Cynthia E, W, 32; Ella May D, 3; Cherokee E D, 2; Fannie E D, 1

10325 BALLARD Barney F, Gravette AR, 44; Edna Pearl D, 15; Nellie G D, 13; Eva M, D, 10; Percy Paul, S, 5; Freeman S, S, 1

25773 BALLARD Daisy B, Tahlequah, OK, 21; 17066 Polly, W, 26; Dawes, Sampson, S of W, 8

31255 BALLARD De Auburn, Nowata, OK, 17; Guy R Bro, 6; By Minnie B. Ballard, Gdn.

10432 BALLARD, George W, Maysville AR, 50

31256 BALLARD, Goldie, Nowata, OK, 20

13064 BALLARD, Henry C, Vinita, OK, 46; 1878 Nancy A, W, 41; Evelyn J D, 12; Mable L, D, 10; James Q, S, 8; Thomas H, S, 6; George W, S, 2

23622 BALLARD, Henry T, Eufaula, OK, 21

13065 BALLARD, James E, Spavinaw, OK, 48; Jno. C, S, 8

27842 BALLARD, James R, Needmore, OK, 25

27937 BALLARD, Jane A, Needmore, OK, 31

[BALLARD, Jesse. See #29484.]   *(Note: entry separate from other family groups)*

36561 BALLARD, John W, Needmore, OK, 20

 2413 BALLARD, Randolph, Needmore, OK, 52; 2388 Miriam M, W, 51; Claude R, S, 17; George B, S, 12; Joe M, S, 9

25861 BALLARD, Robert A, Needmore, OK, 26; 5930 Jessie L, W, 21; Mary Wilma D, 3; Jenevieve[sic] D, 1

29810 BALLARD, Ruth M, Needmore, OK, 19

 5681 BALLARD, Sarah, Maysville AR, 76

 1056 BALLARD, Thomas, Vian, OK, 58

 2802 BALLARD, Thomas, Grove, OK, 43; Jesse Lee, S, 16; Willie A, S, 11; Lulu A D, 8

 2166 BALLARD, Tuxy Braggs, OK, 43; 4724 Mary, W, 34; Alex, S, 17; Elias, S, 15; Dewitt, S, 13; Mabel D, 10; George, S, 8; Jack, S, 6; Thomas, S, 3; Sequoyah, S, 1/12

 2412 BALLARD, William, Echo, OK, 55; 2411 Charlotte, W, 58; Ruth D, 19; Ethel, D, 16; Zoe D, 14

 8799 BALLARD, William, Tahlequah, OK, 54

10593 BALLARD, William Braggs, OK, 31; 10591 Sallie, W, 27; Thomas H, S, 10; John J, S, 8; Carrie M D, 6; Donald L, S, 4; Capitola L D, 2

25772 BALLARD, William H, Tahlequah, OK, 30; 25782 Wenona L, W, 24; William H, Jr, S, 2

30059 BALLARD, William H, Echo, OK, 22; Teesquantee, S, ¼

 577 BALLENGER, Ida Lee Coffeyville, KS, 28; Alma Lee D, 8

13760 BALLEW, Jack Cookson, OK, 27; 13688 Lydia, W, 24

Key: Guion Miller Application Number; Name; Address, Relation (to Head); Age in 1906

26798 BALLEW, Josie Cherokee, OK, 36; Thomas J, S, 14; William F, S, 4; Ellen J D, 2

25427 BALLEW, Ollief(?), Tahlequah, OK, 27; Kermit C, S, 1

10328 BALLINGER, Fannie R, Tahlequah, OK, 28; Maiva O D, 1

23104 BALINGER, Mary Ethel Big Cabin, OK, 4; Achilles Bro, 11; Dewey H Bro, 8; Opal, Sis, 5;   By Bird Ballinger, Gdn.

 3821 BALLOU, George, Vinita, OK, 28

 5886 BALLOU, James Big Cabin, OK, 23; 8902 Alsie (Alice), W, 28; Joe, S, 5; James, S, 1

 3237 BALLOU, Jefferson, Vinita, OK, 30

13301 BALLOU, Louisa, Locust Grove, OK, 46

 8741 BALLOU, Samuel, Locust Grove, OK, 36

14291 BALOU Bird, Locust Grove, OK, 14; Tom Bro, 11; Annie, Sis, 5; By Sam Balou, Gdn.

 8851 BALOU, John, Locust Grove, OK, 32; 8913 Vinnie, W, 39; Charley, S, 5; Sarah D, 1

 6445 BALOU, Thos, Locust Grove, OK, 29; 6446 Sallie, W, 26; Nelson D, 7; Peter, S, 5; Dave, S, 2; Elias D, 1/12

[BANTY, Lila. See #17270]   *(Note: entry separate from other family groups)*

23374 BARBER Cherokee, Westville, OK, 26; Pearl M D, 2

10198 BARBER Dave, Porum OK, 37

13958 BARBER, Jennie, Porum, OK, 62

 1093 BARBER, Mahana Afton, OK, 23; Josephine D, 5

10197 BARBER, Maud, Porum, OK, 16

29821 BARBRE[sic], Phoebe, Webber Falls, OK, 20

28405 BARD, Elizabeth H Chelsea, OK, 37

28404 BARD, Emily L Chelsea, OK, 25

 1178 BARD, Laura Chelsea, OK, 61; Robert B, S, 20

28403 BARD, Laura Chelsea, OK, 33

28406 BARD, Sarah B Chelsea, OK, 35

28402 BARD, Thomas D, Jr Chelsea, OK, 28

24202 BARE, Katie, Westville, OK, 21

24784 BARGER Agnes Chelsea, OK, 26; Bessie D, 9; Carl, S, 7; Claudie, S, 2

30396 BARGER Charles W, Miami, OK, 35; Annie C D, 12; Samuel R, S, 10; Lillie F D, 7; William E, S, 4

30395 BARGER, John W, Miami, OK, 37; Edna Elizabeth D, 12; Myrtle C, D, 8; Jesse R, S, 3

25864 BARGER, Joseph F, Foyil, OK, 31; Maggie C D, 7; Emma Minnie, D, 5; Joseph S, S, 3

30096 BARGER, Samuel F, Miami, OK, 39; Esta M D, 11; Bessie I D, 10; Gilbert E, S, 9; Roy F, S, 7; Lula A D, 6; Cora D, 3

Key: Guion Miller Application Number; Name; Address, Relation (to Head); Age in 1906

25865 BARGER, William E, Talala, OK, 24; Bernice Ina D, 2; Edward R, S, 1/3

2985 BARK Andrew Chapel, OK, 36; 4292   Nannie, W, 27; Webster, S, 11; Sunday, S, 8; Selia D, 6; Lizzie D, 4; Betsy D, 1

5623 BARK Dave, Proctor, OK, 53

10665 BARK, Eliza, Vian, OK, 17

2945 BARK, George W, Locust Grove, OK, 32; 27856 Lillie, W, 19

10710 BARK, John, Vian, OK, 51; 17014 Lizzie, W, 45; Richard, S, 18; Levie, S, 15; Louisa D, 12; Daisy D, 7

[BARK, Loonie. See #3171] *(Note: entry separate from other family groups)*

13996 BARK, Louella Blunt, OK, 25

13693 BARK, Martha A Blunt, OK, 60

16776 BARK, Pearl, Cherokee Orphan Asylum, Tahlequah, OK, 10; By John Bark, Gdn

16664 BARK, Robert, Vian, OK, 23

16774 BARK, Sam, Vian, OK, 14; By John Bark, Gdn.

16773 BARK, Scrub, Vian, OK, 18;   By John Bark, Gdn.

[BARK, Willie. See #13673] *(Note: entry separate from other family groups)*

13542 BARK, William David Blunt, OK, 32; Lemie L D, 1

42969 BARKER, Emma, Gritts, OK, 19

27924 BARKER, Josephine G, Welch, OK, 25

12386 BARKER, Mary A, Welch, OK, 46; Sequoyah, S, 17; Artemus B, S, 14; Dennis, S, 12; Emelese D, 10

42970 BARKER, Susie, Gritts, OK, 50

2289 BARKS, Victoria, Vinita, OK, 35; Hazel D, 12; Grace D, 7; Mathew M, S, 3

7916 BARNARD, Emma W, White Oak, OK, 10; James W Bro, 8; By Ira L. Barnard, Gdn.

36935 BARNES Charles W, Sallisaw, OK, 30; Bonnie D, 8

6442 BARNES, Eliza Akins, OK, 32; Alford F, S, 12; Vivian N, D, 10; Curtis, S, 7; Kate, D, 5; Virgil T, S, 3; Lafayette F, S, 1

24133 BARNES, Ella Zoe Dodge, OK, 22

26965 BARNES, George F, Tahlequah, OK, 21

5038 BARNES, Henry N, Tahlequah, OK, 9; Robert Owen Bro, 6; By Mary C. Barnes, Gdn.

1180 BARNES, Jennie M Chelsea, OK, 30

3789 BARNES, Mattie M, Warner, OK, 25

[BARNES, Maud. See #1090]   *(Note: entry separate from other family groups)*

36934 BARNES, Samuel, Sallisaw, OK, 25; Phoeba D, 1; Phema D, 1

Key: Guion Miller Application Number; Name; Address, Relation (to Head); Age in 1906

37270 BARNES, Turner, Leavenworth, KS, 28
12901 BARNES, Wenona Briartown, OK, 43; Charles, S, 20; Cornelious, S, 16; Oscar, S, 11; Bulah D, 5; Jamie, S, 18
2786 BARNETT Benjamin, Flint, OK, 32
23135 BARNETT, Edward, Miami, OK, 34 R.F.D. #4; Ida S D, 9; Lula A, D, 7; Frank E, S, 5; Arlis D, S, ¼; Alma A D, 2
27844 BARNETT, Frank M, Miami, OK, 37 R.F.D. #4; Jessie L D, 14; Kenney L, S, 12; Georgia L D, 8
2793 BARNETT, George, Flint, OK, 26
3080 BARNETT, Joel, Vera, OK, 27; Leonora D, 1
2787 BARNETT, John, Flint, OK, 20
498 BARNETT, Julia, Leach, OK, 35
4947 BARNETT, Mabel Cleora, OK, 7; By Wm. Barnett, Gdn.
4788 BARNETT, Sarah F, Flint, OK, 20
29276 BARNEY, Minnie Chelsea, OK, 26; Jessie I D, 4
12214 BARNOSKE Cat Campbell, OK, 27
12551 BARNOSKE Charlie, Vian, OK, 26
13611 BAR-NOS-KEE Clo-ny-as-tee Braggs, OK, 34
12549 BARNOSKE Conseen, Vian, OK, 28; Lizzie D, 1
44031 BARNOSKE, Jennie Braggs, OK, 17
12550 BARNOSKE, Nancy, Vian, OK, 22

[BARNWELL, Rutledge. See #24870]   *(Note: entry separate from other family groups)*

[BARR, Ella May. See 5496]   *(Note: entries separate*
[BARR, Thelma. See 5496]   *from other family groups)*

43454 BARRETT Bessie, Vinita, OK, 24
26522 BARRETT, John C Claremore, OK, 33; 26521 Victoria S, W, 27; Flavins L, S, 16; Jack, S, 3
22935 BARRETT, Lee, Vinita, OK, 40; 22937 Elizabeth N, W, 35; Mary D, 11; Alice Bell, D, 6
8669 BARRITT, Susie H, Tulsa, OK, 31; Emory L, S, 8; Archie E, S, 6
9124 BARRICK, Emaline Campbell, OK, 24; Marion F, S, 5; Bessie D, 3
22898 BARROW, Ida H, Muldrow, OK, 24
22896 BARROW, James H, Muldrow, OK, 20
903 BARROW, Jenetta, Muldrow, OK, 52; Mary E D, 18; Cicero, S, 15
22899 BARROW, Lillie A, Muldrow, OK, 26

[BARROWMAN Anna E. See #8138]   *(Note: entry separate from other family groups)*

13068 BARTHEL Annie, Muskogee, OK, 14; Frank, Jr Bro, 12; Mamie, Sis, 10; William W, Bro, 8;   By Frank Barthel, Gdn.

Key: Guion Miller Application Number; Name; Address, Relation (to Head); Age in 1906

919 BARTON Cynthia, Grove, OK, 72

141 BARTON, Mary V Chelsea, OK, 44; Edwin H, S, 16

23317 BASKINS, Rachel Braggs, OK, 22; Annie Augusta D, 5; Leroy, S, 1

1633 BASS, Josephine G, Romona, OK, 34; Robt M, S, 8; Harold E, S, 3

1208 BATES Birdie, Tahlequah, OK, 20

24918 BATES Charles A, Taiban, NM: 27

[BATES, Josephine. See #330]   *(Note: entry separate from other family groups)*

24982 BATES, Mollie, Pryor Creek, OK, 38; Fannie D, 11; Bulah D, 10; Crystal I D, 2

25637 BATEY, Robt. S Denver, CO, 22

1245 BATT Black, Stilwell, OK, 57; 3251 Mary, W, 55

13967 BATT Charley, Wauhillau, OK, 43; 6581 Nannie, W, 43; Jane A D, 6; Anna C D, 2; Mankiller, George, S of W, 16; Mary D of W, 14

1222 BATT Daniel, Oaks, OK, 27

2041 BATT, Eli, Oaks, OK, 48; 9665 Emily, E, 51

12501 BATT, Ellis, Stilwell, OK, 52; 12503 James, S, 15; Hennie D, 11; Daylight, S, 3; Lucy D, 2

28759 BATT, Isaac, Stilwell, OK, 39; Mary E, D, 8; Eva C, D, 6; Richard W, S, 4; Isaac N, S, 4; Willie A, S, 1

1287 BATT, Jack, Stilwell, OK, 69; 4507 Lucy, W, 61

12502 BATT, Jack, Stilwell, OK, 23; 10396 Patsy, W, 21; Earthy, S, 1; Daniel, S, 1

3249 BATT, Jeanna, Stilwell, OK, 16; By Black Batt, Gdn.

22588 BATT, Joe, Stilwell, OK, 30

17167 BATT, Joseph Campbell, OK, 34

23511 BATT, Mose, Stilwell, OK, 26; 1296 Jennie, W, 44

8309 BATT, Ned, Grove, OK, 51; 8308 Eliza, W, 39 [Died Oct, 1906]; 8309 Freeman, S, 5? (Difficult to read age); Adam, S, 13; Mary D, 5; Charles, S, 3

29201 BATTENFIELD, Lillie, Muskogee, OK, 26; La Vanch D, 8; Frantz, S, 3

879 BATTLES, Emily J, Vinita, OK, 62

25255 BATTLES, Stephen D, Pryor Creek, OK, 27

8896 BAUGH, Joel L, Jr Choteau, OK, 13; Roscoe Bro, 11; Edgar Bro, 9; By Joel L. Baugh, Gdn.

26072 BAUGH, Nannie S Choteau, OK, 29

1418 BAUGHMAN Bertha Dutch Mills AR, 20

10743 BAUGHMAN, Temperance W Campbell, OK, 24 [Died June 18 1906]; Nannie L D, 4; 10756 Dora E D, 2; By N.D. Baughman, Gdn.

23203 BAXTER, Stella, Holdenville, OK, 31

1354 BAZZELL, Mittie A, Vinita, OK, 30; Clarence S, S, 9; Jessie D, 5; Fay D, 3; Le Roy, S, 1

1499 BEACH Carrie, Needmore, OK, 26

24431 BEAGLES, Mary B. Cordray, 4th & Dennison St, Muskogee, OK, 18

Key: Guion Miller Application Number; Name; Address, Relation (to Head); Age in 1906

2784 BEAMER Bill, Row, OK, 20;   Rosie, Sis, 14;   By Nancy Beamer, Gdn.

26913 BEAMER, Emiline, Moodys, OK, 21

4943 BEAMER, John, Grove, OK, 46; 24792 Sarah J, W, 37; Oliver C, S, 16; Lula D, 12; Nancy D, 8; Lee F, S, 6; Lola May D, 3

8046 BEAMER, John, Kansas, OK, 50; 8045 Alice, W, 39

9792 BEAMER, Lewis, Moodys, OK, 53; 1638 Alice, W, 53; George, S, 12

27726 BEAMER, Nancy, Moodys, OK, 31; Samson, S, 2

24791 BEAMER, Pearl, Grove, OK, 18

30093 BEAMER, Sam, Moodys, OK, 33

9301 BEAMER, Will Cherokee City AR, 29; 9294 Lucy, W, 24; Jim, S, 5; Jennie D, 1; Ellis, S, ¼

25880 BEAMISH, Mary E Braggs, OK, 25; Russell L, S, 1/6

24376 BEAN, Adam, Baron, OK, 24; 6937 Alcey, W, 30; Webster, S, 2; Blackwood, Nellie, D of W, 12

5631 BEAN Arch, Hulbert, OK, 28; 7919, Annie, W, 27; 5631, Tom, S, 4

6807 BEAN Belle Boyd, Sheep Ranch CA, 40

28301 BEAN Bryant W, Foyil, OK, 23

23618 BEAN Carlos, Kilgore, TX, 25

22576 BEAN Charles, Stilwell, OK, 43; Sam, S, 17; Pearl D, 16; Mack, S, 14; Kate D, 12; Lee, S, 10; George P, S, 5; Madge D, 2; Jennie D, 1/12

17539 BEAN Charles Rawlin Angels Camp, CA, 9;   By Mary E. B. Mallett, Gdn.

28866 BEAN, Edgar Delaware, OK, 35; Mark, S, 6; Mary E D, 5; James C, S, 3

11414 BEAN, Edward R Claremore, OK, 48; Eliza E D, 18; Lorena D, 16; Tot D, 13; Dot , D, 13; Jesse E, S, 9

8757 BEAN, Elizabeth, McKey, OK, 29

[BEAN, Ella. See #8748]   *(Note: entry separate from other family groups)*

6911 BEAN, Geo. Samuel, Sheep Ranch CA, 33; Earl Boyd, S, 6; Leslie Blythe, S, 1

23617 BEAN, Grover, Kilgore, TX, 22

5812 BEAN, Hail, Oaks, OK, 63

384 BEAN, Henrietta, Kilgore, TX, 62

23615 BEAN, J. S, Kilgore, TX, 39; Foster, S, 3; Mary Ann D, 5/12

1776 BEAN, Jack Baron, OK, 65

[BEAN, Jim. See #10253]   *(Note: entry separate from other family groups)*

2704 BEAN, Joel Clayton, NM, 56; Albert, S, 11; Mark, S, 9; Ruby D, 6; Dennis B, S, 4; Henry M, S, 2

8130 BEAN, John, Eureka, OK, 12; Mary Ellen, Sis, 6; Jefferson Bro, 17; By Mary A. Bean, Gdn.

5632 BEAN, Joseph, Hulbert, OK, 52 [Dec'd.]; 5098 Susie, W, 51 [Dec'd.]; John, S, 14; Elic, S, 11; Anna D, 9; Nana D, 7; James, S, 2; Downing Charles, GS, 1

Key: Guion Miller Application Number; Name; Address, Relation (to Head); Age in 1906

[BEAN, Joseph. See #2704]   *(Note: entry separate from other family groups)*

21034 BEAN, Louis Rogers, Pryor Creek, OK, 33
29886 BEAN, Lucy, Hulbert, OK, 23
 4328 BEAN, Lucy J, Foyil, OK, 16;   Nannie, Sis, 12;   By Evaline Grover, Gdn.
11277 BEAN, Mark A, Tahlequah, OK, 37
43767 BEAN, Mary L, Sallisaw, OK, 16; Jennie A, Sis, 14; Thos. H Bro, 12; Jessie B,
        Sis, 9; Everett A Bro, 5; Edna E, Sis, 5;   By Jno. M. Bean, Gdn.
11635 BEAN, Mary S, Eureka, OK, 50
23616 BEAN, N.B, Kilgore, TX, 32; John E, S, 6; Ines D, 4; Tom S, S, 2
 3242 BEAN, Nancy Baron, OK, 58
 5003 BEAN, Nancy A, Sheep Ranch CA, 76

[BEAN, Oce. See #4243] ⎫   *(Note: entries separate*
[BEAN, Eli. See #4243] ⎭   *from other family groups)*

22676 BEAN, Raven Baron, OK, 26; 26236 Eliza, W, 20
11278 BEAN, Robert B, Tahlequah, OK, 33; 8317 Phenia, W, 34; 11278 William M, S,
        10; Robert B, Jr, S, 6; Sidney C, S, 3; Ridge, John P, S of W, 14
 8038 BEAN, Robt. Lee, Groveland CA, 42
 4245 BEAN, Russell, Warner, OK, 35
27948 BEAN, Ruth A, Sallisaw, OK, 18
13712 BEAN, Susan, Warner, OK, 60
10327 BEAN, Thomas A, Tahlequah, OK, 24; 43092 Sarah E, W, 26; Gladys D D, 4
 8131 BEAN, Walter S, Eureka, OK, 20
  383 BEAN, William W, Kilgore, TX, 53;   By John E. Bean, Gdn.
 4514 BEANSTICK Becca, Stilwell, OK, 39
23396 BEANSTICK Charley, Stilwell, OK, 30; 3641 Susan, W, 22

[BEANSTICK Dicey. See #1547]   *(Note: entry separate from other family groups)*

[BEANSTICK, Houston. See #1419]   *(Note: entry separate from other family groups)*

 4515 BEANSTICK, John, Stilwell, OK, 41; Susannah D, 4; Grant, S, 2
  984 BEANSTICK, Peggy, Stilwell, OK, 88

[BEANSTICK, Sut. See #1419]   *(Note: entry separate from other family groups)*

 1420 BEANSTICK, Watta, Stilwell, OK, 69
14209 BEAR Abraham, Spavinaw, OK, 20
22224 BEAR, Johnson Ballard, OK, 8;   By C.E. Holderman, Gdn.
22222 BEAR, Oscar Ballard, OK, 15;   By C.E. Holderman, Gdn.
22223 BEAR, Polly Ballard, OK, 12;   By C.E. Holderman, Gdn.

Key: Guion Miller Application Number; Name; Address, Relation (to Head); Age in 1906

14210 BEAR, Samuel, Spavinaw, OK, 20

22225 BEAR, Simon Ballard, OK, 16;   By C.E. Holderman, Gdn.

1952 BEARD Beulah M Claremore, OK, 23

21987 BEARGREASE, Ellen Braggs, OK, 49; Brown, James, S, 20; Dykes, Katie D, 12; Bud, S, 8

16455 BEARHEAD, Peter, Zeno, OK, 23; 13102 Lucy, W, 26; Nancy D, ¼

16460 BEARPAW Andy, Oaks, OK, 18

6604 BEARPAW Celia, Oaks, OK, 61

8888 BEARPAW Charlie, Stilwell, OK, 40; 6710 Jennie, W, 47

13313 BEARPAW Charlie Cookson, OK, 30; 13323 Addie, W, 29; Lookie D, 7; Stan Watie, S, 4; Nancy D, 2

13135 BEAVER, William Bunch, OK, 32; 12630 Ratt, Susan, W, 26; Beaver, Ola D of W, 1; Ratt, Polly D of W, 6; John, S of W, 3; Hicks, George, S of W, 7

32325 BEAVERS Albert or Rabbit, Webbers Falls, OK, 23; Sam, S, 4

26708 BEAVERS Chas, Webbers Falls, OK, 28

[BEAVERS, Ellen. See #22848]   *(Note: entry separate from other family groups)*

2074 BEAVERS, Sarah M Claremore, OK, 54

2755 BEAVERT, Thomas E, Melvin, OK, 55

10963 BEARPAW Daniel, Oaks, OK, 34; 7464 Jennie, W, 52; 22014 Youngpuppy, John, S of W, 13; 22015 Sallie D of W, 3

[BEARPAW, George. See #30828]   *(Note: entry separate from other family groups)*

11914 BEARPAW, Isaac, Stilwell, OK, 32

13199 BEARPAW, James Bunch, OK, 36; 13664 Annie, W, 31; Emiline D, 4; John, S, 2

13756 BEARPAW, Pollie Bunch, OK, 57

17667 BEARPAW, Sallie, Oaks, OK, 14;   By Celia Bearpaw, Gdn.

13305 BEARPAW, Sar-gy-yah Cookson, OK, 24

16094 BEARPAW, Wa-li-ci, Welling, OK, 17

[BEARPOLE Charlie. See #8888]   *(Note: entry separate from other family groups)*

23909 BEATTIE, Susan Ahniwake, OK, 18

9815 BEATTY Alice Bird R, Grass Valley, CA, 58

13312 BEAVER Bunch, OK, 97

13232 BEAVER Annie Bunch, OK, 51

13218 BEAVER Clem Bunch, OK, 33; Steve, S, 9; Nellie D, 7; Nannie D, 5; Linnie D, 11

[BEAVER Daniel. See #21749]   *(Note: entry separate from other family groups)*

Key: Guion Miller Application Number; Name; Address, Relation (to Head); Age in 1906

[BEAVER, Susie. See #21750]   *(Note: entry separate from other family groups)*

16433 BEAVER, George, Tulsa, OK, 30

18595 BEAVER, Grant, Peggs, OK, 34; 6447 Katie, W, 38; William, S, 17; James, S, 15; Jennie D, 10; Carrie D, 9; Claud, S, 7

13304 BEAVER, Jim Bunch, OK, 56; George, S, 18; Ardie, S, 16; Charlotte D, 13; Lilly D, 10

10944 BEAVER, Nellie Bunch, OK, 36; Collar, Jackson, S, 20

[BEAVER, Ola. See # 12630]   *(Note: entry separate from other family groups)*

369 BEAVER, Runaway, Eucha, OK, 39; 17200 Emma, W, 23; Isaac, S, 6; Maud D, 2

10883 BEAVER, Susie, Marble City, OK, 22

12416 BEAVER, Susie, Vian, OK, 23; Eliza Daugherty D, 6

13291 BEAVER, Susie Bunch, OK, 54

11012 BEAVER, Tom, Webbers Falls, OK, 56; 11489 Alsie, W, 50; Cherrie, D, 16; Mary, D, 12; 17270 Banty, Lila D of W, 14

9904 BEAVER, William, Spavinaw, OK, 35; 6073 Mary L, W, 40; Alice D, 18; Jennie D, 14; Jeff, S, 12; Charlotte D, 10; Eloise D, 8; Henrietta D, 4; Tommie, S, 1

6468 BECK Arthur W, Needmore, OK, 30

17585 BECK Bell Dora Childers, OK, 5; Fannie Leona, Sis, 2; By Carrie Vancuren, Mother

891 BECK Cynthia, Owassa, OK, 35; Jessie B, S, 14; John B, S, 7

5759 BECK Dora, Muskogee, OK, 8; Amy, Sis, 6; Frank Bro, 3; By Dora Beck, Gdn.

10385 BECK, Eliza, Fawn, OK, 32; Claud, S, 14; Lynda, S, 8; Nannie D, 6; Homer, S, 4; Jos. R, S, 2

34813 BECK, Ella V, Ignacio CO, 22   care Southern Ute School

16545 BECK, Frederick Bartlesville, OK, 35

13045 BECK, Guy, Row, OK, 22; Arlilee D, (age ?)

13041 BECK, Harlin, Row, OK, 35

[BECK, Willie Orien. See #13041]   *(Note: entry separate from other family groups)*

413 BECK, Harvey M, Independence KS, 23

5489 BECK, Henry, Row, OK, 49; Cornelious, S, 16; Albert, S, 15; Sina D, 14; Ida, D, 13; Ellen D, 10; Henry, S, 10; Dewey, S, 7; Oscar, S, 6; Icy, S, 5; Clifford, S, 2; Lora D, 11

12240 BECK, James, Tahlequah, OK, 13; Cogin Bro, 11; Tom, Bro, 18; By Wm P. Beck, Gdn.

13044 BECK, Jeffrey, Row, OK, 37

Key: Guion Miller Application Number; Name; Address, Relation (to Head); Age in 1906

27475 BECK, Jesse Cherokee City AR, 27

866 BECK, John, Flint, OK, 35

11595 BECK, John Cherokee City AR, 37; 11597 Ida R, W, 27; Ezekiel, S, 11; George, S, 9; Sabra D, 7; Cherry M, S, 5; Lillie B D, 3

13042 BECK, John, Row, OK, 28

8649 BECK, Joseph, Row, OK, 38

3239 BECK, Klon L, Guertie, OK, 9; By M. O. Smith, Gdn.

17139 BECK, Lucian, Row, OK, 11; By Harlin Beck, Gdn.

8962 BECK, Lytha Alluwee, OK, 64

6799 BECK, Mary, Eureka, OK, 23

17138 BECK, Mary, Row, OK, 9; By Harlin Beck, Gdn.

17137 BECK, Maud, Row, OK, 14; By Harlin Beck, Gdn.

925 BECK, Richard, Flint, OK, 29; 926 Ida A, W, 30; Roy L, S, 10; Maggie M D, 8; Eddie A, S, 4; Nettie M D, 1

5488 BECK, Robt Cherokee City AR, 52

11271 BECK, Robert, Kennison, OK, 24

16653 BECK, Rutherford Cherokee City AR, 31; Homer, S, 12; Stella D, 10; Ary D, 9; Joe, S, 8; Jessie D, 7; Ada P D, 5; Susie D, 2

867 BECK, Sabra, Row, OK, 61

5065 BECK, Samuel, Flint, OK, 33

10497 BECK, Samuel Cherokee City AR, 21

2672 BECK, Sarah, Estella, OK, 51

2201 BECK, Sarah Josephine, Kansas, OK, 57

15077 BECK, Thomas, Estella, OK, 42; Tecumseh, S, 5; Richard, S, 2

12816 BECK, Toney A, Flint, OK, 35; 25987 Sarah A, W, 35; Chessie D, 6; Kermit, S, 1

17140 BECK, Vivian, Row, OK, 13; By Harlin Beck, Gdn.

5360 BECK, Walter R, Independence, KS, 20; William A Bro, 17; Stella M, Sis, 12; By Mary J. Beck, Gdn.

13043 BECK, Weatherford, Row, OK, 25; John H, S, 4; Lottie A D, 2

8798 BECK, William P, Tahlequah, OK, 36; Joseph, S 10; Susie D, 8; Carl D, S, 1/3

13573 BECKNELL, John, Wilson's Mills, MO, 52

859 BEE, Julia A, Flint, OK, 54; Mary Ellen D, 12; Willora C.J. D, 17; Dial, Mattie D, 20

25191 BEEBE, Lillie B, Welch, OK, 23

35455 BEESON, Edward B, Fairland, OK, 20

26785 BEESON, Perry H, Vinita, OK, 31; John Edward, S, 11

26783 BEETS Augusta, Vinita, OK, 27; Bertha D, 9; Everett R, S, 7; Wesley E, S, 5; Nancy A, D, 3

13438 BEFFA, Sarah A, Ramona, OK, 62

18537 BELL, Frances, Peggs, OK, 13; Percy Bro, 11; John Bro, 9; Frank Bro, 7; By Lena Taylor, Gdn.

17196 BELL, George W, Leach, OK, 25; Laura D, 3; George, Jr, S, 1

CHEROKEE DESCENDANTS RESIDING WEST OF MISSISSIPPI RIVER.
VOLUME II   (A – M)

Key: Guion Miller Application Number; Name; Address, Relation (to Head); Age in 1906

2680 BELL, James M, Vinita, OK, 78

2678 BELL, John Martin Chelsea, OK, 47; 2679 Minnie C, W, 44; Andrew L, S, 16; Ella, D, 14; Martin W, S, 11; Fortner D, S, 8; George M, S, 5

2467 BELL, Lizzie, Westville, OK, 58

2205 BELL, Lucien B, Vinita, OK, 68; 2204   Mary F. S, W, 64

29987 BELL, Mattie J, Owasso, OK, 25; Newman, Sallie F D, 10; Toka J D, 4; Van S, S, 3

3638 BELL, Minerva J.E, Ft. Smith AR, 40 524 Carnall Ave; Mary D, 3

3012 BELL, Minnie R. C. Bartlesville, OK, 48; Alfred E, S, 12; Pauline Laura D, 10; Lorena, D, 7

12620 BELL, Stephen, Westville, OK, 41; 12621 Jennie, W, 32; Hooley, S, 14; Jesse, S, 4; John D, S, 5

14240 BELL, Samuel, Westville, OK, 43

547 BELL, Sherman, Leach, OK, 32; Dee A, S, 1

8020 BELL, Tilden, Siloam Springs AR, 31; Pearl D, 7; Daisy D, 1

11671 BELL, William Ballard, OK, 22

16783 BELT, Mary, Oaks, OK, 36; 16784 Adam, Maud D, 18

3876 BELT, Polly, Peggs, OK, 46; Thomas, S, 13; Levi, S, 10

3875 BELT, Stan, Peggs, OK, 22

11908 BELT, Thos, Leach, OK, 37; Liddy D, 7; Scoo-wee, S, 5; Nancy D, 1

18775 BENDABOUT Blunt Cookson, OK, 25

7647 BENDABOUT, James Cookson, OK, 30; 7648 Lizzie, W, 28; Roat, S, 6; Quatie D, 5; John, S, 1

10326 BENDABOUT, Moses Cookson, OK,   77; 10306 Lucy, W, 57

2687 BENDABOUT, Tainey Cookson, OK, 50

22932 BENDURE Charley Choteau, OK, 26

22931 BENDURE, Edward Choteau, OK, 32; 31822 Blanche, W, 17

22934 BENDURE, John B Choteau, OK, 35; Ella M D, 10; Ettie R D, 9; Nettie M D, 8; Lilly A D, 6; Charley E, S, 4; John B, Jr, S, 1

31361 BENEFIELD, Edna Collinsville, OK, 17

7901 BENGE Caroline , Ft. Gibson, OK, 60

[BENGE Cornelius C. See #25943]   *(Note: entry separate from other family groups)*

4486 BENGE David W Akins, OK, 36; Lizzie J D, 13; James M, S, 11; Dooley, S, 7

26475 BENGE, Elinor Adair, OK, 18

[BENGE, Emmett. See #7923]   *(Note: entry separate from other family groups)*

8877 BENGE, George Brushy, OK, 24; Edna Lee D, 1

5395 BENGE, George W, Tahlequah, OK, 54; 5272 Fannie F, W, 50; J. Albert, S, 19; Houston, S, 17; Eliza D, 15; Cora D, 13

26474 BENGE, Georgia A Adair, OK, 22

Key: Guion Miller Application Number; Name; Address, Relation (to Head); Age in 1906

13425 BENGE, Henry, Long, OK, 34; Mack, S, 4; Jesse L, S, 1
14264 BENGE, Henry, Oklahoma City, OK, 36
7902 BENGE, Jack, Ft. Gibson, OK, 25
1630 BENGE, James F, Lynch, OK, 57
7898 BENGE, Jennie, Ft. Gibson, OK, 24
26385 BENGE, Jessie L, Tahlequah, OK, 28

[BENGE, John D. See #4831]   *(Note: entry separate from other family groups)*

8879 BENGE, John Brushy, OK, 35; Sally B D, 13
6967 BENGE, Joseph M Adair, OK, 27
7905 BENGE, Louis, Ft. Gibson, OK, 27; Floyd, S, 6; Thelma D, 4; Robert, S, 2
2743 BENGE, Margaret, Moodys, OK, 59
7895 BENGE, Martin V, Ft. Gibson, OK, 50; 12364 Adna S, W, 35; John A, S, 17;
    Emma, D, 11; Ruth D, 11; Leo, S, 9; Charles S, S, 6; George, S, 3
30539 BENGE, Martin V, Ft. Gibson, OK, 21
15992 BENGE, Medley Braggs, OK, 19; James Bro, 14;   By William Choate, Gdn.
26386 BENGE, Minnie, Tahlequah, OK, 25
6792 BENGE, Nancy, Ft. Gibson, OK, 61
4039 BENGE, Nelson, Long, OK, 34; Mary D, 12; Columbus, S, 11; Lula D, 9
8878 BENGE, Obediah, Jr Brushy, OK, 21
4485 BENGE, Obediah, Sr Akins, OK, 65; Ridge Otto, S, 4; Drewie H, S, 2; Mary D
    D, 1/12
1629 BENGE, Oce P Adair, OK, 57; 3044 Martha A, W, 45; Lelia L D, 14; Dora D,
    11; Lenora D, 4
7904 BENGE, Pickens, Ft. Gibson, OK, 21
9317 BENGE, Pickens, Sallisaw, OK, 50; Houston, S, 13
10702 BENGE, Richard Braggs, OK, 26
18001 BENGE, Riddle, Ft. Gibson, OK, 18
7903 BENGE, Robert, Ft. Gibson, OK, 38; Louis, S, 11; Ollie D, 8; Nora D, 5; Addie
    D, 2
5394 BENGE, Ross L, Whitmire, OK, 46; Lucy D, 11
28277 BENGE, Samuel A, Tahlequah, OK, 27; 28278 Maggie D, W, 18
7900 BENGE, Samuel H, Jr, Ft. Gibson, OK, 34; 29654 Sallie, W, 32; Carrie D, 10;
    Samuel, S, 8; Jack R, S, 4; Jeff M, S, 2
7897 BENGE, Theodore, Ft. Gibson, OK, 32; Richard, S, 5; Maggie D, 4; Ross, S, 2
9177 BENGE, Thomas Brushy, OK, 38

[BENGE, Tuglee. See #25394]   *(Note: entry separate from other family groups)*

1836 BENNETT. Annie C, Muskogee, OK, 34; Anna Lee D, 10; Martha McK, D, 8
207 BENNETT, Emily, Muskogee, OK, 66
1819 BENNETT, Mary Chelsea, OK, 90

Key: Guion Miller Application Number; Name; Address, Relation (to Head); Age in 1906

[BENNETT, Mary. See #25291]   *(Note: entry separate from other family groups)*

8065 BENNETT, Phillip, Hulbert, OK, 53; 7875 Delilah, W, 48
15641 BENTIE Cornelius Campbell, OK, 27
27765 BERD, Nancy E, Ft. Gibson, OK, 26; Beatrice J D, 7; Harold B, S, 5; Evlyn[sic] D, 1
33477 BERNER Cora D, Miami, OK, 20; Ovel R, S, ½
33478 BERNER, Ora B, Miami, OK, 20 R.F.D. #4; Goldia M D, ¼
24459 BERRY Amos E, Fairland, OK, 43
29653 BERRY Charles M Chelsea, OK, 36; Jay Clarence, S, 4; Jessie T D, 1/12
37742 BERRY, Elisha C, Quapaw, OK, 47
24828 BERRY, Etta M, Fairland, OK, 20
2393 BERRY, Flora, Woodley, OK, 22; Clyde A, S, 1
26805 BERRY, Florence L, Webbers Falls, OK, 25; George E, S, 5; Albert K, S, 2
23602 BERRY, Ibbie Afton, OK, 28; Otia R D, 8; Silvia G D, 6; Zim M, S, 2
5733 BERRY, Ida Coffeyville, KS, 33; Ruth J D, 13; Frank E, S, 11; Tacy E D, 7; John Henry, S, 4; Floyd Thomas, S, 1/6
26305 BERRY, John W, Vinita, OK, 34; Brown, George F.C. C, Nep, 3
31257 BERRY, Wesley B Delaware, (OK), 9; Lee B Bro, 7; By Robt. E. Berry, Gdn.
26150 BESHEAR, Mary Catoosa, OK, 18

[BETHEL Clarence W. See #1866]   *(Note: entry separate from other family groups)*

9373 BETHEL, Lillian, Foreman, OK, 35; Dora E D, 13; Dona Bell D, 10; Willie E, S, 8; Madgie L D, 7; Louis L, S, 5; David F, S, ¾; 28344 Talithia May D, 18
326 BETTERTON, Wm. Catharine, Grove, OK, 25

[BEVEART, Lucie. See #5311]   *(Note: entry separate from other family groups)*

[BEZONIA Delitha M. See #571]   *(Note: entry separate from other family groups)*

1537 BIBLE Arthur A Alluwe, OK, 34; George L, S, 5
33621 BIBLES, Louis Chelsea, OK, 13; Jessie, Sis, 11; By Joseph Hildebrand, Gdn.
3837 BIBLES, Margaret M Chelsea, OK, 52; James T, S, 20; Edward, S, 20
23929 BICKFORD, Maggie B, Pryor Creek, OK, 18; Charles H, S, 3; William F, S, 2; Nancy E D, ½
23746 BICKFORD, Mary P, Ft. Gibson, OK, 17

[BIGACORN, Nancy J. See #5353] ⎤   *(Note: entries separate
[BIGACORN, Maud. See #5353] ⎦   from other family groups)*

[BIGACORN, Ollie. See #4917]   *(Note: entry separate from other family groups)*

Key: Guion Miller Application Number; Name; Address, Relation (to Head); Age in 1906

10581 BIG ACORN, Red Bird, Southwest City, MO, 47

26085 BIGACORN, Ezekiel, Locust Grove, OK, 22; 5354 Jennie, W, 22

26047 BIGBEY Abe, Evansville AR, 21

26048 BIGBEY Arthur E, Evansville AR, 26

24716 BIGBY Charles T, Stilwell, OK, 31; Charles T, Jr, S, 4; Jessie Z, D, 3; Claude D, S, 1

28758 BIGBEY David E Dutch Mills AR, 26; 17276 Johann, W, 19

5360 BIGBY David T, Evansville AR, 57; 5218 Nancy J, W, 54; Martha J D, 18; Walter A, S, 16; David L, S, 10

26354 BIGBEY, Edward C, Stilwell, OK, 23

26128 BIGBEY, Henry C, Gideon, OK, 23

16854 BIGBEY, John, Texanna, OK, 48; 8177 Betsy, W, 49

5232 BIGBY, Malinda J, Evansville AR, 54

26046 BIGBEY, Samuel A, Evansville AR, 31; Teetsey Ora D, 4;   Marvin A, S, 1

27486 BIGBEY, Samuel A, Stilwell, OK, 21

23897 BIGBY, Thomas, Stilwell, OK, 33; Edith D D, 10; Clarence G, S, 7; Corda M D, 4; Fred J, S, 2

26689 BIGBEY, Thomas B, Stilwell, OK, 29

5332 BIGBEY, Thomas W, Evansville AR, 58; Sarah D, 18; Minnie C D, 16

1234 BIGBEY, Walter Ahniwake, OK, 51; Samuel, S, 19; Susan D, 14

29316 BIGBEY, Walter D, Stilwell, OK, 35; 5752 Sabina, W, 26; Maud M D, 10; Maymie S, D, 9; William J.B, S, 6; Gladys D, D, 4; Mary C D, 1½

15966 BIGBULLET, Mack, Stilwell, OK, 35

6594 BIGDRUM, Joseph Christie, OK, 47; 6622 Mary, Wm, 50; Jim, S, 19; Grace D, 16; Ada D, 13; Johnson, S, 11

[BIGELOW, Wm. See #9153] }   *(Note: entries separate*
[BIGELOW, Emma. See #9153] }   *from other family groups)*

27103 BIGFEATHER Ben, Jr, Maple, OK, 20

5592 BIGFEATHER Buck, Stilwell, OK, 52; 604 Sallie, W, 58; Scraper, Polly D of W, 13

9325 BIGFEATHER, Jennie, Melvin, OK, 63

6448 BIGFEATHER, Joe, Locust Grove, OK, 32

9796 BIGFEATHER, John, Melvin, OK, 38; 9234 Polly, W, 30; 10309 George, S, 14; Sarah, D, 12; 9234 Keener, Heavy, S of W, 18; Hair, Oscar, S of W, 13; Keener, Hattie D of W, 6; Bigfeather, Nannie D, 4

2828 BIGFEATHER, Lucy, Maple, OK, 56; George, S, 9; Lydia D, 17

10688 BIGFEATHER, Mitchell, Maple, OK, 30; 27105 Mary, W, 25; Lucy D, 5; Gussie, S, 4; Jennie D, 2; Annie D, 1

17469 BIGFEATHER, Ollie, Melvin, OK, 36

24943 BIGFEATHER, Pearl, Maple, OK, 11;   By Wm. W. Miller, Gdn.

27104 BIGFEATHER, Polly, Maple, OK, 22

Key: Guion Miller Application Number; Name; Address, Relation (to Head); Age in 1906

13121 BIGFEATHER, Rider Bunch, OK, 22

5591 BIGFEATHER, Wash Bunch, OK, 49; 13222 Ka-ho-gah, W, 61

3253 BIGGERS, Georgia, Pryor Creek, OK, 21; George, S, 3

13327 BIGGS, Katie Catoosa, OK, 51

3254 BIGGERS, Lillian C, Pryor Creek, OK, 6; By John T. Biggers, Gdn.

1235 BIGHAM, Eva M, Ramona, OK, 29; Addie M D, 5

6533 BIGHEAD, Molly, Melvin, OK, 60

6534 BIGHEAD, Sallie, Hulbert, OK, 22; Carey. Joe, S, 6

1339 BILL, Sallie, Stilwell, OK, 81

40030 BILLINGSLEA, Frank D, Nowata, OK, 29

30057 BILLINGSLEA, Homer A Adair, OK, 11; Robert F Bro, 9; By Elyer B. Neville, Gdn.

6749 BILLINGSLEA, Janet, Vinita, OK, 44; Willie D D, 18; Joe, S, 14

32778 BILLINGSLEA, McLeod, Nowata, OK, 31

19487 BINNS, Lillie, Kelleyville, OK, 33; Roxie C D, 5; James O, S, 10

33638 BIRCHFIELD, John A, Pryor Creek, OK, 24; Cecil, S, 3

32915 BIRD Andrew, Marble City, OK, 20; Andy, S, 1/12

[BIRD Charley. See #9145]   *(Note: entry separate from other family groups)*

[BIRD Cynthia. See #9146]   *(Note: entry separate from other family groups)*

27909 BIRD Charlie Briartown, OK, 23

17082 BIRD Charlotte, Tahlequah, OK, 26

[BIRD Christie. See #7490]   *(Note: entry separate from other family groups)*

5651 BIRD Cornelius Braggs, OK, 24

9452 BIRD Daniel, Tahlequah, OK, 39; 30112 Nancy, W, 30; Nathaniel A, S, 6; Felix P, S, 3; Florence H D, 1

9742 BIRD Dave, Marble City, OK, 41; 9744 Cynthia, W, 44; Winnie D, 5; Still, Mary D of #24461

10748 BIRD Delilah Briartown, OK, 50

[BIRD, Eliza M. See #13673]   *(Note: entry separate from other family groups)*

[BIRD, Esther. See #19646]   *(Note: entry separate from other family groups)*

[BIRD, Eloise. See #4932]   *(Note: entry separate from other family groups)*

1496 BIRD, Emily, Wagoner, OK, 37; Watts, Eddie, S 19; Bird, Lizzie D, 11; Trissie D, 8; Cinda D, 5; Mary D, 3

27908 BIRD, Francis M Briartown, OK, 27; Pearlie D, 4

Key: Guion Miller Application Number; Name; Address, Relation (to Head); Age in 1906

17078 BIRD, James, Tahlequah, OK, 31; 34560 Eliza, W, 28; Shadie D, 1
11230 BIRD, Jesse, Whitmire, OK, 28; 11238 Sis, W, 24; Sand Charley, S of W, 5;
Poorboy, Sallie D of W, 2

[BIRD, John. See #13757]   *(Note: entry separate from other family groups)*

1269 BIRD, John A, Texanna, OK, 40

[BIRD, Joseph. See #922]   *(Note: entry separate from other family groups)*

9706 BIRD, Nancy Bunch, OK, 51; Young, George, GS, 6
16921 BIRD, Nancy, Long, OK, 30; Ton H, S, 2
9733 BIRD, Peter Bunch, OK, 51
8732 BIRD, Rachel, Locust Grove, OK, 31; Joshia, S, 10
2219 BIRD, Sarah, Stilwell, OK, 52; Jenna D, 18; 8085 Nellie D, 13
13288 BIRD, Scott, Stilwell, OK, 27; Thomas, S, 5; Charley, S, 4
3800 BIRD, William, Tahlequah, OK, 64
11684 BIRD, William, Jr, Tahlequah, OK, 20
2810 BIRDCHOPPER Ben, Locust Grove, OK, 33; 5286 Jennie, W, 50;
Kingfisher Dooniah, S of W, 12; Dew, Ella D of W, 8
2760 BIRDCHOPPER Caleb, Hulbert, OK, 44; 6801 Lucy, W, 45
2815 BIRDCHOPPER, Huckleberry, Locust Grove, OK, 44

[BIRDTAIL, John. See #17107]
[BIRDTAIL Dave. See #17107]   *(Note: entries separate*
[BIRDTAIL, Sam. See #17107]   *from other family groups)*

26892 BISHOP Allie H, Ft. Worth, TX, 37 Sta. A
44118 BISHOP, Edward B, Sherman, TX, 15; By Fannie Bishop, Gdn.
26967 BISHOP, Lucy M Chelsea, OK, 24; Lillian L D, 1
22521 BISHOP, Maggie L Chelsea, OK, 23; Selma E D, 3; Ellouise D, 1
25038 BISHOP, Mamie, Ft. Gibson, OK, 23; Eva Lucile D, ½
24355 BITTING, John, Tahlequah, OK, 21
31277 BITTING, Leppoe, Tip, OK, 35; Kellie, S, 9; Emma D, 7; Jackson, S, 2; Mary
D, 1
865 BITTING, Mary J, Tahlequah, OK, 58
31277 BITTING, Nicholas, Tahlequah, OK, 26
31295 BITTING, William, Tahlequah, OK, 23; 31296 Maggie, W, 21; Edgar T, S, 1
9422 BIVIN Adeline, Vinita, OK, 68
24561 BLACK Alcey, Southwest City, MO, 29; Ketcher Andrew, S, 12; Black Calvin,
S, 10; Lucian, S, 8; Benjamin, S, 6; Nellie D, 1
23568 BLACK Cora L, Fairland, OK, 24; Mary Lucile D, 3; Dorus Carl, S, 1/12
29880 BLACK, Kathleen P, Muskogee, OK, 18

Key: Guion Miller Application Number; Name; Address, Relation (to Head); Age in 1906

31866 BLACKARD Clara, Muldrow, OK, 26; Irene D, 7; Joe, S, 6; Vida R D, 2

4190 BLACK BEAR, Locust Grove, OK, 55; 14189 Sallie, W, 49; Lista D, 12; Oh-lee-qu-nee, D, 10; Coo-wie, S, 8; Locust, S, 6; Gor-tu-yoh, D, 3; Oo-da-lar-da, GS,10

14298 BLACKBEAR Car-no-he-yar-deer, Locust Grove, OK, 21

10211 BLACKBEAR, Scale, Locust Grove, OK, 28; 10208 Cynthia S, W, 21; Love D, 3

444 BLACKBEAR, Teach, Eucha, OK, 22

5328 FIXIN BLACKBIRD Alcey, Stilwell, OK, 64

11519 BLACKBIRD Dave, Locust Grove, OK, 17;   By Sarah Dreadfulwater, Gdn.

28797 BLACKBIRD David, Muskogee, OK,   31

11403 BLACKBIRD, Jim, Southwest City, MO, 35; 11458 Lucy, W, 23; Jew-saw-lunt, S, 14; Oo-goo-ne-ya-chee, S, 11; Squal-eest, S, 3

1992 BLACKBIRD, Joe, Uniontown AR, 50; 1200 Nancy, W, 46; John, S, 19; William, S, 13; Rosie D, 10; Annie D, 8

16116 BLACKBIRD, Joseph Baron, OK, 30; 7028 Ollie, W, 20; William, S, 3

4293 BLACKBIRD, Susannah, Peggs, OK, 21

28160 BLACKBIRD, Wilson, Stilwell, OK, 37; 6456 Nellie, W, 30; Speaker, Willie, S of W, 15; Sam, S of W, 14; Blackbird, Susie D, 10; Joe, S, 8; Allie D, 6

[BLACKFOX. See #8859]   *(Note: entry separate from other family groups)*

16880 BLACKFOX Benjamin, Oaks, OK, 21

[BLACKFOX Darky. See #2035]   *(Note: entry separate from other family groups)*

[BLACKFOX David. See #16884]   *(Note: entry separate from other family groups)*

14294 BLACKFOX, Ellis, Hulbert, OK, 51; 17470 Susie, W, 38; James, S, 15; John, S, 7; Jessie D, 6; Lyda D, 4

84 BLACKFOX, Enola Dragger, OK, 67 [Died 9-30-1907]; 85 Alsie, W, 61

5441 BLACK, Henry, Southwest City, MO, 60; White, Lucinda, GD, 10

24060 BLACKFOX, Jim Dragger, OK, 33; 4912 Ahlie, W, 27; Charlotte D, 4

14286 BLACKFOX, John Baptist, OK, 58

8042 BLACKFOX, Nancy, Kansas, OK, 80

5815 BLACKFOX, Ned, Oaks, OK, 36; 5813 Annie, W, 39; Jennie D, 14; Laura D, 2

5725 BLACKFOX, Nellie, Oaks, OK, 64

4308 BLACKFOX, Sallie, Locust Grove, OK, 26

10221 BLACKFOX, Sam, Oaks, OK, 41; 11234 Lucy, W, 41; Joe, S, 19; Susie D, 17; Sallie, D, 15; Jonathan A, S, 13; Charlotte D, 11; Steve, S, 9

[BLACKFOX, Tom. See #8859]   *(Note: entry separate from other family groups)*

Key: Guion Miller Application Number; Name; Address, Relation (to Head); Age in 1906

[BLACKFOX, Wilson. See #4903]   *(Note: entry separate from other family groups)*

15960 BLACKHAW Annie, Tahlequah, OK, 56; 27181 Emma, D, 12 [Minor Died 11-1906]
  1448 BLACKHAWK Coowie, Sallisaw, OK, 50

[BLACKMON, Lou. See #1130]   }   *(Note: entries separate*
[BLACKMON, Jesse L. See #1130] }   *from other family groups)*

  6979 BLACKSTONE Dewitt W, Muskogee, OK, 29
13170 BLACKSTONE, Edward F, Porum, OK, 27
12515 BLACKSTONE, Eliza, San Pedro CA, 21
12517 BLACKSTONE, Frank S, San Pedro, CA, 16
32095 BLACKSTONE, George, Porum, OK, 31; Gracie D, 6   [Died 3-24-1907]; Pearl D, 5; Theoderia, S, 3; Alta D, 2; Venia D, 1/6
13588 BLACKSTONE, George E, Webbers Falls, OK, 21
14667 BLACKSTONE, Kate, Webbers Falls, OK, 20
10110 BLACKSTONE, Mollie L, San Pedro, 282 ½ 4th St CA, 25
13589 BLACKSTONE, Napoleon D, Webbers Falls, OK, 25
  4394 BLACKSTONE, Robert D, Muskogee, OK, 33
  8212 BLACKSTONE, Robert W, Porum, OK, 33; Mae D, 11; John, S, 8; Nora D, 3; Minnie D, 1/6
23325 BLACKWELL, Elizabeth, Gritts, OK, 20

[BLACKWELL, King David. See #9233] }   *(Note: entries separate*
[BLACKWELL, Solomon. See #9233]   }   *from other family groups)*
[BLACKWELL, Hazel. See #9233]   }

  2849 BLACKWOOD Annie Baron, OK, 41; 9408 Jennie D, 9; Wah-le-yah D, 7; George, S, 4
27837 BLACKWOOD Cora A, Siloam Springs, AR, 32; Henry F, S, 12; Minnie M D, 10; James A, S, 7; Ida C D, 5; Nancy G D, 3
  9677 BLACKWOOD Dave Christie, OK, 46
27531 BLACKWOOD, Emma E, Siloam Springs AR, 48; Leander H, S, 17; Isaac Burr, S, 15; John H, S, 12
  1876 BLACKWOOD, Hoolie Baron, OK, 39; 24997 Julia, W, 26; 40793 James, S, 12; Leona D, 15; Youngbird, S, 4; Margaret D, 1; Thornton, Mary D of W, 11
27532 BLACKWOOD, Lida A, Siloam Springs AR, 25
  1944 BLACKWOOD, Lydia Baron, OK, 27
  1924 BLACKWOOD, Martin Baron, OK, 30; 30616 Susie, W, 18

[BLACKWOOD, Nellie. See #6937]   *(Note: entry separate from other family groups)*

Key: Guion Miller Application Number; Name; Address, Relation (to Head); Age in 1906

30204 BLACKWOOD, William I, Siloam Springs AR, 22

3595 BLADON Aggie E Campbell, OK, 14;   By John Bladon, Gdn.

3594 BLADON, Marion Campbell, OK, 17;   By John Bladon, Gdn.

30176 BLAIR, Eliza, Sallisaw, OK, 41; Lee, S, 19; Douglass, S, 16; Callie, S, 14;
Dewey, S, 7

1542 BLAIR, Emma Catoosa, OK, 41; Frank, S, 9

27026 BLAIR, George Akins, OK, 46; Zella L D, 6; Tommie Retta, S, 4; Jewell D, 3

25814 BLAIR, Jesse T Cookson, OK, 25

9460 BLAIR, John Cookson, OK, 40; 12225 Jennie, W, 32; Eliza D, 8; Louie, S, 6;
John, Jr, S, 4; Katie D, 3; Nellie D, 1

[BLAIR, Lila. See #4210]   *(Note: entry separate from other family groups)*

5379 BLAIR, Lizzie Chaffee, OK, 52; Jimmie, S, 15

1050 BLAIR, Thomas, Tahlequah, OK, 62; 1053 Margaret, W, 56; 25815 Pearl D, 18

26038 BLAKE, Georgia A, Pryor Creek, OK,   39; Jennie A D, 17; Neta E, D, 14;
John F, S, 12; Albert W, S, 9; Georgia K D, 6; Mable H D, 3; Hester K D, 1

43246 BLAKE, Lola W, Hobart, OK, 21; Eugene, S, 2

3239 BLAKEMORE, Eliza J, Muskogee, OK, 27

31048 BLAKEMORE, Retta M, Owasso, OK, 14; Gracie D, Sis, 9; Oce, Bro, 6; By
William N. Blakemore, Gdn.

31049 BLAKEMORE, Sarah E, Owasso, OK, 23; Susanna M D, 2; Starkey, Willie,
S, 8; Henry, S, 5

9276 BLANKET, Lucy, Melvin, OK, 42; Welch, Nancy D, 12

9277 BLANKET, Peter, Melvin, OK, 20

26705 BLASENGAME, Elizabeth, Wauhillau, OK, 18

4008 BLEDSOE, Nannie B Choteau, OK, 37; Henry W, S, 17; Sallie M D, 14; Joel C,
S, 11; William A.G, S, 8; Edna D, 5; Fannie G D, 3

24157 BLEDSOE, Susie, Muldrow, OK, 20; Bessie M D, 4; Evert Barney, S, ¾

23333 BLEVINS, George, Grove. OK, 27; Pleasy, D, 8; Burril, D, 4; Mollie, D, 2

22929 BLEVINS, Jackson, Jr, Vinita, OK, 24

26308 BLEVINS, Jeff, Vinita, OK, 34

24774 BLEVINS, John T Dodge, OK, 26

23332 BLEVINS, Joseph, Grove, OK, 39; William V, S, 10; John C, S, 5; Rosa D, 2

22213 BLEVINS, Leroy C, Maysville AR, 45; Willie, S, 15; Apsa D, 13; Edna D, 10;
Jabe, S, 4

38 BLEVINS, Nancy, Vinita, OK, 52

2146½ BLEVINS, Nellie M, Grove, OK, By A. Blevins, Gdn.

[BLEVINS, Ollie. See #19370]   *(Note: entry separate from other family groups)*

23331 BLEVINS, Pleasant, Grove, OK, 34; Joseph, S, 12; Lizzie, D, 10; James, S, 5;
Fred, S, 2

Key: Guion Miller Application Number; Name; Address, Relation (to Head); Age in 1906

23416 BLEVINS, Ross, Vinita, OK, 32

11533 BLISS, Hattie, Spavinaw, OK, 40; Mankiller, Thos. H, S, 18; Beacher, S, 15; Bliss, Luria V D, 2

5002 BLOSSOM, Betsy, Melvin, OK, 50; Lizey, GD, 2

2133 BLOSSOM, Jack, Locust Grove, OK, 22

2917 BLOSSOM, Joe, Locust Grove, OK, 29; Agnes D, 4; Phillips, S, 1; Muggie D, 6

78 BLOSSOM, John, Locust Grove, OK, 33; 3290 Jennie, W, 33; Joe, S, 9; Ocie D, 8; Will, S, 6; Emma D, 2

79 BLOSSOM, Lila, Locust Grove, OK, 58; Grayson, Napoleon, S, 13

18480 BLOSSOM, Maggie, Hulbert, OK, 20

9273 BLOSSOM, Ned, Melvin, OK, 22

2132 BLOSSOM, Tom, Locust Grove, OK, 26; 1288 Jennie, W, 31; Kingfisher, Skake, S of W, 13; Vann Cornelius, S of W, 8; Ezekiel, S of W, 4; Blossom, Sam, S, 1

9621 BLUE, Mardee, Oaks, OK, 8; By Susie Fencer, Gdn.

[BLUE, Martha. See #17050]   *(Note: entry separate from other family groups)*

[BLUEBIRD Charlie. See #9946]   *(Note: entry separate from other family groups)*

[BLUEBIRD, Elias. See #5264]   *(Note: entry separate from other family groups)*

29696 BLUEBIRD, Jack, Locust Grove, OK, 25; 2987 Peggie, W, 28; Lizzie D, 2

26527 BLUEBIRD, Luke, Moodys, OK, 26; 4311 Mary, W, 20; Sam, S, 1/12; Kingfisher, Joe, S of W, 1

16905 BLUEBIRD, Samuel, Locust Grove, OK, 52; 3692 Nellie, W, 29; Oh-ling D, 13; Chee-goo-wa D, 9; Gur-u-jay D, 6; Oo-ly-jay D, 6; Johnson, S, 1

13631 BLYTHE Burton M, Ramona, OK, 22

24166 BLYTHE Cornelius Claremore, OK, 4; By Emma T Bradshaw, Gdn.

793 BLYTHE, Elijah, Ramona, OK, 60

[BLYTHE, Jack. See #4056]   *(Note: entry separate from other family groups)*

10747 BLYTHE, Jackson, Porum, OK, 34

707 BLYTHE, James C Bartlesville, OK, 82

1678 BLYTHE, Jemima S, Vinita, OK, 73

3203 BLYTHE, Napoleon B Afton, OK, 54; John E, S, 18; Aubrey A, S, 13; Erma Lola D, 9; Jesse L, S, 7; Charles F, S, 6

23990 BLYTHE, William H Afton, OK, 22

22703 BOATMAN, Joanna, Webbers Falls, OK, 23; Clara D, 1/12

11642 BOATMAN, Sarah L, Texanna, OK, 24; Edgar, S, 4; Ocie E D, 2; Dovie L D, 1

7480 BOGGS, Katy, Sallisaw, OK, 56

[BOLAND. See BOLEN, BOLIN, BOLYN, and BOWLIN.]

CHEROKEE DESCENDANTS RESIDING WEST OF MISSISSIPPI RIVER.
VOLUME II   (A – M)

Key: Guion Miller Application Number; Name; Address, Relation (to Head); Age in 1906

23441 BOLAND, John, Porum, OK, 24

4081 BOLAND, Ross, Porum, OK, 54; 10733 Kate, W, 48; Lizzie D, 16; Mose, S, 14; Eva, D, 11; Nellie D, 9; Robert, S, 5

[BOLEN. See BOLAND, BOLIN, BOLYN, and BOWLIN.]

17004 BOLEN Charley, Marble City, OK, 57; 11552 Jennie, W, 54

[BOLEN, Lucy. See #3214]   *(Note: entry separate from other family groups)*

4207 BOLEN, Martin, Vian, OK, 56; 4204 Annie, W, 51; Samuel S, 19; Richard, S, 17; John, S, 12

12573 BOLES, Leo B, Texanna, OK, 8; Richard Bro, 5; By Katie Downing, Gdn.

23179 BOLES, Thomas, Texanna, OK, 15; By J.G. Schofield, Gdn.

[BOLIN, See BOLAND, BOLEN, BOLYN, and BOWLIN.]

15963 BOLIN, Jackson, Stilwell, OK, 23

2128 BOLIN, Leonard, Locust Grove, OK, 36; 2941 Jennie, W, 27; Lucile D, 7; Edna D, 4; Ross, S, ½

29487 BOLIN, Lucy, Owasso, OK, 27; Lillie D, 5; Lydia D, 3

6301 BOLIN, Martha Bunch, OK, 31

15962 BOLIN, Qua-ti, Stilwell, OK, 40; Ki-e-ska, Jennie D, 12; Canoe Darber, S, 10; Margaret Peg D, 5; Ti-e-skey Du-del-da-nah D, 1

15964 BOLIN, Ta-ti-yu-lah, Stilwell, OK, 19

11540 BOLIN, William Brent, OK, 24

10314 BOLING Chas, Manard, OK, 32

29260 BOLING, Julia M Claremore, OK, 38

10313 BOLING, Worcester, Manard, OK, 35

[BOLYN, See BOLAND, BOLEN, BOLIN, and BOWLIN.]

10303 BOLYN Charles Cookson, OK, 40; 11700 Sarah, W, 37; Sallie D, 16; John, S, 14; Lydia D, 13; Martha D, 6

2163 BOLYN, Katie Cookson, OK, 39; Wolfe, S, 17; Peggie D, 12; Rattler, S, 10; Jennie , D, 7; Diana D, 5

32731 BOLYN, Will Cookson, OK, 22; 15997 Sadie, W, 15

5205 BOND, Eddie S, Vinita, OK, 19; William P Bro, 14; Albert H Bro, 10; By Sylvester W. Bond, Gdn.

5205 BOND, Nannie, Peggs, OK, 18; Siddie S D, 1

11445 BONDS, Ora M Claremore, OK, 27; Charlotte E D, 2; Archibald C, S, 1/12

6996 BONEY Beckey, Southwest City, MO, 80

11457 BONEY Chic-gu-we, Southwest City, MO, 56

32

CHEROKEE DESCENDANTS RESIDING WEST OF MISSISSIPPI RIVER.
VOLUME II (A – M)

Key: Guion Miller Application Number; Name; Address, Relation (to Head); Age in 1906

6249 BONEY Daniel, Locust Grove, OK, 27; 6248 Sarah, W, 25; Esiah, S, 5; Jew-li-oh-wa, S, 2

6250 BONEY, Nancy, Locust Grove, OK, 50

[BONEY, Rabbit. See #14133]   *(Note: entry separate from other family groups)*

370 BONEY, Sam Cove, OK, 30; 11442 Sa-ka, W, 32; Ollie D, 8; Miller Bertha D of W, 14; Emma D of W, 11

26546 BONHAM Adda, Sallisaw, OK, 33; Vaughn E, S, 15; Nannie A D, 13; Bertha L D, 11; Gertrude I D, 9; Howard B, S, 6

23228 BOOKER, Ethel, Lenapah, OK, 22

31269 BOON, Earl Harnage, Pearsall, TX, 23

31270 BOON, Emma Harnage, Pearsall, TX, 21

32724 BOON, Fannie M, Los Angeles CA, 24 1001 E. 36th St; Nancy Elizabeth D, 2

24608 BOON, Harriet B, Tahlequah, OK, 26; Louria B D, 4

2803 BOONE Betsie H, Grant, OK, 29

5388 BOONE, Maude Claremore, OK, 27; George H, S, 10; Walter, S, 6; Ethel M D, 4

6573 BOONE, Ora C, Chelsea, OK, 26; Cecil W, S, 7; Raymond A, S, 4

1797 BOOT, Eliza, Estella, OK, 69

1796 BOOT, William, Estella, OK, 33; 2459 Nellie, W, 31; Cornelius, S, 11

642 BOOTHE, Rebecca A, Lometa, OK, 41; Frances L D, 15; Grover G, S, 12; Francis M, Jr, S, 9

10253 BOOTS, Polly, Hulbert, OK, 54; Smith, Jim, S, 15; Carey Dick, S, 14; Bean, Jim, S, 12

16675 BOSWELL, Linda, Pensacola, OK, 24; Richard E, S, 6; Iva Delight, D, 4; Lilia May, D, 2; Arvel G, S, 1/12

16624 BOUDINOT, Frank J, Ft. Gibson, OK, 40; 31619 Anna S. M, W, 33; Frank J, Jr, S, 7

16586 BOUDINOT, Richard F Braggs, OK, 51; 8638 Mary C, W, 33; Carrie Mary D, 15; Eleanor M D, 13; Harriet G D, 9; William P D, 6; Rachel C D, 3

[BOUDINOT, Sallie. See #5131]   *(Note: entry separate from other family groups)*

32858 BOWEN Clara A, Fairland, OK, 40; Sanford M, S, 6; Othel M D, 2

29097 BOWEN, I. Thomas, Luling, TX, 29 R.F.D. #2 Box 41

29077 BOWEN, J.L, Yoakum, TX, 32; Seymore C, S, 9; William A, S, 8; Addie M D, 6; Mahala A D, 3; Richard N, S, 1

29098 BOWEN, Joe S, Luling, TX, 23 R.F.D. #2 Box 41

28340 BOWEN, Lydia M, Muldrow, OK, 20; Iva May D, 2; Lillie J D, 5/12

11726 BOWEN, Mahala, Prairie Lee, TX, 56

29096 BOWEN, William H, Luling, TX, 34 R.F.D. #2 Box 41; William B, S, 11

16115 BOWLES Betsy Baron, OK, 23; Jennett D, 4; Riley, S, 1

[BOWLEY, Alton F. See #12556]   *(Note: entry separate from other family groups)*

[BOWLIN. See BOLAND, BOLEN, BOLIN, and BOLYN.]

10400 BOWLIN, Tooka Cookson, OK, 76
38795 BOWMAN Caldonia, Galena, KS, 36; Hughs Alice D, 18; Arthur, S, 12; Emma, D, 11

[BOWMAN, Clara D. See #7991]   *(Note: entries separate*
[BOWMAN, Delilah. See #7991]   *from other family groups)*

1543 BOYD, Florence J Catoosa, OK, 50
32435 BOYD, Sallie C Claremore, OK, 29; Ruby A D, 9; Henry A, S, 4
  692 BOYDSTON, Minnie Akins, OK, 36; Wica, S, 15; Domah R D, 13; Beulah D, 11; Manuel, S, 9; Willie E, S, 6; Gracie D, 4; Indianola D, 2
5225 BOYLES, George W Cookson, OK, 38; 3214 Peggie, W, 37; Bolen, Lucy D of W, 10; Boyles Charley, S, 6; Lydia I D, 3; Beulah Jane D, 1
3498 BOYLES, Margaret Cookson, OK, 59
2692 BOYLES, Martha, Tahlequah, OK, 52; William H. H, S, 13
22545 BOYLES, Oliver O, Tahlequah, OK, 24; 21031 Mary, W, 21; Mamie D, 4; Georgia, D, 1
4194 BRACKETT Adam Brushy, OK, 60; Lizzie M D, 15; Annie D, 10; 24377 Benjamin, S, 20
7982 BRACKETT Augustus, Wauhillau, OK, 28
4071 BRACKETT Benjamin, Sallisaw, OK, 57
12422 BRACKETT Charles A Claremore, OK, 22
4078 BRACKETT Daniel, Sallisaw, OK, 62
24843 BRACKETT Daniel R, Sallisaw, OK, 35; Callie M D, 7; Clara E D, 5; Vernie J, S, 3
24680 BRACKETT, James, Ft. Gibson, OK, 39; Alice D, 14; Jeff, S, 11; Dovey D, 9; Josie, D, 8
6683 BRACKETT, Jefferson, Sallisaw, OK,19; Thomas Bro, 17; By J. R. McMurtry, Gdn.
401 BRACKETT, Margaret, Vinita, OK, 78
6970 BRACKETT, Mige L, Stilwell, OK, 36; Elizabeth J D, 12; Annie M D, 6; Martha D, 4; Nancy D, 1
7552 BRACKETT, Robert L, Moodys, OK, 41
6612 BRACKETT, Sarah, Wauhillau, OK, 59
35917 BRACKETT, Sarah, Ft. Gibson, OK, 29; Israel, Loyd, S, 4; Brackett, Rosa D, 2
5101 BRACKETT, William B, Sallisaw, OK, 26; Voil D, 3
31784 BRACKETT, William H, Sallisaw, OK, 33; 8940 Lucinda, W, 23; Bayliss, S, 6; Jesse, S, 4; Willie, S, 1
26472 BRACKETT, William T, Sallisaw, OK, 30

Key: Guion Miller Application Number; Name; Address, Relation (to Head); Age in 1906

25127 BRACY, Margaret E, Stilwell, OK, 20

11994 BRADFORD Buff Baron, OK, 7;   By Joe Bradford, Gdn.

11993 BRADFORD, Mamie Baron, OK, 9;   By Joe Bradford, Gdn.

11992 BRADFORD, Riley Baron, OK, 4;   By Joe Bradford, Gdn.

25383 BRADLEY Bertha M, Hanson, OK, 22

12433 BRADLEY Cynthia A, Hanson, OK, 50; Robert, S, 20; Benjamin, S, 16;
Frederick, S, 16; Walter, S, 13; George, S, 11

30480 BRADLEY David, McKey, OK, 28; Edna Cherokee D, 1

27054 BRADLEY, Jesse, Hanson, OK, 30

24381 BRADLEY, John Q, Hanson, OK, 26

 4387 BRADLEY, Myrtle, LaJunta CO, 35

24196 BRADLEY, Nora, Hanson, OK, 24

 6614 BRADSHAW, Emma T Claremore, OK, 57; Albert H, S, 19

23651 BRADSHAW, George A, Pryor Creek, OK, 29

14002 BRADSHAW, James L, Keefeton, OK, 23

27426 BRADSHAW, Jesse P Claremore, OK, 22

 3669 BRADSHAW, John H, Pryor Creek, OK, 53; John Milton, S, 20; Fred Carl, S,
11; Lottie Caroline D, 8

21706 BRADSHAW, Mary, Vian, OK, 27; Willie R, S, 8; Dixie A D, 5; James Kerman,
S, 3; Ford Allen, S, 1/3

[BRADY, Etheral. See #17970]   *(Note: entries separate*
[BRADY, Edgar. See #17970]   *from other family groups)*

13540 BRADY, George W, Hillside, OK, 25; Wm. F Bro, 19

32733 BRADY, Jallah, Wagoner, OK, 18

42963 BRADY, Rachel C, Tulsa, OK, 31; Ruth T D, 10; Bessie L D, 9; Henry T, S, 6;
John, D, S, 3

 5798 BRADY, Vance, Owasso, OK, 46; Addie E D, 18; Zeb A, S, 16; Phoebe B D,
14; Calvin L, S, 11

31342 BRAMWELL, Lorenda P, Siloam Springs AR, 24; Lillie M D, 5

11228 BRANAN, Emma, Webbers Falls, OK, 29; Clifford B, S, 12; Edward H, S, 10;
William C, S, 7; Virgil C, S, 4; George F, S, 2

 5860 BRANDEWIEDE, Sallie, Sallisaw, OK, 36; 22635 Simpson, Oma D, 19; 5860
Brandewiede, Frank, S, 10

24179 BRANDON, Jimmie, Lynch, OK, 15

23273 BRANNON, Elizabeth, Mark, OK, 22; Lawrence A, S, 4; Jesse E, S, 2

23272 BRANNON, Lillie, Mark, OK, 16

31061 BRANNON, Lucile S, Tulsa, OK, 19

24163 BRANSON, Emma, Pryor Creek, OK, 32; Liza D, 11; Lucy D, 9; William F, S,
4

27505 BRANSON, Laura E, Owasso, OK, 31; Charles R, S, 5; John E, S, 3

 5852 BRANTLEY, Mary A.E, Proctor, OK, 15

Key: Guion Miller Application Number; Name; Address, Relation (to Head); Age in 1906

13244 BRAY, John, Ochelata, OK, 36
27481 BRAY, Louisa, Warner, OK, 27; Elita D, 4; Charles, S, 2; Bertie D, 1
 6494 BREAD Arheater [or Mush], Hulbert, OK, 60
 1988 BREAD Cherokee, Hulbert. OK, 26
17503 BREAD, Jennie, Tahlequah, OK, 19
 6064 BREAD, Mary, Melvin, OK, 18
17504 BREAD, Nancy, Hulbert, OK, 27; Houston, S, 4; Downing, Stacey D, 1

[BREAD, Samuel. See #4664]   *(Note: entry separate from other family groups)*

 6065 BREAD, Wilson, Leach, OK, 32; Ben, S, 2; Jennie D, 1/12
 7709 BRECKER Annie E, Vinita, OK, 29; Louis H, S, 7; Flossie B D, 5
 3724 BREEDEN Clara A, Adair, OK, 22; Mary E D, 4
32393 BREEDEN, Rebecca Claremore, OK; Bessie D, 11; John, S, 7; Raymond E, S, 4; Velma M D, 1¼,
43775 BREEDEN, Susie Claremore, OK, 51; Gertie D, 10
22670 BREEDLOVE, Mary B, Muldrow, OK, 24; Willoughby W, S, 4; Jack Thompson, S, 2; William Curtis, S, ¼

[BREHMN, Sam M. See #804]   ⎫   *(Note: entries separate*
[BREHMN Amos. See #804]   ⎬   *from other family groups)*

29876 BREUNINGER Charlotte G, Pipestone, MN, 27; Louis D, S, 3; Mary L D, 1/12
26718 BREWER David B, Rex, OK, 27; Bennie F, S, 6; George F, S, 3 [Died 10-1906] Gertie L D, 1
12726 BREWER Delilah, Muskogee, OK, 72

[BREWER, George. See #8981]   *(Note: entry separate from other family groups)*

12678 BREWER, George W, Locust Grove, OK, 48; Richard R, S, 10; Cherokee D, 8; Lucile G, D, 5; Nannie M D, 4
26331 BREWER, Jack W, Rex, OK, 35; 26332   Fannie E, W, 31; Charles E, S, 7; Jack W, S, 5; William S, S, 2
 5233 BREWER, John W, Stilwell, OK, 35; 24788 Thurza, W, 26; Floyd, S, 13; Sallie D, 11; Jewel D, 6; John, S, 4
12971 BREWER,. Mack Black Gum, OK, 45; Alice D, 1
10782 BREWER, Oliver P, Muskogee, OK, 35
28618 BREWER, Pearlie, Muskogee, OK, 23
26717 BREWER, Richard, Rex, OK, 23
29008 BREWER, Thomas F, Rex, OK, 38; Chooie, S, 15; William S, S, 13; Eva D, 11; Thomas F, Jr, S, 8

Key: Guion Miller Application Number; Name; Address, Relation (to Head); Age in 1906

[BREWER, Thos. J. See #10959]   *(Note: entries separate*
[BREWER Commodore P. See #10959]   *from other family groups)*

12677 BREWER, Walter P, Locust Grove, OK, 42; Carrie B D, 19; William M, S, 17; John T, S, 15; Mary G D, 9
28618 BREWER, William D, Muskogee, OK, 49; Alfred, S, 19; Nellie D, 16; Edith D, 11; Earl, S, 11
 5671 BREWER, William S, Rex. OK, 70

[BRICE Charles M, See #11301]   *(Note: entries separate*
[BRICE Annie L. See #11301]   *from other family groups)*
[BRICE, Walter J. See #11301]

25479 BRICKEY, Gertrude Collinsville, OK, 31; Mamie R D, 11; Mary N D, 9; James S, S, 7; Burnice C D, 1
  184 BRIDGE, Runaway, Locust Grove, OK, 33; 2811 Nellie, W, 27; Nancy D, 6; Susie, D, 2
16107 BRIDGES Augusta A Catoosa, OK, 22
16106 BRIDGES, Fannie Catoosa, OK, 28
27260 BRIECE, Nannie, Muskogee, OK, 21; Thelma D, 2

[BRIGGS, Purdie. See #27503]   *(Note: entry separate from other family groups)*

  131 BRIGHT Barsha, Westville, OK, 57
27853 BRIGHT Chas, Westville, OK, 29; Hiram, S, 1
23369 BRIGHT, F. Marion, Westville, OK, 27; Henry, S, 4; John W, S, 2
22656 BRIGHT, John H, Westville, OK, 33; Gatsie H D, 3
23642 BRIGHT, Letha, Westville, OK, 33
23643 BRIGHT, Noah, Westville, OK, 35; Jewel D, ¼
  130 BRIGHT, Sally, Westville, OK, 65
11927 BRILEY, Tennessee V Black Gum, OK, 23; William E, S, 8; Nettie M D, 6; Lela E, D, 1
16009 BRIMAGE Alex, Porum, OK, 26; Ethel May D, 6
22702 BRIMAGE, Fred, Webbers Falls, OK, 29; Cora F D, 5; Harvey, S, 3; Mary D, 2

[BRIMAGE, Mary. See #9191]   *(Note: entry separate from other family groups)*

16011 BRIMAGE, Thos, Webbers Falls, OK, 21; Christie, S, 4
25850 BRINK, Geo. F Dewey, OK, 21
25849 BRINK, Lydia, Nowata, OK, 41; Charley N, S, 17½; Albert L, S, 16; William T, S, 12; Hooley S, S, 6; James, S, 5; Laura E D, 1/12
25851 BRINK, Mary A, Nowata, OK, 19
24084 BROADDUS, Rebecca J, Grove, OK, 26; Burnell, S, 1/3

Key: Guion Miller Application Number; Name; Address, Relation (to Head); Age in 1906

31506 BROCK Chas. R, Lawton, OK, 32; Robert E, S, 9

22995 BROCK, Joe C, Pryor Creek, OK, 9; Lula G, Sis, 6; Mary M, Sis, 4; By Hugh Brock, Gdn.

38496 BROCK, Walter J, Fairland, OK, 20; 3809 Susie E, W, 30; George, S, 6½; Gleeson, S, 5½; James C, S, 3

588 BROOKING, Lettie M, Talala, OK, 19

26464 BROOKS, Samantha, Zena, OK, 22

10302 BROOKS, Sophia J, Webbers Falls, OK, 41; Scales, Joseph A, Jr, S, 12; Frank V, S, 10; Brooks, Eunice G D, 3

26277 BROWER, Josie M Bartlesville, OK, 22

558 BROWN Abbie, Lenapah, OK, 75

24523 BROWN Addie J, Narcissa, OK, 20

7448 BROWN Annie B Chelsea, OK, 23; Lilla Emily D, 3

3152 BROWN Anna E, Tahlequah, OK, 76

23773 BROWN Belle, Ft. Gibson, OK, 36; Ada D, 2

24419 BROWN Belle, Ft. Gibson, OK, 36; Ada D, 19; Mary D, 15; Charley, S, 12; Louis, S, 10; John, S, 7; Finis, S, 5; Joseph, S, 3

2790 BROWN Celie, Vinita, OK, 69

6607 BROWN Charley, Grove, OK, 37; Frank J, S, 17; Pearly J D, 15; Charles A, S, 12; George R, S, 10; Eula V D, 7; Anna L D, 4; Norena D, 2

973 BROWN, Eliza Chance, OK, 73

8797 BROWN, Ella May, Spavinaw, OK, 26;   Ida A D, 9; Lelia F D, 7; Ruth E D, 6; Samuel F, S, 5; Jewel E D, 2; Cecil E, S, 1

[BROWN, Eve. See #8299] *(Note: entry separate from other family groups)*

26284 BROWN, Flora, Gideon, OK, 22; Maggie May D, 2

22970 BROWN, Florence Chance, OK, 21

22966 BROWN, Florence M, Sr Chance, OK, 35

12670 BROWN, Frank, Welch, OK, 24; Geneva A D, 2; Frederick C, S, 1

13630 BROWN, Franklin G, Narcissa, OK, 68; Mary M D, 16; Tennessee B D, 16; Fanny A, D, 14; Frederick F, S, 12; Nancy I D, 8; Robert E. L, S, 5; Ruth May D, 2

25936 BROWN, George C, Ottawa, OK, 21

[BROWN, George. See #26305]   *(Note: entry separate from other family groups)*

557 BROWN, Geo. Hammer, Lenapah, OK, 67

25862 BROWN, Henry F, Ketchum, OK, 20

22974 BROWN, Henry M Chance, OK; 2216 Mary M, W, 56; William, S, 17; Sarah, D, 15

22969 BROWN, Ida Chance, OK, 31

CHEROKEE DESCENDANTS RESIDING WEST OF MISSISSIPPI RIVER.
VOLUME II   (A – M)

Key: Guion Miller Application Number; Name; Address, Relation (to Head); Age in 1906

10315 BROWN, Ida B, Hubert, OK, 38; Roscoe, S, 11; Geneva D, 7; Charley, S, 5; Fannie, D, 3; John, S, 1/6

16550 BROWN, Jack, Muskogee, OK, 19; Narcissa, Sis, 14; John, Jr Bro, 12; Kellah, Sis, 11; By John L. Brown, Gdn.

[BROWN, James. See #21987]   *(Note: entry separate from other family groups)*

465 BROWN, James Chicotah, OK, 53 [Died 5-5-1907]; Wady, S, 14; James, Jr, S, 13; By James Barnes, Gdn.

23145 BROWN, James Chance, OK, 41; Martha D, 20; Arta, S, 16; Bertha D, 3

6437 BROWN, James Henry Cleora, OK, 26; 24877 Bertha A, W, 24; Homer E, S, 3; Henry L, S, 1

[BROWN, Jesse B. See #10335]   *(Note: entry separate from other family groups)*

23557 BROWN, Jennie E, Tip, OK, 19; Herbert Reen, S, 2

12722 BROWN, John, Muskogee, OK, 59 923 S. 2nd St; 12724 Ollie, W, 26; Jack, S, 19; Narcissa D, 16; John, Jr, S, 14; Kellah D, 12; Akie D, 3

14226 BROWN, John Claremore, OK, 22 Box 31

974 BROWN, John W Chance, OK, 57; Robert A, S, 19; Demeria D, 17

1702 BROWN, Johnnie Collinsville, OK, 38; Laura E D, 17; John L, S, 14; Addie M D, 12; Martha Ellen D, 9; Elijah M, S, 4; Robert D, S, 2

17716 BROWN, Josie, Tahlequah, OK, 22 [Insane]; By C. M. Rose, Gdn.

27664 BROWN, Julia, Stilwell, OK, 35

22741 BROWN, Julia Catoosa, OK, 35

16605 BROWN, Larkin, Kinnison, OK, 32; Martha A D, 13; Elmer L, S, 11; Sybil F D, 9; Bertha M D, 7; William H, S, 5; Bessie G D, 3; Mary L D, 1

6242 BROWN, Louis, Nowata, OK, 30; Ebben W, S, 6; Ida May D, 4; Leslie L, S, 2

32079 BROWN, Maggie, Vian, OK, 23; Nannie D, 5; Vera D, 2

[BROWN, Marvin. See #9167]   *(Note: entry separate from other family groups)*

908 BROWN, Mary, Ketchum, OK, 63; Fannie M, GD, 10; Bertha L, GD, 9; Sadie M, GD, 5

972 BROWN, Mary A Chance, OK, 61

[BROWN, Mary E. See #12410]   *(Note: entry separate from other family groups)*

[BROWN Addie V. See #10188] ⎤   *(Note: entries separate*
[BROWN Bertha E. See #10188] ⎦   *from other family groups)*

22973 BROWN, Matta Chance, OK, 20

26028 BROWN, Maud F Cookson, OK, 21

Key: Guion Miller Application Number; Name; Address, Relation (to Head); Age in 1906

[BROWN, Minnie. See #24618]   ⎤   *(Note: entries separate*
[BROWN, Emma. See #24618]   ⎦   *from other family groups)*

16604 BROWN, Morris, Welch, OK, 33; Helen D, 11; Ena M D, 10; Mable O D, 8; Floyd F, S, 5; Georgia D, 2

22971 BROWN, Myra Chance, OK, 24

3149 BROWN, Nannie E, Tahlequah, OK, 40; 8138 Anna E D, 17; 8139 Catherine D, 15

23321 BROWN, Pearl, Lenapah, OK, 29; Jeromie, S, 2

26916 BROWN, Perlenie B, Gideon, OK, 18

15076 BROWN, Polly Afton, OK, 49; George F, S, 11

6419 BROWN, Rachel, Keefeton, OK, 34; Samuel T, S, 17; Joseph, S, 10; Jennettie D, 7

22968 BROWN, Richard Chance, OK, 22

12728 BROWN, Robert, Muskogee, OK, 56; 42524 Viola D, 8

9233 BROWN, Rosa, Nowata, OK, 36; Blackwell, King David, S, 18; Solomon, S, 15; Hazel, D, 11

5879 BROWN, Rufus H Collinsville, OK, 33; Bessie M D, 13; Letha F D, 11; Florence B, D, 9; Nora L D, 5; Fay D, 5/6; Fern D, 5/6

16853 BROWN, Ruth M Choteau, OK, 15; Ernest R, ½ Bro, 12; Rebecca A, ½ Sis, 10; William M, ½ Bro, 8; By Geo. A McCord, Gdn.

266 BROWN, Sarah A, Narcissa, OK, 41; Jesse C, S, 16; Garland A, S, 14; Effie E D, 9; Stella Maud D, 7

23230 BROWN, Silas, Lenapah, OK, 38; Willie, S, 19; George S, 15; Viola, D, 5; Towney, S, 2

31368 BROWN, Tennessee, Tahlequah, OK, 22

29702 BROWNING Charlotte B, Grove, OK, 20; Thelma L D, 3; Lawford L, S, 1

30804 BROWNING, Fanny M, Los Angeles, CA, 25

4219 BROWNING, Mary J, Los Angeles CA, 50; Robbie E, S, 16

16432 BRUERE, Lydia J Chelsea, OK, 35

16432 BRUERE, Louisa S Catoosa, OK D of Lydia (Above), 16; Charles A Bro, 12; Susie J, Sis, 10; Louis V Bro, 8; Clarinda, Sis, 6; By Louise Bruere, Gdn.

19202 BRUNER, Geo. S Centralia, OK, 40; Mary E D, 12; Ivory I, S, 9; Rice A, S, 6; Samuel L, S, 1; Amos C, S, 4

1546 BRUNER, Isaac N, Stilwell, OK, 43; Clarence N, S, 17; Jalina C D, 7; Leonard N, S, 1

8117 BRUNER, John R Copan, OK, 46; Claude, S, 16

13293 BRUNER, Lydia Bunch, OK, 42

8087 BRUNER, Theodore S, Wauhillau, OK, 37; Mary M D, 10; Florence E D, 8; Josey H, D, 6; Gertrude C D, 3; Allie M D, 1

9371 BRUTON Calvin, Sallisaw, OK, 28; Walter C, S, 5; Jesse B, S, 2; Bonnie D, D, 1

4496 BRYAN, Maggie J, Locust Grove, OK, 30; Jessie Mae D, 4; Clement, S, 3

Key: Guion Miller Application Number; Name; Address, Relation (to Head); Age in 1906

3924 BRYAN, Rachel B Claremore, OK, 40; Joseph L, S, 4; Mamie A D, 2

8266 BRYANT Benjamin F, Siloam Springs, AR, 44; Leona D, 17; Rhoda D, 14

3174 BRYANT, Jennie, Locust Grove, OK, 13

5511 BRYANT, Lottie S, Leach, OK, 18; Bertha M, Sis, 16; Benjamin F Bro, 13; Lucinda, Sis, 11; William C Bro, 9; Inola, Sis, 7; Jessie V, Sis, 4; By Wm D. Sanders, Gdn.

15592 BRYANT, Minnie B, Pryor Creek, OK, 24; Clarence R, S, 4; Margaret D, D, 2

26557 BRYANT, Myrtle B Centralia, OK, 27; Luther R, S, 6; Calvin A, S, 5; Theodore O, S, 4

26470 BRYANT, Valena, Spavinaw, OK, 27; Eleanor D, 3; Hazel C D, 1

23150 BUCHANAN Bertha L, Webbers Falls, OK, 17

7908 BUCHANAN Bessie Coffeyville, KS, 24; Martha D, 2

13765 BUCK, John Cookson, OK, 27; Aggie D, 8; Isaac, S, 5; Enolie, S, 3

27108 BUCK, Jumper, Spavinaw, OK, 31; 468 Nellie, W, 41; Hair, Jefferson, S of W, 17; Jack, S of W, 16; Lizzie D of W, 14; George, S of W, 11; Charlotte D of W, 9

27109 BUCK, Noah, Spavinaw, OK, 28; 23844 Avey, W, 25; Proctor, Lucy D of W, 7; Buck, Lydia D, 4; Mollie D, 1

459 BUCK, Steve, Spavinaw, OK, 63; 446   Betsey, W, 56

26063 BUCK, Taylor, Spavinaw, OK, 35; 463 Jennie, W, 51; 4615 William, S, 16

11793 BUCKET Dave, Grove, OK, 47; 1740 Aggie, W, 51; Jack, S, 19; Dawes, S, 17; Samuel, S, 14; Lou D, 12

16081 BUCKHORN, George, Tahlequah, OK, 20

4597 BUCKHORN, Jack, Tahlequah, OK, 33; 11777 Lizzie, W, 19; Arch, S, 3; Spade, S, 1/12

16080 BUCKHORN, Nannie, Tahlequah, OK, 14

16587 BUCKNER, Martha A, Stilwell, OK, 34; Ivy C D, 16; Arphenia L D, 14; Lola E, D, 11; Strauther R, S, 8; Tams E, S, 5; Wales S, S, 1

16649 BUCKNER, Mary C, Stilwell, OK, 50; Joel M, S, 17; Leland D, S, 12; James C, S, 10; Neoma V D, 7

14206 BUCKSKIN, James, Locust Grove, OK, 27; 3694 Alice, W, 31; Jennie D, 8; Emily, D, 2; Ar-ne-che-, Levi, S of W, 15; Bud, S of W, 5

[BUCKSKIN, Joe. See #6988]   *(Note: entry separate from other family groups)*

[BUCKSKIN, Polly. See #8328]   *(Note: entry separate from other family groups)*

[BUCKSKIN, Joe M. See #5780½]   *(Note: entry separate from other family groups)*

[BUCKSKIN, Josie. See #5353]   *(Note: entries separate*
[BUCKSKIN, Susie. See #5353]   *from other family groups)*
[BUCKSKIN, Zeke. See #5353]

Key: Guion Miller Application Number; Name; Address, Relation (to Head); Age in 1906

2818 BUCKSKIN, Little Bird, Locust Grove, OK, 44; 181 Littlebird, Katie, W, 57; 11526 Buckskin, Frank, S, 14; Smith, S, 12

10616 BUCKSKIN, Sam, Kansas, OK, 26

[BUDD. See BUDDER.]

9131 BUDDER David, Eucha, OK, 38; 10207 Sallie D, W, 30; Ned, S, 12

1699 BUDDER, Jack, Eucha, OK, 24; 24151 Polly, W, 27

1559 BUDDER, Jesse, Eucha, OK, 45; 4925 Nellie, W, 36; Harry, S, 13; Jennie D, 11; Canuka, S, 9; Watt, S, 7; Oochalah, S, 3

657 BUDDER, Lewis, Eucha, OK, 42

42148 BUFFINGTON Alex, Vinita, OK, 23; John E, S, 1/12

9171 BUFFINGTON Alex C, Maple, OK, 35; 33942 Estella May, W, 31; Annie L D, 11; William E, S, 9; Georgia L D, 7; Jessie A D, 3; Clayton D, S, 1/3

22 BUFFINGTON Charles Chelsea, OK,   44; George N, S, 1/12

878 BUFFINGTON Daniel W, Vinita, OK, 50

982 BUFFINGTON, Fannie E, Westville, OK, 52; John D, S, 17

29594 BUFFINGTON, Isaac Grover Anadarko, OK, 22

1649 BUFFINGTON, James Caney, KS, 42; Hazel M D, 8; Jessie M D, 6; Susan N D, 4

8613 BUFFINGTON, John E, Vinita, OK, 25

3287 BUFFINGTON, John R Chapel, OK, 42; Nannie J D, 14; Carrie R D, 13; Chas. R, S, 12; Hallie H D, 9; Joel W, S, 8; Mary J D, 6; Cherry S D, 5

42146 BUFFINGTON, Lucien, Vinita, OK, 25

10158 BUFFINGTON, Lucien W, Vinita, OK, 49; 10159 Nannie E, W, 39

23908 BUFFINGTON, Mollie C, Stilwell, OK, 34; Culbert W, S, 10; Stella K D, 8; Thomas C, S, 5; Bruce G, S, 3; Pink D, 1

15995 BUFFINGTON, Susie Braggs, OK, 5; By Susie Lyman, Gdn.

34551 BUGHER, Florence, Pryor Creek, OK,   35; Charley, S, 14; Oma D, 10

8141 BULL, Thomas, Tahlequah, OK, 20

14260 BULLETT, John Bunch, OK, 22

43434 BULLETT, Lewis, Hulbert, OK, 14; By Alec Johnson, Gdn.

14262 BULLETT, Lydia Bunch, OK, 24

[BULLETT, Watt. See #14271] ⎤   *(Note: entries separate*
[BULLETT, Emma. See #14271] ⎦   *from other family groups)*

10680 BULLFROG, Deh-yeh-ni, Whitmire, OK, 73

7893 BULLFROG, Nancy, Whitmire, OK, 66

3880 BULLFROG, Thomas, Locust Grove, OK, 56

32298 BUMGARNER, Viola W, Gans, OK, 20; Ruper K, S, 2

1323 BUNCH Alex, Stilwell, OK, 46; Lizzie D, 15; Jesse, S, 13; Nance D, 11; Jack, S, 9; Sam, S, 5

Key: Guion Miller Application Number; Name; Address, Relation (to Head); Age in 1906

1068 BUNCH Becca, Stilwell, OK, 61

1508 BUNCH Charley, Stilwell, OK, 38; 42202 Nannie, W, 39; James, S, 17; Jack, S, 12; Mary D, 9; Adeline D, 6; Lee, S, 5; Sam, S, 2

[BUNCH, Eli. See #1670]   *(Note: entry separate from other family groups)*

9450 BUNCH, Henry Bunch, OK, 29; 9393 Annie, W, 43

9715 BUNCH, Jennie Bunch, OK, 50

9667 BUNCH, John Bunch, OK, 15; By Jennie Bunch, Gdn.

42173 BUNCH, John Bunch, OK, 21

1588 BUNCH, Jug Bunch, OK, 47; 1589 Annie, W, 49; Esther D, 16; Jack, S, 14; Susie, D, 10; Nancy D, 6

42224 BUNCH, Levi, Stilwell, OK, 25; 8086 Nannie, W, 26; Quatie D, 9; Lila D, 4; Richard, S, 2

8980 BUNCH, Missouri Bunch, OK, 56; 8981 Jennie, W, 54; Bird [Ah-ko-wah], S, 12; Brewer, George, S of W, 19

790 BUNCH, Noah, Stilwell, OK, 32; 784 Ollie, W, 32; Christie, Rachel D of W, 15

9668 BUNCH, Peggie Bunch, OK, 17; By Jennie Bunch, Gdn.

1506 BUNCH, Quatie, Stilwell, OK, 28; Chair, Kate D, 7; Rabbit, S, 5

9669 BUNCH, Richard Bunch, OK, 19; By Jennie Bunch, Gdn.

9451 BUNCH, Sarah Bunch, OK, 21

6457 BUNCH, Tom, Stilwell, OK, 56; 6452   Ollie, W, 54; Tunie D, 16; Jim, S, 13

24992 BURCHETT, Flora M, Tahlequah, OK, 24; Leo B, S, 3; Susie B D, 1

11628 BURCKHALTER, Tom C, Vinita, OK, 25; Opal L D, 6; Frances L D, 4; Tom C, S, 1

22541 BURGESS, Jessie M, Stilwell, OK, 30

27111 BURGESS, Louona V Collinsville, OK, 35; Flora E D, 16; Laura M D, 12; Sidney E, S, 9; Ben, S, 7; Eva F D, 1

23825 BURK, Fanny Morgan, Warner, OK, 54; Eva D, 14; Fanny R D, 13; Otto P, S, 10

15873 BURKART, Ollie Dewey, OK, 17

10729 BURKE Austia L Coffeyville, KS, 16

[BURKE, William R. See #33641]   *(Note: entry separate from other family groups)*

12238 BURNETT Dannie H, Sapulpa, OK, 31; William James, S, 2

29261 BURNETT, Pearl Ethel, Snyder, OK, 26; Alta C D, 5; Archie C, S, 4

24973 BURNS, Mary, Hanson, OK, 22; Sue D, 1

25472 BURNS, Sallie Bell, Turley, OK, 20; Viola D, 4; Bob, S, 2

16006 BURR Benjamin F, Webbers Falls, OK, 45; Charles, S, 19; Josie D, 15; Frank, S, 10; Sylvia D, 6; Cordelia D, 1

9832 BURR, George W, Vera, OK, 41; Calvin, S, 11; Alexander, S, 8; Gladys Pearl D, 3; Myrtle D, 1

34485 BURR, Rachel Columbus, KS, 17; Jones, Willie E, S, 1/12

5885 BURROW, Sarah A, Hanson, OK, 40; Chas. H, S, 17; Wm D, S, 15; Bertha L D, 9; Jos W, S, 7; Franklin E, S, 5; Susie M D, 3

16866 BURROWS Chas C Claremore, OK, 26; Eva C D, 11/12

16867 BURROWS Christopher C Claremore, OK, 15;   By Claud C. Burrows, Gdn.

16869 BURROWS, Edw. M Claremore, OK, 19

4070 BURROWS, James, Muskogee, OK, 33; Walter Raymond, S, 9; Lela D, 3

16865 BURROWS, John Claremore, OK, 20

16868 BURROWS, Thos C Claremore, OK, 19

4232 BURROWS, Tobe Braggs, OK, 28; Samantha L D, 6; William R, S, 3

210 BURROWS, Whit, Talala, OK, 31; Williams A, S, 8; Alta M D, 6; Lawrence E, S, 2

6072 BURT Alice, Melvin, OK, 36

25306 BURT, Loduskie Chelsea, OK, 41; Joseph L, S, 19; Eva L D, 15; Alice D, 13; Roscoe T, S, 11; Francis S, S, 9; Ivey M D, 8; James E, S, 4; Lottie M D, 17; Ettie P, D, 4; Roy R, S, 1

28229 BURT, Max O Bunch, OK, 21

5497 BURTON, Maud E Collinsville, OK, 26; Gladys D, 6

[BUSE, Onie M. See #14105]
[BUSE Charles F. See #14105]
[BUSE Ada E. See #14105]   *(Note: entries separate*
[BUSE, Samuel F. See #14105]   *from other family groups)*
[BUSE, Sherman. See #14105]

9639 BUSH Dave, Marble City, OK, 38; 1178 Bettie, W, 28; Sam, S, 6; Ben, S, 4; Nancy, D, 3; Easter D, 1

9497 BUSH, Eliza Braggs, OK, 22; Edna D, 5; Hallie D, 2; Wheeler, S, 1

14310 BUSHEYHEAD Dennis W Baptist, OK, 26

7912 BUSHEYHEAD, James B, Tahlequah, OK, 22

213 BUSHEYHEAD, Jesse, Southwest City, MO, 53; 252 Jane Snail, W, 41; John, S, 20; Maggie D, 16; Cornelius, S, 14; Eddie, S, 11; Lucinda D, 9; Rufus, S, 7; Louisa D, 2

13464 BUSHEYHEAD, Jesse C Claremore, OK, 36; Oowala D, 7; Edward R, S, 3; Jesse C, S, 4; Dennis W, S, 2

[BUSHEYHEAD, Louis. See #16311] *(Note: entry separate from other family groups)*

8734 BUSHEYHEAD, Robert L, Longmont, CO, 30; Virgil Lee, S, 1

31560 BUSHEYHEAD, William, Southwest City, MO, 24

6576 BUSHYHEAD Delilah, Oolagah, OK, 57

5226 BUSHYHEAD, Edward W, San Diego, CA, 74

5878 BUSHYHEAD, Eloise P. B, Tahlequah, OK, 17

CHEROKEE DESCENDANTS RESIDING WEST OF MISSISSIPPI RIVER.
VOLUME II (A – M)

Key: Guion Miller Application Number; Name; Address, Relation (to Head); Age in 1906

11774 BUSHYHEAD, George Braggs, OK, 51; 11499 Nancy, W, 52; 17056 Rattlinggourd, Jennie D of W, 15; 17061 John, S of W, 13; 17057 Walker, Jack, S of W, 20

3576 BUSHYHEAD, George W, Locust Grove, OK, 39

27119 BUSHYHEAD, Geo. W, Oolagah, OK, 57; 6577 Martha, W, 50; William T, S, 19; Charlotte D, 16; James W, S, 11

3577 BUSHYHEAD, Jacob, Locust Grove, OK, 27; 4503 Maggie, W, 22

16466 BUSHYHEAD, Ka-haw-ker, Oaks, OK, 77 [Dead]; By John Pigeon, Gdn.

11197 BUSHYHEAD, Larenda Braggs, OK, 35; Swimmer, Lizzie D, 14; Ned, S, 10; Micco, Jim, S, 6; Bessie D, 4

21701 BUSHYHEAD, Smith Claremore, OK, 57; Mamie E D, 9; Augustus, S, 4

9316 BUSSEY Dottie Collinsville, OK, 34; 26290 Dora D, 18; Francis M, Jr, S, 15; Fred M, S, 13; Millard F, S, 10; John H, S, 9; George W, S, 5; Earl William, S, 3

[BUSSEY, Emma B. See #10335]   *(Note: entry separate from other family groups)*

35628 BUSSEY, Martha Claremore, OK, 25; Hec. B, S, 6; Nicholas C, S, 5; Charles P, S, 3

[BUSTER Doosda. See #16185]   *(Note: entry separate from other family groups)*

18864 BUSTER Dora J, Oolagah, OK, 22

[BUSTER, E-ja-gar. See #14800] ⎤   *(Note: entries separate
[BUSTER, George. See #14800] ⎦   from other family groups)*

6752 BUSTER, Hunter Campbell, OK, 53; Gee-gu-wee D, 18; Polly D, 16; Dargie D, 14; Cealie D, 11; Lipsy, S, 8; Tiger, S, 6

12552 BUSTER, Nannie, Vian, OK, 45; Wilson, Nannie D, 11; Morris, Watt, S, 9; Emma Yahola D, 3

14801 BUSTER, Nellie Campbell, OK, 53

7662 BUSTER, Rachel, Vian, OK, 60

[BUSTER, Scar-lup-ka. See #14807] *(Note: entry separate from other family groups)*

[BUSTER, Tom. See #14808]   *(Note: entry separate from other family groups)*

3004 BUTLER Aaron H Claremore, OK, 48; 3862 Nora, W, 47; Charles C, S, 12

3636 BUTLER Carrie, Pryor Creek, OK, 21;   Roland F, S, 2

12900 BUTLER, Catherine, Tahlequah, OK, 30; Daniel R, S,16; James L, S, 13; Pierce P, S, 8

Key: Guion Miller Application Number; Name; Address, Relation (to Head); Age in 1906

[BUTLER, Frank L. See #3161] ⎤   *(Note: entries separate*
[BUTLER, Myrtle A. See #3161] ⎦   *from other family groups)*

6628 BUTLER, George, Hulbert, OK, 47; 9802 Charlotte, W, 44; Susie D, 19; Sam, S, 15; Charley, S, 12; Curtis, S, 5; George A, S, 3
33323 BUTLER, Helen, Muldrow, OK, 44; Elizabeth M D, 19; Helen M D, 14
4271 BUTLER, James, Grove, OK, 46; 4270 Nancy, W, 48; James, S, 9

[BUTLER, James. See #5626]   *(Note: entry separate from other family groups)*

5890 BUTLER, John E Big Cabin, OK, 44; 5891 Sallie, W, 45;   Lucien, S, 18
26505 BUTLER, Lydia, Webbers Falls, OK, 34; Bertha D, 3; Minnie D, 1/6

[BUTLER, Richard. See #2848] ⎤   *(Note: entries separate*
[BUTLER, Samuel H. See #2848] ⎦   *from other family groups)*

15797 BUTLER, William, Grove, OK, 51
22483 BUTLER, William Claremore, OK, 28
22774 BUTTS, Ella S Collinsville, OK, 26; Harvey W, S, 7; Sylvia E D, 5; Goldie M D, 3

[BUTTS, Naeta M. See #13167] ⎤   *(Note: entries separate*
[BUTTS Cherokee. See #13167] ⎦   *from other family groups)*

24281 BUTY, Helen, Muskogee, OK, 23; Helen Rebecca D, 2; Emily Elizabeth D, 5/12
11412 BUZZARD Cornelius Cove, OK, 36; 1430 Lucy, W, 19; Nancy D, 1
13361 BUZZARD Dan, Southwest City, MO, 22; Loyd, S, 2; Lona D, 1/12
3818 BUZZARD, Eliza, Estella, OK, 59
13279 BUZZARD, George Bunch, OK, 16; By Nellie Buzzard, Gdn.

[BUZZARD, Jackson. See #6995]   *(Note: entry separate from other family groups)*

16471 BUZZARD, Jackson, Southwest City, MO, 32; 13087 Sallie, W, 37; Cennie D, 6; Mary D, 3; William, S, 2
18556 BUZZARD, Jessie, Vian, OK, 13; By Cynthia Park, Gdn.
16440 BUZZARD, John, Southwest City, MO, 26; Lon, S, 2
13669 BUZZARD, Johnson Bunch, OK, 24
14269 BUZZARD, Ludia Cookson, OK, 19
9292 BUZZARD, Nancy Cove, OK, 48; Joe, S, 17
13752 BUZZARD, Nettie Bunch, OK, 36; Rat, James, S, 16; Sanders, Charles, S, 14; Berry, S, 12; Howard, S, 12; Curtis, S, 9
13200 BUZZARD, Sallie Bunch, OK, 17

CHEROKEE DESCENDANTS RESIDING WEST OF MISSISSIPPI RIVER.
VOLUME II (A – M)

11443 BUZZARD, Sam Cove, OK, 46; 11405 Lese, W, 42; John, S, 5; Israel, S, 3

2342 BUZZARD, William Afton, OK, 34; 9496 Lucy, W, 39; Jackson, S, 5; Elmer, S, 2

36795 BYERS Alfred, Evansville AR, 21

8342 BYERS Annie, Vian, OK, 57; 8341 Eliza D, 14

9128 BYERS, Cornelia, Cookson, OK, 15; Nicodemus, Bro, 11; By Margaret Ann Byers, Gdn.

33624 BYERS, Emma A, Fairland, OK, 35; Willa A D, 6; Jesse M D, 5; Georgia M D, 2

9121 BYERS, Ezekiel Cookson, OK, 21

34462 BYERS, Henry C, McKey, OK, 26

9122 BYERS, James Cookson, OK, 27

36794 BYERS, Joe, Evansville AR, 27

9129 BYERS, Margaret Ann Cookson, OK, 56

920 BYERS, Nick, Evansville AR, 75; 3295 Ellen, W, 61

4192 BYERS, William H, McKey, OK, 47; 3089 Ellen Elizabeth, W, 49; Charles W, S, 20; Sarah A D, 18; Leona M D, 16; Mary C D, 14; Offie D, 12; Enoch, S, 9; John, S, 6

4455 BYERS, Wilson, McKey, OK, 36

26911 BYNUM, Janie A, Hulbert, OK, 17

[BYRD, Maggie. See #6307] *(Note: entry separate from other family groups)*

22524 BYRD, Daisy D, Chelsea, OK, 26

22523 BYRD, Henry H Chelsea, OK, 29; Daisy E.L, D, 6; Claris C D, 4; Edna M D, 1

5865 BYRD, Jane Chelsea, OK, 51

13432 BYRD, Nina, Wann, OK, 30; Alfred, S, 12; Maudie May D, 10; Minnie Lee D, 8; Louisa J D, 6; Bulah B D, 3; Thomas, S, 1

[CABBAGEHEAD, Jennie. See #5642] *(Note: entry separate from other family groups)*

[CA-GA-A-LES-KE. See Henry Walkabout #6062]
(Note: entry separate from other family groups)

12886 CALDWELL Annie Claremore, OK, 47; Isaac, S, 16; Elsie D, 14; Frank, S, 9; Tulle, S, 9; Annie D, 3

4248 CALDWELL Benjamin M, Vinita, OK, 17; Joella May, Sis, 15; Lula, Sis, 13; By John D. Caldwell, Gdn.

9323 CALDWELL, John Lynch, Salina, OK, 23

21158 CALLAHAN Drury Q, Sallisaw, OK, 20; Benjamin P Bro, 17; William R Bro, 15; James A Bro, 13; Georgia C, Sis, 8; By Green B. Callahan, Gdn.

27582 CALLISON, Emily H, Porum, OK, 33; Bertha E D, 7; Walter C, S, 2

24591 CALVERT, Berilla A Adair, OK, 26; Iola B D, 1

Key: Guion Miller Application Number; Name; Address, Relation (to Head); Age in 1906

34699 CALVERT, Sarah A, Montoya, NM, 38; Amanda A D, 16; Charlie E, S, 13; Lela D, D, 5; Jasper F, S, 1

15956 CAMERON, John, Wauhillau, OK, 40; 12596 Olce, W, 44; Will, S, 10; Susie D, 6; Andrew, S, 3; 12597 Flute, Josie D, 18; 12596 Charlotte D, 15; Aikey [Aggie] D, 10

15955 CAMERON, Wilson, Wauhillau, OK, 51

4642 CAMPBELL Abraham, Oaks, OK, 37

2103 CAMPBELL Alice, Hulbert, OK, 22; Henry E, S, 2

25765 CAMPBELL, Emma, Miami, OK, 20

[CAMPBELL, Flora. See #36628]   *(Note: entry separate from other family groups)*

29189 CAMPBELL, Francis, Park Hill, OK, 41; Alluwaa D 1

24190 CAMPBELL, George L, Owasso, OK, 41; Gay Lena D, 8; Charles H, S, 6; Flora D, 3; George L, S, ¼

28756 CAMPBELL, Hettie Sixkiller, Muskogee, OK, 22; Bessie Gertrude D, 2

10750 CAMPBELL, Jim, Porum, OK, 19

14736 CAMPBELL, John, Porum, OK, 37; Miles, S, 5; Ellis, S, 3; Sam, S, 1

18535 CAMPBELL, John Choteau, OK, 25; Clarence R, S, 1

18536 CAMPBELL, Joseph Choteau, OK, 30; 21038 Mande, W, 22; Joseph M, S, 1

1821 CAMPBELL, Lucy Collinsville, OK, 69

861 CAMPBELL, Mary, Peggs, OK, 24

23687 CAMPBELL, Mary E Collinsville, OK, 47

9598 CAMPBELL, Nancy Brent, OK, 28

[CAMPBELL, Olcie or Aulsa. See #12596]
    (Note: entry separate from other family groups)

28727 CAMPBELL, Sallie B, Muskogee, OK, 22; Harris Bonnie A D, 7; Campbell Beauregard, S, 3; Earl, S, 1

30775 CAMPBELL, William R, Tulsa, OK, 39; Flora D, 12

35585 CANADA, Henry L, Oolagah, OK, 23

12887 CANARY, Anola J, Caney, KS, 34; Emma P D, 15; Simeon C, S, 14; James H, S, 11; Elmira L D, 9

24445 CANDILL, Lou Big Cabin, OK, 19

8803 CANDY Allen, Ft. Smith AR, 19

14171 CANDY, George Cookson, OK, 17; Nancy, Sis, 16; By Jess Candy, Gdn.

267 CANDY, George T, Rose, OK, 28

14172 CANDY, Jess Cookson, OK, 31

14169 CANDY, John Cookson, OK, 25

16088 CANDY, Mable, Tahlequah, OK, 12; By Betsy Greece, Gdn.

14170 CANDY, Mary Cookson, OK, 13; By John Candy, Gdn.

24833 CANDY, Rachel Braggs, OK, 26; Louis J, S, 6

Key: Guion Miller Application Number; Name; Address, Relation (to Head); Age in 1906

9274 CANDY, Wyly, Melvin, OK, 27
17099 CANNADA, Fannie E Bartlesville, OK, 40
18477 CANNON Ada, Ray, OK, 21; James Leonard, S, 1
7446 CANNON Ada N Chelsea, OK, 21
7888 CANNON Al Ballard, OK, 7
25742 CANNON Charles L Ballard, OK, 30
23501 CANNON Claud Dragger, OK, 23; 11674 Roxie, W, 20; Mattie E D, 4;
Effie L, D, 2
3165 CANNON Cora, Ray, OK, 21
349 CANNON, Edwin B Ballard, OK, 51; Aud, S, 18; Caud, S, 15; Ruth D, 11
22250 CANNON, George L, Hydro, OK, 25
26769 CANNON, Ira Dragger, OK, 28; Cora V D, 6; Alvin A, S, 2
348 CANNON, John C, Siloam Springs AR, 37; 8019   Lee, W, 29; Walter, S, 9;
Bular D, 7; Cora D, 5; Tilden, S, 3; Price, S, 1/3
804 CANNON, Katie, Sleeper, OK, 24; Brehmn, Sam M, S, 3; Amos Rogers, S, 1
25743 CANNON, Maud Ballard, OK, 21
343 CANNON, Oscar Ballard, OK, 40; Bertha D, 16; Wirt, S, 11; Maggie M D, 5;
Fannie, D, 2
34641 CANNON, Robert L Duenweg, MO, 23
7447 CANNON, Spencer W Adair, OK, 30; Spence W, S, 1; Florence W D, 1
576 CANNON, Sterling P, Siloam Springs, AR, 43
350 CANNON, Wilson L, Siloam Springs, AR, 46; Alice D, 17;   Grover, S, 15;
Frank, S, 11; Mance, S, 7; Adah D, 4; Fred, S, 1
17251 CANNON, Zoe M Checotah, OK, 24; Leonard L, S, 5; James D, S, 2 [Died 1-
1907]

[CANOE Ben. See #13302]   *(Note: entries separate*
[CANOE, Louisa. See #13302]   *from other family groups)*

[CANOE Darber. See #15962]   *(Note: entries separate*
[CANOE, Margaret P. See #15962]   *from other family groups)*

4227 CANOE, Ellis, Stilwell, OK, 30; 16764 Katie Silk, Long, OK, W, 26; Hooper,
Nancy, D, 5; Canoe Charley, S, 2
9745 CANOE, George Bunch, OK, 46; 9746 Nellie, W, 48; 13129 Waterdown, Joe, S
of W, 18; 13128 Ellis, S of W, 12; 13127 Steve, S of W, 7; 6228 Canoe
Beaver, S, 14

[CANOE, Martin. See #8971]   *(Note: entries separate*
[CANOE, Nancy. See #8971]   *from other family groups)*

2958 CANOE, Sam, Locust Grove, OK, 25; 26752 Katie, W, 19

Key: Guion Miller Application Number; Name; Address, Relation (to Head); Age in 1906

23254 CANTRELL Charles, Marble City, OK, 5; Floyd Leslie, Bro, 2; By Richard D. Cantrell, Gdn.

2438 CANTRELL, Ida B, Needmore, OK, 30; Mabel Lee D, 10; Louis E, S, 6

16757 CANTRELL, Maud M Cleora, OK, 27; Ruthie M D, 9; Walter J, S, 6; John F, S, 4; Hiram J, S, 1

[CANUP, Harry T. See #638]*(Note: entry separate from other family groups)*

8379 CAPPS Amanda E, Marble City, OK, 26; Leoneath L, S, 8

[CAPPS, Lillie May. See #1593]   *(Note: entry separate from other family groups)*

9610 CAPPS, Louisa M, Muskogee, OK, 64

16508 CAPPS, Romie, Welch, OK, 14; Ethel, Sis, 12; By Walter A, Holland, Gdn.

[CAR-CAR-WEE, Ross. See #9942]   *(Note: entry separate from other family groups)*

5204 CARD Carrie E, Pryor Creek, OK, 15; By Charlotte E. Stiles, Gdn.

11510 CARDEN Anna, Honolulu, HA, 46 1520 Fort St.; William Thomas, S, 18; John Joseph, S, 16; Edward W, S, 14; Mary A D, 11

5531 CAREY Anna, Melvin, OK, 37; James, S, 15; Jessie D, 13; Samuel, S, 10; Dewey, S, 8; Joe, S, 5; Dollie D, 2

6051 CAREY Caty, Melvin, OK, 23

25396 CAREY Clem, Hulbert, OK, 32; 25080 Nellie, W, 27; Mary D, 4; Lesie D, 1

17471 CAREY Daniel, Melvin, OK, 24

29703 CAREY David L, Grove, OK, 32

[CAREY Dick. See #10253] *(Note: entry separate from other family groups)*

496 CAREY, Edmund D, Grove, OK, 74; 497 Lydda A, W, 56; George B, S, 17

29701 CAREY, Edmund L, Grove, OK, 23

321 CAREY, Flona V, Nowata, OK, 11; Sansa V, Sis, 9; Majora B, Sis, 8; William V Bro, 6; By Emma M. Carey, Gdn.

[CAREY, Frances. See #1202]   *(Note: entry separate from other family groups)*

16955 CAREY, George G, South West City, MO, 20

[CAREY, Jesse. See #43641]   *(Note: entry separate from other family groups)*

[CAREY, Joe. See #6534]   *(Note: entry separate from other family groups)*

320 CAREY, Lelia M, Nowata, OK, 21

CHEROKEE DESCENDANTS RESIDING WEST OF MISSISSIPPI RIVER.
VOLUME II   (A – M)

Key: Guion Miller Application Number; Name; Address, Relation (to Head); Age in 1906

2409 CAREY, Madison, Porum, OK, 27; 14288 Allie, W, 27

5628 CAREY, Mike, Hulbert, OK, 38; 9202 Jennie, W, 39; Oglesby, Okla D of W, 15; Carey, Nora D, 7

43496 CAREY, Nelson, Hulbert, OK, 28

16952 CAREY, Rhoda A, South West City, MO, 12

5627 CAREY, Richard, Hulbert, OK, 58; 5630 Jennie, W, 44; Linnie D, 15

2727 CAREY, Robert E. Lee, Grove, OK,37; Lillie D, 13; Lucy D, 11; Winnie D, 7; Ray E, S, 5; Thomas, S, 3; Joseph S, S, 1

24675 CAREY, Robin L, Zena, OK, 13; Rachel J, Sis, 7; By Nancy C. Carey, Gdn.

[CAREY, Ruth. See #965] ⎤   *(Note: entries separate*
[CAREY, William R. See #965] ⎬   *from other family groups)*
[CAREY, Joella. See #965] ⎦

4443 CAREY, Sallie, Hulbert, OK, 56; 43641 Jesse, S, 18

19722 CAREY, Silas, Hulbert, OK, 26; Tom, S, 9; Harlin, S, 7; Robert, S, 4

4438 CAREY, Steve, Hulbert, OK, 50; 4445 Amanda, W, 48; Mollie D, 12

29700 CAREY, Stonewall J, Grove, OK: 34; Bruce, S, 13

16953 CAREY, Thomas L, South West City, MO, 17

16954 CAREY, Walter L, South West City, MO, 18

17168 CAR-LER-SAR-YO-HA, Sam Campbell, OK, 65

[CARLETON, William. See #24870]   *(Note: entry separate from other family groups)*

6809 CARLEY, Mary E, Sheep Ranch CA, 40; Alvin F, S, 13

10741 CARLILE Charles Campbell, OK, 31

27092 CARLILE, Henry H Cookson, OK, 31; Lizzie M D, 8; Thomas K, S, 4; Dollie Josie, D, 2

24795 CARLILE, John, Tahlequah, OK, 37; 2725 Johnan, W, 47; Ada B D, 17; Alice B, D, 9; Thomas S, S, 3

[CARLILE, Maggie. See #1124]   *(Note: entry separate from other family groups)*

12655 CARLILE, Mary Cookson, OK, 19

11436 CARLILE, Robert B Campbell, OK, 32; 11437 Piercie J, W, 29; Senareste D, 2

27096 CARLILE, Stephen F,Cookson, OK, 34; Willie T, S, 13; Mattie Mary D, 7; Callie, D, 4

16304 CARLILE, Stephen N Bakersfield CA, 29

5241 CARLILE, Thomas, Sallisaw, OK, 44; Myrtle D, 15; Arthur, S, 13; Noland E, S, 4; Minta Ellen D, 2

25424 CARLILE, Thomas J, Park Hill, OK, 44; 25423 Viana, W, 39; Thomas H, S, 19; John H, S, 17; Walter E, S, 15; Edward A, S, 12; Levi, S, 10; Virgil D, S, 7; Clarence G, S, 4; Homer E, S, 2

CHEROKEE DESCENDANTS RESIDING WEST OF MISSISSIPPI RIVER.
VOLUME II (A – M)

Key: Guion Miller Application Number; Name; Address, Relation (to Head); Age in 1906

8903 CARLILE, William, Vian, OK, 47; Lon [or Wm. A], S, 18; Leo, S, 15; Maud D, 14; Effie D, 11; Mary D, 5; Alma D, 2

27064 CARLILE, William K, Park Hill, OK, 38; 3037 Emma, W, 30; Annie May D, 11; Carrie E D, 10; Henrietta D, 9; William K, S, 7; Bluie J D, 5; Levi, S, 3

23034 CARLOCK, Mattie B Centralia, OK, 22; Jewel L D, 1/3

39774 CARMAN Caroline D Collinsville, OK, 19; Lawrence, S, 3; Samuel C, S, 1

24063 CARMAN, Katie J Adair, OK, 33; Hugh, S, 14; Daniel, S, 12; William A, S, 10

26243 CARNES Andrew J, Flint, OK, 48; Maudie J D, 15; George W, S, 11; Earl J, S, 9; Hazel A. F, D, 2

25999 CARNES Annie F, Flint, OK, 31

2202 CARNES, Dianna, Flint, OK, 73

2203 CARNES, Elizabeth, Flint, OK, 57

24209 CARNES, George Robert, Kansas, OK, 26; 24219 Ella A, W, 24

24919 CARNES, George W, Kansas, OK, 51; Lizzie Nora D, 15; Walter Rosco, S, 12; Ada Ann D, 8

27283 CARNES, Henry Arthur, Flint, OK, 23

27282 CARNES, Jeff D, Flint, OK, 45; John Jefferson, S, 19; Dempsey A.N, S, 16; Oscar, S, 10; Angie D, 6; Aubrey, S, 3

24935 CARNES, John W, Kansas, OK, 40; 2199 Susan, W, 33; Roscoe, S, 10; Coney, S, 6; Gertrude D, 4; Jewel D, 1/8

26244 CARNES, Joseph E, Flint, OK, 23

25023 CARNES, Robert H. L, Kansas, OK, 28; Dorothy M D, 1

[CAR-NO-HE-YAR-DEER Blackbear. See #14298]

(Note: entry separate from other family groups)

242 CARPENTER Angeline, Talala, OK, 24; Lorenzo, S, 9; Grace D, 6; Leonard, S, 3; Mamie D, 1

25832 CARPENTER Claude, Warner, OK, 17; By Samuel W. Carpenter, Gdn.

6521 CARPENTER, Olive, Woodley, OK, 26; Alma Lewis, S, 4; Evelyn Grace D, 2

23035 CARR, Fannie J, Grove, OK, 22

26275 CARR, Frank M Bartlesville, OK, 28

8240 CARR, John G, Hudson, OK, 32; John L, S, 1/6

617 CARR, Sarah Ann Bartlesville, OK, 58; Beulah M D, 4

2150 CARR, Susan M, Grove, OK, 58

26276 CARR, William A, Mound Valley, KS, 33

8329 CARRICK, Lydia, Kansas, OK, 39; Robert, S, 15; Maggie D, 11; Lelia D, 9; Ila D, 7; Cornelias, S, 5; Thomas R, S, 2; Ella B D, ½

28533 CARRIER, Laura E, Owasso, OK, 19

42819 CARROLL Adorium, Lincolnville, OK, 25; Lena M D, 3; John E, S, 1

10678 CARROLL Charley, Oaks, OK, 7; By John Edwards, Gdn.

5496 CARROLL, Ella May, Vinita, OK, 24; Barr, Thelma D, 2

30368 CARROLL, Hattie E, Zena, OK, 19

Key: Guion Miller Application Number; Name; Address, Relation (to Head); Age in 1906

[CARROLL, Henry L. See #23591]   *(Note: entry separate from other family groups)*

35564 CARROLL, Julia A, Los Angeles, CA, 38; Nelson, Eddie, S, 16; Arthur, S, 14; Myrtle, D, 12; John, S, 9; Carroll Charles L, S, 6

27972 CARROLL, Mary C, Vinita, OK, 30; Clemmie, S, 10; Myrtle J D, 12; Gillie M D, 8; Jesse L, S, 6; Julia D, 2

29384 CARROLL, Newton Claremore, OK, 34; 29383 Nellie, W, 39

8002 CARROLL, Tottie, Vinita, OK, 28

5325 CAR-SE-LAH-WEE, Joe, Porum, OK,   36

7710 CARSELOWEY Arthur A, Okoee, OK, 22

10257 CARSELOWEY, Charles V, Okoee, OK, 26; 25183 Mary D, W, 24; Charles M, S, 1/12

13315 CARSELOWEY, James R Adair, OK, 31; James M, S, 4; Leverna G D, 1

8275 CARSELOWEY, Kate A, Vinita, OK, 53

1216 CARSON, Sarah E, Ramona, OK, 21

25074 CARTER Carrie Etta, Ft. Gibson, OK,   29; Sue Amy D, 11; James P, S, 6

13034 CARTER, Ellen, Hulbert, OK, 39; Hughes, Maggie D, 18; Hughes, Mattie D, 11

2222 CARTER, Mary, Muskogee, OK, 60

25569 CARTER, Mary B Campbell, OK, 36; Minnie L D, 15; Pearl I D, 13; Ada P D, 10; Albert E, S, 5; Ora B D, 3; Charles W, S, 3; D. L, ?, 1/6; D. N, ?, 1/6

27756 CARTER, Minnie E Campbell, OK, 19

26813 CARTER, Nancy C, Etta, OK, 31; James, S, 14; Lula D, 8; Albert, S, 6; Sarah May D, 4; Houston, S, 2; John E, S, 1

29055 CARTER, Ola M Afton, OK, 40; 27185 Florence E D, 19; 39474 Mai M D, 18; William S, S, 16; Allie Alma D, 13; Frank, S, 11; Clifton, S, 4; Sara E D, 2

[CARVER, Emma. See #21033]   *(Note: entry separate from other family groups)*

26499 CARVER, Josie, Metory, OK, 31; Jerry, S, 10; Dona[sic] D, 5; Bessie D, 2

35106 CARVER, Nannie, Muskogee, OK, 34;   Frank, S, 16; 35109 Joanna D, 18

11575½ CARVER, Walter, Muskogee, OK, 18; Pearl, Sis, 13; By James F Carver, Gdn.

5238 CASE, Martha, Muskogee, OK, 47

[CASE, Maud. See #23295]
[CASE, Emma. See #23295]   *(Note: entries separate*
[CASE, Robert. See 23295]   *from other family groups)*
[CASE, May. See #23295]

1298 CASEY Arch Carthage, MO, 34; Gladys Elizabeth D, 2

25991 CASEY Bertie E Collinsville, OK, 23; Hirschell E, S, 1

2184 CASEY, John, Ft. Gibson, OK, 31

5043 CASH, Nancy E.B, Briartown, OK, 53; James M, S, 18

Key: Guion Miller Application Number; Name; Address, Relation (to Head); Age in 1906

25319 CASS Bruce Alonzo, Los Angeles CA, 220 W 40th St, 23; 25320 Joseph H, S, 1

22368 CASS, Iddo Grant, Vinita, OK, 39; Corbet, S, 15; Mary E D, 7; Jessie D, 5; Paul, S, 2

34487 CASS, Lewis P, Welch, OK, 34; 28037 Ora A, W, 28; Ruby May D, 10; Pearl M D, 9; Grace B D, 7; Cornelia C D, 5; Lewis P, S, 4

[CATCHER. See KETCHER.]

10425 CATCHER Andrew, Locust Grove, OK, 25; 6975 Emma, W, 21; Cenie D, ½
6273 CATCHER Charlotte Dutch Mills AR, 52
6920 CATCHER, Ellis Baron, OK, 59; 6913 Lucy, W, 56; Sallie D, 17
6270 CATCHER, George Ann Dutch Mills, AR, 16
6922 CATCHER, John, Stilwell, OK, 46; 9898 Susie, W, 48 [Died 1-'09]; Charley, S, 11; John, S, 5; 39394 Lettie D, 17

[CATCHER, John H. See #6261] ⌉   *(Note: entries separate*
[CATCHER, Vance. See #6261] ⌋   *from other family groups)*

27962 CATCHER, Louis, Evansville AR, 34; Sarah D, 12; Emma D, 8; Frank E, S, 5; A. A, S, 3; Ora L D, 1/6
6255 CATCHER, Mollie Dutch Mills AR, 24; Adair Clauda D, 4; Cleo D, 1
5772 CATCHER, Neal Dutch Mills AR, 35; 5757 Bettie, W, 26; Willie, S, 13; Rosa D, 9; Clo D, 7; George, S, 2; Losier, S, 1/6
8325 CATCHER, Price, Eucha, OK, 50; 8326 Nancy, W, 30; Jirs-gar-yo-yih, S, 17; Si-nar-s-der D, 15; Gar-do-yoh-eh D, 13; Yoli-neh-qua, S, 10; Jih-nar-sar D,7

[CATCHER, Sis. See #8917] *(Note: entry separate from other family groups)*

23997 CATES, Emma C, Westville, OK, 36; Leona A D, 16; Edmond, S, 12; Sibble E, S, 9; Newton L, S, 6; Raymond, S, 3
27550 CATRON, Jefferson D, Wauhillau, OK, 23
1484 CATRON, John, Wauhillau, OK, 47; Lafayette, S, 19; George, S, 17; Thomas, S, 15; Maude B D, 13; Ola D, 11; Etta D, 7; Mary D, 3; John Emma D, 2
27549 CATRON, Julius, Wauhillau, OK, 28; Frank L, S, 5; Lorvetta J D, 3; Lisey G D, 1
1478 CATRON, Lafayette, Wauhillau, OK, 76; Joseph, S, 20; Louanna G D, 14
24254 CATRON, Maggie, Wauhillau, OK, 21
11990 CATRON, Mary, Welling, OK, 28; Peggie D, 3; Maggie D, 1

[CAU-DES-KE. See #6043]   *(Note: entry separate from other family groups)*

2452 CAUDILL, Elrilda, Grove, OK, 57; Peyton, Nancy D, 16

Key: Guion Miller Application Number; Name; Address, Relation (to Head); Age in 1906

28172 CAUDREY, Eliza, Tahlequah, OK, 49; 6060 Jennette D, 18
23508 CAULK, Fannie M Chelsea, OK, 28
11521 CAVALIER, Eliza E Choteau, OK, 33; Cicero T, S, 17; Theodore P, S, 15;
  Markham, S, 12; Scott, S, 10; Curtis, S, 8; Walter A, S, 2

[CAVALIER, John. See #26940]   *(Note: entry separate from other family groups)*

31365 CAYWOOD, Joe, Southwest City, MO, 28; 11973 Agnes, W, 26; Agie or
  Cartayah, D, 8; Wolfe or Ool-skas-te Dah-me- or John Davis, S, 3
  4785 CAYWOOD, Lizzie, Flint, OK, 50; Fannie D, 13; Albert, S, 11; Bruce, S, 9;
  Joseph, S, 7; Thomas P, S, 6; Lafayette, S, 3; Jessie N D, 1
23137 CAYWOOD, Mary E Big Cabin, OK, 22; William M, S, 5; Walter, S, 3
18633 CAYWOOD, Moses S, Siloam Springs, AR, 30
31287 CEARLEY, John G Big Cabin, OK, 26
31286 CEARLEY, Sarah L Big Cabin, OK, 48; Charles S, S, 8
42986 CEARLEY, Sion A, Tulsa, OK, 28; Opal M D, 2

[CETCHER. See KETCHER and CATCHER.]

34156 CHAIR Benjamin, Tahlequah, OK, 23
42088 CHAIR Bettie, Tahlequah, OK, 31; Annie D, 12; Phoebe D, 12; Cora M D, 3

[CHAIR, Kate. See #1506]   *(Note: entries separate*
[CHAIR, Rabbit. See #1506]   *from other family groups)*

24848 CHAIR, Nannie, Welling, OK, 31
  6806 CHAIR, Stout, Welling, OK, 58; 10209 Margaret, W, 50; James, S, 15; Nahsee
  D, 12; Lydia D, 8
  4275 CHAMBERLIN Arthur F, Vinita, OK, 49; Dollie E D, 19; Catherine B D, 13;
  Arthur, Jr, S, 6
  4273 CHAMBERLIN Clara E, Vinita, OK, 25
  6511 CHAMBERLAIN, Edward R, Vinita, OK, 18; John R Bro, 13; Ethel L, Sis, 10;
  Marthan[sic] E, Sis, 7; By Sarah E. Chamberlain, Gdn.
  4272 CHAMBERLAIN, Laura H, Vinita, OK, 20
  4276 CHAMBERLAIN, Nelson B Centralia, OK, 56; Erastus, S, 16; Mary E D, 14;
  Clarence E, S, 11
26545 CHAMBERLAIN, Ollie Cherokee City, AR, 20; William O, S, 1
  3304 CHAMBERLAIN, Robert L, Vinita, OK, 41; Amory P, S, 13; Freda Eunice D,
  10
  4287 CHAMBERLAIN, William C, Vinita, OK, 55; Winifred C D, 18; Margaret L D,
  13; Milo R, S, 11; Cline L, S, 9; Quate E D, 7
28492 CHAMBERLAIN, William N Centralia, OK, 23
24827 CHAMBERS Bertha, Fairland, OK, 22; Harold J, S, 2

23913 CHAMBERS Bulah, Miami, OK, 16

9976 CHAMBERS David, Tiawah, OK, 49

16092 CHAMBERS, Elsie, McKey, OK, 45; Correll, Minnie D, 17; Bullett, neph, 20; Charlotte, niece, 14; Sadie, niece, 12; Nola, niece, 9; Phillip, neph, 5; Perry, neph, 2

11266 CHAMBERS, Ezekiel P, Tiawah, OK, 31

11267 CHAMBERS, George S, Tulsa, OK, 52

29265 CHAMBERS, Hallie O Collinsville, OK, 21

24191 CHAMBERS, Henry, Talala, OK, 21

[CHAMBERS, James. See #8070]   *(Note: entries separate*
[CHAMBERS, John Q. See #8070]   *from other family groups)*
[CHAMBERS Clementine. See #8070]

1326 CHAMBERS, Jennie D Claremore, OK, 52; Vann S, S, 19; Clarence, S, 16; Clora or Alsie C D, 16; Joanna D, 12

11650 CHAMBERS, Jesse S, Tiawah, OK, 22

36394 CHAMBERS, Joe Claremore, OK, 21

11264 CHAMBERS, John Q Claremore, OK,   25

40158 CHAMBERS, Joe W Claremore, OK, 23

25947 CHAMBERS, Louis R Claremore, OK, 24

9831 CHAMBERS, Mack Collinsville, OK,   26

4195 CHAMBERS, Mary F, Sallisaw, OK, 72

15735 CHAMBERS, Maxwell, Tiawah, OK, 34; Jones, Henrietta D of W, 4; Florence V, D of W, 1

16871 CHAMBERS, Pickens Claremore, OK, 35; Bessie L D, 11; Floyd, S, 9; Teesey D, 7

5060 CHAMBERS, Robert, Tiawah, OK, 48

24274 CHAMBERS, Robert, Porum, OK, 21

9978 CHAMBERS, Tarchechee Claremore, OK, 23

17146 CHAMBERS, Teesey Claremore, OK, 51; 38330 Minnie L, W, 41; Evans, S, 18; Claud S, S, 16

40159 CHAMBERS, Tuxy H Claremore, OK, 21

28470 CHAMBERS, William, Vinita, OK, 32

43197 CHAMBERS, William A Claremore, OK, 41; 15733 Maud B D, 13; 43197 William L, S, 19; Mary E D, 9; Katie D, 7; Robert P, S, 4; Hurt C, S, 2

9975 CHAMBERS, William D, Tiawah, OK, 29; Henry F, S, 3; Jennie P D, 2

41172 CHAMBERS, William E Claremore, OK, 47; 12159 Nannie E, W, 44; Teesey, S, 12

107 CHAMBERS, William M Claremore, OK, 48

1371 CHAMBERS, William W, Tiawah, OK, 72; Leo, S, 20; Joe Henry, S, 18

27636 CHANCE Annie, Vian, OK, 21; Arthur, S, 3; Jasper O, S, 1; L. J, S, 1/12

Key: Guion Miller Application Number; Name; Address, Relation (to Head); Age in 1906

24583 CHANCE, Maggie Chance, OK, 34; James, S, 16; Myrtle D, 15; Ida D, 12; William, S, 9; Tilman G, S, 4

23038 CHANDLER Claud A, Fairland, OK, 27

1725 CHANDLER Cornelia C, Fairland, OK, 45; Benjamin Harrison, S, 18; Fannie Wanira, D, 15; Homer Edward, S, 12; Robert Elmer, S, 10; Otto Cornelius, S, 8; Lura Corinne, D, 6; Rebecca Caroline D, 4; John Dewitt, S, 20

30205 CHANDLER David L, Siloam Springs, AR, 23

1723 CHANDLER, Fannie E, Ogeechee, OK, 51; Ethel May D, 11; Ben. Edward, S, 13; John Willey, S, 16; Jeanettie B, D, 19

23570 CHANDLER, Felix Chester, Fairland, OK, 25; 23567 Dona[sic] M, W, 25; Thelma, D, 1

23040 CHANDLER, James A, Ogeechee, OK, 25

24721 CHANDLER, John C, Siloam Springs, AR, 32; 3874 Emma M, W, 22; Lillian D, 1

16751 CHANDLER, Mary M, McLain, OK, 27; George, S, 8; Frances D, 3; John, S, 1

23039 CHANDLER, Myrtie May, Fairland, OK, 22

24796 CHANDLER, Oliver K, Muskogee, OK, 22

35584 CHANDLER, Pearl, Pryor Creek, OK, 19

[CHANDLER, Richard. See #10728]   *(Note: entry separate from other family groups)*

24709 CHANDLER, Sam W, Siloam Springs, AR, 29

868 CHANDLER, Susannah, Siloam Springs AR, 54

41210 CHANDLER, William P, Tahlequah, OK, 35; 31638 Josie, W, 39

28821 CHANDOIN, Jane Ann, Moody, OK, 27; Mary I D, 7; Elva D, 5; Della D, 3; Curtis, S, 2

24864 CHANDOIN, Mary, Manard, OK, 23; Johnnie, S, 1

1407 CHANEY Artie Collinsville, OK, 36; Williams, Jennie D, 15; Thomas J, S, 10; Edna, D, 4

28466 CHANEY Charles E Centralia, OK, 31; James D, S, 7; Charles E, Jr, S, 5; Leona C, D, 3

30892 CHANEY, Eliza Coodys Bluff, OK, 22

10315 CHANEY, Florence, Eureka, OK, 15; By Alfred H. Chaney, Gdn.

22519 CHANEY, Florence, Lenapah, OK, 20

19194 CHANEY, Julia Coodys Bluff, OK, 50; Della D, 17; Ethel D, 15; Lou E D, 11; George W, S, 9; Florence E D, 5

15671 CHANEY, William H Chelsea, OK, 24

16456 CHANLEY Alice, Zena, OK, 26; Mary E D, 1

31594 CHANLEY, Josie B Afton, OK, 24; Maggie M D, 6; Gracie E D, 5; Ralph, S, 3; Welbern, S, 1/12

[CHARBONEAU, Mary M. See #38484] ⎤   *(Note: entries separate*
[CHARBONEAU, John H. See #38484] ⎦   *from other family groups)*

Key: Guion Miller Application Number; Name; Address, Relation (to Head); Age in 1906

5014 CHARLES, Elizabeth, Westville, OK, 17; Mary Alice D, 1
7031 CHARLES, John, Stilwell, OK, 25
1212 CHARLES, Nancy, Stilwell, OK, 49
6261 CHARLES, Nannie Dutch Mills AR, 22; Catcher, John H, S, 3; Vance, S, 1

[CHARLES, Thompson. See #7417]   *(Note: entry separate from other family groups)*

31418 CHARLESWORTH, Fred W, Vinita, OK, 23
1729 CHARLESWORTH, Mary J, Vinita, OK, 44; Oliver E, S, 18; Henry A, S, 16; Blanche, D, 14
31417 CHARLESWORTH, Walter M, Vinita,   OK, 24; 31466 Eugenia K, W, 23
7981 CHARLEY, Elizabeth C, Turley, OK, 23; William C, S, 2; Athia L D, ½
3503 CHARLEY, Sophia L Cookson, OK, 49; 13369 Silk, Charles, S, 17; Susan D, 14; Jennie D, 12
23720 CHASTAIN, Martha Bell Afton, OK, 18
568 CHASTAIN, Mary E, Fairland, OK, 31
2990 CHASTAIN, Nancy J, Eureka, OK, 31; Robert, S, 9; Bertha D, 6; Bell D, 4; John, Jr, S, 2; James B, S, 1
27146 CHASTAIN, Rhoda Chelsea, OK, 25; Elvin, S, 8; Ernest, S, 5; Roland, S, 2
18491 CHASTAIN, Rosa, Sallisaw, OK, 21
29381 CHASTINE, Martha W, Hulbert, OK, 20
7559 CHEATER Asy, South West City, MO, 37; E. Shut-ta D, 13
26252 CHEATER Benjamin, South West City, MO, 30; Mary D, 10
6993 CHEATER Charley, South West City,   MO, 33; 24560 Sarah, W, 19
358 CHEATER, Enole, Grove, OK, 57 [Died 7-17-1906]; Katie or Ca-hu-cah, W, 57
6991 CHEATER, George, South West City, MO, 45; 6995 Peggy, W, 27; Gah-la-chi, S, 9
12922 CHEATER, Ike, Maysville AR, 52; 13359 Jane, W, 61
9332 CHEATER, John, South West City, MO, 22
11432 CHEATER, John Cove, OK, 39; 11409 Oo-squi, W, 48
16450 CHEATER, Joseph, South West City, MO, 19
5982 CHEATER, Lacy, South West City, MO, 66; 5980 Caty, W, 56; Nick, S, 19
9931 CHEATER, Maria, South West City, MO, 24
9010 CHEE-GOO-WA, Tah-la-la, Locust Grove, OK, 33; Wood, Small, S, 14
10739 CHEEK, Rosa Atkins, OK, 36; Myrtle D, 16; George, S, 15; Roy, S, 13; Beatrice, D, 9; Nina D, 7; Margie D, 6; Evie D, 4; Seba D, 2
13255 CHE-KE-LE, Nancy Bunch, OK, 54
5732 CHENEY, Thomas C Chance, OK, 21
27638 CHERRY, Ruth E, Paw Paw, OK, 24; Jessie H D, 3; Edith G D, 1
24846 CHESTNUT, Holly, Sapulpa, OK, 15; By William H. Chestnut, Gdn.

[CHETIE Caty or CHETEE Caty. See #5980]
(Note: entry separate from other family groups)

CHEROKEE DESCENDANTS RESIDING WEST OF MISSISSIPPI RIVER.
VOLUME II   (A – M)

Key: Guion Miller Application Number; Name; Address, Relation (to Head); Age in 1906

[CHEWEE, Sam. See #16935]   *(Note: entry separate from other family groups)*

14312 CHEWEY, Talala, Stilwell, OK, 39 [Blind];   By John Hogner, Gdn.

[CHEWIE. See CHUWEE.]

30615 CHEWIE, John, Stilwell, OK, 16
30613 CHEWIE, Looney Baron, OK, 10;   By Susie Blackwood, Gdn.
17671 CHEWIE, Lucy, Whitmire, OK, 8;   By Annie Snake, Gdn.
7863 CHEWIE, Sarah, Oaks, OK, 64

[CHEWIE, William. See #6036]   *(Note: entry separate from other family groups)*

[CHICKEN, Nancie. See #6678]   *(Note: entry separate from other family groups)*

10632 CHICKEN, Ned, Spavinaw, OK, 31; 10429 Cora, W, 33; Jackson, S, 6; High, S, 3
10627 CHICKEN, Night, Locust Grove, OK, 42; 10649 See-kee, W, 24
620 CHILDERS, John C Copan, OK, 46
27422 CHILDERS, Luella Brushy, OK, 32; James A, S, 7
9149 CHILDERS, Thomas B, Welch, OK, 20
537 CHILDERS, William, Wann, OK, 46; Wilie S, S, 19; Landy S, S, 15; Sophia N D, 13; Ben F, S, 10; Sarah V D, 7; Gladys A D, 4; Vera E D, 2
1452 CHILDRESS, John, Sallisaw, OK, 75; 1456 Nancy, W, 60
7417 CHILDS, Thomason, Stilwell, OK, 52
9673 CHINARCHE, John Afton, OK, 37; William T, S, 10
31813 CHISHOLM, Eliza, Melvin, OK, 25; Woodall, Looney, S, 8; Chisholm Buster, S, 5; Chancy, S, 3; Enos, S, 1
24871 CHISHOLM, Mary, Melvin, OK, 27; Clark Ada D, 13; Ethel D, 9
3676 CHITWOOD, Lucy A, White Oak, OK, 32; Walter, S, 15; Mamie J, D, 12; Floyd H, S, 7
24374 CHOATE Bettie May, Gans, OK, 4; James Anderson Bro, 3;   By Rosa Choate, Gdn.
24603 CHOATE, Felix R, Marble City, OK, 24
13385 CHOATE, George W, Jr, Marble City, OK, 28
8625 CHOATE, George W, Sr, Marble City, OK, 63; 5616 Lizzie C, W, 50; Rufus, S, 19; Jennie D, 15; Douglass, S, 12
63 CHOATE, John B, Pryor Creek, OK, 43; Robert M, S, 13; Isabella D, 10
2346 CHOATE, John C, Tahlequah, OK, 35; 5115 Fannie L, W, 33; Juanita D, 2
2345 CHOATE, Joshua, Sallisaw, OK, 51
11484 CHOATE, Lillian, Sallisaw. OK, 30
29299 CHOATE, Lorettia, Gans, OK, 56
6441 CHOATE, Marion D Brushy, OK, 38

Key: Guion Miller Application Number; Name; Address, Relation (to Head); Age in 1906

2347 CHOATE, Richard B Bunch, OK, 43; 8304 Lydia E, W, 43; Robert M, S, 11; Edward E, S, 7

62 CHOATE, Rufus M, Pryor Creek, OK, 49; William P, S, 13

13643 CHOATE, Sam Cookson, OK, 19; By Sam Massey, Gdn.

15996 CHOATE, William Braggs, OK, 27; 15994 Mary, W, 24; Charlie, S, 5; Georgia V, D, 2

14297 CHOONOOSTOOT, Josiah, Locust Grove, OK, 37; William, S, 17

[CHOO-WA-LOO-KIE. See #21749] *(Note: entry separate from other family groups)*

[CHOO-WA-LOO-KIE. See #21750] *(Note: entry separate from other family groups)*

14109 CHOOWEE, Nancy Christie, OK, 68

[CHOOWEE, Nannie. See #42528]   *(Note: entry separate from other family groups)*

11200 CHOOWEE, Sarah Christie, OK, 48

655 CHOPPER Daylight, Eucha, OK, 57; 654 Jennie, W, 57

1199 CHOPPER, Joe, Eucha, OK, 20;   By Emma Fox, Gdn.

5858 CHRISMAN, Ida, Southwest City, MO, 30; Willie, S, 12; Allen, S, 9; Preston James, S, ½

27919 CHRISMAN, Rachel L, Southwest City, MO, 18; Gilbert, Earl G, S, 3; Preston, Lewis P, S, 2

40291 CHRISTIAN, Ethel, Vinita, OK, 12 R.F.D. #1; Ora, Sis, 10; Samuel Bro, 8; Ray, Bro, 5;   By M. C. Christian, Gdn.

24678 CHRISTIAN, James W, Tahlequah, OK, 8; Orlando O, Bro, 3; By Bessie Pearl Christian, Gdn.

17697 CHRISTIAN, William F, Wagoner, OK, 35; Pearl D, 4; Willie, S, 2; Belle D, 1

9158 CHRISTIE Alex, Proctor, OK, 29; 9187 Ada, W, 23

[CHRISTIE Alice (or Ollia). See #2156] *(Note: entry separate from other family groups)*

[CHRISTIE Angie M. See #1459]   *(Note: entries separate*
[CHRISTIE, May C. See #1459]   *from other family groups)*

8806 CHRISTIE Arch, Tahlequah, OK, 23; 33401 Nannie, W, 26

364 CHRISTIE Buffalo, Welling, OK, 47; 6510 Akey, W, 44; Jewey D, 16; Richard, S, 14; George, S, 12; Nannie D, 9; Mary D, 7; Annie D, 4

24132 CHRISTIE Charley, Welling, OK, 21

2933 CHRISTIE Charlie, Locust Grove, OK, 24

1458 CHRISTIE Cherokee, Sallisaw, OK, 23

31605 CHRISTIE Cynthia, Gideon, OK, 17

13107 CHRISTIE Dick Cookson, OK, 20

Key: Guion Miller Application Number; Name; Address, Relation (to Head); Age in 1906

39159 CHRISTIE, Ezekiel Bunch, OK, 22

23658 CHRISTIE, George W Christie, OK, 47; Mary B D, 13; Ollie, S, 11; Ella D, 8; Jennie, D, 5; Blanch D, 2

11876 CHRISTIE, Goback, Wauhillau, OK, 41; 11877 Susan, W, 25

10712 CHRISTIE, Isaac, Vian, OK, 20;   By James Foster, Gdn.

13596 CHRISTIE, Israel, McKey, OK, 24

17194 CHRISTIE, Jack, Welling, OK, 22

24206 CHRISTIE, James Christie, OK, 34; 24207 Lula C, W, 34; Lucy J D, 11; Ella M D, 6; Annie E D, 4

 4794 CHRISTIE, Jennie Christie, OK, 73

 5536 CHRISTIE, Jennie, Gideon, OK, 45; Sallie D, 12; Arch, S, 10; Daniel, S, 9

13670 CHRISTIE, Jennie, Wauhillau, OK, 38

13828 CHRISTIE, Jennie, Marble City, OK, 17;   By Nelly Christie, Gdn.

24131 CHRISTIE, Jennie, Welling, OK, 24

12418 CHRISTIE, Jess Cookson, OK, 20

 7989 CHRISTIE, Jess S, Tulsa, OK, 28

13827 CHRISTIE, John, Marble City, OK, 23

39157 CHRISTIE, John Bunch, OK, 20

 6588 CHRISTIE, Katie Bunch, OK, 50; Daniel, S, 13; John, S, 10; Lacy, S(?), 5

13829 CHRISTIE, Lillie, Marble City, OK, 19;   By Nelly Christie, Gdn.

 1651 CHRISTIE, Nancy, Wauhillau, OK, 62

23659 CHRISTIE, Nancy E Christie, OK, 42

39166 CHRISTIE, Nellie Bunch, OK, 17

12512 CHRISTIE, Nellie Phillips, Locust Grove, OK, 22

 4203 CHRISTIE, Nelly, Marble City, OK, 50

17274 CHRISTIE, Nelly, Wauhillau, OK, 47

 2391 CHRISTIE, Pheasant, Stilwell, OK, 45; 2396 Lucy, W, 39

 2867 CHRISTIE, Polly Bunch, OK, 20

[CHRISTIE, Rachel. See #784]   *(Note: entry separate from other family groups)*

13830 CHRISTIE, Richard, Marble City, OK, 14; By Nelly Christie, Gdn.

21749 CHU-WA-LOO-KIE Daniel, Wauhillau, OK, 34; 21750 Susan, W, 33

43082 CHRISTIE, Sallie, Vinita, OK, 20; Lydia D, 2

12650 CHRISTIE, Taylor, Wauhillau, OK, 45; 17478 Annie, W, 27; Fannie D, 17; Albert, S, 16; Annie D, 13

 9658 CHRISTIE, Walker Bunch, OK, 57; 9659 Sallie, W, 60

23398 CHRISTIE, William, Etta, OK, 27; 6569 Hester, W, 28; William, Jr, S, 1

[CHRISTIE, Wilson. See #43361]   *(Note: entry separate from other family groups)*

 6990 CHRISTMAN Agness[sic], Southwest City, MO, 30; Audrey S D, 1; Barnes, Servetus B, S, 10; George D, S, 9; Oscar E, S, 5

CHEROKEE DESCENDANTS RESIDING WEST OF MISSISSIPPI RIVER.
VOLUME II   (A – M)

Key: Guion Miller Application Number; Name; Address, Relation (to Head); Age in 1906

2494 CHRISTY Betsey, Locust Grove, OK, 60

2953 CHRISTY Dick, Locust Grove, OK, 30

13177 CHRISTY, Lily, Melvin, OK, 30

19832 CHRISTY, Springfrog, Wauhillau, OK, 26

2954 CHRISTY, William, Locust Grove, OK, 28

26650 CHRONISTER, Mary, Etta, OK, 21[Died 6-22-1906]; Lawrence, S, 3; Ella D, 3

29221 CHUALOOKY Beaver, Eucha, OK, 24; 9291 Sallie, W, 20; Steen [or Steve], S, 3

612 CHU-A-LU-KEE Chick-a-le-le, Eucha, OK, 56; 720 Chewanah, W, 32; Lee, S, 13; Annie M D, 10; Walsie, S, 6; Olcie D, 3; Polly D, ½

364 HU-A-LU-KE David, Eucha, OK, 67; 378 Lean, W, 60; Liddie D, 19; Taylor, S, 15

3928 CHUCALATE Charley, Sallisaw, OK, 21

3927 CHUCALATE, Ellis, Sallisaw, OK, 55; 4843 Eliza, W, 37; Peggie D, 16; David, S, 14; Levi, S, 6; Duval, S, 4

10709 CHUCALATE, Jessie, Vian, OK, 31

[CHUCKALATE, Hyatt or Hyde. See #43787] ⎤ *(Note: entries separate*
[CHUCKALATE, Ose or Oscar. See #43787] ⎦ *from other family groups)*

2814 CHUCKELUCK, Tyler, Locust Grove, OK, 34

[CHUCKULUCK, Tom. See #3288]   *(Note: entry separate from other family groups)*

[CHUCKULUCK, Nancy. See #22006]
(Note: entry separate from other family groups)

9648 CHUCULATE Bush Bunch, OK, 24; Ella May D, 3

5927 CHUCULATE Charley, Sallisaw, OK, 49; 12487   Sarah, W, 52

9741 CHUCULATE Con-sene Bunch, OK, 34; 9740 Sarah, W, 28

8015 CHUCULATE, George W, Sallisaw, OK, 38; 6714 Elmira, W, 34; Perry, S, 15; Beulah D, 12; George, S, 9; Moses, S, 6; Emma C D, 2

3942 CHUCULATE, Isaac, Sallisaw, OK, 31; 6735 Nellie, W, 26

42532 CHUCULATE, James, Vian, OK, 23; Gussie D, 3

3943 CHUCULATE, John, Sallisaw, OK, 35 [Died 1908]; 981 Lizzie, W, 35; Ben, S, 8; Berman, S, 6; Frye, Nancy D of W, 17; Walter, S of W, 14; Mary D of W, 11

9647 CHUCULATE, John Bunch, OK, 26; Nellie D, 3

5926 CHUCULATE, Lizzie, Marble City, OK, 60

1450 CHUCULATE, Mose, Sallisaw, OK, 90

4845 CHUCULATE, Rachel, Sallisaw, OK, 84

3541 CHUCULATE, Sally, Sallisaw, OK, 29

10937 CHUCULATE, Sally, Sallisaw, OK, 19

Key: Guion Miller Application Number; Name; Address, Relation (to Head); Age in 1906

960 CHUCULATE, Sam, Sallisaw, OK, 31; 3365 Venie, D, 9; Bonie, D, 6; Samuel, S, 3

31629 CHUCULATE, Tom, Hulbert, OK, 31; 38484 Rebecca, W, 31; Nancy D, 3; Downing, Mary D of W, 7

14268 CHUCULATE, Walker Bunch, OK, 32

3865 CHUCULATE, Wesley, Sallisaw, OK, 59; Charlie, S, 17

25281 CHUCULATE, Wesley, McKey, OK, 11; By George King, Sr, Gdn.

34725 CHUCULATE, Wyley, Muskogee, OK, 9; By C. E. Holderman, Gdn.

5934 CHUKERLATE Alex, Marble City, OK, 51

39176 CHUKERLATE Boone Bunch, OK, 25

13131 CHUKERLATE Daniel, Sallisaw, OK, 53

9738 CHUKERLATE, Eli Bunch, OK, 55; 9713 Louisa, W, 50; Alex, S, 16

9680 CHUKERLATE, Fields Bunch, OK, 29; 9394 Lucy, Stilwell, OK, 29; Sam, S, 9 John, S, 6; Lizzie D, 4; Henry, S, 2

9636 CHUKERLATE, Ice, Sallisaw, OK, 28; 28604 Katie, W, 27; Duck, Mary D of W, 12; Chukerlate, William, S, 1

9635 CHUKERLATE, Jennie, Marble City, OK, 48

13192 CHUKERLATE, Jennie Bunch, OK, 14; By Ella Thrower, Gdn.

[CHUKERLATE, John. See #5802]   *(Note: entries separate*
[CHUKERLATE, Robert. See #5802]   *from other family groups)*

39171 CHUKERLATE, Nannie Bunch, OK, 22

39170 CHUKERLATE, Zeke Bunch, OK, 31; 4865 Lizzie, W, 28; Josie D, 10; John, S, 4; Lewis, S, 2

4072 CHULIO, Jack, Stilwell, OK, 42; 42196 Lucinda, W, 20

4076 CHULIO, John, Stilwell, OK, 40; 8357 Nancy, W, 36; Lizzie [Liza] D, 9; Rattler, S, 8; Bear, S, 5; Margaret D, 1

[CHULIO, John. See #39158]   *(Note: entry separate from other family groups)*

[CHUNESTUDY, John & Wm. and families. See #13090 et. seq.]
                          (Note: entry separate from other family groups)

5266 CHURCHILL, Julia Claudia, Vinita, OK, 21

[CHU-WA-LOOKY Che-wa-nes. See #720]
                          (Note: entry separate from other family groups)

9145 CHU-WA-LU-KY Crying Bird, Eucha, OK, 61 9146 Bird Cynthia, W, 61

611 CHUWALOOKY, Lydia, Eucha, OK, 67

624 CHUWA-LOOKY Dick Chloeta, OK,   38; 1646 Lizzie, W, 32; John, S, 13; Cora D, 10; Ella D, 8; Lucy D, 6; Mary D, 2

CHEROKEE DESCENDANTS RESIDING WEST OF MISSISSIPPI RIVER.
VOLUME II (A – M)

Key: Guion Miller Application Number; Name; Address, Relation (to Head); Age in 1906

650 CHU-WA-LU-KE, Quatie, Eucha, OK, 24

[CHU-WEE. See CHEWIE.]

8113 CHU-WEE Annie Braggs, OK, 16; By Ah-le Miller, Gdn.

[CHEWEE, Samuel. See #16935]   *(Note: entry separate from other family groups)*

11625 CLAGHORN, Peggie Catoosa, OK, 27

[CLAPP Bettie Ray. See #8082] ⎤   *(Note: entries separate*
[CLAPP Davie (or Dovie) D. See #8082] ⎦   *from other family groups)*

22875 CLAPPER, Elouise M Centralia, OK, 22; Carl E, S, 3; Arthur H, S, ¼
5637 CLAPPER, Emma J, Miles, OK, 26; Zella May D, 7;Ora Lee, S, 4

[CLARK Ada. See #24871] ⎤   *(Note: entries separate*
[CLARK, Ethel. See #24871] ⎦   *from other family groups)*

24963 CLARK Albert Checotah, OK, 24
3748 CLARK Alice, Warner, OK, 27; Wicked, Lillie D, 9; Clark, Stella O D, 7;
   Charley A, S, 5; Myrtle D, 3; Emma O D, 2; Earnest, S, 1/12
2991 CLARK Bertha Chelsea, OK, 21; Charles H, S, 4; Herbert Eugene, S, 1
30529 CLARK Blue D Dewey, OK, 22
29067 CLARK Bud Alluwe, OK, 29; Charles Edward, S, 1/12
2889 CLARK, Elizabeth J, Grove, OK, 45
2121 CLARK, Emily L Chelsea, OK, 59; Emily L D, 16
2919 CLARK, George W, Vinita, OK, 63; 2920 Lydia A, W, 60; R. R, S, 16; May D,
   14
22945 CLARK, George W, Jr, Vinita, OK, 21
4718 CLARK, Jay T Cookson, OK, 51; Jesse J, S, 15; Jennie R D, 13; Maggie C D,
   9; Frank C, S, 7; Clarence J, S, 4; Levi S, S, 2; Viola D, 1/12
24964 CLARK, John Checotah, OK, 26; Velma Lee D, 1
30542 CLARK, Levi K Dewey, K, 26; 30543   Mary, W, 20
11958 CLARK, Lottie A, Sumas, WA, 37; Pattie Cora E D, 4; Frederick H, S, 3;
   Sophie F, D, 1
13073 CLARK, Lucinda C Checotah, OK, 55; Austin, S, 19; Elita D, 16; Ruth D, 11
17172 CLARK, Lucy, Webbers Falls, OK, 26; Pawnee, S, 2/3
2112 CLARK, Mary A, Talala, OK, 30; George W, S, 5; Ansie D, 3; Lester Wayne, S,
   1
3235 CLARK, Olola, Vinita, OK, 18
24641 CLARK, Perry, Hadley, OK, 15; Jennie, Sis, 13; Myrtle, Sis, 11; By Charles
   Clark, Gdn.

Key: Guion Miller Application Number; Name; Address, Relation (to Head); Age in 1906

31369 CLARK, Robert L Dewey, OK, 25; Martin V, S, 5; Owen B, S, 3; Peachie D, 1

7029 CLARK, Silas D Dewey, OK, 25; 30530 Jennie D, 19; Elvin P, S, 9; Joel M, S, 16

8626 CLARK, Taylor, Tahlequah, OK, 46; 4040 Dilla, W, 43; Lila D, 20; Silas D, S, 17; Jay T, S, 13

2147 CLARK, William, Grove, OK, 27; John F, S, 6; William, S, 4; George W, S, 3; Nancy Iola D, 1

30378 CLARK, William, Ft. Gibson, OK, 21 (or 27 unable to read last number.)

5055 CLARK, William A. Alluwe, OK, 45; Joseph J, S, 13; Lucy J D, 13; Marey L D, 9; Clerinda S D, 6; William A, Jr, S, 4; Lillie B, Jr[sic] D, 4

22748 CLARK, William H Chelsea, OK, 40; 22749 Lella J, W, 32; James W, S, 10; Mabel C, D, 8; Raleigh P, S, 6; Rosa B, D, 4; William H, Jr, S, 2

28676 CLARKE Addie C Chelsea, OK, 18

31802 CLARKE, Lucy C Chelsea, OK, 21

28677 CLARKE, Sarah E, R Chelsea, OK, 23

25090 CLASBY, Fannie Afton, OK, 32; Annie M D, 15; Philip R, S, 11; Robert L, S, 9; James R, S, 7; Thomas M, S, 5

32441 CLAWSON, Vinita I, Tulsa, OK, 26; Mirah Catherine D, 4; Lucile D, 3

11452 CLAY Columbus, Fawn, OK, 42

[CLAY, Henry. See #9488]   *(Note: entry separate from other family groups)*

33833 CLAY, Henry, Eureka Springs AR, 8; By Sarah Leach, Gdn.

5124 CLAY, James, Welling, OK, 42; Susie J D, 6; Abraham L, S, 2

26114 CLAY, Lovely Braggs, OK, 21

17224 CLAY, Rachel, Fawn, OK, 18

5122 CLAY, Riley, Welling, OK, 52; James A, S, 8; William, S, 5; Mammie D, 1/12

14137 CLAY, Tommy, Peggs, OK, 12; By C. C. Manus, Gdn.

29651 CLAYTON, Sarah E Chelsea, OK, 22

23582 CLELAND, Emmett Shaw, Wagoner, OK, 43; Emmett Shaw, S, 14; Marion Wilson, D, 9

4333 CLELAND, George W, Wagoner, OK, 78

24693 CLELAND, George W, Wagoner, OK, 45; Catherine W D, 14; James Brown, S, 11

23583 CLELAND, James Bancroft, Wagoner, OK, 33; Thomas T, S, 4; Wheeler Bancroft, S, 1

2477 CLEVELAND Bark F Blue Jacket, OK, 32; 5067 Cornelia C, W, 28; Byron F, S, 5; Cathaleen H D, 2

2040 CLEVENGER, Nellie, Vinita, OK, 51

14751 CLEVENGER, Sarah J, Vinita, OK, 32

73 CLIFTON, Mattie, Owasso, OK, 14; By George Clifton, Gdn.

31601 CLINE Ben D, Wimer, OK, 31; 6477 Dora C, W, 28; Johnie[sic] R, S, 9; Raymond D, S, 6; Ray L, S, 4; Ross A, S, 1; Lilla L D, 1

Key: Guion Miller Application Number; Name; Address, Relation (to Head); Age in 1906

38445 CLINE, Eli Buckeye, WA, 23

455 CLINE, Ezekiel, Ruby, OK, 52; Albert R, S, 20; Amanda M D, 16; William P, S, 8; Timothy E, S, 6; Maude D, 5; Annie D, 2

30009 CLINE, John T, Wimer, OK, 27; 24129   Nettie, W, 21

1427 CLINE, William Bunch, OK, 51; 13662 John, S, 17; 13663 Sallie D, 10; 1427 Bettie, D, 14; Harvey, S, 1/12

24822 CLINGAN Cora M, Gibson Sta, OK, 28

1541 CLINGAN, Judge K Chelsea, OK, 69

25386 CLINGAN, Samuel D, Rex, OK, 23

24356 CLINGAN, Sherman A, Melvin, OK, 30

8097 CLINGAN, William D, Gibson Sta, OK, 73

2478½ CLINKSCALES, Albert S, Vinita, OK, 13; John H Bro, 9; By Albert M. Clinkscales, Gdn.

26079 CLINKSCALES, Lewis Dupree, Vinita, OK, 22

28984 CLOUD Arch, Locust Grove, OK, 28; 28984 Jennie, W, 32

31895 CLOUD Charles C, Lenapah, OK, 46; 406 Mary J, W, 56; Caldonie D, 16; Joel B, S, 18; Pearl D, 13

911 CLOUD Cricket, Locust Grove, OK, 62

28876 CLOUD, George S, McKey, OK, 29; Jessie D, 5; Jo, S, 3

1204 CLOUD, Henry L, Wellston, OK, 32; Riley H, S, 2; Lucile D, 1

37497 CLOUD, James H, Foyil, OK, 7; By B. S. Tinsley, Gdn.

31945 CLOUD, James L, Lenapah, OK, 39; 22755 Sarah J, W, 32; 31945 Thomas, S, 16; James S, S, 12; Emma J D, 9; John C, S, 7; Clousee D, 2

28877 CLOUD, John E, McKey, OK, 34

22757 CLOUD, John M, Lenapah, OK, 23

13118 CLOUD, Joshua Chapel, OK, 29; Annie Lee D, 2

16086 CLOUD, Katie, Tahlequah, OK, 24; Richard H, S, 6; Joanna D, 3; Sallie D, 1

346 CLOUD, Martha C, McKey, OK, 66

22756 CLOUD, Mattie B, Lenapah, OK: 20

1471 CLOUD, Noah, Tahlequah, OK, 23

5751 CLOUD, Robert, Stilwell, OK, 41; Noah S, S, 14; Susan D, 12; Robert, S, 10; William, S, 10; Leona D, 7

28879 CLOUD, William M, McKey, OK, 25; Embra M D, 4

5152 CLYNE, John Baron, OK, 16; Emma B, Sis, 18;   By Edward A. Clyne, Gdn.

14231 COAST Alice M, Ramona, OK, 29; Clara Belle D, 4; Albert F, S, 2

410 COATS Canzadie, Bloomfield AR, 12; Novadia, Sis, 11; 13031 Beck, Willie Oren, ½ Bro, 2; By Laura Beck, Gdn.

35465 COATS Charles F Blue Jacket, OK, 32; Lillie E D, 8

2063 COATS, Henry L, Welch, OK, 37; Carrie Mayes D, 9; William M, S, 6; Lillie May D, 3; Bee Atris D, 1

3299 COATS, James, Pryor Creek, OK, 40; 8676 Susie D, W, 31; Jennie B D, 12; James M, S, 10; Elmer Earl, S, 4; Captolia U D, 2; Lula May D, 1/3

Key: Guion Miller Application Number; Name; Address, Relation (to Head); Age in 1906

34479 COATS, James E, Blue Jacket, OK, 37; Annie M D, 12; Claude E, S, 10; Robert P, S, 4

410 COATS, John Choteau, OK, 40; 3604 Lucy, W, 33; Lillia May D, 21; 3607 Still, Enos, S of W, 9

27797 COATS, John H, Welch, OK, 21

40574 COATS, John M Adair, OK, 32; 40535 Ada, W, 22; Mary J D, 4; William P, S, 2

37129 COATS, John W Blue Jacket, OK, 29; Floyd, S, 8; Lewis H, S, 1

9423 COATS, Louisa J, Welch, OK, 54

1935 COATS, William, Miami, OK, 46; George M, S, 19; William P, S, 16; Charles J, S, 13

3723 COATS, William Adair, OK, 17; Thomas M Bro, 10;   By Jane Sandidge, Gdn.

31887 COBB Alexander C, Wagoner, OK, 42; Gilbert B, S, 17; Mary I D, 15; William A, S, 7; Irene D, 6; Harry F, S, 4; Kedzie P, S, 2

34534 COBB Andrew Jackson, Muskogee, OK, 21; 30052 Lucy, W, 19; James A, S, 1/12

30557 COBB Charles H, Muskogee, OK, 23 Robison Street; 30556 Addie, W, 19

5931 COBB, Evaline C, Wagoner, OK, 71

30534 COBB, Isabel, Wagoner, OK, 48

4240 COBB, James, Lometa, OK, 24

26461 COBB, James E, Muskogee, OK, 25; 35269 Sarah C, W, 19

4634 COBB, James H, Keefeton, OK, 55; William W, S, 18; Susie M D, 16

4244 COBB, Jefferson, Lometa, OK, 21

40523 COBB, Jennie Fields, Muskogee, OK, 24

31126 COBB, Joseph B, Wagoner, OK, 43; Evelyn D, 11; Florence D, 9; Joseph J, S, 8; Isabel D, 5; Thomas, S, 3

24395 COBB, Lillie E, Nowata, OK, 25; Charlie R, S, 8; William McD, S, 6; Theodore R, S, 1; Florence L D, 1

2797 COBB, Mary E, Craig, OK, 51; 25481 Artie, S, 18; 2797 Samuel A, S, 17; Mary Ellen, D, 14; Clarice D, 12; Hutton V, S, 9

2049 COBB, Rufus B, Muskogee, OK, 58; 208 Mary E, W, 51; Benjamin R, S, 20; Edith M, D, 17; Grover C, S, 15; Ula E D, 13; Mary E D, 7

30533 COBB, Samuel S, Wagoner, OK, 41; Phil H, S, 11; Paul P, S, 9; Samuel S, Jr, S, 6; Carolyn E D, 4; Ruth Isabel D, 2/3

23097 COBB, Simpson C, Muskogee, OK, 23

23229 COBBELL Anna, Lenapah, OK, 32; Safrona D, 6; Earl, S, 3

29774 COBLE, Robert, Oklahoma City, OK, 22

24409 COBSTILL, Martha J, Fawn, OK, 36; Mark, S, 14; Lucinda D, 12; Jesse, S, 10; Pearl, D, 6; Bessie D, 3; Bettie D, ¼

16582 COCHRAN, Jennie, Westville, OK, 20

25004 COCHRAN Alexander Cookson, OK, 34; Joseph, S, 9; Jesse, S, 7; William, S, 4; Jack, S, 2

Key: Guion Miller Application Number; Name; Address, Relation (to Head); Age in 1906

[COCHRAN Annie. See #4291]   *(Note: entry separate from other family groups)*

13516 COCHRAN Annie Braggs, OK, 20

26796 COCHRAN Arch Cookson, OK, 37; Joseph Loyd, S, 10; Zell, S, 7; Edwin Levi, S, 5; Ora May D, 3; Bessie Ella D, 1/6

[COCHRAN Charlotte. See #14133]   *(Note: entry separate from other family groups)*

6453 COCHRAN Cintha, Stilwell, OK, 37

12565 COCHRAN Clarence Chelsea, OK, 22; 36556 Minda, W, 33; Hall Andrew Z, S of W, 16

12567 COCHRAN Clinton Chelsea, OK, 24

32859 COCHRAN Dollie, Ray, OK, 29; Sanders, Murrel, S, 3; Sanders, Charley, S, 1; Cochran, Jesse,

5300 COCHRAN, Eve, Stilwell, OK, 29; Jim, S, 14; Sallie D, 12; Narcissus D, 6

[COCHRAN, George. See #4719]   *(Note: entry separate from other family groups)*

7011 COCHRAN, George, Melvin, OK, 29; 34570 Vina, W, 20; Landon, S, 4; Lula D, 2; Eliza D, 1

11503 COCHRAN, George, Stilwell, OK, 72; 12538 Charlie, S, 18

5685 COCHRAN, George, Jr, Stilwell, OK, 46; 5683 Stacy, W, 40; Jack, S, 16; Curtis, S, 7

14768 COCHRAN, George W Catoosa, OK, 40; 14769 Julia, W, 30; 14770 George, S, 17; Joseph, S, 8; Jay, S, 3; Lethie May D, 1

6454 COCHRAN, Henry, Stilwell, OK, 36; 5393 Eve, W, 34; Lydia D, 8; Jemmie[sic] or James, S, 6; Lucy D, 4; Joe, S, 2

14223 COCHRAN, Henry C Chelsea, OK, 34

38483 COCHRAN, Holley, Ray, OK, 23

17914 COCHRAN, Isabella, Melvin, OK, 17

4992 COCHRAN, Jack, Melvin, OK, 28

31344 COCHRAN, James, Hulbert, OK, 34; Lilley D, 10; Jennie D, 4; Walker, S, 1

88 COCHRAN, Jennie, Locust Grove, OK, 44; William, S, 14;   Stop, S, 11

12566 COCHRAN, Jesse, Jr Chelsea, OK, 32; 14777 Lettie J, W, 25

5285 COCHRAN, John, Locust Grove, OK, 24; 10644 Maud, W, 18

6450 COCHRAN, John, Stilwell, OK, 35; 6972 Ni-yo-see, W, 24; Annie D, 5; Grover, S, 2

[COCHRAN, John. See #7024]   *(Note: entry separate from other family groups)*

13404 COCHRAN, John Chelsea, OK, 23; Willie, S, 1

[COCHRAN, Landon. See #2446]   *(Note: entry separate from other family groups)*

Key: Guion Miller Application Number; Name; Address, Relation (to Head); Age in 1906

1071 COCHRAN, Lewis, Stilwell, OK, 49; 1115 Betsey, W, 54; Jennie D, 17; Watt, S, 15; Felix, S, 12; 23896 Annie D, 18

26848 COCHRAN, Lome, Oaks, OK, 34; 9444 Cynthia, W, 35; Spade, Robert, S of W, 18; Cochran, William, S, 13; 26848 Cochran Charley or Too-late, S, 12; Annie, D, 8

17909 COCHRAN, Maly Cookson, OK, 14; Carrie, Sis, 13; By Thomas J. Pettit, Gdn.

[COCHRAN, Mariah. See #516]
[COCHRAN, Jessie. See #516]   *(Note: entries separate*
[COCHRAN Alex. See #516]   *from other family groups)*
[COCHRAN, Minnie. See #516]

10351 COCHRAN, Ned, Greenbrier, OK, 26; 873 Willie A, W, 27

151 COCHRAN, Price, Hulbert, OK, 63; 18100 Eliza, W, 41; 31858 Susie D, 19; Lewis, S, 13; Dollie, D, 6; Celie D, 4; 31857 Anna D, 20; Rosa Lee D, 1/6

5137 COCHRAN, Rufus, Stilwell, OK, 48; Josie D, 17; Dora D, 13; Henry, S, 9; Cora D, 7

25294 COCHRAN, Russel, Stilwell, OK, 45

42089 COCHRAN, Sallie, Stilwell, OK, 21

26096 COCHRAN, Sallie, Stilwell, OK, 43

[COCHRAN, Sallie P. See #4461]   *(Note: entries separate*
[COCHRAN, Henry C, See #4461]   *from other family groups)*

11915 COCHRAN, Sanders, Stilwell, OK, 27; 12535 Nancy, W, 22; Jesse, S, 7

3535 COCHRAN, Sarah, Melvin, OK, 27; Davis, Mary D, 10

10218 COCHRAN, Sequoyah, Gideon, OK, 34; 24082 Maggie, W, 25

[COCHRAN, Silas. See #2445]   *(Note: entry separate from other family groups)*

4546 COCHRAN, Susie Chelsea, OK, 57

5549 COCHRAN, Taylor, Wagoner, OK, 25; 16358 Alex, S, 2

152 COCHRAN, Walker, Hulbert, OK, 62; 3088 Nancy, W, 59; 29885 Juda D, 18

1495 COCHRAN, William, Hulbert, OK, 33; Lena M D, 14; Lydia D, 9; Price, S, 1

22568 COCHRAN, William, Stilwell, OK, 23;   Oscar Bro, 21

29883 COCHRAN, Wind, Hulbert, OK, 24; 29884 Eliza, W, 23

11854 COCHRUM, Sallie, Manard, OK, 19; James A, S, 4

[COCKRAN Ada. See #38651]   *(Note: entry separate from other family groups)*

7894 COCKRAN, Nancy, Leach, OK, 61

6256 COCKRELL, Mary Cherokee City AR, 32; Lillie D, 12; Percy, S, 9; Pearl D, 8; Stella D, 6; Francis M, S, 3; Hilda D, 1

Key: **Guion Miller Application Number; Name; Address, Relation (to Head); Age in 1906**

[COCKRUM, Lizzie. See #13172] ⎫   *(Note: entries separate*
[COCKRUM, Ned. See #13172]   ⎭   *from other family groups)*

16673 COFFEE, George Choteau, OK, 21
5117 COFFEE, Lila G, Tahlequah, OK, 31; Ruby L D, 9; Violet P D, 4
7996 COFFEY, George Big Cabin, OK, 36; Lincoln B, S, 1/3
29309 COFIELD, Laura, Muskogee, OK, 33
13510 COGGLE, Lucelle, Texanna, OK, 26; Cecil W, S, 2; Huston, S, 1
5345 COKER, Eliza J Coodys Bluff, OK, 45; Lizzie D, 12; Samuel C, S, 9; Varina E
    D, 8; Manassa M, S, 4
27180 COKER, Mary A, Ramona, OK, 23; Harrod, Julian, S, 5

[COLDWEATHER Dave. See #16076] ⎫   *(Note: entries separate*
[COLDWEATHER, Johnson. See #16076] ⎭   *from other family groups)*

23912 COLDWELL Arthur, Inola, OK, 24
23821 COLE Cora L, Tip, OK, 41; Pearl C D, 1
3677 COLE, Mary J. E, Salina, OK, 40; Maudie D, 16;   Effie D, 14; Paul A, S, 9;
    Daniel Boone, S, 5
12903 COLEMAN Akie, Long, OK, 26
11220 COLEMAN Arch, Vian, OK, 48; 11221 Peggie, W, 40; Emma D, 17; Chi D,
    16 [Died 1-21-1906]; Esther, D, 12; Ed, S, 9; Gooestah, S, 6; Samuel, S, 1[Died
    6-24-1906]
6308 COLEMAN, Ella, Texanna, OK, 26; Myrtle D, D, 3; Alexander C, S, 1/3
37297 COLEMAN, Ella, Ft. Gibson, OK, 20
37172 COLEMAN, Eva, Ft. Gibson, OK, 23
1493 COLEMAN, Ida V, Ft. Gibson. OK, 35
12 COLEMAN, James A, Ft. Gibson, OK, 59; 13 Nannie, W, 61; Tim, S, 17
13995 COLEMAN, John, Porum, OK, 77; 10442 Nancy, Gritts, OK, W, 55
1213 COLEMAN, Kire Bushy, OK, 57
30932 COLEMAN, Newton E, Porum, OK, 34 [Died 6-13-1906]; By Nancy A.
    Coleman, Admr.; Becky D, 11; Joel, S, 8; Willis, S, 6
1708 COLEMAN, Samuel, Eucha, OK, 52; Lydia D, 8
18509 COLEMAN, Samuel G, Porum, OK, 32; Bertha Lee D, 5
37296 COLEMAN, Tommie, Ft. Gibson, OK,   21
43311 COLEMAN, Will, Muskogee, OK, 29

[COLLAR, Jackson. See #10944]   *(Note: entry separate from other family groups)*

15984 COLLIER Bettie, Pryor Creek, OK, 36; Missouri A D, 12; Jasper N, S, 11;
    Alice M, D, 8; William A, S, 6; Eliza E D, 3; Lula B D, 1

Key: Guion Miller Application Number; Name; Address, Relation (to Head); Age in 1906

[COLLIER Charlotte. See #15985] ⎤   *(Note: entries separate*
[COLLIER, Edgar. See #15985]   ⎦   *from other family groups)*

9434 COLLIER, Flora A, Tiawah, OK, 26

13636 COLLIER, James Braggs, OK, 9;   By Abraham Collier, Gdn.

29599 COLLIER, Jesse Brent, OK, 19; Hattie M, Muldrow, OK, Sis, 11; By Arthur Collier, Gdn

3999 COLLIER, Joseph, Sadie, OK[?], 22

13634 COLLIER, Katie Braggs, OK, 17; Mattie D, 1

19777 COLLIER, Mack, Winslow AZ, 28

12211½ COLLINS Andy, Sallisaw, OK, 23; William R, S, 3; Caroline D, 1

29656 COLLINS Annie, Turley, OK, 33; Mary F D, 14; Albert H, Jr, S, 13; Eli H, S, 10; Augusta B D, 7; Thomas J, S, 2

25948 COLLINS Arizona Afton, OK, 24; Evaline G D, 4; Allmon A, S, 1

1765 COLLINS Clark L, Moody, OK, 40; Ira J, S, 16

22828 COLLINS Delana A, Pryor Creek, OK, 35; Clarence A, S, 7; John E, S, 3

11893 COLLINS, Henry, Kennison, OK, 31; 7705 Ara Addie, W, 29; Lula E D, 8; George D, S, 7; Elmer H, S, 4

24412 COLLINS, Henry, Jr, Ft. Gibson, OK, 29; Gracie D, 5

28159 COLLINS, Ira J, Moody, OK, 25; 1926 Rachel, W, 28; Nora E D, 4; Nannie M D, 1

11269 COLLINS, James B, Kennison, OK, 21

25530 COLLINS, James D Campbell, OK, 19

8009 COLLINS, Jeffery, Ketchum, OK, 25

26710 COLLINS, John H, Lowrey, OK, 38; 26711 Jennie, W, 29; Mollie D, 12; Mary, D, 10; Thomas, S, 6; Sallie D, 3; Harry, S, 1/6

935 COLLINS, John Parker, Moody, OK, 67

23394 COLLINS, John W, Stilwell, OK, 18; By Rudason H. Land, Gdn.

1232 COLLINS, Mary E, Tahlequah, OK, 10;   By Carrie A. Harris, Gdn.

11022 COLLINS, Mary M Black Gum, OK, 28; Wyoming, S, 12; Sirl, S, 9; Lindsey, S, 8; U. Grant, S, 5; John Robert, S, 2

26241 COLLINS, Nancy J, Westville, OK, 46; Alberty, William W, S, 19; Mose, S, 16; Pete, S, 14

[COLLINS, Nannie. See #26498]   *(Note: entry separate from other family groups)*

12912 COLLINS, Narcissa, Porum, OK, 45; Thompson, William, S, 17; Gracie D, 15; Katie, D, 13

5773 COLLINS, Robert, Stilwell, OK, 51

12211 COLLINS, Robert V, Paris AR, 49; Dave, S, 10

6239 COLLINS, Ruth M, Stilwell, OK, 9;   By Emma Franklin, Gdn.

20181 COLLINS, Tennessee Collinsville, OK, 28; Ada B D, 11; Benjamin F, S, 9; Nellie D, 8; Hazel D, 5; Columbia D, 3; Robert Warren, S, 1

CHEROKEE DESCENDANTS RESIDING WEST OF MISSISSIPPI RIVER.
VOLUME II   (A – M)

Key: Guion Miller Application Number; Name; Address, Relation (to Head); Age in 1906

24242 COLLIPRIEST, Emma D, Loup City, NB, 22

[COLSTON Cyntha. See #1704] ⎤   *(Note: entries separate*
[COLSTON, Fannie. See #1704] ⎦   *from other family groups)*

13949 COLSTON, Louis R. B Catoosa, OK,   25
 5938 COLSTON, Samuel, Maysville AR, 22; 28868 Rachel, W, 25
 8862 COLSTON, Sterling, Vinita, OK, 54
29279 COLTON, Neina Pearl Chelsea, OK, 24; Lillian W D, 1
 8855 COLVIN Callie Big Cabin, OK, 16
32068 COMER, Mary E, Tahlequah, OK, 33; Leona D, 15; William J. B, S, 10
34173 COMER, Mary M Claremore, OK, 31; Charles M, S, 7; Sadie E D, 3; Susie D, 1
 5842 COMFORT Dora, Vinita, OK, 28; William, S, 8; Florence D, 4; Bertha M D, 2

[COMING. See CUMMING.]

39505 COMING, John, Kansas, OK, 22; 43402 Lydia, W, 23; Huckleberry, S, 2
43942 COMING, Richard, Kansas, OK, 21
 1887 COMING, Wilson, Locust Grove, OK, [Died 10-1906] 63

[COMINGDEER. See CUMMINGDEER.]

13132 COMINGDEER, George, Sallisaw, OK, 14;   By Daniel Chukerlate, Gdn.
 7675 COMINGDEER, Hunter, Tahlequah, OK, 33; Bessie D, 4; John, S, 1/8
 6988 COMINGDEER, Joe, Southwest City, MO, 79; 8328 Polly, Eucha, OK, W, 65
13125 COMINGDEER, Joe, Marble City, OK, 16;   By Jennie Chukerlate, Gdn.
 7490 COMINGDEER, Mollie, Tahlequah, OK, 36; Bird Christie, S(?), 5
 1981 COMINGDEER, Nick, Tahlequah, OK, 61; 1757 Eliza, W, 62
25079 COMPSTON, Margaret Big Cabin, OK, 21
20202 COMSTOCK, Nita, Elder, OK, 25
 1317 CONDREAY Barbara A, Westville, OK, 39; Charley, S, 18; Hattie D, 15; Mary D, 12; Harris, S, 10; Minnie D, 7; Sadie D, 2
22759 CONDREY, Edward, Westville, OK, 21
23505 CONDRY, Rebecca Chelsea, OK, 41; Joseph S, S, 15; Georgia A D, 6; Lola B D, 5; Monte Lafayette, S, ¼
 1915 CONEY, Eliza J, Vinita. OK, 55
28077 CONEY, George, Vinita, OK, 26
 9120 CONLEY, Carrie A Cookson, OK, 31; Meed, Sarah D, 11; Conley, Ruth D, 8; Charles W, S, 4; Nancy D, 2
26732 CONLEY, Jessie A, Vian, OK, 28; Sarah D, 5; Fannie D, 3; Modie D, 1
25732 CONNER Alonzo, Vinita, OK, 29; 25733 Kate Eugene, W, 28; Nevada M D, 9; Lon Jay, S, 6; Clifton S, S, 4

Key: Guion Miller Application Number; Name; Address, Relation (to Head); Age in 1906

32246 CONNER Crawford, Fairland, OK, 25; 32247 Anna M, W, 29; Francis W, S, 4; Marvin R, S, 3; Millard L, S, 1

1127 CONNER, Lucy J Afton, OK, 61

2739 CONNER, Rebecca J, Fairland, OK, 48; Leonard, S, 17

26676 CONNER, Susan N, Nowata, OK, 24

13896 CONRAD, George Braggs, OK, 48; 12837 Jennie L, W, 53

32754 CONRAD, George B Braggs, OK, 25

32755 CONRAD, Jeff [or Medly J] Braggs, OK, 23

13941 CONRAD, John Braggs, OK, 54

5799 CONSEEN Dora, Rose, OK, 22

26753 CONSEEN, Eliza, Locust Grove, OK, 37; Margie D D, 18

194 CONSEEN, Thomas F, Locust Grove, OK, 30; 24700 Lillie M, W, 32; Wright, Ellis D(?), 9; Ella W D, 7; Conseen, Frank, S, 4; Pliney S D, 2

11571 COODEY Annie F Cannon, OK, 14;   By R.B. Butts, Gdn, Muskogee, OK

2386 COODEY Benjamin L, Fawn, OK, 10;   By Martha L Coodey, Gdn.

11572 COODEY Bessie Cannon, OK, 9;   By R.B. Butts, Gdn, Muskogee, OK

11570 COODEY Callie Cannon, OK, 11;   By R.B. Butts, Gdn, Muskogee, OK,

71 COODEY Daniel R, Jr, Porum, OK, 29; Daniel, S, 6; Andrew M, S, 4; Sequoiah, S, 2

11569 COODEY, Jesse Cannon, OK, 19;   By R.B. Butts, Gdn, Muskogee, OK

11714 COODEY, Lavena Gaylor, Eufaula, OK, 24

2385 COODEY, Lewis W, Fawn, OK, 12;   By Martha L. Coodey, Gdn.

2387 COODEY, Myrtle U, Fawn, OK, 14   By Martha L. Coodey, Gdn.

7997 COODY Daniel R, Vera, OK, 48; Edward, S, 18;   Mary D, 16; Alice D, 15; Charles, S, 13; Lila D, 12; Sallie, S, 10; Bettie D, 8; Robert, S, 6; Susie D, 4

23777 COODY, Lida R Big Cabin, OK, 4; Daniel H Bro, 6; Bessie D, Sis, 2; By John Skillman, Gdn.

8771 COODY, Mary A, Nowata, OK, 37[?]

21757 COODY, Richard Henry, Nowata, OK, 26; Samuel, S, 3; Joseph, S, 1

8664 COODY, Sarah E, Miami, OK, 11;   By Betty M. Coody, Gdn.

11567 COODY, William S Cannon, OK, 22

25115 COOK, Florence N Dawson, OK, 29

25117 COOK, Henry A Dawson, OK, 37

583 COOK, Susan, Vinita, OK, 56

25116 COOK, Thomas M Dawson, OK, 24

27223 COOK, William D, Vinita, OK, 35

44765 COOK, Zerelda Belle, St. Louis, MO, 10 3831 Windsor Place; By Zerelda Masdon, Gdn.

5301 COOKINGHEAD, Jackson, Stilwell, OK, 27; Charlotte D, 4; Lucy D, 2; 5301 Cookinghead, Johnson, Long, OK, S, 8;   By Joseph Boyd, Gdn.

10794 COOKSEY, Maggie, McKey, OK, 31; Johnnie, S, 14; Benton, S, 12; Nannie D, 10; Robert, S, 9; Floyd, S, 5

26927 COOKSON Andrew G Cookson, OK, 54; Mary Arla D, 18; Anna L D, 16

Key: Guion Miller Application Number; Name; Address, Relation (to Head); Age in 1906

27187 COOKSON, E. Levi Cookson, OK, 52; 2159 Aggie, W, 44; Ogden L, S, 16; Ellinor B, D, 14; John H, S, 11; Andrew F, S, 4

26931 COOKSON, Jack Cookson, OK, 25

11603 COOKSON, John H Cookson, OK, 80

27945 COOKSON, Joseph Cookson, OK, 51; 2164 Eliza, W, 44; Clement, S, 19; Ella D, 16; Betty D, 12; Reese, S, 7

27955 COOKSON, Lem M Cookson, OK, 21

[COOKSON, Levi. See #3499] ⎫   *(Note: entries separate*
[COOKSON Andrew. See #3499] ⎭   *from other family groups)*

26930 COOKSON, Levi, Jr Cookson, OK, 23

 1079 COOKSON, Lizzie B Cookson, OK, 29; Lucinda E D, 11; George H, S, 9; William K, S, 7

26929 COOKSON, Maggie L Cookson, OK, 23

32922 COOKSON, Thomas J, Tahlequah, OK, 21

 2651 COOLEY, Ethel Mable, Fairland, OK, 23

 1091 COOLEY, Ida M, Fairland, OK, 27; Curtis B, S, ½

 1419 COOLEY, Sut, Stilwell, OK, 54; 1547 Beanstick Dicey, W, 54; 1419 Houston, S, 11

27086 COON Amy Cawanah, OK, 23; Claude O, Jr, S, 2; Eva D, 1

12420 COON, Ella, Nowata, OK, 39; Alice D, 13; Bertha D, 11; Annie D, 8

12683 COON, John, Stilwell, OK, 44; 12685 Dargery, W, 40; Boles, S, 17; Joe, S, 12; Chow-wee-yuk, S, 9; Tarepin, S, 3

 8075 COON, Linnie, Stilwell, OK, 33; Goodrich, George, S, 9

 8076 COON, Richard, Stilwell, OK, 30; 29012 Venia, W, 27

 2869 COON, Sarah, Stilwell, OK, 57; 8077 Mary D, 16; 8074 Franklin [Rabbit], S, 18

17021 COON, Yute, Stilwell, OK, 24

28578 COOPER, J. Glenn, Santa Cruz CA, 24

 5937 COOPER, Joanna, Edna, KS, 48; Oceola, S, 5

  887 COOPER, Joseph, Mark, OK, 50; 1173 Safronia, W, 44

 9775 COOPER, Katie E, Ft. Gibson, OK, 18

17474 COOPER, Laura E, Vinita, OK, 48

32248 COPELAND Cordelia J, Fairland, OK, 39

 5212 COPELAND Dollie, Sallisaw, OK, 32; Robert F, S, 13; William M, S, 9; Nola E D, 6; Loreno D, 4; Theodore E, S, 2

 3857 COPELAND, Nancy E, Fairland, OK, 42; Rabit[sic] B, S, 19; Bertha M D, 17; George W, S, 15; Cordelia D, 12

 2798 COPELAND, Urena, Sadie, OK, 35; Charlotte D D, 14; Anderson, S, 12; Jackson, S, 10; Polly E D, 8

[COPPINGER, William. See #26498]   *(Note: entry separate from other family groups)*

Key: Guion Miller Application Number; Name; Address, Relation (to Head); Age in 1906

6455 CORAM, Ollie, Stilwell, OK, 28; Verley M D, 4; Sarah D, 1

24893 CORBIN, Frances, Lenapah, OK, 21; Lona, S, ¼   [Died 1907]

[CORDERY. See CAUDREY CORDRAY, CORDREY and CORDRY.]

4281 CORDERY Andy, Metory, OK, 45

14093 CORDERY Belle C, Tahlequah, OK, 8 By D. N. Leerskov, Gdn.

14092 CORDERY, Emma C, Tahlequah, OK, 10; By D. N. Leerskov, Gdn.

11868 CORDERY, Mary, Ft. Gibson, OK, 13; Sarah, Sis, 11; Charlotte, Sis, 9; By John B. Smith, Gdn.

4025 CORDERY, Thomas, Muskogee, OK, 58; Hugh, S, 18; Ada D, 13; Clifford, S, 6 [Died 1-1908]; Clem, S, 1/12

11858 CORDERY, Thomas J, Ft. Gibson, OK, 27; Ada B D, 8; Josie Ann D, 7; James B, S, 1/3

29102 CORDILL, Nora, Nubia, TX, 19; Irene D, 1

9135 CORDON, Martha M Campbell, OK, 26; Fannie M D, 8; Mamie M D, 5

[CORDRAY. See CORDERY CORDREY and CORDRY.]

22807 CORDRAY, Henry H, Westville, OK, 26; Mary Ann D, 33; Noah T, S, 1

22829 CORDRAY, James T, Westville, OK, 21

4714 CORDRAY, Mary E, Westville, OK, 48; Edward C, S, 17; Althie M D, 16; Nannie B, D, 14; Alley B D, 11; George W, S, 8; Leona B D, 6; Albert S, S, 4

8782 CORDREY Bradley Centralia, OK, 29

11648 CORDREY, James, Manard, OK, 24

[CORDREY, Jennette. See #6060]   *(Note: entry separate from other family groups)*

4025½ CORDREY, Kerney, Muskogee, OK, 3; Annie, Sis, 1; By Grace Cordrey, Gdn.

[CORDREY, Willie A. See #26232]   *(Note: entry separate from other family groups)*

4230 CORDRY Andy, Metory, OK, 57; May D, 18; Annie D, 16; Cornell, S, 13

16978 CORDRY Annie, Vinita, OK, 40; Wofford, Jackson E, S, 19; Pearl D, 17

13612 CORDRY, Joseph, Ft. Gibson, OK, 36; James A, S, 5; Bertha M D, 2

2437 CORDRY, William, Kaw City, OK, 43

26733 CORLEY, Ida, Vian, OK, 18

8441 CORMICLE Allen F, Talala, OK, 29

8442 CORMICLE Annie J Catale, OK, 20

8440 CORMICLE Clarence L Catale, OK, 22

Key: Guion Miller Application Number; Name; Address, Relation (to Head); Age in 1906

8439 CORMICLE, Walter Catale, OK, 18; Thomas C Bro, 15; Mary E, Sis, 14; Levi P Bro, 12; Lincoln R Bro, 9; Milton R Bro, 9; Eva, Sis, 3; By Nathan Cormicle, Gdn.

26230 CORN Dora, Tahlequah, OK, 27; Alvina D, 6; Kruger C, S, 5

16434 CORN, Ethel L, Kinnison, OK, 31; James A, S, 13; Callie M D, 12; Grace E D, 10; Emma L D, 9; Percy J, S, 5; Evelyn Anna D, 4; Dwight S, S, 2; Juanita J D, 1/12

3136 CORN, Hannah, Nowata, OK, 54

6515 CORNELIOUS, Henry, Locust Grove, OK, 34; 4500 Susie B, W, 33

[CORNELIUS, Peter. See #3171]   *(Note: entry separate from other family groups)*

5735 CORNSHUCKER, George, Southwest City, MO, 42; 5737 Sallie, W, 46; Tom, S, 19; Samuel, S, 17; Waity, S, 15; Arch, S, 13

8254 CORNSILK Charley Afton, OK, 27; 8255 Eliza, W, 30; Nora D, 5; Rosa D, 1

2271 CORNSILK, Jennie, Stilwell, OK, 50; 12542 Johnson, S, 11

9417 CORNSILK, Lucy, Lometa, OK, 96

16552 CORNSILK, Steve, Webbers Falls, OK, 32

12543 CORNSILK, William, Stilwell, OK, 25; 26356 Kate, W, 30; Scott, Emma D, 10; Mary, D, 11; John, S, 6; Buelah[sic] D, 4

661 CORNSTALK, Eucha, OK, 60; 648 Se-we, W, 36

22013 CORNSTALK, John Cherokee City, AR, 54

1905 CORNSTALK, Lizzie, Maysville AR, 25; Claude, S, ½

1590 CORNTASSEL Adam, Westville, OK, 48; 1386 Lutetia, W, 47; Benjamin, S, 17; Mary Ann D, 10; Johnnie, S, 11

3236 CORNTASSEL, Jesse Afton, OK, 28

1873 CORNTASSEL, John, Vinita, OK, 56; 10895 Jane, W, 47; 10894 Walker, Susanna, D of W, 16

8955 CORNTASSEL, Nancy, Westville, OK, 75

6282 CORNTASSEL, Sarah Bunch, OK, 62

1595 CORNTASSEL, Tom, Westville, OK, 46; 25021 Johnnie, S, 18; Jonanna [Jennie] D, 15; Jimmie, S, 9; Tommie, S, 7; Bertha D, 3

[COSTEN Cassie B. See #26134]   *(Note: entry separate from other family groups)*

[COSTEN, Edna B. See #26133]
[COSTEN, Robert. See #26133]
[COSTEN, Samuel H. See #26133]   *(Note: entries separate*
[COSTEN, William T. See #26133]   *from other family groups)*
[COSTEN, Meredeth G. See #26133]
[COSTEN, Elizabeth L. See #26133]
[COSTEN, Eula W. See #26133]

Key: Guion Miller Application Number; Name; Address, Relation (to Head); Age in 1906

5240 COSTEN, Mollie, Wann, OK, 10; By George W. Patrick, Gdn.

4864 COTTREL, Nannie Braggs, OK, 40; Pierce Charles P, S, 16; Claud, S, 14; Ruth D, 11; Edna D, 9; Stella D, 7; May D, 5

23528 COUCH Addie, Westville, OK, 22; William T, S, 1

1334 COUCH Dondenah M, Vinita, OK, 51; Thomas L, S, 14

44348 COUCH, Floy Edward Alluwe, OK, 8; By Jesse T. Couch, Gdn.

22610 COUCH, George F, Vinita, OK, 24; Ruth C D, 1

4375 COUCH, Georgia, Redland, OK, 7; By A.J. Couch, Gdn.

11261 COUCH, John F Chelsea, OK, 39

33124 COUCH, L. Lewelyn, Porum, OK, 27; Ina D, 8; Frankie, S, 6

28696 COUCH, Maggie S Cleora, OK, 21

6460 COUCH, Mitchell M, Nowata, OK, 47

26338 COUCH, Mont L [or Lorenzo M], Vinita, OK, 22

23686 COUCH, Stella I, Westville, OK, 28; Thelma Lucile D, 6; Alfred B, S, 4; Roger R, S, 1

3644½ COUGHRAN, Katie, Fawn, OK, 19; Bertie D, 5; Bessie D, 3

579 COUNTRYMAN Andrew J, Needmore, OK, 62; Robert A, S, 17; Jackson A, S, 15; Clara B D, 9

25309 COUNTRYMAN, George A Afton, OK, 32; Zimeroshew D, 6; Andrew, S, 4; Arthur W, S, 2; Ralph, S, 1

1325 COUNTRYMAN, George W, Needmore, OK, 67; 1324 Manerva, W, 65

27808 COUNTRYMAN, James T, Needmore, OK, 32; Eliza D, 11; Fay H, S, 8; Henry, S, 7; Sam, S, 5; Oliver, S, 2

27904 COUNTRYMAN, John A, Needmore, OK, 34; 27905 Jane A, W, 24; W. T, S, 4; Velvie I D, 2; Thomas F, S, 1

1330 COUNTRYMAN, John M Afton, OK, 69; Norine D, 5

22628 COUNTRYMAN, John M, Needmore, OK, 24

42098 COURTNEY Ann E, Neosho, MO, 48; Jessie Lee D, 14; Lulu B D, 8; Ethel C D, 6; Opal D, 4; Hellina D, 1/6

29469 COURTNEY, Edward E Afton, OK, 23

8047 COURTS, Sarah E, Watova, OK, 53; John W, S, 11

26788 COVEL, Ella Mae, Tahlequah, OK, 26

29195 COVEL, Jesse Crawford, Tahlequah, OK, 23

3546 COVEL, John H. Tahlequah, OK, 58; 9930 Lizzie, W, 52; Henry Owen, S, 15

29462 COVEY, Susan, Raton, NM, 34; Beulah L D, 16; Preston C, S, 14; Bessie L D, 12; George R, S, 7; Tena M D, 1

8012 COWAN Alexander C, Wagoner, OK, 45; Cherra D, 16; Terry, S, 14; Louis, S, 11; Georgia H D, 8; Alexander F, S, 7; Andrew F, S, 4; Margaret E D, 2

8786 COWAN, Felix Grundy, Vinita, OK, 40

6307 COWAND, Mary, Warner, OK, 30; Byrd, Maggie E D, 8; Cowand, Johnnie L, S, 6; Henry, S, 2

10384 COWAND, Thomas W, Warner, OK, 13; By Thomas J. Cowand, Gdn.

23989 COWART, James S, Stilwell, OK, 22

Key: Guion Miller Application Number; Name; Address, Relation (to Head); Age in 1906

23987 COWART, Mary A, Stilwell, OK, 20

12135 COWART, Slater, Muskogee, OK, 53; John, S, 18; Alice D, 15; Cynthia D, 12; Mary, D, 10; Collins, S, 8; Nettie D, 6

1229 COWART, William L, Stilwell, OK, 44; 23988 Laura V, W, 44; William L, Jr, S, 17; Charles M, S, 14; John E, S, 10; Jesse T, S, 8; Martha E D, 2; Herbert C, S, 1/12

4933 COWDEN, Myrtle, Spavinaw, OK, 25; Annie M D, 4; Fay Maud M D, 2

5034 COWELLS Caleb W Afton, OK, 26

25867 COWLES, Edmond, Fairland, OK, 24

6459 COX, Emma J, Estella, OK, 32; Elledge, Roy P, S, 12; Cena B D, 10;   Cox, Zeno M, S, 4; Sarah A D, ¼

10730 COX, Frances, Vinita, OK, 21

31581 COX, Fred F, Leavenworth, KS, 25

[COX, J. D. See #24874]   *(Note: entries separate*
[COX, Elvy. See #24874]   *from other family groups)*

38554 COX, Martha J, Grove, OK, 29; Dovie D, 12; Marshall, S, 9; Leonard, S, 8; Dillard, S, 3

27380 COX, Maude Elsie, Red Rock, NM, 17

4323 COX, Nannie B, Grove, OK, 35

8013 COX, Pearl Chanute, KS, 30; Ailem W D, 1

2102 COX, Sallie, Hulbert, OK, 30; Fish, Nellie D, 8

[COX, William Jerome. See #31442]   *(Note: entry separate from other family groups)*

[COX, Lena Leoto. See #31443]   *(Note: entry separate from other family groups)*

27430 COYNE Abbie O Centralia, OK, 18

8101 COYNE, Isabella J Centralia, OK, 31; Patrick W, S, 10; Ibbie Jane D, 8; James J, S, 7; John A D, 4; Catherine A D, 2

[CRAIG Buell. See #3207]
[CRAIG, Leonard. See #3207]   *(Note: entries separate*
[CRAIG Annie May. See #3207]   *from other family groups)*
[CRAIG Burley. See #3207]

26382 CRAIG Arthur, Proctor, OK, 24

27779 CRAIG Carl E, Welch, OK, 33

10892 CRAIG Charles S Dixon CA, 49; Annie T D, 20; Charles A, S, 18; Gladys P D, 5

[CRAIG Coleman. See #26968]   *(Note: entry separate from other family groups)*

Key: Guion Miller Application Number; Name; Address, Relation (to Head); Age in 1906

23318 CRAIG Delilah Braggs, OK, 20; Thomas, S, 3; Lizzie D, 1
9421 CRAIG, Elgie C, Welch, OK, 22; Hugh C, S, 1
2724 CRAIG, Ermina, Proctor, OK, 59
27777 CRAIG, George F, Kingsburg CA, 30; Anna J D, 7
9424 CRAIG, Granville C, Welch, OK, 57
9419 CRAIG, Laura, Welch, OK, 17;   By Catherine Craig, Gdn.
28600 CRAIG, Nannie Braggs, OK, 32; Addie D, 13; Amon H, S, 11; Clifford C, S, 9;
Warren R, S, 6
10891 CRAIG, Robert W, Kingsburg CA, 28
26383 CRAIG, Sam, Proctor, OK, 21
11898 CRAIG, William L, Pinole CA, 41; Claud M, S, 17; Hazel O D, 15; Harry G, S,
13; Arthur O, S, 11; Lucinda A D, 8
27776 CRAIG, William L, Miles, OK, 38; Clara R D, 11
26384 CRAIG, Willie, Proctor, OK, 10; Fredy Bro, 8; Elor C, Sis, 6; Josie, Sis, 4;
Callie, Sis, 1;   By Elizabeth Craig, Gdn.
1904 CRAIL, Linnie J, Wagoner, OK, 43; Della D, 15; John H, S, 13; Myrtle J D, 10;
Dora B, D, 6; Leonard, S, 4; Lewis, S, 2
10751 CRAIN, George, Porum, OK, 25; Etter E D, 3; Eva May D, 1
2752 CRAIN, Luella, Moody, OK, 26

[CRAIN, Mary M. See #40697]   *(Note: entry separate from other family groups)*

5749 CRAIN, Nancy, Ft. Gibson, OK, 67; Bonie D, 14; Bessie May D, 12; Richard,
S, 4; William Luther, S, 2

[CRAMP, Johnson. See #1549]   *(Note: entry separate from other family groups)*

1759 CRAMP, Tilden, Porum, OK, 35; John, S, 2; Eugene, S, 1
28310 CRANE, Ella, Porum, OK, 15
28309 CRANE, Frances, Porum, OK, 19
23599 CRANE, Henry O Checotah, OK, 37; Sarah C D, 6; Arthur L, S, 4
23427 CRANSTON Marcia P, Ft Sam Houston, San Antonio, TX, 30
25977 CRAPO Albert Campbell, OK, 30
25976 CRAPO, George Campbell, OK, 24

[CRAPO, James. See #8999]   ⎤   *(Note: entries separate*
[CRAPO, Collins. See #8999] ⎦   *from other family groups)*

9260 CRAPO, Linda Campbell, OK, 59
25974 CRAPOE, Nelson L Campbell, OK, 34; Lela D, 11; Lewis B, S, 5
11454 CRAVEN, Kate, Tahlequah, OK, 49
23945 CRAWFORD, Edna E, Wagoner, OK, 26; Lawrence [or Hickey], S, 6; Charley L,
S, 1

Key: Guion Miller Application Number; Name; Address, Relation (to Head); Age in 1906

11295 CRAWFORD, Jack, Melvin, OK, 25

7013 CRAWFORD, Jennie, Melvin, OK, 23; Jessie, S, 2

17045 CRAWFORD, Ned Braggs, OK, 23

24066 CRAWFORD, Ruth Claremore, OK, 25; Carl F, S, 3; Alice L D, ½

17110 CRAWLER, Joe, Vian, OK, 25

24314 CREECH Alice Collinsville, OK, 23

759 CREECH, Jeff, Howe, OK, 24

929 CREECH, Rebecca E Collinsville, OK, 51; William, S, 18

13691 CREEDEN, Ida L Campbell, OK, 36; Nellie L D, 15

16457 CREEK-KILLER, Frank, Zena, OK, 20; 16448 Linnie, W, 23

16449 CREEK-KILLER, Jeff, Zena, OK, 48; 16469 Liddie, W, 46; Sarah D, 13; Rebecca, D, 5

16468 CREEK-KILLER, Lucy, Zena, OK, 23; Mary D, 10; Oo-lu-gee D, 7

11455 CREEK-KILLER, Mary, Southwest City, MO, 40; 11459 Rachel D, 15; Lydia D, 5

[CRIGBIN, James O. See #39436] ⎤   *(Note: entries separate*
[CRIGBIN, Mattie O. See #39436] ⎦   *from other family groups)*

29754 CRIM, Lou Della, Kilgore, TX, 38; J. Malcolm, S, 18; Pauline D, 16; John Thompson, S, 13; Robert Lee, S, 11; Leggette, S, 7; William Philip, S, 4

3078 CRIPPS, Josie E, Oolagah, OK, 24; Helen C D, 3; Amy Louisa D, 1

[CRITTENDEN Albert C. See #13025] *(Note: entry separate from other family groups)*

5743 CRITTENDEN Alex, Tahlequah, OK, 41; 5629 Katie, W, 26; Willis, S, 4

4801 CRITTENDEN Charles, Proctor, OK, 22

23371 CRITTENDEN Charles L, Westville, OK, 25; Lena E D, ¼

33435 CRITTENDEN Charlie, Flint, OK, 26; 16988 Lucy, W, 20; Washburn, S, 1/12

11465 CRITTENDEN Clem, Proctor, OK, 51; 9294 Tom, S, 19

7869 CRITTENDEN Cornelius N, Oaks, OK, 63; 7891 Jinnie[sic], W, 36; Susie D, 12; Martin, S, 16; Hummingbird, S, 10; Lydia D, 7; Jackson, S, 4

25971 CRITTENDEN Cornelius C, Hadley, OK, 25

4944 CRITTENDEN, Electa, Grove, OK, 17   By James F Crittenden, Gdn.

33436 CRITTENDEN, Ella, Flint, OK, 23; Crust D, 4

10404 CRITTENDEN, Felix Baron, OK, 25

5274 CRITTENDEN, George W, Westville, OK, 62?; 23453 Nancy J, W, 47; Jessie D, 14; Georgia A D, 12; Dewey, S, 8; Charles D, S, 6; Rebecca A D, 15

5850 CRITTENDEN, Heddge[sic], Proctor, OK, 9

5251 CRITTENDEN, Henry C, Westville, OK, 49; 23370 Mary S, W, 49; Thomas R, S, 15; Susan F D, 12; Cicero, S, 20

1787 CRITTENDEN, Isaac Baron, OK, 33; 24353 Lydia, W, 28; Joe, S, 11; Taylor, S, 9; Mitchell, S, 7; John, S, 3

Key: Guion Miller Application Number; Name; Address, Relation (to Head); Age in 1906

4797 CRITTENDEN, Jack, Proctor, OK, 21

10401 CRITTENDEN, Jack Baron, OK, 30; Luke, S, 6

8348 CRITTENDEN, James Baron, OK, 20

16898 CRITTENDEN, James, Stilwell, OK, 80; Riley, S, 16; Ella D, 14; Maud D, 12; Cicero, S, 11; Maggie M D, 9; Mattie D, 7

4948 CRITTENDEN, James F, Grove, OK, 43; Electa D, 17

11828 CRITTENDEN, James W, Warner, OK, 16;   By Margaret Hence, Gdn.

11739 CRITTENDEN, Jess Chance, OK, 39

4847 CRITTENDEN, Jesse, Locust Grove, OK, 54; 8071 Ary, W, 61

8099 CRITTENDEN, John Collinsville, OK, 40; Arthur D, S, 12; Susan A D, 2

23456 CRITTENDEN, John H, Westville, OK, 20; Georgia Clyde D, 1

23454 CRITTENDEN, Joseph H, Westville, OK, 34; 22851 Nancy L, W, 31;   Carl, S, 9

5851 CRITTENDEN, Lela, Proctor, OK, 19

11829 CRITTENDEN, Leroy, Warner, OK, 10;   By Margaret Hence, Gdn.

27391 CRITTENDEN, Lydia, Tahlequah, OK, 24

6505 CRITTENDEN, Mary, Stilwell, OK, 50

12610 CRITTENDEN, Mary, Flint, OK, 59

11827 CRITTENDEN, Mary J, Warner, OK, 14

8311 CRITTENDEN, Minnie, Whitmire, OK, 34; Rebecca D, 9; James, S, 10

12544 CRITTENDEN, Minnie B Claremore,   OK, 30

9231 CRITTENDEN, Ned, Proctor, OK, 32; 11704 Callie, W, 28; Blue, S, 11; Lucinda, D, 8; William, S, 5; Mary D, 1/6

13366 CRITTENDEN, Rachel Claremore, OK, 52; Musgrove Cassie V, GD, 8; Snow, Flora C, GD, ¼

33434 CRITTENDEN, Sam, Flint, OK, 38; Henry, S, 16;   Watt, S, 12; Carrie D, 9

12537 CRITTENDEN, Sanders, Stilwell, OK, 52; Mary A D, 16; Ora A D, 13; Thomas C, S, 10

23455 CRITTENDEN, Vinnie R, Westville, OK, 36

13831 CRITTENDEN, Walter, Hulbert, OK, 20

16585 CRITTENDEN, William Baron Fork, OK, 56

4020 CRITTENDEN, William C, Tahlequah, OK, 47

24379 CRITTENDEN, William H, Westville, OK, 23

12399 CRITTENDEN, William P, Stilwell, OK, 54

26078 CRITTENDEN, Wilson, Hulbert, OK, 29; 6071 Becky, W, 25

[CRITTENDON Albert C. See #13025]
(Note: entry separate from other family groups)

10311 CRITTENDON Annie, Tahlequah, OK, 23

8318 CRITTENDON, Peggy Baron, OK, 57

4587 CRITTENTON Alice, Westville, OK, 65

9584 CRITTENTON Barbara A, Greenbrier, OK, 14;   By George Crittenden, Gdn.

Key: Guion Miller Application Number; Name; Address, Relation (to Head); Age in 1906

1743 CRITTENTON Ben, Proctor, OK, 57; Emly[sic] D, 14; Louis, S, 12; David, S, 11; Lula D, 9; Walter, S, 6

9583 CRITTENTON, Christina B, Greenbriar, OK, 7;   By George Crittenden, Gdn.

40801 CRITTENTON, George W, Greenbriar, OK, 31; 8062 Jessie B, W, 32

8064 CRITTENTON, Martin M, Westville, OK, 25

8063 CRITTENTON, Richard H, Westville, OK, 29; 27154 Nannie E, W, 34; Allie F D, 8; Robert L, S, 5; Jannie M D, 3; Mary S D, 1

3397 CROCKETT, Mary Alice, Fairland, OK, 48; Bertha Inez D, 16

26924 CROFTON, Mary C, Tahlequah, OK, 43; 26800 Mary Louise D, 18; 26924 Kathleen, D, 16; Susan E D, 12

[CROMWELL, Zeddie R. See #8697] *(Note: entry separate from other family groups)*

13167 CROOK Cordelia, Webbers Falls, OK, 29; Butts, Naeta M, D, 7; Cherokee D, 4

15602 CROOKSHANK, Mary, Pryor Creek, OK, 25; Tom Sam, S, 1/12

38678 CROOM, Jessie Morton, Muskogee, OK, 31; Joseph Newton, S, 10; Marvin Earle, S, 8; Willie Lea, S, 5; Elmer Clement, S, 2

13979 CROSSLAND, Elizabeth, Webbers Falls, OK, 59

25644 CROSSLAND, Josephus, Webbers Falls, OK, 25

24042 CROSSLAND, Mahala, Ft. Gibson, OK, 22; Dora D, 4; Emmet, S, 2; Walter, S, 1

9405 CROSSLIN Buck, Gans, OK, 19

13298 CROSSLIN, Lizzie, Gans, OK, 16; Bettie, Sis, 14; Alfred Bro, 12; Ada, Sis, 11; Effie, Sis, 9; Leo Bro, 6;   By Sallie Hill, Gdn.

27197 CROSSLIN, Maud, Gans, OK, 16; Rudie, Sis, 14; Squirrel Bro, 12; Ruth, Sis, 10; Minnie, Sis, 6;   By Ida May Davis, Gdn.

3310 CROSSLIN, Richard, Gans, OK, 46; Calvin, S, 17; Samuel, S, 17; Samuel, S, 15; George, S, 13; John, S, 2

13819 CROTHERS, Sarah, Liberal, KS, 28

1401 CROTZER, Emma Lee, Fairland, OK, 42; Willie I, S, 2; Lucile G D, 4; Carl L, S, 7; Edward F, S, 12; Effie L D, 14; Stella M D, 16

7707 CROUCH, Stella E, Okoee, OK, 19; Mary Lucile D, 1

23660 CROW Andrew J, Tahlequah, OK, 32; Lou D, 1

23664 CROW Charley, Tahlequah, OK, 26; James, S, 3 [Died 8-1906]; William, S, 1

30013 CROW Claud Collinsville, OK, 16; Clarence Bro, 14; William Bro, 12; By Hugh C. Crow, Gdn.

23665 CROW, John, Tahlequah, OK, 21

3796 CROW, Laura E Alluwe, OK, 40; Anabel D, 7

1648 CROW, Margaret, Tahlequah, OK, 76; Jessee, GS, 18

[CROW, Polly. See Polly YAHOLA.]

23663 CROW, Thomas, Tahlequah, OK, 34

Key: Guion Miller Application Number; Name; Address, Relation (to Head); Age in 1906

23662 CROW, William, Tahlequah, OK, 47

43148 CROWDER Charles, Proctor, OK, 32; 3793 Martha A, W, 31; Robert Lee, S, 1; Ryan, Emmette, So of W, 10; Calvin, S of W, 8; William H, S of W, 6

22841 CROWDER, Nelson, Westville, OK, 29; Polly D, 7; Culvin, S, 3; Louner M D, 1

836 CROWDER, Polly, Westville, OK, 61

22842 CROWDER, William P, Westville, OK, 21

39461 CROWELL Allie B Afton, OK, 20; 27786 Laura Elva, W, 21

29928 CROWELL, Elizabeth Afton, OK, 48; Frank, S, 18; Hunter K, S, 15

29929 CROWELL, Erda Afton, OK, 23

30793 CRUSE, Dora J, Siloam Springs AR, 19

12925 CRUTCHFIELD Claude, Inola, OK, 26; Ray Bro, 18; Henry G Bro, 16

9911 CRUTCHFIELD David V, Kansas City, 548 Main St., MO, 30

1333 CRUTCHFIELD, Edward, Spavinaw, OK, 49

3010 CRUTCHFIELD, James M Chelsea, OK, 23; 26547 Ida L, W, 20; Joseph M, S, 1/3

17226 CRUTCHFIELD, John H, Vinita, OK, 22

27224 CRUTCHFIELD, John K, Inola, OK,40; Leory C, S,14; Ewing H,S, 12; Willie M, S, 10

[CRUTCHFIELD, Nannie. See #8971] *(Note: entry separate from other family groups)*

16170 CRUTCHFIELD, Orah, Graham, TX, 30?; Millie D, 9; Johnie, S, 4

15948 CRUTCHFIELD, Taylor F, Vinita, OK, 25

977 CRUTCHFIELD, Vinita, Tulsa, OK, 15;   By Josephine Crutchfield, Gdn.

25344 CULLEY Betsey Walker Chelsea, OK, 25; Thelma D, 3; Ira B, S, 1/6

32327 CULVER, Maggie, Vian, OK, 24; Maggie D, 6; Bettie E, D, 4; Bluford, S, 1

24970 CULVER, Mamie Z Bluejacket, OK, 15;   By Missouri B, Wickizer, Gdn.

25913 CUMIFORD, Henry S, Southwest City,   MO, 23; John E, S, 2; Zeta May D, 1

7560 CUMIFORD, Pleas, Southwest City, MO, 52; Bula D, 16; Wat, S, 13; Margaret D, 6

25912 CUMIFORD, Robert S, Southwest City,   MO, 25

[CUMMING. See COMING.]

4617 CUMMING, Joseph, Kansas, OK, 53; 4616 Lizzie, W, 41; Nancy D, 14; David, S, 10; Samuel, S, 1

[CUMMING, Peter. See #16455]   *(Note: entry separate from other family groups)*

[CUMMINGDEER. See COMINGDEER.]

Key: Guion Miller Application Number; Name; Address, Relation (to Head); Age in 1906

7488 CUMMINGDEER, Nancy, Eucha, OK, 29; Mouse, Joe [Hominy], S, 8; 17972 George, S, 6

9205 CUMMINGS, Wilson, Vian, OK, 59; 9216 Maggie, W, 33

1966 CUMMINS, Evans, Vian, OK, 23; Albert, S, 1

1963 CUMMINS, Fannie, Vian, OK, 47; Frank, S, 19; Jessie D, 16; Rebecca D, 13; Lewis, S, 8

6729 CUMMISKY, Jessie, Lusk, WY, 18

6047 CUMPTON, James L Claremore, OK, 26

4604 CUMPTON, Thomas M, Muskogee, OK, 42; Chelia D, 14; Emmett, S, 12; Glenn, S, 10; Charles, S, 7; John B, S, 5; Ruth D, 3

6046 CUMPTON, Willis C, Muskogee, OK, 28

3051 CUNINGAN, George, Southwest City, MO, 44; 318 Sarah, W, 32; Cynthia D, 6

25753 CUNNINGHAM Albert S, Tahlequah, OK, 33

9400 CUNNINGHAM Alfred C Bartlesville, OK, 46

27674 CUNNINGHAM Andrew B, Tahlequah, OK, 37; 5872 Sammie, W, 33

25249 CUNNINGHAM Belle, Tahlequah, OK, 25

16757 CUNNINGHAM Callie, Pawhuska, OK, Box 255, 23

37413 CUNNINGHAM, Fannie Chelsea, OK, 20; Wilma D, ¼

23521 CUNNINGHAM, Henry M, Spavinaw, OK, 23

5174 CUNNINGHAM, Jeter T, Tahlequah, OK, 63; 5173 Keziah, W, 56

24993 CUNNINGHAM, Jeter T, Jr, Tahlequah, OK, 33

30940 CUNNINGHAM, Lizzie, Rex, OK, 48;   By Columbus Phipps, Gdn.

28235 CUNNINGHAM, Mabel C Afton, OK, 15; Neva, Sis, 14; James W Bro, 12; Lew Orin Bro, 10;   By James L. Cunningham, Gdn.

10333 CUNNINGHAM, Mary, Spavinaw, OK, 49; James M, S, 17; Lizzie P D, 15; Charles F, S, 13; Maggie D, 8; Lee Vann, S, 11

25250 CUNNINGHAM, Roxie, Tahlequah, OK, 21

25202 CUNNINGHAM, Thomas F, Ft. Gibson, OK, 26; 25203 Emma S, W, 25; John C, S, 2

4452 CUNNINGHAM, William C, ?, 27; 4453 Emma, W, 24; Foster B, S, 6; Royal W, S, 3; David B, S, 1

5699 CUNNINGHAM, William P, Maysville, AR, 30; 33479 Dora O, W, 27; A. Ward, S, 5; Jeter T, S, 3; James Oliver, S, 1

32001 CURREY Charles T, Southwest City, MO, 22

25391 CURREY, Clarence E, Southwest City, MO, 28

812 CURREY, Francis S, Southwest City, MO, 51; Albert W, S, 20; Florence, D, 18; Benjamin F, S, 15; Claud P, S, 13; May D, 11

36328 CURREY, George B, Southwest City, MO, 25

29124 CURRY, Charles J Coffeyville, KS, 25

[CURTIS, Joe W. See #9183]   *(Note: entries separate*
[CURTIS Dave T. See #9183]   *from other family groups)*

CHEROKEE DESCENDANTS RESIDING WEST OF MISSISSIPPI RIVER.
VOLUME II   (A – M)

Key: Guion Miller Application Number; Name; Address, Relation (to Head); Age in 1906

6957 CURTIS, Mary A Afton, OK, 34; Dulsa I D, 13; Annie O D, 11

26352 CURTIS, Maudie A, Ft. Gibson, OK, 19

31547 CYPHERS, Sallie M, Spokane, WA, 21 1205 Coeur D'Alene St.

1900 CZARNIKOW, Robert Dora AR, 60; Charley, S, 18; Joel B Mays, S, 16; George, S, 14; Beula A D, 12; Mandy D, 19; Bertha D, 6; Robert S, 4; J. Warren, S, ½; Jessie, S, 1/12; Bessie D, 1/12

9965 DAGGETT, Pearl W, Pryor Creek, OK, 21; Lois, S, 5; Ray, S, 2

[DAIL, Mary F, See Mary E, Han, #13633]   *(Note: entries separate*
[DAIL, Mark L, See Mary E, Han. #13633]   *from other family groups)*
[DAIL, Springee (or Springer), See Mary E Han. #13633]

995 DALE, Joseph Alice, Nowata, OK, 21

2338 DALEY, Homer, Vian, OK, 21

1376 DALEY, Marshall, Webbers Falls, OK, 33

2336 DALEY, Timothy Brushy, OK, 41; Rufus L, S, 10; James M, S, 4

7952 DAMERON Byrd A, Vinita, OK, 19

7954 DAMERON, Henry A, Joplin, MO, 25 1710 Bird St.

7953 DAMERON, John T, Vinita, OK, 12;   By Mattie L. Dameron, Gdn.

7955 DAMERON, Lee L, Vinita. OK, 17;   By Mattie L. Dameron, Gdn.

7957 DAMERON, Mattie L, Vinita, OK, 41

7956 DAMERON, Nancy, Vinita, OK, 20

7951 DAMERON, Rex E, Vinita, OK, 22

4419 DAMSELL, Stella, Healdsburg CA, 31; Ernest Glanvill, S, 10; Genevive L D, 8; Alvin J, S, 6; Merrill Curtis, S, 5; Gwendolin D, 1

1094 DANDERSON, John O Catoosa, OK, 13;   By Frank F. Danderson, Gdn.

8801 DANIEL Allen W, Tahlequah, OK, 40; Virgil A, S, 14; Osceola P, S, 12; John C, S, 10; Lilla B D, 8; Brewer, S, 3; Peachie D, 1/6

[DANIEL Annie. See Annie DEERINWATER. See #11765]
(Note: entry separate from other family groups)

536 DANIEL, George Bartlesville, OK, 57; Lucinda D, 12; Georgie, S, 10; Maggie D, 4; William R, S, 2

[DANIEL, Geo, with Charley Fencer. See #8043]
(Note: entry separate from other family groups)

1916 DANIEL, Jennie, Evansville AR, 51

11687 DANIEL, John Afton, OK, 12; Aylce, Sis, 10; Adolphus Bro, 8; Katie, Sis, 6; By William Buzzard, Gdn.

Key: Guion Miller Application Number; Name; Address, Relation (to Head); Age in 1906

9988 DANIEL, John A, Miami, OK, 29; Lula M D, 7; William A, S, 6; John F, S, 4; Opal V, D, 3; Homer L, S, 1/6

3529 DANIEL, John M, Vinita, OK, 64; Martha J.E. D, 19; Emma E D, 17; William A, S, 15; Edgar J, S, 12; Walter S, S, 8

22622 DANIEL, John R, Vinita, OK, 25; 22623 Druvilla M, W, 25; Mabel E D, 5; Ralph C, S, 3; Opal Ray D, 2

[DANIEL, Lydia with Jack Bellew. See #13688]

(Note: entry separate from other family groups)

34626 DANIEL, Marma D, Vinita, OK, 28; 34627 Louisa, W, 24; Freeman, S, 6; Ethel L, S(?), 3

3530 DANIEL, Marmaduke, Vinita, OK, 62;   Lavonia S D, 14

13319 DANIEL, Oce, Ochelata, OK, 40   By Geo. Daniel, Gdn.

1728 DANIEL, Robert, Vinita, OK, 56

4370 DANIEL, Ros T, Tahlequah, OK, 33; Josie B D, 13; Asie A, S, 8; Eliza B D, 6; Emma B, D, 6; Leon R, S, 3; Samuel J, S, 1/3

32300 DANIEL, Tom, Eucha, OK, 20

36409 DANIELS, Edna, Verd, OK, 5;   By Henry Hays, Gdn.

2912 DANIELS, Ella, Westville, OK, 33; 13119 Mary D, 1; 13150 Andy, S, 7

2951 DANIELS, George, Locust Grove, OK, 46; Sarah D, 12; Peggie D, 5; Willie, S, 1

706 DANIELS, Richard, Ochelata, OK, 22

24368 DANNENBERG Alice N Chelsea, OK, 20

22552 DANNENBERG Daniel E, Nan Tung Chow, China, 30; By John C. Dannenberg

22551 DANNENBERG, John C, Tahlequah, OK, 32; Yancey N. S, 7; Okla, D, 3

1655 DANNENBERG, John H, Stilwell, OK, 64

29913 DANNENBERG, Joseph R, San Francisco CA, 29

5758 DANNENBERG. Louis L, Stilwell, OK, 53

8027 DANNENBERG, Nathaniel B Chelsea, OK, 46; 5485 Sarah E, W, 46; H. Grady, S, 16; Waldemar, S, 12

1652 DANNENBERG, Richard M, Tahlequah, OK, 55; Fannie A/ D, 17; Richard M, S, 10

24925 DANNENBERG, Robert C, Manard, OK, 29; 1870 Mary, W, 28

3252 DANNENBERG, William Dutch Mills, AR, 66

22661 DANNENBERG, William H, Stilwell, OK, 31; George L, S, 6; Opal C D, 4; Madge N, D, 5/12

22823 DANNENBERG, Louis B, Stilwell, OK, 32; 23911 Mary, W, 26; Susie D, 1

24704 DANNENBURG, Thomas N. Adair, OK, 36; George R, S, 17; Lewis B, S, 13; Jane E, D, 12; John F, S, 10; Leonard L, S, 8; Gladys D, 5; Robert O, S, 2

9144 DAR-YOU-LE-SI-NI,Will, Southwest City, MO, 43; 9211 Polly, W ,40

30197 DAUGHERTY Ada, Stilwell, OK, 27; Hester D, 4; Lula D, 1

Key: Guion Miller Application Number; Name; Address, Relation (to Head); Age in 1906

3730 DAUGHERTY Belle C Catoosa, OK, 22; Lou T D, 4; Thomas W, Jr, S, 2; Oce C, S, 1/12

4228 DAUGHERTY Bob, Stilwell, OK, 52

[DAUGHERTY, Eliza. See #12416] *(Note: entry separate from other family groups)*

15033 DAUGHERTY, Elizabeth Dewey, OK, 37; 15032 Fields, Patrick, S, 19; 15031 Mike, S, 17; 15033 Stella D, 14; Emmett, S, 12; Catherine D, 10; Amy D, 8; Mary E D, 6; Dorothy D, D, 3; Elizabeth A D, 1

4403 DAUGHERTY, Elk, Stilwell, OK, 48

18534 DAUGHERTY, Ellen Choteau, OK, 33

8995 DAUGHERTY, George Blackgum, OK, 42; 14244 Mary, W, 45

8998 DAUGHERTY, Henry, Vian, OK, 32; 5680 Nannie, W, 28; 8998 Blue, S, 3; Jeff, S, 1

4733 DAUGHERTY, James, Evansville AR, 11;   By Chicululu Selers, Gdn.

2272 DAUGHERTY, Jennie, Stilwell, OK, 21

9193 DAUGHERTY, Lydia, Long, OK, 27; Ellen D, 13; Toy-nee-che D, 9; Jack, S, 7; Lilla, D, 3; Mary D, 1/3

8265 DAUGHERTY, Money, Remy, OK, 55

13133 DAUGHERTY, Rachel, Vian, OK, 31

3555 DAUGHERTY, Robert E, Grove, OK, 34

8319 DAUGHERTY, Runabout, Stilwell, OK, 43; Walter, S, 14; Robert, S, 11; Andrew, S, 9; Thomas, S, 3

23543 DAUGHERTY, Scott, Stilwell, OK, 22

1070 DAUGHERTY, Silk, Stilwell, OK, 55; Ellen D, 15; Mary D, 8; Eva D, 4; Katie D, 2

13575 DAUGHERTY, William Braggs, OK, 33

7950 DAUGHERTY, William H, Grove, OK, 43; Claude H, S, 18; William H, S, 14; John H, S, 11; Percy C, S, 6

13388 DAVE, Key Cookson, OK, 17;   By Sequichie Squirrel, Gdn.

[DAVE, Little. See #17211] *(Note: entry separate from other family groups)*

4954 DAVENPORT, Millard G, Vinita, OK, 12; Grace, Sis, 10; Dorothy, Sis, 9;   By Jas. S. Davenport, Gdn

924 DAVID Betsy, Tahlequah, OK, 19

900 DAVID, Nellie, Tahlequah, OK, 57

922 DAVID, Polly, Tahlequah, OK, 25; Bird, Joseph, S, 3

1746 DAVIDSON, Emma, Moodys, OK, 29; Annie L D, 7; Ruth D, 4; Athelene D, 2

11723 DAVIDSON, George W, Edith, TX, 42; Earl, S, 10; Roxie D, 7; Dollie D, 4

30116 DAVIDSON, Percy Ray Chelsea, OK, 6;   By Robert A. Davidson, Gdn.

29790 DAVIDSON, Ruth E Chelsea, OK, 29; Marvin Wayne, S, 3; Robert Donnell, S, 1

Key: Guion Miller Application Number; Name; Address, Relation (to Head); Age in 1906

29100 DAVIS, Albert E, Nocona, TX, 18; Edith, Sis, 15; Joseph K Bro, 14; By Nancy Ellen Skeen, Gdn

11554 DAVIS, Alex Cherokee City AR, 25

11997 DAVIS, Alexander D, Ramona, OK, 30

3562 DAVIS, Alford, Sallisaw, OK, 24; Jennie Bell D, 1

27737 DAVIS, Alice V Chelsea, OK, 47; Arthur C, S, 17; Mabel D, 15; Frank, S, 11

13458 DAVIS, Ammon H Briertown, OK, 16; Jeter Bro, 12; By Malinda Evans, Gdn.

3178 DAVIS, Andrew Bartlesville, OK, 27; James, S, 4; Edith D, 1

13447 DAVIS, Andrew J, Muskogee, OK, 22

27963 DAVIS, Annie, Maysville AR, 26; John, S, 6; Foreman, Richard, S, ½

29257 DAVIS, Burwell M Claremore, OK, 26

17164 DAVIS, Charley, Webbers Falls, OK, 20

698 DAVIS, Charlie, Sallisaw, OK, 42; Barney, S, 15; Mary D, 8

13900 DAVIS Cicero, Fort Smith AR, 47 [Deceased 9-11-'06 By Sidney Davis - Wife]; Rachel D, 15; Nannie D, 13; Pauline D, 4; Sidney Cicero, S, 1

24352 DAVIS Daniel B, Okoee, OK, 32; Duell A, S, 4

18166 DAVIS Dave Cherokee City AR, 28

[DAVIS David. See David Fixing, #14131]
(Note: entry separate from other family groups)

[DAVIS, Joseph. See David Fixing, #14133]
(Note: entry separate from other family groups)

2352 DAVIS David C, Hulbert, OK, 62

25012 DAVIS, Edna E Chelsea, OK, 34; Mack O, S, 15; Leah O D, 12; Roy, S, 10; Arizona, D, 8; Louis H, S, 6; Nancy M D, 4

1707 DAVIS, Fixing, Spavinaw, OK, 54; 1705 Susie, W, 31; 13571 John, S, 17; 1703 Will, S, 1; 9942 Car-car-wee, Ross, S of W, 13

7487 DAVIS, George Cherokee City AR, 35; 7977 Annie, W, 24; 7487 Dick, S, 1/6

9302 Davis, George, Peggs, OK, 40?

5512 DAVIS, Geo. W, Ketchum, OK, 31; Mary L, D, 5; James A, S, 3; Ruth May D, 1

13566 DAVIS, Hannah M, Vera, OK, 49; Joe, M, S, 20; Theodore, S, 17; Asa, S, 15; Isaac, S, 13; John W, S, 12; Sidney M, S, 11

5459½ DAVIS, Hattie Collinsville, OK, 14;   By John W. Hudgepath, Gdn.

42966 DAVIS, Hattie, Webbers Falls, OK, 22

8907 DAVIS, Jack Cherokee City AR, 31

3560 DAVIS, James, Sallisaw, OK, 34; Ora E D, 9; Annie L D, 6; Marvin, S, 3

25692 DAVIS, James, Valeda, KS, 30; Laura D, 10; Alla D, 7; Ray A, S, 3; Jessie J D, 1

29099 DAVIS, James W Baggs, WY, 43; Ruby E D, 3; Chas. Willard, S, 1

30266 DAVIS, Jane, Tahlequah, OK, 31; Richard J, S, 2; William A, S, 1

Key: Guion Miller Application Number; Name; Address, Relation (to Head); Age in 1906

5748 DAVIS, Jeff Claremore, OK, 44

4178 DAVIS, John Collinsville, OK, 19; Mack Bro, 17; By Jas. R. Stout, Gdn.

5356 DAVIS, John Claremore, OK, 60

9684 DAVIS, John, Muskogee, OK, 42; Joe Lynch, S, 15; Sam Tate, S, 13; Caroline, D, 11; Jack, S, 8

12393 DAVIS, John Anna Afton, OK, 20

98 DAVIS, John B Claremore, OK, 46; Jeff, S, 16; Jesse, S, 12; Jetar, S, 7; Ezekiel, S, 4; Ella D, 2

27736 DAVIS, John B Chelsea, OK, 23

5513 DAVIS, John W, Ketchum, OK, 33; Violet D, 7; William T, S, 4

2407 DAVIS, Joseph W Adair, OK, 56; Joseph J, S, 19; Hattie M D, 16; Mattie B D, 13; James H, S, 11

17248 DAVIS, Katie, Porum, OK, 18

4180 DAVIS, Kim Collinsville, OK, 23

24031 DAVIS, Kyle, Gritts, OK, 28

23234 DAVIS, Lee F Collinsville, OK, 22

17757 DAVIS, Lenora, McLain, OK, 22; Sarah Ann D, 8; Tempie Susan D, 5; John T, S, 3

22567 DAVIS, Lowery, Stilwell, OK, 35

25979 DAVIS, Lucy Cleora, OK, 22; Eugene Farmer, S, 1/12

10000 DAVIS, Lukie, Porum, OK, 16

27738 DAVIS, Lyta Chelsea, OK, 19

11790 DAVIS, Martha A, Nocona, TX, 71

[DAVIS, Mary. See Sarah Cochran, #3535]
(Note: entry separate from other family groups)

24670 DAVIS, Mary Ballard, OK, 18

29258 DAVIS, Mary Claremore, OK, 29

[DAVIS, Mary. See #43404]   *(Note: entries separate*
[DAVIS, Johnson. See #43404]   *from other family groups)*

23741 DAVIS, Mary L, Muskogee, OK, 31

17271 DAVIS, Mollie, Webbers Falls, OK, 26

26794 DAVIS, Narcena Adair, OK, 23

25129 DAVIS, Neffie, Warner, OK, 27; Cherry D, 2; Willie, S, ¼

32427 DAVIS, Neppie W. F, Muskogee, OK, 23

8910 DAVIS, Nick Cherokee City AR, 24

37228 DAVIS, Perry B, Muskogee, OK, 33

13456 DAVIS, Robert L, Porum, OK, 36; Robert S, S, 2/3

10001 DAVIS, Sallie, Porum, OK, 24

CHEROKEE DESCENDANTS RESIDING WEST OF MISSISSIPPI RIVER.
VOLUME II   (A – M)

Key: Guion Miller Application Number; Name; Address, Relation (to Head); Age in 1906

11272 DAVIS, Sallie A Bartlett, KS, 26; Edna G D, 9; Ellis L, S, 6; Mable B D, 4; Katie M, D, 2

18635 DAVIS, Sam, Kansas, OK, 27; 43406 Lizzie, W, 23; Josephine D, 1/12

12916 DAVIS, Samuel, Porum, OK, 56; 12914 Lucinda, W, 66

25577 DAVIS, Sanford L, Webbers Falls, OK, 12; Leo J Bro, 10; Lorena G, Sis, 9; Ellen E, Sis, 3;   By Josephus Crossland, Gdn.

13419 DAVIS, Stand W, Stigler, OK, 27; Watie Elmer, S, 6

24613 DAVIS, Susie J, Muskogee, OK, 17 705 S. Third St.

4257 DAVIS, Thomas Collinsville, OK, 58; Napoleon, S, 15

10942 DAVIS, Thompson, Peggs, OK, 44; 10194 Lucy, W, 25; Geo. Annie D, 3

23939 DAVIS, William Collinsville, OK, 26

5374 DAVIS, William H, Stilwell, OK, 68; 9650 Eliza L, W, 60

13066 DAVIS, Winnie, St. Louis, MO, 19 309 N Compton St.

24752 DAWES Cora B. Chelsea, OK, 18

2964 DAWES, Johnathan W Chelsea, OK, 47; 42105 Phoebe J, W, 28; Mary E D, 10; Sallie D, 9; Ida D, 7; Ada D, 7; Opal D, 4; Lloyd, S, 2;   Edith B, S, 1/3

2961 DAWES, Lloyd R Chelsea, OK, 49; Claud, S, 16; Essie D, 7

2963 DAWES, Martha Chelsea, OK, 45

4415 DAWES, Mary Malissa, Vinita, OK, 57

[DAWES, Sampson. See #17066]   *(Note: entry separate from other family groups)*

24957 DAWES Dora Claremore, OK, 27; James E, S, 11; Samuel, S, 9; Charles, S, 5; Author Floyd, S, 3; Zola Ada D, 13

3279 DAWSON, Fannie L, Nowata, OK, 30; John Hubert, S, 4; Jewel P D, 1

30131 DAWSON, Geo. H Claremore, OK, 16;   By Henry Dawson, Gdn.

30663 DAWSON, Laura Centralia, OK, 32; Stephen E, S, 12; Jeff, S, 10; Joseph, S, 8; Bessie J D, 3; Nora E D, 1

22744 DAWSON, Martha Afton, OK, 31; Lorene M D, 1

30142 DAWSON, Rebecca Claremore, OK, 17

5969 DAY, John Parks, Spavinaw, OK, 32; 23828 Ellen, W, 16

360 DAY, William A Big Cabin, OK, 43; Ruth S D, 13; Mary E D, 11; William A, Jr, S, 7; Mattie D, 5; Bennie W, S, 3; Louis E, S, 1

8731 DAY-GUR-US-TE, Welleah, Locust Grove, OK, 58

25875 DAYHOFF, Octavia Z, San Antonio, TX, R.F.D. #9 Box 59 25

1896 DAYLIGHT, Sarah, Short, OK, 32

25462 DAYTON, Etta L Claremore, OK, 20; Charles E, S, 1

6700 DAZZLER Aggie Braggs, OK, 53; Oce, S, 19; Charles, S, 12

25102 DAZZLER, James L Braggs, OK, 22

25101 DAZZLER, John W Braggs, OK, 24

2038 DEAL Charles, Stilwell, OK, 35

18887 DEAL, Edgar Chelsea, OK, 10; Ethel, Sis, 8; Cornelius Bro, 6; Sallie, Sis, 3; By Sarah Deal, Gdn.

Key: Guion Miller Application Number; Name; Address, Relation (to Head); Age in 1906

6243 DEAL, John H, Stilwell, OK, 31; Clara O D, 6; Addie D, 4; Joseph, S, 1

8016 DEAL, Joseph, Stilwell, OK, 19

8080 DEAL, Robert Lee, Fairland, OK, 21

2983 DEAL, Susan, Estella, OK, 23; Sadie May D, 1

22205 DEAL, William W Chelsea, OK, 38

23907 DEAN, Nancy J, Gideon, OK, 47; William A, S, 16; Jefferson D, S, 13; Percy S, S, 7; Ena E D, 10; Mamie E D, 4; James E, S, 2

11490 DEAN, Nannie Braggs, OK, 32; Claud, S, 8; Bessie D, 5

23904 DEAN, Presha M, Gideon, OK, 23

1293 DEATHERAGE, Mariah A, Tahlequah, OK, 30; Sallie M D, 4; Callie M, S, 2; Clara E D, ¼

5151 DECKEY Callie E, Lenapah, OK, 25; Effie E D, 6; Pearl May D, 4

7641 DECKMAN Amanda, Ketchum, OK, 29; Charles, S, 9; Joseph A, S, 4; John W, S, 2

8868 DEE-GAH-NEE-SKI, Elsie, Locust Grove, OK, 45

25252 DEEMS, John Bristow, OK, 28

14287 DEERHEAD, John Choteau, OK, 31; 10882 Lizzie, W, 47

15605 DEERHEAD, Nannie Choteau, OK, 12; By M.L. Lindsey, Gdn.

8945 DEER-IN-WATER Alex, Welling, OK, 44; 10381 Annie, W, 40

11765 DEERINWATER Annie, Pryor Creek, OK, 42; 17107 Birdtail, John, S, 19; Birdtail Dave, S, 13; Birdtail, Sam, S, 11

1295 DEERINWATER, George, Evansville, AR, 57; 2487 Lucinda, W, 55; Charley, S, 20; Sallie D, 18; Tom, S, 16; John, S, 14

10955 DEERINWATER, George Cookson, OK, 50

18430 DEERINWATER, Jennie Braggs, OK, 12; By Katie Brown, Gdn.

17175 DEERINWATER, John, Muldrow, OK, 49; 17244 Lizzie, W, 56; 17175 Charlie, S, 19

10388 DEERINWATER, Katie Braggs, OK, 34

10957 DEERINWATER, Keener Cookson, OK, 33

8735 DEERINWATER, Levi, Locust Grove, OK, 58; Josiah, S, 4

18431 DEERINWATER, Richard Braggs, OK, 8; By Katie Brown, Gdn.

[DEERINWATER Star. See Susie Perdue #12401]
(Note: entry separate from other family groups)

24420 DEESE, Joe Anna Baron, OK, 26; Hugh John, S, 3

2671 DEETRICK, Lillie B, Vinita, OK, 25; Beulah D, 5; Evelyn D, 1

43344 DEGE, John J, Yuma AZ, 32

32305 DEGE, Laura A, Pryor Creek, OK, 60

32306 DEGE, Mary E, Pryor Creek, OK, 25

[De GROOT Carrie H. See #7553] *(Note: entry separate from other family groups)*

CHEROKEE DESCENDANTS RESIDING WEST OF MISSISSIPPI RIVER.
VOLUME II   (A – M)

Key: Guion Miller Application Number; Name; Address, Relation (to Head); Age in 1906

[DEGUADEHI, Groundhog. See #5675] ⎫   *(Note: entries separate*
[DEGUADEHI, Tincup. See #5675]   ⎭   *from other family groups)*

11434 DE-KA-HOO-GEE-SKIE [or WATERMELLON], Southwest City, MO, 72;
11433 De-ka-hoo-gee-skie Ancy, W, 74

4523 DELAY Clara C, Pryor Creek, OK, 9;   By J.B. Delay, Gdn.

29999 DELAY, Kate, Pryor Creek, OK, 30; Dora Gladys D, 1

13569 DELGADO, Fannie Braggs, OK, 18; Delphia D, 1

12694 DELLUS, George, Uniontown AR, 35

29285 DELOZIER, Evaline Chelsea, OK, 35

10653 DELOZIER, Georgia V Adair, OK, 38; Fountain G, S, 18; Manford E, S, 15;
John Edward, S, 13; Ralph A, S, 10; Hazel M D, 8; Vivian D, 4

23102 DELOZIER, Lueda Adair, OK, 19; Clara J D, 7/12

29284 DELOZIER, Virginia S Chelsea, OK, 28; Joseph W, S, 4

34460 DeMOTT, Liddia, Pryor Creek, OK, 24; Fay D, 2; Emory, S, 1

13147 DEMPSEY, Sallie, Fawn, OK, 26; James W, S, 11; Jennie M D, 7; Charles
Oscar, S, 4; Jackson, S, 2

3727 DENBO, John L Catoosa, OK, 32; 4564 Laura A, W, 33; Robert E, S, 6; John L,
S, 5; James R, S, 1 [Died 1907]

3729 DENBO, Oceola C Catoosa, OK, 24; Bertha O D, 2

3728 DENBO, Robert L, Rocky Ford CO, 26; Milton D, S, 3; Ida M D, 2

36529 DENNIS, Nancy, Zena, OK, 20

35717 DENNIS, Oscar, Zena, OK, 23

13088 DENNIS, Peter, Zena, OK, 45; 16454 Mary, W, 47; 13088 Rachel D, 18;
Susie D, 15; Jennie D, 10; Jimmie, S, 8

25842 DENNIS, Viola, Vinita, OK, 29; Samuel B, S, 5; Basil B, S, 3; Harold J, S, 1/3

16008 DENNY Alice J Claremore, OK, 54

9380 DENNY, Harriette E Brushy, OK, 35; Fouts, Irvin, S, 11; Maggie M D, 7;
Denny, Phoeba D, 5; Nathan, S, 1

32043 DENNY, Noble, Hudson, OK, 32; Louis J, S, 6; Emmett A, S, 5; Ralph V, S, 2

243 DESHANE, Rosettie Catale, OK, 27; Alfred, S, 11; Ida M D, 8; Leetha D, 4

8364 DE-S-QUA-NI, Eucha, OK, 60

6931 DEVAN, Mahala, Lenapah, OK, 35; Addie D, 14; Carrie D, 11; Eva D, 7;
Benjamin, S, 5

8083 DeVAUGH Arthur E, Marble City, OK, 33

16428 DeVAUGHN Daniel R, Uniontown, AR, 28; Lillie A D, 2

16428 DeVAUGHN, George F, Uniontown, AR, 20

8082 DeVAUGHN, Sarah L, Muldrow, OK, 21; Clapps, Bettie Ray D, 3; Dovie D, D,
1

27060 DEVINE Chas. W, Westville, OK, 25;   James T, S, 4; Robert L, S, 1

27059 DEVINE, James T, Westville, OK, 24; George O, S, ¼

4637 DEVINE, Thomas M, Westville, OK, 44; Joel M, S, 19; William R, S, 17;
Jackson, S, 15

Key: Guion Miller Application Number; Name; Address, Relation (to Head); Age in 1906

6058 DEW Charlotte, Tahlequah, OK, 41; 16076 Coldweather, Johnson, S, 17; Buffington, Susie D, 4

10596 DEW, George, Moodys, OK, 18

10639 DEW, George, Locust Grove, OK, 18;   By Quatie Vann, Gdn.

[DEW, Ella or Ailsey. See #5286]   *(Note: entry separate from other family groups)*

2228 DEW, Fay, Tahlequah, OK, 14;   By Jesse Sixkiller

3661 DEW, Fremus, Oaks, OK, 23

4504 DEW, Jack, Locust Grove, OK, 32; 13258 Fannie, W, 38; Hawkins, Nancy D of W, 17; Jesse, S of W, 13; Jim, S of W, 11; Nannie D of W, 4

11985 DEW, Jim, Moodys, OK, 23

10695 DEW, Willie, Moodys, OK, 24

[DIAL, Mattie. See Julia A. Bee, #859] *(Note: entry separate from other family groups)*

33439 DIAL, Thomas, Oaks, OK, 27; 1504 Mattie, W, 19

9602 DICK Andrew, Peggs, OK, 44; 2499 Sack, Rachel, W, 23; Welling, S of W, 2

1475 DICK Annie, Peggs, OK, 48

41515 DICK Annie Cookson, OK, 19

[DICK Betsy. See #24064]   *(Note: entry separate from other family groups)*

7645 DICK Charles A, Tahlequah, OK, 28

6753 DICK Coleman Cookson, OK, 57; 11766 Katie, W, 44; Watt, S, 15; Josie D, 11

246 DICK, George Catale, OK, 34

8665 DICK, George, Peggs, OK, 29; 3744 Margaret D, 3; Jesse T, S, 1

16964 DICK, George, Welling, OK, 23; 17188 Bell, W, 18

4934 DICK, Ira May Chloeta, OK, 16; Mary E, Sis, 13; Joanna, Sis, 10; Isaac J Bro, 8; By Cynthia Dick, Gdn.

713 DICK, Jacob, Ochelata, OK, 54; Ellen D, 13; Bessie D, 11

11989 DICK, John, Welling, OK, 15;   By Mary Catron, Gdn.

35126 DICK, John H, Tahlequah, OK, 37; 24407 Sallie E, W, 41

23050 DICK, Joseph, Ochelata, OK, 25; Arvil L, S, 1

5744 DICK, Lizzie, Welling OK, 23; George, S, 3

244 DICK, Mary Catale, OK, 61

11641 DICK, Nancy, Welling, OK, 47; Sooky D, 13

5346 DICK, Oce, Tulsa, OK, 46

4936 DICK, Thomas E Chloeta, OK, 22

29385 DICK, Walter Chelsea, OK, 18; George Bro, 15; Myrtle, Sis, 14; Ellis Bro, 12; May, Sis, 10; Lorenzo Bro, 8;   By Laura C. Quigley, Gdn.

247 DICK, Washington Catale, OK, 41; Arthur, S, 13;   Ada D, 11; Bessie M D, 9; Effie, D, 6; Eura D, 3; Verna D, 1

Key: Guion Miller Application Number; Name; Address, Relation (to Head); Age in 1906

41510 DICK, William Cookson, OK, 34; 12408 Sally, W, 25; 41510 Jennie D, 8; Maggie, D, 4; Henry, S, 1

[DICK, William E. See #3458]   *(Note: entries separate*
[DICK, Ellis. See #3458]   *from other family groups)*

5517 DICK, Wuttie, Welling, OK, 49
12144 DICKENS, Irene Alexander, Alexandria, LA, 32; Miriam Cherokee D, 10
96 DICKSON Cynthia Achelata, OK, 38; Claude, S, 14; Serena D, 12; Paul, S, 10; Beulah D, 8; Thoman Benton, Jr, S, 6; Cleva Latitia D, 3; Lucile D, 5/12
3224 DICKSON, Sarah H, Humble, TX, 38; Mattie L D, 13; Joseph E, S, 11; Arthur E, S, 5; John S, S, 1
25313 DILDINE, James, Oglesby, OK, 21
4908 DILDINE, Rachel, Kansas, OK, 45; Lethy D, 16; Hester D, 18; Andy, S, 11; Silas, S, 9; Isaac, S, 6; Jacob, S, 6; Sarah D, 4; Anna M D, 1
29317 DINSMORE, Susie Choteau, OK, 19
480 DIRTEATER Charley, Moodys, OK, 39; 12592 Annie, W, 34; 480 Stand, S, 13; Dick, S, 9; Henry, S, 7; 12592 Rogers Annie D of W, 16
3879 DIRTEATER, Joe, Locust Grove, OK, 40; Lizie[sic] D, 9
6571 DIRTEATER, Mary, Hulbert, OK, 26; Su-agee, S, 1
4366 DIRTEATER, Robin, Moodys, OK, 35; 17067 Ella, W, 33; 4366 Maggie D, 11; Sarah D, 3; Jack, S, 1
9798 DIRTSELLER, Jessie, Melvin, OK, 31
43355 DIRTSELLER, Mary, Southwest City, MO, 20
8373 DIRTSELLER, Rider, Southwest City, MO, 34; 11964 Oo-squin-ne, W, 40; 8373 Ooyustutah, S, 14; La-le D, 4; Oo-ki-li, S, 1/12

[DIRT TRACK, Mary with Joe James. See #8331]
                    (Note: entry separate from other family groups)

11855 DISNEY Alice, Manard, OK, 26; Minnie D, 2
3492 DIVER Bunch, Stilwell, OK, 22
30108 DIXON, Henrietta, Welch, OK, 32; Edith D, 12; Issac[sic] Earl, S, 10; Mabel L D, 6; George W, Jr, S, 3
147 DIXON, Isaac Claremore, OK, 24
146 DIXON, William, Gideon, OK, 12;   By Isaac Dixon, Gdn.
854 DOBBINS, James, Gideon, OK, 50

[DOBBS, William R. See #27741]   *(Note: entry separate from other family groups)*

28579 DOBBYN, Maude K, Red Bluff CA, 28; Irma D, 6; Lloyd, S, 4
1061 DOBKINS Ben, Welch, OK, 27; Juanita D, 1

Key: **Guion Miller Application Number; Name; Address, Relation (to Head); Age in 1906**

[DOBSON Bonnie See #16609]   *(Note: entry separate from other family groups)*

24124 DOBSON, Harry L, Eureka, OK, 21
26543 DOBSON, Mary J, Eureka, OK, 23
4706 DOBSON, Sarah, Eureka, OK, 42; Arthur Ray, S, 16; Eugenia D, 14
24126 DOBSON, Wallace, Eureka, OK, 25; 27022 Matttie[sic] S, W, 20
16746 DOCTOR, Lizzie, Tahlequah, OK, 6;   By Mose Fulin, Gdn.

[DODSON Alma Pearl. See #2125]   *(Note: entry separate from other family groups)*

6245 DODSON, Nancy J Claremore, OK, 34; Jessie I D, 12; Waitey F D, 10; Dewey
Lee, S, 8

[DOG, Nancy. See #9623]   *(Note: entry separate from other family groups)*

927 DOHERTY, James R, Ramona, OK, 27 Box #82; Edna D, 4; Clarisa J D, 1
9826 DOHERTY, John M, Ramona, OK, 23
8096 DOHERTY, Robert, Roff, OK, 52
7949 DOHERTY, Walter L, Grove, OK, 36; 33601 Mary E, W, 34; Elizabeth C D, 11;
William L, S, 10; Ella M D, 8; Letha E D, 6; James E, S, 5; Roger E, S, 3;
Annie B, D, 1

[DOLEN, Ida May. See #21032] ⎤   *(Note: entries separate*
[DOLEN Clarry M. See #21032] ⎦   *from other family groups)*

2484 DOLLAR, Sarah, Stilwell, OK, 24
30541 DONALDSON, Frank M Afton, OK, 28; William Henry, S, 3; Frankie F, S, 1/12
7703 DONALDSON, Maggie B, Vinita, OK, 21
2286 DONALDSON, Ola M Afton, OK, 18?; Jessie Annie, Sis, 16; Arthur Bro, 14;
By William H. Donaldson, Gdn.
30540 DONALDSON, William C Albia, OK, 26
25188 DONNELLY, Emma, Vinita, OK, 22
3532 DONNELLY, Emma J, Vinita, OK, 56; Ada D, 15
25187 DONNELLY, James, Vinita, OK, 34; Mattie A D, 9; James O, S, 6; Ray E, S, 3;
Bernice M D, 1/6
28480 DONNELLY, Paul, Vinita, OK, 21
35236 DONNELLY, Thomas A Canon City, CO, 28; 18481 Mary E, W, 29; Gladys D,
5
28479 DONNELLY, William, Vinita, OK, 30
4565 DONOHOO, Lucile, Joplin, MO, 13;   By Phillip Donohoo, Gdn.

[DONOHOO, Madeline. See #26295] ⎤   *(Note: entries separate*
[DONOHOO, Paul Langley. See #26295] ⎦   *from other family groups)*

CHEROKEE DESCENDANTS RESIDING WEST OF MISSISSIPPI RIVER.
VOLUME II   (A – M)

Key: Guion Miller Application Number; Name; Address, Relation (to Head); Age in 1906

23248 DOOLEY, George W, Eastland, TX, 39; Esther D, 14; Jennie D, 11; Birdie D, 8; Myrtle D, 4; Clarence, S, 2

26039 DOOLEY, Margaret J Choteau, OK, 44; Myrtle D, 16; Earle M, S, 14; Ruby Esther, D, 12

767 DOOLEY, Melissa C Catoosa, OK, 59

12557 DORGELOH, Edna V, San Francisco, CA, 731 Fulton St., 28

4510 DOTSON, Lucy R, Marble City, OK ,26; Lewis B, S, 3; Charles, S, 1

[DO-TSU-LE-NAR Arlie. See #21987] *(Note: entry separate from other family groups)*

17227 DOTTS Beulah C Bluejacket, OK, 27; Daniel Oliver, S, 7; Bessie May D, 6

3628 DOUBLEHEAD Bert, Estella, OK, 23

3486 DOUBLEHEAD Blackbird, Stilwell, OK, 54; Lula D, 17; Joe, S, 14

14295 DOUBLEHEAD, Isaac, Locust Grove, OK, 48

[DOUBLEHEAD, Jennie. See #18722] *(Note: entry separate from other family groups)*

14148 DOUBLEHEAD, John, Welling, OK, 21; Henry, S, ¼

[DOUBLEHEAD, John A. See #1269] *(Note: entry separate from other family groups)*

1822 DOUBLEHEAD, Levi, Vinita, OK, 19

3484 DOUBLEHEAD, Peter, Stilwell, OK, 55; 3491 Peggy, W, 44; 3484 John, S, 18; Nanny D,, 16; Caroline D, 11

12761 DOUGHERTY Dianna, Stilwell, OK, 20

10927 DOUGHERTY, Soap, Stilwell, OK, 23 [Died 1908]; Jimmie, S, 3; Katie D, 1/3

3189 DOUGLASS, Effie D, Vinita, OK, 23

26001 DOWELL Bessie Canadian, OK, 20

[DOWELL Claude E. with Henry W. Hines. See #22106]
(Note: entry separate from other family groups)

32107 DOWELL, Henry H, Tulsa, OK, 21

[DOWNING Abraham. See #14209] *(Note: entry separate from other family groups)*

10496 DOWNING Alex Baron, OK, 26

24861 DOWNING Alex, Tahlequah, OK, 43; 17118 Nancy, W, 43; 24861 Joel, S, 14

2444 DOWNING Allie, Hadley, OK, 60

9800 DOWNING Andy, Melvin, OK, 28; 11294 Jennie, W, 30; Charles, S, 4 [Hoo-lon-da-ke]

1883 DOWNING Annie, Locust Grove, OK, 21

13434 DOWNING Benjamin, Muskogee, OK, 29

CHEROKEE DESCENDANTS RESIDING WEST OF MISSISSIPPI RIVER.
VOLUME II   (A – M)

Key: Guion Miller Application Number; Name; Address, Relation (to Head); Age in 1906

[DOWNING Caldonia with Mary Kelley. See #23788]
(Note: entry separate from other family groups)

858 DOWNING Caroline, Tahlequah, OK, 54

[DOWNING Charles. See #12619] ⎤   *(Note: entries separate*
[DOWNING, Pumpkin. See #12619] ⎦   *from other family groups)*

24851 DOWNING Chester, Peggs, OK, 31; **34186** Annie, W, 29

[DOWNING Clorinda. See #254]   *(Note: entry separate from other family groups)*

12806 DOWNING Cull, Ft. Leavenworth, KS, Box #7 27
 2134 DOWNING Cynthia, Locust Grove, OK, 20
  849 DOWNING Daniel, Locust Grove, OK, 69; **3608** Martha, W, 68
17673 DOWNING Daniel, Whitmire, OK, 18
 1225 DOWNING Dave, Peggs, OK, 55; **10184** Samuel, S, 12; Sissie D, 7
12575 DOWNING Dave, Vian, OK, 62
 2463 DOWNING Dave Baron, OK, 28
  191 DOWNING David, Locust Grove, OK, 31; Mink, S, 10; Lizzie D, 4
14136 DOWNING Dick, Locust Grove, OK, 52; **10148** Wakey, W, 46; **14134** Niecer
         [Nayesah] D, 19; Dave [Chuuwahneeski], S, 17
 2057 DOWNING Drucilla, Hadley, OK, 17;   By Jos. Downing, Gdn.
13509 DOWNING, Edward, Texanna, OK, 24
 1337 DOWNING, Eliza Claremore, OK, 51
 6449 DOWNING, Eliza, Locust Grove, OK, 46; **16907** Joe, S, 16; Willie, S, 14
16998 DOWNING, Ely, Uniontown AR, 26; **24434** Amanda, W, 31; Needles, Jug, S of
         W, 14; Miller, Martha D of W, 10; Downing, Laura D, 2
 2669 DOWNING, Felix, Estella, OK, 50; **1872** Lizzie, W, 36; Nancy D, 13
 2056 DOWNING, George, Hadley, OK, 12   By Jos. Downing, Gdn.
 3267 DOWNING, George, Texanna, OK, 73
 9326 DOWNING, George, Melvin, OK, 21
12513 DOWNING, George, Estella, OK, 32; **13062** Mollie, W, 26; **12513** John, S, 10;
         Zuma, S, 10; Adam, S, 4; Noyah, S, 2
13062 Hawk, Lucy D of W, 13

[DOWNING, George. See #31190]   *(Note: entry separate from other family groups)*

  857 DOWNING, George B, Westville, OK, 49; James Louis, S, 19; Effie Ala D, 17;
         William A, S, 13; Susie D, 11; Jesse, S, 4
22662 DOWNING, George G, Rose, OK, 25
  522 DOWNING, Henry, Locust Grove, OK, 52; **189** Mary, W, 58; Carrie D, 18
25597 DOWNING, Henry, Owasso, OK, 30; **22944** Mary, W, 21

Key: Guion Miller Application Number; Name; Address, Relation (to Head); Age in 1906

379 DOWNING, Houston, Southwest City, MO, 39; 429 Elizabeth, W, 38; Nancy D, 16; Mary D, 14; Rebecca D, 11; Hill, S, 9; Charley, S, 6; George, S, 4; Louisa D, 2

5130 DOWNING, Jack, Foyil, OK, 63; 5131 Sallie, W, 51; Benjamin, S, 17; Alice D, 18 Bondinot(?), Sallie D of W, 16

17242 DOWNING, Jackson, Muldrow, OK, 35; Josie D, 14; Joshua, S, 12

7507 DOWNING, James, Spavinaw, OK, 54; 3877 Lucy, W, 38; Eliza D, 1/12; Stealer, Lewis, GS, 8; Necer D, 4

9384 DOWNING, James, Lometa, OK, 21

24110 DOWNING, James, Locust Grove, OK, 39; 2940 Emma, W, 30; 24110 Blue, S, 8; Johnson, S, 5; Jessie D, 2; 2940 Sixkiller, Josie D of W, 13

10157 DOWNING, Jane, Southwest City, MO, 56; 10154 Willie, S, 19; 10156 Mike, S, 15

4201 DOWNING, Jess, Row, OK, 30

[DOWNING, Jesse. See #10900]   *(Note: entry separate from other family groups)*

[DOWNING, Joel. See #5558] ⎤   *(Note: entries separate*
[DOWNING, Lafayette. See #5558] ⎦   *from other family groups)*

10498 DOWNING, Joshua Baron, OK, 13

178 DOWNING, Johnson, Peggs, OK, 72; 10 Jennie, W, 60

2059 DOWNING, Joseph, Hadley, OK, 64; 23481 Callie, W, 27; 2059 Edward, S, 5; Stephen, S, 4; Maggie D, ¼; Lucy D(?), 65 [Insane Sister]

1120 DOWNING, Katie, Tahlequah, OK, 77

30366 DOWNING, Katie, Tahlequah, OK, 19

12580 DOWNING, Katie, Texanna, OK, 55; 12578 George H, S, 20; Maud D, 16

2054 DOWNING, Louis, Hadley, OK, 17   By Jos. Downing, Gdn.

[DOWNING, Lizzie with John Deerhead. See #10882]
(Note: entry separate from other family groups)

2944 DOWNING, Lucy, Locust Grove, OK, 46

10083 DOWNING, Lydia, Pryor Creek, OK, 86

13559 DOWNING, Mack, Hadley, OK, 47; 13560 Sallie, W, 33; 13559 Cora, D, 9; Robert, S, 4

[DOWNING, Mary. See #38484]   *(Note: entry separate from other family groups)*

1897 DOWNING, Mose, Uniontown AR, 36; John, S, 8; Charley, S, 6; Mary D, 4; Joannie, D, 2

[DOWNING, Nannie. See #4905]   *(Note: entry separate from other family groups)*

Key: Guion Miller Application Number; Name; Address, Relation (to Head); Age in 1906

4303 DOWNING, Nannie, Peggs, OK, 35; Charlotte D, 9; Elizabeth D, 5; Fannie D, 2

1108 DOWNING, Ned, Welling, OK, 50; 1110 Sallie, W, 52

2135 DOWNING, Ned, Peggs, OK, 23

3690 DOWNING, Ned, Locust Grove, OK, 34; 4341 Susie, W, 25; Sallie D, 4; Nancy D, 2

[DOWNING, Nellie. See #27258]   *(Note: entry separate from other family groups)*

2058 DOWNING, Peggy, Hadley, OK, 15   By Jos. Downing, Gdn.

11101 DOWNING, Richard Childers, OK, 43; Roy, S, 12; Simpson, S, 10; Susie D, 6; Maggie D, 3

1006 DOWNING, Rufus Baron, OK, 48; Henry, S, 2; Owen Brady, S, 1

7729 DOWNING, Ruth Baron, OK,10; Sanders, Peggy, Sis, 12; By Elizabeth Tieaspie, Gdn.

[DOWNING, Samuel. See #14210]   *(Note: entry separate from other family groups)*

29014 DOWNING, Samuel B, Peggs, OK, 24

16739 DOWNING, Samuel H, Peggs, OK, 33; 34559 Jennie, W, 26; Susie D, 4; Mollie D, 3; Alex, S, 1

13272 DOWNING, Susan B Baron, OK, 11   By William P. Downing, Gdn.

[DOWNING, Susie Bell. See #1994]   *(Note: entries separate*
[DOWNING, Lucy. See #1994]   *from other family groups)*

17186 DOWNING, Scott, Tahlequah, OK, 24

[DOWNING, Stacey with Nancy Bread. See #17504]
(Note: entry separate from other family groups)

7939 DOWNING, Thomas, Texanna, OK, 40; Jessie D, 16; Maggie D, 12; Lewis, S, 9; George, S, 7; Robert, S, 4

28590 DOWNING, Thomas B Choteau, OK, 35

10500 DOWNING, Tom Baron, OK, 19

1226 DOWNING, Thompson, Peggs, OK, 49; 2969 Sallie, W, 48; Lucy D, 16; Nancy D, 12

[DOWNING, Tommie. See #4300]   *(Note: entry separate from other family groups)*

3312 DOWNING, Walter Claremore, OK, 34

24108 DOWNING, Walter, Locust Grove, OK, 34

Key: Guion Miller Application Number; Name; Address, Relation (to Head); Age in 1906

8997 DOWNING, Wash Blackgum, OK, 37; 9587 Elsie, W, 28; 8997 Laura D, 13; Belle, D, 8; Mose, S, 3

[DOWNING, Will. See Jess Sanders, #1338]
(Note: entry separate from other family groups)

2468 DOWNING, William Baron, OK, 37; Willie May D, 1/12

24109 DOWNING, William, Locust Grove, OK, 32

1275 DOWNING, William A, Rose, OK, 51; 22663 Eliza J, W, 41; 1275 Samuel S, S, 17; Nannie M D, 17; Elodie V D, 15; Ella V D, 12; Elizabeth D, 10; William A, Jr, S, 8; David M, S, 5; Thomas B, S, 3

5634 DOWNING, William, Muskogee, OK, 30; 2848 Ruth K, W, 40; Butler, Richard V, S of W, 17; Samuel H, S of W, 12; Sykes Bertha I D of W, 6; Kirk, Ora Ethel D of W, 2

12153 DOWNING, William H Chelsea, OK, 30; Lewis W, S, 6; Anna L D, 4

21791 DRAGGER, John, Welling, OK, 20

5780 DRAGGER, Lewis Dragger, OK, 50; 26083 Nellie, W, 38

8103 DRAGIN, Geo, Oaks, OK, 78; 8104 Lina, W, 65

2916 DRAKE Dora M Big Cabin, OK, 29; Nettie F D, 10; Delia M D, 7; William J, S, 5; James F, S, 5; Mary A. M D, 2; Nora M. C D, ¼

35539 DRAKE, Emeline, Sallisaw, OK, 38; Emma E, D,13; Raymond P, S, 6; Seymour B, S, 2

3077 DRAKE, Emily J Chelsea, OK, 60

25346 DRAKE, Nannie E Chelsea, OK, 18

5175 DRAKE, Rachel C, Muskogee, OK, 36 Box 674

8914 DREADFULWATER, Ned, Locust Grove, OK, 17; 6056 Annie, W, 23; John, S, 4; Charles, S, 1

2748 DREADFULWATER, Henry, Gideon, OK, 55; John, S, 18

8865½ DREADFULWATER, John, Locust Grove, OK, 47; 8272 Nakie, W, 56

2748 DREADFULWATER, Peggy, Gideon, OK, 74 [Died 10-1906] By her son, Henry Dreadfulwater.

8865 DREADFULWATER, Wilson, Locust Grove, OK, 25; 2939 Sarah, W, 37; 8865 Andrew, S, 15; Nancy D, 13; Willie, S, 5; Joel, S, 3

13022 DREW, George, Pueblo CO, 34; Eugene H, S, 10; Richard E, S, 7; Eunis P D, 4

8011 DREW, Jamia Chanute, KS, 22

13455 DREW, Jesse B, Fairview, OK, 35; Pauline D, 10; Nena D, 9

12446 DREW, William H Chanute, KS, 63

8993 DREW, Mollie E, Ft. Gibson, OK, 48; John T, Jr, S, 20; James M, S, 13; Mary E D, 11

8012 DREW, Ruby Chanute, KS, 22

29664 DREW, Sarah E, Ft. Gibson, OK, 23

11492 DREW, William P, Muskogee, OK, 26

Key: **Guion Miller Application Number; Name; Address, Relation (to Head); Age in 1906**

[DRINKER, Jennie. See #12921]   *(Note: entry separate from other family groups)*

4302 DRUM, Groundhog, Peggs, OK, 25
22221 DRY Agnes, Oaks, OK, 14   By C.E. Holderman, Gdn.
1505 DRY Barker, Oaks, OK, 17   By Lizzie Stover, Gdn.
24898 DRY Daisy, Fairland, OK, 25; Robert L. S, 2; John Everett, S, 4; Floyd Albert, S, 6
22220 DRY, John, Oaks, OK, 12   By C. E. Holderman, Gdn.
7557 DRY, Phillip, Hulbert, OK, 47; Darkie, W, 39; Jumper, S, 12; Lydia D, 7; Scraper D, 5; Gu-you-chie D, 2
722 DRY, Samuel, Kansas, OK, 37; 1188 Charlotte, W, 28; Mary D, 9; Elia, S, 7; Jim, S, 1; Lucy D, 3
9441 DRY, Tom or Hunter, Oaks, OK, 38; 9442 Celia, W, 35; Susie D, 14; Steve, S, 12; Johnson, S, 11; Will, S, 1
22219 DRY, Walter, Oaks, OK, 11   By C.E. Holderman, Gdn.
3663 DRYWATER, George Bunch, Rose, OK, 43; 4697 Susanna, W, 28; 3663 Chu-nee-qua-le-skee, S, 4; Dick, S, 2
14292 DRYWATER, Jesse, Locust Grove, OK, 55; 14290 Lila, W, 26
14694 DRYWATER, Jesse, Tahlequah, OK, 21
540 DRYWATER, John, Oaks, OK, 63
14211 DRYWATER, Lucy, Sallisaw, OK, 22
11847 DRYWATER, Mink, Oaks, OK, 35; 9663 Elsie, W, 39; Oo-gher-we-yu, S, 7; Marie D, 16
5783 DRYWATER, Nancy, Rose, OK, 57
6475 DRYWATER, Samuel, Locust Grove, OK, 34
16561 Jennie, W, 33; Jesse, S, 12; Susie D, 7
5532 DuBOIS, Nancy J, Tahlequah, OK, 42; Osage, Eben E, S, 16; Mary E D, 11
479 DuBOIS, William R, Grove, OK, 17; Susan M, Sis, 15   By Jacob Dubois.
5802 DUCK, George, Stilwell, OK, 35; 2266 Lydia, W, 30; 5802 Tim, S, 16; Rachel D, 14; Frank, S, ¼; Adair, Mack, S of W, 14; Chukerlate, John, S of W, 6 Robert, S of W, 2
2506 DUCK, Jennie, Evansville AR, 27; Satarni D, 8; Charley, S, 6; Nick, S, 4; Tom, S, 2
2505 DUCK, Jesse, Evansville AR, 51; 13357 Willie, S, 19
261 DUCK, John Claremore, OK, 36; Ola D, 2
15959 DUCK, John, Wauhillau, OK, 22
35582 DUCK, Levi, Stilwell, OK, 20
1931 DUCK, Lucy, Evansville AR, 56

[DUCK, Mary. See #28604] *(Note: entry separate from other family groups)*

2488 DUCK, Nancy, Evansville AR, 25; Lizzie D, 4; Davis, S, 1
3882 DUCK, Nancy, Spavinaw, OK, 58; Ellis, Susie, GD, 5

Key: Guion Miller Application Number; Name; Address, Relation (to Head); Age in 1906

9008 DUCK, Nancy, Locust Grove, OK, 50

43212 DUCK, Nancy, Oaks, OK, 22; Nellie D, 1

14289 DUCK, Neppie, Locust Grove, OK, 19

13300 DUCK, Susie, Locust Grove, OK, 46

2508 DUCK, Yose, Evansville AR, 22

890 DUCUAH, Polly Bartlesville, OK, 17

22648 DUDLEY, Mollie E, Westville, OK, 36; Fannie B D, 17; Floyd F, S, 15; Maggie M D, 11; Mamie G D, 6; Nina D, 4

23157 DUDLEY, Nannie L, Stilwell, OK, 28; William C, S, 7; Richard E, S, 5; Mattie E D, 4; Edith M D, 1

9689 DUDLEY, Phoeby, Stilwell, OK, 25; Hazel D, 2

9013 DUFF, Virginia C, Wauhillau, OK, 44; Bettie D, 17; Jennie B D, 13; Linnie D, 10

33936 DUFFIELD Annie, Moodys, OK, 35; George, S, 15; William H, S, 13; Eli, S, 8; Leroy, S, ¼

9314 DUFFIELD, Everet, Inola, OK, 9;   By Geo. Duffield, Gdn.

9315 DUFFIELD, Thomas, Inola, OK, 7;   By Geo. Duffield, Gdn.

9313 DUFFIELD, Wallace, Inola, OK, 13;   By Geo. Duffield, Gdn.

5553 DUGGER, Polly, Lometa, OK, 24; William, S, 7; Daisy D D, 5; Bessie E D, 2

[DUGGER, Samuel E. See #12423]   *(Note: entry separate from other family groups)*

25873 DUKE Alice A, San Antonio, TX, 23 R.F.D. #9 Box #59

25945 DUKE Andrew O Dallas, TX, 28 309 Flora St.

25872 DUKE Caroline M, San Antonio, TX, R.F.D. #9 Box #59 27

25874 DUKE, Oliver C, San Antonio, TX, 22 R.F.D. #9 Box #59; Nora D, 1

11719 DUKE, William, San Antonio, TX, 58 R.F.D. #6 Box #3; Mahala E D, 18; Jesse Bowen, S, 16; William H, S, 14; Robert E, S, 11; Buford A, S, 8

44512 DUKES Beulah Choteau, OK, 5   By Richard Dukes, Gdn.

10298 DUKES, Hooley B Choteau, OK, 14   By Richard Dukes, Gdn.

34944 DUNAGAN Cicero S, Porum, OK, 30

12915 DUNAGAN, Georgia Ann, Porum, OK, 58

34945 DUNAGAN, James B, Porum, OK, 14   By Cicero S. Dunagan, Gdn.

34946 DUNAGAN, Lula, Porum, OK, 18

34947 DUNAGAN, Mary O, Porum, OK, 24

1487 DUNAWAY, Eliza J, Estella, OK, 25

[DUNCAN Annie. See #35537]   *(Note: entry separate from other family groups)*

26544 DUNCAN Charles Cleora, OK, 20; 22840 Rosa, W, 18; Thelma Marie D, 5/12

44104 DUNCAN Charley Braggs, OK, 33; Janie D, 11; Annie D, 5; Charley, S, 3; Rosevelt[sic], S, 1

5871 DUNCAN Claud E, Tahlequah, OK, 25

Key: Guion Miller Application Number; Name; Address, Relation (to Head); Age in 1906

25628 DUNCAN Clint Baron, OK, 23

10787 DUNCAN, Elizabeth S, Tahlequah, OK, 74

13069 DUNCAN, Fred B Chetopa, KS, 32; Inola Josephine D, 1

17101 DUNCAN, James, Texanna, OK, 19; Maggie, Sis, 16; Lou, Sis, 13; Johnson Bro, 11; By John Bigby, Gdn..

  341 DUNCAN, James D Blunt, OK, 45; Franky M, S, 17; Lovey N D, 14; Luther S, S, 12; Olivet M D, 4; Martha M C, 2

3048 DUNCAN, James N, Fairland, OK, 27; Herman, S, 3; Oran W, S, 4

  969 DUNCAN, James R, Echo, OK, 77

16738 DUNCAN, James W, Tahlequah, OK, 45; 8289 Lucinda B, W, 27; 16738 Vera S, D, 9; L. Buffington, S, 5; Mary Nettie D, 2

31373 DUNCAN, John, Stilwell, OK, 24

29773 DUNCAN, John C, Ochelata, OK, 46

  6693 DUNCAN, John R, Tahlequah, OK, 28

31372 DUNCAN, Joseph, Stilwell, OK, 26; 32746 Nancy, W, 29; 31372 Leona D, 6; Peona, D, 4; Lena D, 1

  4023 DUNCAN, Joshua L Bluejacket, OK, 42; 29135 Charlotte P D, 19; Dellen R D, 15; Charles T, S, 13; Lucy E D, 7

  3241 DUNCAN, Lizzie Baron, OK, 44; 25630 Cleo D D, 19; 3241 Felix, S, 9; Josie, D, 5

  8696 DUNCAN, Lucy A Afton, OK, 59

  354 DUNCAN, Marion, Sallisaw, OK, 56; George, S, 17

  357 DUNCAN, Martha Blunt, OK, 69

15986 DUNCAN, Martha, Pryor Creek, OK, 26; Andrew, S, 12; Thomas, S, 11; Sarah L D, 9; Samuel G, S, 7; Eva M D, 5; Charles D, S, 3; William F, S, ¾

25629 DUNCAN, Mary Baron, OK, 23; Vemen, S, 5

13070 DUNCAN, Mary N, Vinita, OK, 33

  1910 DUNCAN, Narcissus Chetopa, KS, 46; Luther L, S, 19; 23308 Kate L D, 17; Louie E, S, 15; Alva R D, 13; Neoma I D, 10

31374 DUNCAN, Nathaniel, Stilwell, OK, 21

  3050 DUNCAN, Nolan L, Fairland, OK, 22

  3049 DUNCAN, Oran A, Fairland, OK, 25

  1360 DUNCAN, Sarah A Afton, OK, 66

  7708 DUNCAN, Susie E, Rose, OK, 32; Ellis C, S, 16; Robert S, S, 14; Cathleen N D, 12; Albert C, S, 10; Walter A, S, 7; Johnnie M, S, 4; Charles D, S, 1

11980 DUNCAN, Taylor, Stilwell, OK, 52; 31191 Lydia, W, 46; 11980 Hubert, S, 19; Sallie, D, 17; Emma D, 15; Annie D, 13; Felix, S, 11; Charlie, S, 9

  7436 DUNCAN, Walter E, Tahlequah, OK, 26

16111 DUNCAN, Walter T, Edna, KS, 40; Ethel D, 13; Geneva D, 9; Ruth D, 3

23285 DUNHAM Charles A, Summit, OK, 24

23292 DUNHAM, James W, Muskogee, OK, 30

23294 DUNHAM, John W, Summit, OK, 25

23293 DUNHAM, Marcus L, Summit, OK

Key: Guion Miller Application Number; Name; Address, Relation (to Head); Age in 1906

23286 DUNHAM, May, Summit, OK, 20

83 DUNHAM, Muggie M, Locust Grove, OK, 22; Vann, S, 5; Addie E D, 3; William Albert, S, ¼

3919 DUNHAM, Susan, Summit, OK, 56

23291 DUNHAM, William H, Summit, OK, 32

3047 DUNIPHIN, Ellen F, Fairland, OK, 29; David N, S, 11; May E D, 5; Marion A D, 4; Samantha J D, 1

31793 DUNN Amanda, Maple, OK, 47

19085 DUNN, Lizzie, Skiatook, OK, 25 [Dead]

[DUNN, Mairn P with Nancy Frasher. See #6539] ⎱ *(Note: entries separate*
[DUNN, Ellen with Nancy Frasher. See #6539] ⎰ *from other family groups)*

2478 DUPREE Charlotte B, Vinita, OK, 84

23757 DUPREE, Elmer, Vinita, OK, 24

23771 DUPREE, Emma, Vinita, OK, 18

26473 DUPREE, Maud Effie, Vinita, OK, 41

23772 DUPREE, William E, Vinita, OK, 50; Herbert, S, 20; Wright, S, 17; Elizabeth D, 15; Fred, S, 12; Ann D, 8; Elise D, 3

1063 DURALL Ada, Welch, OK, 27; Harold, S, 8; Hugh A, S, 4; Geo. M, S, 1

11610 DURALL, Edna Earl, Welch, OK, 26; Benoni F, S, 8; George R, S, 6

16665 DUVAL Benjamin, Vian, OK, 28; 23327 Alice, W, 26; Richard, S, 5; Mack, S, 2; Coleman, S, 1

3866 DUVALL, Samuel, Sallisaw, OK, 35; 1453 Linda, W, 29; 3866 Logan, S, 3; 1453 Leaf, Mary D of W,

9788 DUVAL, William, Vian, OK, 32; Tom, S, 7

27239 DYER, Elizabeth, Hanson, OK, 36; J. Blair, S, 3; Sill Word, S, 1

5010 DYKES Arabella , Tahlequah, OK, 40; Bunk, S, 16; David A, S, 12; Toney R, S, 10; Walter V, S, 8; Rocksey B D, 6; Henry J, S, 4

[DYKES, Katie. See #21987] ⎱ *(Note: entries separate*
[DYKES Bud. See #21987] ⎰ *from other family groups)*

23985 DYKES, Lou E Chelsea, OK, 26; Julius O, S, 10; Chester J, S, 5

29685 DYKES, Nettie C, Tahlequah, OK, 18

6279 EADES, Penelope Bunch, OK, 29; Emmet, S, 5/6

[EAGLE Adam. See #3870]   *(Note: entry separate from other family groups)*

[EAGLE Annie. See #23423]   *(Note: entry separate from other family groups)*

11924 EAGLE, Ida, Stilwell, OK, 37; Josiah, S, 13; William, S, 5

Key: Guion Miller Application Number; Name; Address, Relation (to Head); Age in 1906

[EAGLE, Israel. See #16763] ⎤   *(Note: entries separate*
[EAGLE, Jennie. See #16763] ⎦   *from other family groups)*

[EAGLE, John. See #5508] (Deceased 3-'07)
        (Note: entry separate from other family groups)

1996 EAGLE, Malinda, Long, OK, 35; Rogers, Jack, S, 15; Austin, Lizzie D, 12; Minnie D, 11; Josie D, 8; Willie, S, 6

16767 EAGLE, Rufus, Muldrow, OK, 36; 41529 Caroline, W, 26; Betsy K D, 10; Kee-Kee, D, 4; Henry, S, 6; Charlie, S, 2 [Appl. Died 3-1907]

6247 EAGLE, William Bunch, OK, 38; 6246 Peggie, W, 50; Ida D, 15; George S, 14

4342 EARBOB, George, Locust Grove, OK, 26; 1001 Takey, W, 41; 10320 Tee Hee, Peggy, D of W, 19; 10370 Jesse, S of W, 20; 10371 Charlie, S of W, 14; 4342 Earbob, Nancy D, 10; Mary D, 5

14200 EARBOB, Nancy Choteau, OK, 11   By Dakey Earbob, Gdn.

30527 EARBY, Martha, Foyil, OK: 44; Dora D, 20; John W, S, 19; Mollie A D, 17; Mattie L, D, 13; Robert R, S, 11; Ida B D, 8; Mollie D, 6; Dovie D, 2

5242 EARNEST, Ellen, Fayetteville, AR, 45; 627 Leverett St; Lee Roy, S,18; Albert N, S, 16

29044 EARP Cynthia, Row, OK, 22 [Dec'd.]; John L, S, 2;   By R.L. Earp, Gdn.

25022 EARP, Maggie M Cherokee City AR,   21; Jay R, S, 2; William J, S, ¼

26541 EARP, Minnie L Bartlesville, OK, 21; 35127 Joe, S, 6; Mattie D, 2; Hattie D, 2

26361 EARP, Priscilla, Maysville AR, 24; Cora D, 5; Oscar L, S, 3

6467 EASKY, Caleb, Evansville AR, 44; 6032 Patsey, W, 35; Edward, S, 17; Joseph, S, 14; Lulu D, 13; Andy, S, 12; Billie, S, 8; Jim, S, 4; John Ann, S, 1/6

27672 EASKY, Lenora, Tahlequah, OK, 20

20192 EASKY, Lula, Leach, OK, 14; 20190 Eli Bro, 16;   By Margaret C, Grider, Gdn.

17277 EASKY, Mary, Evansville AR, 78

1335 EATON, Ellis M Claremore, OK, 45; 23778 Lelia D, 19; Richard E, S, 16; William S, 13; Edgar W, S, 7

[EATON, John E. See #27389]   *(Note: entry separate from other family groups)*

[EATON, Rose. See #9293] ⎤   *(Note: entries separate*
[EATON, John. See #9293] ⎬   *from other family groups)*
[EATON, James. See #9293] ⎦

10928 EATON, Walter R Claremore,. OK, 38; Mary E D, 10; Raleigh, S, 8; Frank, S, 5

19635 ECKERT, Louisa Jane, Warner, OK, 33; Lula E D, 10; Lydia F D, 6; Lillie May D, 4; Sarah Jane D, 1

9293 EDEN, Rosie Cove, OK, 23; John, S, 8; James, S, 6

Key: Guion Miller Application Number; Name; Address, Relation (to Head); Age in 1906

2296 EDENS, FRANCES R, Needmore, OK, 36

1400 EDENS, Nancy, Wann, OK, 33; Rena D, 5; George W, S, 3; Eloise D D, 1/12

16429 EDINGTON, Isabel May, McLain, OK, 4   By Joseph R. Eddington[sic], Gdn.

33370 EDMINSTON, Elsie D Baron, OK, 4   By Edward Walkingstick, Gdn.

29388 EDMONDS, Ella Jay, Southwest City, MO, 21

26688 EDMONDSON Beulah Benton, Maysville, AR, 22

837 EDMONDSON, Florence E, Maysville, AR, 46

31514 EDMONDSON, James T, Maysville, AR, 29; 31459 Julia A, W, 31; A.Vann, S, 7; Hugh A, S,, 5/12

4278 EDMONDSON, Lula, Pryor Creek, OK, 42; Estella O D, 17; Kate D D, 10; Laura H, D, 13

3293 EDMONDSON, Nancy M, Maysville, AR, 68

404 EDWARDS, Lucy I, Oglesby, OK, 33; Stark, Mattie S D, 13

27241 EDWARDS, Winona, Porum, OK, 28

40058 EGGLESON, Julia, Pryor Creek, OK, 38; Omer, S, 18; Noah, S, 13; Zora D, 15; Josia, S, 11; Nellie D, 9; Dewey, S, 7; Callie D, 5; Mamie D, 3; Lola D, 1

25073 EIFFERT Cecil E, Ft. Gibson, OK, 32

25072 EIFERT, Henry, Jr, Ft. Gibson, OK, 23

2175 EIFFERT, Washington Henry, Ft. Gibson, OK, 57; Sallie May D, 14

24785 ELAM, Lillie Chelsea, OK, 24; Clara E D, 5; James R, S, 3; Cora B D, 1

9464 ELDERS Alice Braggs, OK, 39; William, S, 10; George, S, 9; Thomas, S, 6; Charlie, S, 2

31389 ELDRIGE Alfred, Pryor Creek, OK, 16   By Mary Brown, Gdn.

30119 ELDRIDGE Andrew, Pryor Creek, OK, 22

34459 ELDRIDGE, Harold E, Sageeyah, OK, 3 By Hulda E. Stockton, Gdn.

32436 ELDRIDGE, Martin B Claremore, OK, 26

17743 ELDRIDGE, Taylor, Tiawah, OK, 24; 30115 Jessie B, W, 19

317 ELDRIDGE, William J, Oolagah, OK, 28; Mabel C D, 5; Jewel D D, 1

18631 ELDRIDGE, William J, Pawpaw, OK, 21

7879 ELE, James G Coffeyville, KS, 14   By J.N. Ele, Gdn.

9817 ELK or ELEX, William, Tahlequah, OK, 54; 29997 Sarah, W, 20

16699 ELGIN Astor C, Sallisaw, OK, 12   By W. T. Kelleare, Gdn.

4405 ELI Annie, Stilwell, OK, 29

14320 ELI, Tom, Evansville AR, 38; 2483, Lydia, W, 48; George, S, 14; Sallie D, 10; Jemmea D, 8

9368 ELK Chinkie, Vian, OK, 37

12415 ELK, Lizzie Cookson, OK, 52

12628 ELK, Nannie, Sallisaw, OK, 25; Willie, S, ¼

[ELK, William. See #9817]   *(Note: entry separate from other family groups)*

17402 ELKINS, Kate, Marble City, OK, 25; Jim, S, 8; Nora May D, 4; Gladis D, 2

5317 ELKINS, Margaret, Westville, OK, 43

26134 COSTEN Cassie B D, 19; 26133 Edna B D, 17; Robert, S, 15; Samuel H, S, 14; William T, S, 12; Meredith C, S, 11; Elizabeth L D, 9; Eula W D, 7

[ELLEDGE, Roy P. See #6459]   *(Note: entries separate*
[ELLEDGE Cena B. See #6459]   *from other family groups)*

10584 ELLICK, Jim, Southwest City, MO, 56; 10585, Nellie, W, 55; Polly D, 19; 26064, Coon, S, 18; 15085, Johnson, S, 14
26062 ELLICK, Lyda Chloeta, OK, 25; Buck, S, 3
15874 ELLINGTON, Nettie, Wagoner, OK, 24; Elmo, S, 4; Marie D, 2
29116 ELLIOTT Ben T, Pryor Creek, OK, 24; Ralph, S, 1
17511 ELLIOTT Cordelia, Tulsa, OK, 18
11789 ELLIOTT David I, Pryor Creek, OK, 53
17614 ELLIOTT, Henry A Collinsville, OK, 21
  1396 ELLIOTT, Hiram Big Cabin, OK, 48; Hiram, Jr, S, 14; Samuel, S, 12; Vera M D, 10; Lucullus, S, 7; Lucien B, S, 5; Ruth D, 1
  2993 ELLIOTT, James E Adair, OK, 31, Sadie M D, 3
29115 ELIOTT[sic], James T, Trawick, TX, 25
11784 ELLIOTT, James W, Pinehill, TX, 49; Mollie V D, 18; David I, S, 14; Emma H D, 10; Fannie M D, 5; John H, S, 1
17631 ELLIOTT, Jessie M, Pensacola, OK, 14   By O.P. Showers, Gdn.
18888 ELLIOTT, John, Kismet, MT, 33
  4446 ELLIOTT, Katie, Muskogee, OK, 25; Winfield S, S, 4; Francis Lee, S, 3
11786 ELLIOTT, Riley, Pryor Creek, OK, 16; Addie, Sis, 10   By Lizzie Griffin, Gdn.
  5701 ELLIOTT, Robert, Muskogee, OK, 34; Robert, Jr, S, 7; George, S, 5; William, S, 2
  5920 ELLIOTT, Sabra E Bartlett, KS, 23
21618 ELLIOTT, Walter L Coffeyville, KS, 23
11787 ELLIOTT, William T, Pryor Creek, OK, 20
  3085 ELLIS Charley, Locust Grove, OK, 34; 2936, Sallie, W, 34; 3086, Ga-ga-nee, S, 9; Elizie D, 5; 2936, Stealer, Jimmie, S of W, 13; Lizzie D of W, 11; Sara D of W, 9
25292 ELLIS, George, Sallisaw, OK, 24

[ELLIS, Harvey N. with Josephine McAllister. See #25658]
                    (Note: entry separate from other family groups)

  8861 ELLIS, Jackson W, Muskogee, OK, 47; Charlotte D, 16; Nellie D, 12; Jackson N, S, 10; Dick, S, 8; Blair, S, 6
11649 ELLIS, Mary J Centralia, OK, 29
26130 ELLIS, Mary M, Echelata, OK, 22; Gladys W D, 1

[ELLIS, Minnie. See #4051]   *(Note: entry separate from other family groups)*

Key: Guion Miller Application Number; Name; Address, Relation (to Head); Age in 1906

8112 ELLIS, Mitchel, Sallisaw, OK, 51; Henry, S, 16; Robert R, S, 11; Mitchel, Jr, S, 9; Clara D, 6; Nathaniel B, S, 4

23502 ELLIS, Nannie E, Westville, OK, 29; Arthur T, S, 10; Walter C, S, 8; Ernest C, S, 5; Gracie L D, 3; Maggie F D, 2

[ELLIS, Susie with Nancy Duck. See #3882]

(Note: entry separate from other family groups)

9125 ELLISON, Ida Blunt, OK, 16;   Minnie V D, 1/12

1455 ELMORE Armstrong Brent, OK, 31; Nancy D, 11; Gracie D, 1/12

9262 E-LOW-EE, Jennie Campbell, OK, 88;   By Linda Crapo, Gdn.

27533 ELROD Cora E, Siloam Springs AR, 20; Russel C, S, 3

23762 ELY, Mary Ellen Coodys Bluff, OK, 22; Goldie D, 5

1653 EMERSON, Louisa H Decatur, TX, 54

10331 ENGLAND Annie, Locust Grove, OK,   24

15925 ENGLAND Bessie, Muskogee, OK, 23

16648 ENGLAND Charles Baron, OK, 29; 1783, Mary, W, 18

4154 ENGLAND Charlotte Baron, OK, 14   By Lincoln England, Gdn.

9212 ENGLAND Dave, Southwest City, MO, 29

4401 ENGLAND Dora, Stilwell, OK, 28; Robert, S, 8; Killie, S, 4; Elick, S, 2

27817 ENGLAND, George, Stilwell, OK, 22

4103 ENGLAND, George W, Grove, OK, 31; Flossie M D, 7; Lurie B D, 5; Georgie D, 2

10329 ENGLAND, Himon, Locust Grove, OK,   26; 4300, Ada, W, 21; Downing, Tommie, S of W, 3; Robison Della Edna D of W, 1

24097 ENGLAND, Joe C Chelsea, OK, 21

1048 ENGLAND, John, Fairland, OK, 25; Harmon, S, 5; Beulah L D, 1

3052 ENGLAND, John Chelsea, OK, 44; 4529, Belle, W, 40; Elvie D, 16; Beulah D, 15; Bennie, S, 12; Emma D 10; McGlarthin, S, 8; Mattie D, 6; John R, S, 1/6

3554 ENGLAND, Joseph M, Grove OK, 36; 22753, Sarah, W, 26; William L, S, 8; Virgil, S, 5; Pauline D, 4; Dudley, S, 3; Henry, S, 1

4490 ENGLAND, Killey, Stilwell, OK, 24; Ida May D,, 3; Mitchel, S, 1; Daisy D, 1

11017 ENGLAND, Levena Baron, OK, 19

4152 ENGLAND, Lincoln Baron, OK, 58; 4715, Eliza, W, 30

4609 ENGLAND, Martin, Southwest City, MO, 29

1046 ENGLAND, Maud M, Fairland, OK, 23; Opal V D, 2

4942 ENGLAND, Ollie, Stilwell, OK, 56

15633 ENGLAND, Permilia Baron, OK, 18

329 ENGLAND, Sally Dodge, OK, 71

515 ENGLAND, Samuel, Locust Grove, OK, 56; 10330, Madie D, 20

12491 ENGLAND, Samuel Afton, OK, 18; By R.L. England, Gdn.

24592 ENGLAND, Susan M Adair, OK, 27; Fred, S, 8; Pauline D, 5; Doc H, S, 2

12492 ENGLAND, Susie Lee Afton, OK, 15;   By R. L. England, Gdn.

Key: Guion Miller Application Number; Name; Address, Relation (to Head); Age in 1906

2934 ENGLAND, Tillman, Locust Grove, OK, 34; 10217, Mary, W, 33; Mattie E D, 14; James T, S, 12; Claude W, S, 8; Cullus M, S, 4; Myrtle V D, 2

10155 ENGLAND, Wash, Southwest City, MO, 45; 4873, Catie, W, 52; Pigeon, S, 16; Study, John, S of W, 20; England Betsy D, 14; Andrew, S, 10; John, S, 8

4710 ENGLAND, William, Stilwell, OK, 30; 30614, Nancy, W, 24; Lyd-da D, 8; Mary D, 2

17415 ENGLAND, William W Afton, OK, 22; 37544, Narcissa, W, 19

23262 ENGLISH, Saline T, Tip, OK, 20

16970 ENGLAND, Wilson, Southwest City, MO, 22

24722 ENYART, Florence B, Sallisaw, OK, 20

27402 EPPERSON Bettie Rex, OK, 24; Willie C, S, 3; Lowern F, S, 1

31395 EPPERSON Dora M Big Cabin, OK,   26; Arthur R, S, 1

23131 ERVIN Allie B Afton, OK, 20; Eva E D, 5/6

30674 ERWIN Charles G Chelsea, OK, 34; Mary Q D, 8

9256 ESAW, Mary, Melvin, OK, 29; Heavy, S, 11; Maggie, D, 9; Leachum,S, 5; Season, S, 1

13557 ESLINGER, Emma, Peggs, OK, 18

23630 ESSEX Addie B Chelsea, OK, 32; Cole C, S, 13; Susie I D, 8; John S, S, 6; Paul R, S, 3

3651 ESTES, Sarah Choteau, OK, 22; Bertha L D, 1

1596 ETHRIDGE Artemiza Claremore, OK,   56; John, S, 16

8115 ETTER, Lizzie Bigheart, OK, 33; Lenard[sic] A, S, 8

3041 ETTER, Sarah V, Evansville AR, 43

29633 EUBANKS, Margaret, Stilwell, OK, 16

4481 EUBANKS, William, Tahlequah, OK, 65; 4480, Eliza C, W, 52; Samuel V, S, 20

2860 EVANS Annie, Kansas, OK, 49; Ratcliff, Ella D, 15; Gregory, Lawrence, S, 11

5008 EVANS Catherine, Keefeton, OK, 36

28030 EVANS, Effie M Claremore, OK, 24

28890 EVANS, Florence S, Lometa, OK, 35; Lennon, Florence C D, 8; John E. E, S, 7; Evans, Mary D, 1; Mark P, S, 1/12

385 EVANS, James P Claremore, OK, 28

1726 EVANS, Martha I, Fairland, OK, 64

12403 EVANS, Robert H Cookson, OK, 26; 12404, Elizabeth, W, 26; Katie, M D, 5/6

1951 EVANS, Ruth B, Tulsa, OK, 37; Ross Bettie D of W, 17; Evans, Mattie D, 11; Henry, S, 8; Albert Lee, S, 4

2714 EVANS, Susan Centralia, OK, 46

13716 EVANS, Walter N, Jr Cookson, OK, 12

[EVERS Arvin B with Zora W Kessler. See #24150] ⎤   *(Note: entries separate*
[EVERS, Jesse B with Zora W Kessler. See #24150] ⎦   *from other family groups)*

3872 EVERSOLE Dave Bunch, OK, 38; 3869, Lulu, W, 38

17684 EVERSOLE, Rosella, Gans, OK, 25; Teague, Myrtle D of W, 7

Key: Guion Miller Application Number; Name; Address, Relation (to Head); Age in 1906

22876 EWERS, Emmett Centralia, OK, 31; Charles E, S, 9; Veva Lee, S, 1
 2400 EWERS, Geo W, Hollow, OK, 42; Maland E, S, 8; Tams Bixby, S, 5; Charles, S, 3; Alice May D, 2; Ethel M D, 2; George P, S, 7/12
 9160 EWERS, Ida H Centralia, OK, 53; William A, S, 19
22877 EWERS, John T Centralia, OK, 29; Yuba D D, 6; Roscoe G, S, 2
 6066 EXSTINE[sic], Melvina, Hulbert, OK, 52

22952 FAIN Charlotte, Owassa, OK, 30; Stella W D, 1
18534 FAIR Dora, Pryor Creek, OK, 13; Jacob Bro, 12   By Lewis K, Fair, OK
 833 FAIR, Rena Ross, Pryor Creek, OK, 50
21032 FAIR, Sarah, Pryor Creek, OK, 34; Clyde, S, 2; Dolen, Ida May D of W, 8; Clarry M, D of W, 14
 946 FALLEN, Jess Collinsville, OK, 53; 884, Lucinda, W, 47
17799 FALLEN, Malinda, Wann, OK, 32; Nannie D, 12; Sarah D, 9; Susie D, 7; May Bell, D, 5; Ellie D, ¼
 1907 FALLING Blossom, Eucha, OK, 43; Johnson, S, 13; Sapsucker, S, 10
42982 FALLING Calvin E, Foyil, OK, 28; 13063, Jennie, W, 22;   George, S, 1

[FALLING Car-na-noo-lis-kie. See #24698]
(Note: entry separate from other family groups)

 988 FALLING Charley Claremore, OK, 29
 7913 FALLING, Henry, Estella, OK, 49 [Deceased.]; Freddie, S, 17; Maggie D, 15; Viola, D, 9; Lilard D, 6; Gilben, S, 3; Henry, S, 1;   By Lizzie Falling, Gdn.
 27 FALLING, Jack Claremore, OK, 52; 1721, Nancy, W, 46 [Deceased]; Lizzie D, 8; Jennie D, 4; Jesse, S, 2; Raincrow, Susie D of W, 11
10421 FALLING, Jim, Spavinaw, OK, 34; 17279, Quaity, W, 23; Laura D, 8
 989 FALLING, John Collinsville, OK, 31; 5142, Delilah, W, 24; Delia R D, 5
11257 FALLING, Johnson, Vinita, OK, 52; 2154, Mary, W, 49
13257 FALLING, Nick, Spavinaw, OK, 29; 10646, Onie, W, 26; Katie D, 6; John, S, 3; Joe, S, 5/12
11627 FALLING, Rider, Spavinaw, OK, 64

[FALLINGPOT Betsy. See #87] (Dec'd.)
(Note: entry separate from other family groups)

 662 FALLINGPOT, Grant, Eucha, OK, 36; Maudie D, 5; Lacy D, 1
31787 FARBRO, Sadie Coodys Bluff, OK, 24; Clell E, S, 5
23581 FARGO, Benj. F, Muldrow, OK, 29; May E D, 3; Benjamin E, S, 1
 917 FARGO,Charles A, Muldrow, OK, 62; Pearl, D, 12; Edna, D, 10; Mable, D, 7; Ina, D,4
25284 FARGO Chas A, Jr, Gans, OK, 32; May Narcissa D, 11; Clarence A, S, 6; Joe W, S, 3

CHEROKEE DESCENDANTS RESIDING WEST OF MISSISSIPPI RIVER.
VOLUME II   (A – M)

1624 FARGO Cora H, Muldrow, OK, 24

9182 FARGO Delilah, Muldrow, OK, 46

22958 FARGO, Edward, Muldrow, OK, 22; 5094, Maud, W, 24

1621 FARGO, Joel B, Muldrow, OK, 16; 1622, Myrtle, Sis, 19; Walter Bro, 14; David Bro, 12;   By Delila Fargo, Gdn

1620 FARGO, Saladen A, Muldrow, OK, 33

1625 FARGO, William L, Muldrow, OK, 35; Olive D, 6; Murphy, S, 1/3

22743 FARLESS, Lillie M Catoosa, OK, 25; Maybelle D, 2; Frank, S, 1/12

26978 FARMER, Isabelle, Fawn, OK, 41; Grace L D, 19; Minnie M D, 13; Mintie D, 10; Georgia D, 7; Frankie O D, 3

[FARRAR, Oliver M with Wm H Scudder. See #888]

(Note: entry separate from other family groups)

23400 FARRAR, Sallie M, Talala, OK, 30; Jessie M D, 10; Bruce, S, 8

4487 FARRINGTON, Elizabeth V, Welch, OK, 28; Columbus, S, 5; Mary Belle D, 4; Abram, Jr, S, 6/12

23894 FAULKNER Benj. F Akins, OK, 33; Lelah B D, 12; John S, S, 7; Robert, S, 5

9455 FAULKNER Bertha L, Hanson, OK, 25

12894 FAULKNER David J Claremore, OK, 32; 12895, Jennie, W, 28; Janice M D, 5; Lavinah H D, 3; Frank F, S, 1

11599 FAULKNER David M, Hanson, OK, 64; 9458, Penelope A D, 17; Willie R, S, 3; Winnie L D, 3; Hastings M, S, 1

904 FAULKNER, Florence V, Muldrow, OK, 33; Allie L D, 1

9457 FAULKNER, Frank T, Hanson, OK, 34

25638 FAULKNER, George Akins, OK, 29

9456 FAULKNER, Henry I, Hanson, OK, 23; 30201, Della D, W, 20; James Fillman, S, 2

11553 FAULKNER, Jinnie, Wauhillau, OK, 43; John F, S, 17; Joseph H, S, 9; Jennie M D, 2

9902 FAULKNER, John W, Hanson, OK, 37

25639 FAULKNER, Walter Akins, OK, 27; Leroy F, S, 4; Alice R D, 2

20191 FAUSETT, Mamie, Leach, OK, 20; Florence D, 4

738 FAWLING, Geo W, Wann, OK, 51; Nannie D, 9; Sarah D, 7; Susie D, 5; Mable D, 2; Ellie D, 1

5296 FAY, Frederick A Chelsea, OK, 14;   By J.K. Clingan, Gdn.

7456 FEATHER Dave, Stilwell, OK, 33

14181 FEATHER, Ella, Locust Grove, OK, 21

42192 FEATHER, James, Stilwell, OK, 29

4189 FEATHER, Jennie, Locust Grove, OK, 26

4043 FEATHER, Jesse, Stilwell, OK, 70; 2281, Annie, W, 41; Sam, S, 15

7453 FEATHER, Joe, Stilwell, OK, 21

42200 FEATHER, Joseph, Stilwell, OK, 27; Grant, S, 4; Lydia D, 2

Key: Guion Miller Application Number; Name; Address, Relation (to Head); Age in 1906

[FEATHER, Lizzie. See #7035]   *(Note: entries separate*
[FEATHER, Mary. See #7035]   *from other family groups)*

[FEATHER, Margaret. See #13390]   *(Note: entry separate from other family groups)*

16897 FEATHER, Nancy, Marble City, OK, 54

[FEATHER, Polly. See #2298]   *(Note: entry separate from other family groups)*

1169 FEATHER, Sallie, Stilwell, OK, 67
8018 FEATHER, Skale, Stilwell, OK: 45; 2280, Jennie, W, 56; 42201, George, S, 20
6499 FEATHERHEAD, Mose, Southwest City, MO, 52; 6500, Linnie, W, 30; Ketcher, S, 7; 11968, Jeremiah, S, 16
3878 FEELING, James, Locust Grove, OK, 35; 2130, Annie, W, 29; Samuel, S, 6; Jeff, S, 2; Andrew, S, 1
4502 FEELING, Johnson, Spavinaw, OK, 49; 8900, Eva, W, 38; Susan D, 14; Mike, S, 6
2211 FEELING, Lewis, Kansas, OK, 34; 2210, Maria, W, 24; Adam, S, 5; Maud D, 1
11689 FEELING, Moses, Tahlequah, OK, 30; 10304, Rachel, W, 50
23129 FELTON, Georgia L Afton, OK, 33
10628 FENCE, George, Kansas, OK, 23; Dick, S, 1
18097 FENCE, George O Coffeyville, KS, 24
8044 FENCER Celie, Oaks, OK, 69
8041 FENCER Charley, Oaks, OK, 44; 9617, Fencer Carrie, W, 37; Betsy D, 13; William, S, 12; 8043, Daniel, George, S of W, 19
8040 FENCER, Jim, Oaks, OK, 34; Willie, S, 5; Jesse, S, 2; Nannie D, 3

[FENCER, Nancy. See #605] *(Note: entry separate from other family groups)*

10684 FENCER, Sam, Oaks, OK, 39; 10677, Polly, W, 25; Dick, S, 5; Gar-coo-s-der-dy, S, 3; Jesse, S, 1
9620 FENCER, Susie, Kansas, OK, 40; Youngbird, James, S, 18
2995 FERGUSON Allie E, Stilwell, OK, 43
9892 FERGUSON Annie, Stilwell, OK, 34; Callie D, 12; George, S, 9; Mamie D, 7; Ruth, D, 4; Cookson, S, 2
28488 FERGUSON, John W, Whitmire, OK,25
27132 FEUERSTINE, Rosa Coffeyville, KS, 28; Frank Leslie, S, 9
6518 FIELD, Thomas M Chetopa, KS, 42; Esther M D, 12; Luther T, S, 8; Denney P, S, 6
23103 FIELDER, Rosa E Chelsea, OK, 17
5659 FIELDING, George, Oaks, OK, 58
5032 FIELDING, Jennie, Southwest City, MO, 14;   By Waitie Old Kingfisher, Gdn.

Key: Guion Miller Application Number; Name; Address, Relation (to Head); Age in 1906

2170 FIELDS Albert Blue Jacket, OK, 36; Stella V D, 14; William H, S, 13; George M, S, 9; Lillie E D, 8; James E, S, 6; Chas M, S, 4; Viola D, 2; Jo, S, 1/12

25927 FIELDS Alice, Southwest City, MO, 20

5283 FIELDS Andrew J, Stilwell, OK, 41; John S, S, 13; Benjamin H, S,11; Clarence S, S, 7

3980 FIELDS Anna Campbell, OK, 55; Betsy D, 17

9470 FIELDS Anna E, Fairland, OK, 20

7699 FIELDS Aurelia, Muldrow, OK, 25

4689 FIELDS Benjamin F, Grove, OK, 36; 965, Louella, W, 33; Carey, Ruth D of W, 14; William Ross, S of W, 13; Joella D of W, 11; Ward, Louella D of W, 7

1971 FIELDS Bettie, Southwest City, MO, 45; Rufus, S, 18; Mary D, 16; Henry, S, 14; Lulu D, 11; Ray, S, 9; John, S, 6; Claud, S, 4

5088 FIELDS Calvin L, Warner, OK, 18; By S.J. Rogers, Gdn.

5961 FIELDS Caroline, Vinita, OK, 59

27973 FIELDS Charles Big Cabin, OK, 30

3637 FIELDS Charlotte E, Webbers Falls, OK, 72

5086 FIELDS Carnelius[sic] B, Warner, OK, 27; John T, S, 2

2168½ FIELDS, Edward Chetopa, KS, 16; By Nellie Fields, Gdn

14713 FIELDS, Elmer, Pryor Creek, OK, 20

810 FIELDS, Ezekiel Big Cabin, OK, 57; Ines L D, 6; Edna A D, 4; James E, S, 1

1394 FIELDS, Ezekiel, Southwest City, MO, 64

24135 FIELDS, Ezekiel, Jr Dodge, OK, 24; William, S, 2; Gladys May D, 1/12

27471 FIELDS, Freeman, Southwest City, MO, 31; William Edgar, S, 9; Ella M D, 6; Ethel, D, 4; Bertha D, 2

29462 FIELDS, George, Jr, Southwest City, MO, 24; 8921, Lulu J, W, 25

23339 FIELDS, George F Collinsville, OK, 25

1641 FIELDS, George W, Southwest City, MO, 67; 1868, Sarah, W, 52; 29659, Bertha D, 8; 1868, Jeff, S, 15; Minnie D, 13; Perry, S, 10

6443 FIELDS, Geo. W, Marble City, OK, 60; 5608, Martha J, W, 54; James F, S, 19; Charles H, S, 16; Mattie M D, 13

963 FIELDS, George W, Fairland, OK, 29

25348 FIELDS, Geo W, Jr, Marble City, OK, 21

4214 FIELDS, Henry Frank, Pryor Creek, OK, 30; Mabel D, 5; Owen, S, 2; Ollie D, 1/6

17507 FIELDS, James F, Webbers Falls, OK, 31

3670 FIELDS, James L, Salina, OK, 43; Henry R, S, 14; Rachel D, 11; Ruth D, 8; Cherokee R, S, 4

24180 FIELDS, James M, Fairland, OK, 26; Bertha G D, 8; Clyde E, S, 5; Freda M D, 1

5919 FIELDS, James W, Stilwell, OK, 20

29649 FIELDS, Joel Big Cabin, OK, 21

5391 FIELDS, John, Stilwell, OK, 46; 3868, Nannie, W, 46; Florence D, 16; Williams Delilah, M of W, 70

Key: Guion Miller Application Number; Name; Address, Relation (to Head); Age in 1906

16510 FIELDS, John R, Webbers Falls, OK, 33

6438 FIELDS, Johnson, Vinita, OK, 38; Victoria D, 15; George, S, 10; Rebecca D, 8

28721 FIELDS, Joseph A, Warner, OK, 20

9770 FIELDS, Kiowa R Campbell, OK, 15;   By J.W. Sosbee, Gdn.

22593 FIELDS, Louis, Talala, OK, 22

17015 FIELDS, Lucinda, Vian, OK, 20; Tema or Teemon D, 6; Tola or Telly D, 6; Fannie, D, 3; Ross, S, ¼

3303 FIELDS, Mathew, Estella, OK, 31; Ruby May D, 11; Lowie F, S, 10; Strausie Lee D, 6; Sylvia C D, 3; Mildred B D, 1

[FIELDS, Mike. See #15031]   *(Note: entry separate from other family groups)*

1631 FIELDS, Mollie, Texanna, OK, 32

1927 FIELDS, Mollie, Moodys, OK, 50

2481 FIELDS, Moses O Collinsville, OK, 39; John L, S, 11; James S, S, 9; Thelma D, ¼

33261 FIELDS, Ora, Pryor Creek, OK, 10;   By May Fields, Gdn.

[FIELDS, Patrick. See #15032]   *(Note: entry separate from other family groups)*

2064 FIELDS, Pleasant, Fairland, OK, 37

5085 FIELDS, Richard, Warner, OK, 9; 5089, Ada, Sis, 11; 5083, Ella E, Sis, 15; 5087, Rachel E, Sis, 13   By W. H. Stewart, Gdn.

5308 FIELDS, Richard, Stilwell, OK, 50

24142 FIELDS, Richard Dodge, OK, 33

31582 FIELDS, Richard, Locust Grove, OK, 21; 6974, Linda, W, 19

24136 FIELDS, Richard A Dodge, OK, 36; Arthur Earl, S, 11; Mable Pearl D, 2; Sherman P, S, 1/6

716 FIELDS, Richard M Dewey, OK, 53; 715, Texana, W, 41; Charles, S, 20; Wirt, S, 17; Jesse, S, 16; Prince, S, 12

9772 FIELDS, Robert B Campbell, OK, 24; George B Bro, 18

3735 FIELDS, Robert W, Tahlequah, OK, 30

2915 FIELDS, Sabra E, Grove, OK, 61

18145 FIELDS, Sam Braggs, OK, 51; 11491, Maggie, W, 35; Jim, S, 14; Jinsie D, 11; Betsy, D, 7; Nancy D, 4; Willie, S, 2

9147 FIELDS, Sam T Campbell, OK, 24

32851 FIELDS, Samuel, Southwest City, MO, 20

1365 FIELDS, Samuel I, Maysville AR, 68; Isa Cora D, 16

4483 FIELDS, Squirrel, Vian, OK, 59; 4210, Nannie, W, 35; James, S, 6; Charley, S, 2; Pearle D, 1; Blair, Lila D of W, 9

[FIELDS, Stella. See #15033]   *(Note: entry separate from other family groups)*

Key: Guion Miller Application Number; Name; Address, Relation (to Head); Age in 1906

11573 FIELDS, Susie M, Warner, OK, 3;   By John Hood, Gdn.

25829 FIELDS, Thomas J, Southwest City, MO, 28; Alva L, S, 7; Leslie Earl, S, 5; Edna I, D, 2

25843 FIELDS, Thomas J, Maysville AR, 22

[FIELDS, Thomas M And family. See #6518]
(Note: entry separate from other family groups)

7644 FIELDS, Thomas R Bovina, TX, 32; 9952, Ada W, W, 28; Clarence Ray, S, 7

811 FIELDS, Timothy, Grove, OK, 43; Lee, S, 17; Ulysses Grant, S, 15; Ruth C D, 11; Virgil, S, 9; Harvey E, S, 7; Marshal P, S, 5

33620 FIELDS, Vinnie, Porum, OK, 28; Willie, S, 12; Nellie D, 10; Edward, S, 8; Keller, S, 6; Green, S, 4; Ollie D, 2; Ida D, 1/6

29390 FIELDS, Walker, Southwest City, MO, 30; 29391, Annie, W, 22; Cephus, S, 4; Ollie, D, 3; Rutha D, 1/12

[FIELDS, Walter. See #5189]   *(Note: entry separate from other family groups)*

3082 FIELDS, Walter G, Warner, OK, 59

24134 FIELDS, Wesley Dodge, OK, 38; Lela Bama D, 9; Ethel Vand D, 7; Maggie C D, 4; Jackson T, S, 1

2667 FIELDS, William, Fairland, OK, 35; 8124, Sarah E, W, 27; Irene M D, 6; Nora D, 4; Mamie L D, 2; George E, S, 1/3

13190 FIELDS, William H Chetopa, KS, 47; Roy J, S, 13; Arthur C, S, 10

24634 FIELDS, William H, Vinita, OK, 40; George A, S, 18; William E, S, 15; Howard, S, 12; Nora M D, 7; Louis B, S, 1

29268 FIELDS, William J Collinsville, OK, 27

3668 FIELDS, William L, Pryor Creek, OK, 33

5081 FIELDS, William S, Warner, OK, 20;   By W. H. Stewart, Gdn.

2168 FIELDS, William W, Las Animas CO, 47; Jess, S, 18; Birdie D, 16; Dora D, 14; Della, D, 13; Eugene, S, 11; Howard, S, 9; Cledah, D, 6; Inez D, 5; Rose D, 3; Alpha, D, 1

14733 FILMORE, Emma, Warner, OK, 53; Ella D, 14; Della D, 14; Emma D, 6

24882 FILMORE, George, Warner, OK, 21; Della D, 2; Millard, S, 1/3; James, S, 1/3

32208 FINCHER, James V Adair, OK, 11; Alvin R Bro, 7; Luther M Bro, 6; By Thomas J. Fincher, Gdn.

23448 FINE, Elizabeth, Peggs, OK, 24

27240 FINE, Flora L Akins, OK, 20; Calvin D, S, 2; Indarla D, 1

33619 FINLEY Anna R, Tahlequah, OK, 25

4484 FINLEY, Emily J, Tahlequah, OK, 56

9153 FINLEY. Ruth E, Nowata, OK, 57; Bigelow, William, S, 15; Emma D, 12

30814 FINLEY, Thomas, Tahlequah, OK, 31; 25781, Viola D, W, 31; George C, S, 4

30813 FINLEY, Travis C, Tahlequah, OK, 27; Gean[sic] A D, 1/12

Key: Guion Miller Application Number; Name; Address, Relation (to Head); Age in 1906

14715 FINNEY, Minnie Lee, St. Louis, MO, 6111-A Virginia Ave., 26

26740 FISCHER, Grover G, Oakland CA, 22, 1269 Twelfth St.

6930 FISCHER, Leoda T, Sheep Ranch CA, 43; Robert M, S, 11; Dewey, S, 7

25828 FISCHER, Viva C, Sheep Ranch C, 20

2104 FISH, Eddy Claremore, OK, 39; Dennis, S, 15; Laura D, 7; Joseph, S, 1

9471 FISH, Fannie M Claremore. OK, 10; By Laura Barris, Gdn.

[FISH, John. See #14197]   *(Note: entry separate from other family groups)*

[FISH, Nellie. See #2102]   *(Note: entry separate from other family groups)*

26787 FISHER Amebelle, Wagoner, OK, 29; Mary Ann D, 5; William Elzie, S, 4; Ivy Merinda D, 1

[FISHER David with Nellie Hicks. See #27258]
(Note: entry separate from other family groups)

3650 FISHER, Eliza Choteau, OK, 42

3738 FISHER, Eliza Snow, Scipio, UT, 50; Leffel, S, 18; Nahomi D, 15; Eliza D, 10; Willard L, S, 8

26253 FISHER, Francis M, Jr, Scipio, UT, 24

27025 FISHER, Geo. W, Scipio, UT, 22

5016 FISHER, Isaac Choteau, OK, 26; 41789, Maggie, W, 21; Mose Wiley, S, 4; Lillie, D, 1

3606 FISHER, Jessie Choteau, OK, 16; Joe Bro, 14; Eva, Sis, 8; North L Bro, 4; By Rufus Fisher, Gdn.

5019 FISHER, Johnson, Jr Choteau, OK, 35; 9412, Rachel, W, 23; Elizabeth D, 9; Nancy, D, 6; Rabbit Carrie D of W, 5

5018 FISHER, Moses Choteau, OK, 32

3605 FISHER, Rufus Choteau, OK, 35; 3609, Charlotte, W, 38; Maggie D, 17; Aggie D, 14; Viola D, 12; Foster W, S, 9

[FISHER, Steve. See Jess Sanders. #1338]
(Note: entry separate from other family groups)

1246 FISHINGHAWK, James, Stilwell, OK, 51; Betsy D, 9

1285 FISHINGHAWK, Joe, Stilwell, OK, 46; Chekelie, S, 12; Salie[sic] D, 10; Jesse, S, 8; Dawes, S, 5

5710 FISHINGHAWK, Lydia, Stilwell, OK, 25; Wolf, Katie D, 4

4730 FISHINGHAWK, Nancy, Stilwell, OK, 27; Tehee, Tieasky, S, 6; Gott, William, S, 2

23264 FISK, Minerva, Pryor Creek, OK, 39; Harry A, S, 19; Cora May D, 17

Key: Guion Miller Application Number; Name; Address, Relation (to Head); Age in 1906

22573 FITE, Julia P, Muskogee, OK, 39; William P, S, 16; Frances D, 13; F. Barto, S, 11; Edward H, S, 8

5711 FITE, Nannie K, Tahlequah, OK, 44; Augustus W, S, 14; Sarah C D, 12; John W. S, S, 8; Laura T D, 5; Denman Wyly, S, 3

3223 FITZGERALD, Martha J Chetopa, KS, 40; Nora D, 16; William R, S, 10; Francis L, D, 5; Jesse E, S, 2

12822 FIVEKILLER, Frost, Porum, OK, 29; 8985, Susan, W, 26

5216 FIVEKILLER, Joseph, Wauhillau, OK, 47; Cleveland, S, 19; Callie D, 17; Spencer, S, 13; Annie D, 11; Onie or Anie D, 9

15042 FIVEKILLER, Wattie, Hanson, OK, 20

[FIXIN Alcey Blackbird. See #5328]   *(Note: entry separate from other family groups)*

3674 FIXIN, Tom Cookson, OK, 23; 5620, Ah-le, W, 20

14131 FIXING David, Spavinaw, OK, 30; 14133, Annie D, W, 31; Boney, Rabbit, S of W, 16; Cochran Charlotte D of W, 13; Fixing, Joseph, S, 7; Susie D, 3; Susanna D, 1

24316 FLANAGAN Charles A, Watova, OK, 25

23595 FLANAGAN, Effie, Peggs, OK, 21; Orville H, S, 4; Robert E, S, 2

22620 FLANAGAN, Frank J, Watova, OK, 23

17255 FLANAGAN, Mike, Watova, OK, 18; Tinda H Bro, 14; Rena I, Sis, 11; By Patrick Flanagan, Gdn.

23938 FLANAGAN, William, Watova, OK, 27; Ruby M D, 3; Ruth A D, 2

9272 FLANDERS, Lyman G, Kansas City, MO, 19

621 FLEETWOOD Delila E Copan, OK, 26

3996 FLEMING, Maria L, Fairland, OK, 61

2181 FLENOYE, Kate, Ft. Gibson, OK, 36; Alberty Cornelious, S, 15

8307 FLESHER, Lucinda Bushyhead, OK,38; Nora B D, 15; Eliza E D, 13; William H, S, 9

22638 FLESHER, Viola M Bushyhead, OK, 17

24168 FLETCHER Annie, Oologah, OK, 29; Martha D, 10; Maggie D, 7; Mary D, 5; Willie H, S, 1

25119 FLETCHER Benjamin G, Stilwell, OK, 47; 5362, Harriette, W, 46; 25120, Dora M, D, 19; Ellis R, S, 10; Della J D, 14; Nettie L D, 16; Eva A D, 18

25122 FLETCHER Calvin L, Stilwell, OK, 21; 25118, Maggie M, W, 20

4489 FLETCHER Charlotte E, Stilwell, OK, 68

29629 FLETCHER, James T, Marble City, OK, 32; 20630, Josie M, W, 31; Ada D, 11; Ruth, D, 9; Charlotte D, 7; Josie D, 5; Jinnie D, 1/12

22660 FLETCHER, John T, Stilwell, OK, 37; Dora M D, 15; Nora D, 14; Charlotte D, 10; Ben, S, 6

23910 FLETCHER, Robert N, Stilwell, OK, 22

12853 FLETCHER, Thomas T Braggs, OK, 34

24452 FLINT Charley, Fairland, OK, 22

Key: Guion Miller Application Number; Name; Address, Relation (to Head); Age in 1906

1331 FLINT Delila, Fairland, OK, 48; Daphna D, 2; Opal D, 9; Ballard, S, 11; Albert, S, 14; Nana F D, 16

511 FLINT, Sabra A Coffeyville, KS, 45; Eva D, 16; James E, S, 13; 31588, Essie, D, 19

23566 FLINT, William, Fairland, OK, 27; 24457, Ida C, W, 26; Jessie Jaunita[sic] D, 1

29050 FLINT, William P Coffeyville, KS, 24; Lillian E D, 3; Harold W, S, 1

16516 FLIPPIN Bernice M, Verdigris, OK, 27

[FLIPPIN, Mary L. See #b9491]
[FLIPPIN, Mary T. See #b9491]   *(Note: entries separate*
[FLIPPIN, Ruth A. See #b9491]   *from other family groups)*
[FLIPPIN, Rebecca L, See #b9491]

19645 FLOATING ICE, Sallie, Spavinaw, OK, 60

3923 FLOURNOY Anna Chelsea, OK, 51

29144 FLOURNOY, Rollin D Chelsea, OK, 30; Eldridge D. C, S, 8; Berniece D, 6; Cherrie, D, 4

29203 FLOURNOY, Walter G Chelsea, OK, 25; Laura May D, 8; Mercer W, S, 6; Dennis, S, 3; Clifton, S, 1

9675 FLUKE, George Cleora, OK, 28

9676 FLUKE, Henry, Vinita, OK, 25; Lula D, 4; Susan D, 2

2284 FLUKE, Lula Cleora, OK, 35; Lizzie D, 13; Andrew, S, 11; Edward F, S, 9; Fred W, S, 6; Francis M D, 4; Annie B D, 2

15090 FLUTE Annie, Hulbert, OK, 17

17281 FLUTE, Jesse, Wauhillau, OK, 17; Rhoda, Sis, 13; Watt Bro, 11; Wash Bro, 10; By Callie Terrapin, Gdn.

6271 FLUTE, John, Marble City, OK, 41; 4511, Esther, W, 36; John, Jr, S, 18; George, S, 9; Lizzie D, 6

FLUTE, Josie. See #12597]   *(Note: entry separate from other family groups)*

[FLUTE Charlotte. See #12596]   *(Note: entries separate*
[FLUTE Aikey. See #12596]   *from other family groups)*

15089 FLUTE, Tom, Hulbert, OK, 25; 15091, Nancy, W, 33

9304 FLYING Alsey, Melvin, OK, 67

32426 FLYING Crawford D, Keefeton, OK, 29; Lela D, 1/12

12627 FLYING, James Braggs, OK, 16;   By Looney Hammer, Gdn.

618 FLYNN, Martha E Dewey, OK, 44; Jesse G, S, 13

1591 FODDER Betsy, Westville, OK, 76

11498 FODDER Charlie Braggs, OK, 48

16602 FODDER, John, Leach, OK, 47; 5330, Nannie, W, 43

1639 FODDER, Katie, Westville, OK, 92

CHEROKEE DESCENDANTS RESIDING WEST OF MISSISSIPPI RIVER.
VOLUME II   (A – M)

Key: Guion Miller Application Number; Name; Address, Relation (to Head); Age in 1906

[FODDER, Lizzie with Mattie Poorbird. See #26516]
(Note: entry separate from other family groups)

1170 FODDER, Smith, Uniontown AR, 27; 16922, Susana[sic], W, 20; William, S, 4
9011 FODDER, Stephen, Westville, OK, 27
9913 FOGG Bird, Stilwell, OK, 31; Gibb, S, 4
6240 FOGG Charley, Stilwell, OK, 42; 6237, Nancy, W, 38; Eli, S, 18; Lydia D, 16;
Jim, S, 12; Susie D, 8

[FOGG Dick with #3485] ⎤   *(Note: entries separate*
[FOGG, Wakie with #3485] ⎦   *from other family groups)*

16614 FOGG, John, Evansville AR, 24
9909 FOGG, White, Stilwell, OK, 21; 5389, Betsy, W, 20
8079 FOGG, William Bunch, OK, 39; 8026, Sarah, W, 41; Nelson, S, 14; Tu-na-we, S,
9; Wah-le-sa D, 7; Nannie D, 5; Linnie D, 1
27169 FOGLE, Nancy B Bluejacket, OK, 22; Opal D, 1
22850 FOLSOM, Evaline, Westville, OK, 41
1719 FOOL, William, Porum, OK, 31; Beulah D, 5; Richard, S, 3; Bessie D, 1
16662 FOOY, Susie L Braggs, OK, 27; Maggie D, 6; Madaline D, 1
22787 FORBES, Frances E, Westville, OK, 46; Pearl D, 18
14241 FORBES, Mary E Chelsea, OK, 24; Frances E D, 1
1107 FORBES, Nancy E, Westville, OK, 67
22849 FORBES, Robert J, Westville, OK, 39; Ora D, 12; Rasmus, S, 10; Ola Belle D,
5; Fannie D, 2; Nancy E D, 1/6
9627 FORBES, Rutha, Gideon, OK, 27; Alice D, 7; Eva D, 5; Albin[sic], S, 2
4104 FORD, Minnie B, Ft. Gibson, OK, 20
23419 FORD, Stella Cowan, Melvin, OK, 19
10390 FOREMAN Ada Laura Claremore, OK, 25
5119 FOREMAN Agnes, Proctor, OK, 21
11439 FOREMAN Alexander S, Vian, OK, 27
11794 FOREMAN Araminta R, Vinita, OK, 51
14776 FOREMAN Austin W, Vinita, OK, 51; George A, S, 5; Margaret E D, 2
26296 FOREMAN Charles D Chelsea, OK, 22
2789 FOREMAN Charles L Afton, OK, 48
16148 FOREMAN David McNair, Ochelata, OK, 28

[FOREMAN Delila E. See #621]   *(Note: entry separate from other family groups)*

8906 FOREMAN, Elam Cherokee City AR, 46; Arch, S, 16; Katie D, 14; Noah, S,
10
5847 FOREMAN, Elias, Oaks, OK, 30; 43413, Florence A, W, 24; Amos W, S, 6;
Andy J, S, 3; Charlie E, S, 1

119

CHEROKEE DESCENDANTS RESIDING WEST OF MISSISSIPPI RIVER.
VOLUME II (A – M)

Key: Guion Miller Application Number; Name; Address, Relation (to Head); Age in 1906

4243 FOREMAN, Ellen Bean, Warner, OK, 25; Bean, Ora, S, 3; Eli, S, 1/4

4904 FOREMAN, Elmer, Westville, OK, 30; 43205, Venia, W, 24; Clint, S, 8; Dennis, S, 3

4156 FOREMAN, Emeline, Tahlequah, OK, 55; 5116, Bluford W, S, 19; Eliza D, 16

25459 FOREMAN, Essie Chelsea, OK, 21

13078 FOREMAN, Frank, Tahlequah, OK, 11;   By Houston B. Tehee, Gdn.

9766 FOREMAN, George B Campbell, OK, 31; Ruth D, 2; Cherokee D, 1

17278 FOREMAN, George D, Vian, OK, 25

9436 FOREMAN, James, Wann, OK, 54; James W, S, 18; Joseph T, S, 14; Charles F, S, 12; John, S, 10; Rebecca J D, 7

4717 FOREMAN, James E, Westville, OK, 37; Thomas H, S, 16; James E, Jr, S, 14; Claud C, S, 12; William E, S, 10; Dennis W, S, 7

1816 FOREMAN, John A, Talala, OK, 62; Leonard Wallace, S, 17

8241 FOREMAN, John D Christie, OK, 6;   By Charlotte, Wright, Gdn.

13081 FOREMAN, John D. R, Tahlequah, OK, 19;   By Houston B. Tehee, Gdn.

1634 FOREMAN, John E, Ramona, OK: 35

704 FOREMAN, John T, Sallisaw, OK, 37; Charlie, S, 13; Sarah D, 11

28486 FOREMAN, John W, Moodys, OK, 23

13944 FOREMAN, Johnson, Warner, OK, 49; Charles H, S, 17; Jesse E, S, 13; Susan A D, 11; Nannie E D, 7; Katie A D, 5; John J, S, 2

4036 FOREMAN, Joseph A, Pryor Creek, OK, 40; Steve, S 19; Maud D, 14; Thomas, S, 13; Jackson, S, 11; Oce, S, 9

5486½, FOREMAN, Laura Arkansas City AR, 7; James Bro, 3; By Hugh Foreman, Gdn.

4901 FOREMAN, Leander, Westville, OK, 21

[FOREMAN, Leroy. See #33936]   *(Note: entry separate from other family groups)*

11878 FOREMAN, Luke, Stilwell, OK, 20

1677 FOREMAN, Lydia, Proctor, OK, 42

43414 FOREMAN, Lydia, Eucha, OK, 27; Ka-nee-qua-yo-kee, Liza D, 7

1210 FOREMAN, Mary, Lowrey, OK, 67

4238 FOREMAN, Nannie, Warner, OK, 25

8354 FOREMAN, Nannie E, Vian, OK, 52; Ada R. D, 15

2293 FOREMAN, Nelson Chelsea, OK, 46; 25460, Laura Lewis D, 18; 2293, Ellis William, S, 17; James Leslie, S, 13; Custis Lee, S, 10; Randolph L, S, 7; Nelson Clifton, S, 5

9910 FOREMAN, Peggy, Stilwell, OK, 59

9495 FOREMAN, Polly, Vian, OK, 51; 13798, Jennie D, 17

[FOREMAN, Reuben. See #1190]   *(Note: entry separate from other family groups)*

[FOREMAN, Richard. See #27963]   *(Note: entry separate from other family groups)*

Key: Guion Miller Application Number; Name; Address, Relation (to Head); Age in 1906

5486 FOREMAN, Rider Cherokee City AR, 60?; 7976, Subina, W, 29

14090 FOREMAN, Robert, Tahlequah, OK, 34

1756 FOREMAN, Samuel, Tahlequah, OK, 33; Eveline D, 10; Leroy, S, 8; George C, S, 2

8889 FOREMAN, Samuel, Stilwell, OK, 30; 13287, Lizzie, W, 31

16640 FOREMAN, Samuel, Texanna, OK, 37; Sallie F D, 12; Thomas E, S, 8; Jack T, S, 4

27852 FOREMAN, Sarah E. P, Proctor, OK, 18

188 FOREMAN, Stephen, Locust Grove, OK, 54

13080 FOREMAN, Susan A. E, Tahlequah, OK, 21

3307 FOREMAN, Switchler, Oaks, OK, 32; 23633, Lila A, W, 31; Maggie M D, 12; Mary L, D, 10; Effie G D, 8; Nettie E D, 6; Lila A D, 3

11996 FOREMAN, Taylor W Claremore, OK, 18; Pery A Bro, 16; By Ada C. Foreman, Gdn.

16523 FOREMAN, Thomas, Locust Grove, OK, 29

1385 FOREMAN, Thomas A, Oolagah, OK, 34; Leo E, S, 3

7691 FOREMAN, Thomas J, Tahlequah, OK, 29

11886 FOREMAN, Thomas W, Tahlequah, OK, 46; 11281, Cherrie, W, 36; William E, S, 20; Watie C, S, 16; Thomas A, S, 12

10674 FOREMAN, Tom, Vian, OK, 34; 25879, Alice, W, 32

1744 FOREMAN, Tommie, Westville, OK, 22

943 FOREMAN, William, Moodys, OK, 74; 3140, Lutesha, W, 60

13512 FOREMAN, William, McKey, OK, 24

1758 FOREMAN, William B, Lowrey, OK, 37; 5509, Nellie, W, 38

20238 FOREMAN, William H, Keefeton, OK, 48; William H, Jr, S, 18; Susan A D, 17; Johnson, S, 15; Alice D, 12; Frank, S, 10; Mary D, 8

779 FOREMAN, William J, Westville, OK, 28; Jewel M D, 2

4705 FOREMAN, William T, Westville, OK, 32; Ellis, S, 16; Eddie, S, 10; Jesse R, S, 8; Bertha A D, 6

1949 FOREMAN, William W Centralia, OK, 35; 22878, Belle L, W, 26; James A, S, 8; Bessie J D, 6; Jesse, S, 3

8297 FORKED TAIL, Mary Cherokee City,   AR, 22

6929 FORTNER Anna W, Pawpaw, OK, 45; Samuel H, S, 20; Ralph H, S, 15

27201 FORTNER Benjamin F, Texarkana, TX, 21

24916 FORTNER, Norah, Ft. Gibson, OK, 51; Jack, S, 18

23916 FOSTER Allen B, Tahlequah, OK, 21

25179 FOSTER Artimissa Catoosa, OK, 46; Newton M, S, 11; Denver J, S, 3

17264 FOSTER Ben, Porum, OK, 17

12599 FOSTER Betsy, Wauhillau, OK, 32; Mary D, 13; John, S, 10

10711 FOSTER, James, Vian, OK, 34; 6669, Annie, W, 26; Peter, S, 12; Mary D, 7; Maggie, D, 5; Sallie D, 2

12594 FOSTER, John, Wauhillau, OK, 10; Mary, Sis, 13;   By Betsy Foster, Gdn.

Key: Guion Miller Application Number; Name; Address, Relation (to Head); Age in 1906

12933 FOSTER, John Claremore, OK, 37; 12932, Susan, W, 36; Jane D, 14; Margaret D, 12; Annie D, 10; James, S, 5; Joseph, S, 2; William, S, 1/12

12423 FOSTER, Mary J, Tiawah, OK, 26; Dugger, Samuel E, S, 3

4016 FOSTER, Mary M, Tahlequah, OK, 47; Robert F, S, 16; William, S, 14; Thomas L, S, 11

28028 FOSTER, Myrtle, Hillside, OK, 21; Harvey B, S, 1

13541 FOSTER, Samuel C Claremore, OK, 48; Sylvia E D, 15

23719 FOSTER, Sarah E, Hollow, OK, 27; Cyrus W, S, 12; Goldie M D, 9; Rubie L D, 6; Elmer L, S, 4; William N, S, 2; Mary L D, 1/6

4836 FOSTER, Thomas J, Texanna, OK, 43 [Died 3-1907]; Ben, S, 17; Blue, S, 14; Mary E, D, 10; By R. L. Pearl, Gdn. and Adm. of T. J. Foster

11263 FOSTER, Thomas S Claremore, OK, 31; Emmett H, S, 1

31838 FOSTER, Walter, Melvin, OK, 9;   By William Battie, Gdn.

12548 FOURKILLER Charley, Stilwell, OK, 25

7036 FOURKILLER, Grant, Stilwell, OK, 24

6971 FOURKILLER, Katie, Stilwell, OK, 49; 9914, Judge F, S, 8

17019 FOURKILLER, Larkin, Stilwell, OK, 23

8367 FOURKILLER, Richard, Stilwell, OK, 27; 12541, Sarah, W, 27

16647 FOURKILLER, Sampson, Stilwell, OK, 19;   By Katie Fourkiller, Gdn.

8081 FOURKILLER, Spade, Stilwell, OK, 25

10934 FOURKILLER, Takie Christie, OK, 65

17018 FOURKILLER, William, Stilwell, OK, 21

30621 FOUST, Rebecca Bluejacket, OK, 25; John S, S, 4; Mamie M D, 2; Minnie O D, 1

[FOUST, Thomas J. See #25298] ⎤   *(Note: entries separate*
[FOUST, James M. See #25298] ⎦   *from other family groups)*

[FOUTS, Irwin. See #9380] ⎤   *(Note: entries separate*
[FOUTS, Maggie. See #9380] ⎦   *from other family groups)*

23585 FOUTS, Maggie V Adair, OK, 37; Jacob R, S, 17; Richard L, S, 16; Mildred N D, 12; Ella M D, 10; Amy D, 9; Ruby D, 6; Eula D, 3; Nellie D, 1

12715 FOWLER Ada E, Owassa, OK, 10; Bessie R, Sis, 8;   By Wesley E. Fowler, Gdn.

23390 FOWLER, Emeline, Gans, OK, 32; William C, S, 11; Polly V D, 7; Eva Lou D, 3

8073 FOWLKS, Laura, Skiatook, OK, 31; 29157, Lowery, Omer D, 15; 29154, Peter B, S, 14; 29159, Charles, S, 9; 29158, Fowlks, Mamie, D, 6; 29155, Anna, D, 2; 29156, George M, S ,1

13265 FOX Diane Bunch, OK, 28

24144 FOX, Emma, Grove, OK, 21

CHEROKEE DESCENDANTS RESIDING WEST OF MISSISSIPPI RIVER.
VOLUME II   (A – M)

1568 FOX, Joe, Southwest City, MO, 63; 4269, Susan, W, 53; Callie D, 19; Darcis D, 16

644 FOX, Joe C, Jr, Eucha, OK, 28; 658, Emma, W, 27; John, S, 1/12; Cul Swimmer, S, 3

[FOX, Linda. See #21988]   *(Note: entries separate*
[FOX, Lillie. See #21988]   *from other family groups)*

5782 FOX, Sallie, Leach, OK, 26

24127 FOX, Walter, Grove, OK, 29; 6699, May, W, 18

1651 FOYIL Charlotte, Foyil, OK, 54; Milo, S, 20

29253 FRANCES, Lula P Dodge, OK, 26

24098 FRANCIS, Frances Chelsea, OK, 18

28716 FRANCIS, Maggie May Dodge, OK, 18

5665 FRANKLIN, May, Ft. Gibson, OK, 21; Ella Kizelle D, 3

27858 FRANKS, Lula Pearl, Houston, TX, 26, 513 Main St.

9688 FRANTZ, Emma S, Edna, KS, 32; William F, S, 10; Martha J D, 8; Louisa D D, 6; Laura A D, 4

6539 FRASHER, Nancy Blackgum, OK, 49; Fulton, Myrtle D, 18; Joe, S, 19; William, S, 15; Fannie D, 13; Dunn, Mairm P D, 10; Ellen D, 7

26270 FRAYSER, Lydia M, Vinita, OK, 32

9997 FRAZIER Daniel, Wann, OK, 53; 11576, Elizabeth, W, 53; Daniel, Jr, S, 18; Robert, S, 16; Walter S, 14; Lucy D, 11; 9997, James, Warner, OK?, 9; Peter, S, 7

23191 FRAZIER, John, Warner, OK, 32; Ethel D, 8; Eva D, 6; Gracie D, 2

3709 FRAZIER, John F, Warner, OK, 69; Ines D, 16; Lewis, S, 13; Wilson, S, 12; Ebb, S, 10; Peggy D, 8

25312 FRAZIER, Lela A Claremore, OK, 36; Mattie E D, 14; Charles, S, 12

27237 FREE, Ruth C, Long, OK, 19; Clarence R, S, 2; Maggie M D, 1

28521 FREELAND, Lee Logan, Roswell, NM, 25; Douglas C, S, 1/3

39393 FREEMAN Alzira J, Stilwell, OK, 23

11801 FREEMAN Carrie B, Maysville AR, 24

24288 FREEMAN Cora, Tahlequah, OK, 29; Kidd, James C, Tahlequah, OK, S, 11; Roxsey, D, 6

2652 FREEMAN Daniel W, Fairland, OK, 54

26797 FREEMAN, George Cookson, OK, 34; Henry P, S, 2; Jack A, S, 2/3

29104 FREEMAN, George W, Mount Judea, AR, 24

11803 FREEMAN, Girlie L, Maysville AR, 20

39390 FREEMAN, John B, Stilwell, OK, 20

39391 FREEMAN, Keith, Stilwell, OK, 18;   By W. P. Patterson, Gdn.

24913 FREEMAN, Lee B Big Cabin, OK, 23; Howard E, S, 2

3769 FREEMAN, Loula Ella, Maysville AR, 45

11725 FREEMAN, Missouri J, Mount Judea, AR, 46; Rhoda A D, 15; William H, S, 12

Key: **Guion Miller Application Number; Name; Address, Relation (to Head); Age in 1906**

[FREEMAN, Peggy. See #5905]   *(Note: entry separate from other family groups)*

27452 FREEMAN, William C, Fairland, OK, 21
11802 FREEMAN, William D, Maysville AR, 21

[FRENCH Curtise C. See #28748] ⎤   *(Note: entries separate*
[FRENCH Dory V. See #28748]   ⎦   *from other family groups)*

13393 FRENCH, George, Melvin, OK, 18; Beulah, Sis, 14; Cabel Bro, 12; Joe Bro, 9; Jack, Bro, 5;   By J. M, French, Gdn.
26000 FRENCH, Geo. E, Rosala, WA, 26
13396 FRENCH, Gypsey, Melvin, OK, 19
29322 FRENCH, Henry C, Oglesby, OK, 23; 13114, Dora A, W, 22; Leona M. M D, 2; John H, S, 1/3
 9807 FRENCH, James, Moodys, OK, 51; 31192, Malinda, W, 22
25518 FRENCH, Jane Anne, Los Angeles CA, 51; Joseph A, S, 19; Richard T, S, 17; Eliza C, D, 14; Marguerete[sic] F D, 8

[FRENCH, Joel B, See #142]   *(Note: entry separate from other family groups)*

14765 FRENCH, John H Catoosa, OK, 34; 14774, Jas. Fannie F, W, 28; Warren, John H, S of W, 13; Willie D, S of W, 7
25519 FRENCH, Johnson T, Los Angeles CA, 25
13570 FRENCH, Joseph M, Ray, OK, 50; Gypsey, S, 19; George Yes, S, 18; Beulah D, 14; Cabele, S, 13; Jos. M, S, 8; John F, S, 3; Nina D, 2; Walter, S, 1/6
13398 FRENCH, Louis, Melvin, OK, 24
26498 FRENCH, Nannie, Metory, OK, 34; James, S, 12; Coppinger, William, S, 6
 2279 FRENCH, Necked, Stilwell, OK, 64; 2269, Charlotte, W, 48; Weavel, Nannie D of W, 12; Frog Cowan, S of W, 7

[FRENCH, Peggy. See #13136]   *(Note: entry separate from other family groups)*

11745 FRENCH, Thomas B, Inola, OK, 37; 13422, Lila, W, 29; Thomas F, S, 11; Walter P, S, 2
25520 FRENCH, Thomas F, Los Angeles CA, 23
13094 FRENCH, William, Stilwell, OK, 28; 13093, Eliza, W, 21; Maggie D, 4; Maud D, 1
 1807 FRENCH, William L, Tahlequah, OK, 33
 9804 FRICK, Nannie N. B, Redding CA, 46
24633 FRITZ Callie, Estella, OK, 18
10732 FRITZ, Edward, Vinita, OK, 30; 5967, Nelly, W, 18
10731 FRITZ, Katie, Vinita, OK, 17;   By Francis Fritz, Gdn.

Key: **Guion Miller Application Number; Name; Address, Relation (to Head); Age in 1906**

[FROG Cowan. See #2269] *(Note: entry separate from other family groups)*

[FROG, Lizzie. See #4404] *(Note: entry separate from other family groups)*

11406 FROG, Nancy Cove, OK, 32

2344 FROGG, Thompson, Stilwell, OK, 55; 2298, Susie, W, 56; Feather, Polly D of W, 15

12156 FRY Cullie Claremore, OK, 28; Gertrude D, 8; Cecil R, S, 6; Lettie Marie D, 4

12160 FRY, Maxwell Claremore, OK, 35; Pearl D, 11; Merritt L, S, 6; Cora V D, 4; Robert L, S, 1

12154 FRY, William H Claremore, OK, 38; Paul W, S, 16; Robert E, S, 9; Victorine C D, 7; Mary D, 4

11495 FRYAR, Mary Braggs, OK, 30; Voisie D, 8; Andy, S, 6; Archie Severe, S, 4; Vance, S, 1/3

11008 FRYE Charles O, Sallisaw, OK, 52; Roy, S, 19; Argyle, S, 17; Raymond, S, 14; Charles O, S 12; Pliny S, S, 9; Catherine, D, 7; Mamie, D, 4; Harriette, D, 2; Thomas, S, ¼

13473 FRYE, Edward M, Sallisaw, OK, 27

26526 FRYE, Eliza J, Sallisaw, OK, 36; Edgar Mathes, S, 16; Hattie Midget D, 14

23275 FRYE, George, Mark, OK, 24

13687 FRYE, Hattie, Sallisaw, OK, 14; Mathew, S, 15;   By Eliza Frye, Gdn.

1940 FRYE, Maggie, Mark, OK, 46; Sam, S, 20; Henry, S, 18; Minnie D, 14; Mary D, 12; Louis, S, 10; Joe, S, 8

[FRYE, Nancy. See #981]
[FRYE, Walter. See #981]   *(Note: entries separate*
[FRYE, Mary, See #981]   *from other family groups)*

40273 FULLER, Robin V, Tahlequah, OK, 24; 40274, Cornelia E, W, 27

1859 FULLER, Rosa L, Ft. Gibson, OK, 37; Nellie R D, 16; James P, S, 13; Robert W, S, 8

43793 FULLER, Willard S, Tahlequah, OK, 13;   By Robert C. Fuller, Gdn.

25283 FULSOM, John F, Ft. Gibson, OK, 27

5282 FULSOM, Mary E, Stilwell, OK, 62

26820 FULTON, James Blackgum, OK, 22; Frank A, S, 1

[FULTON, Myrtle. See #6539]
[FULTON, Joe. See #6539]   *(Note: entries separate*
[FULTON, William. See #6539]   *from other family groups)*
[FULTON, Fannie. See #6539]

31014 FULTON, Willie Coffeyville, KS, 26

Key: Guion Miller Application Number; Name; Address, Relation (to Head); Age in 1906

33607 GABRIEL Devere, Valeda, KS, 24; Edna M D, 7; Clifford O, S, 5; Tracy E D, 3; Lloyd E, S, 2

[GAH-SEE-LAH-WEE, Lizzie. See #9257]
(Note: entry separate from other family groups)

25761 GAINES, Lula M, Narcissa, OK, 21; Willie J, S, 5/12
  368 GALCATCHER Charley, Eucha, OK, 47; 1701, Peggie, W, 36; Lee, S, 20; Nancy D, 17; Laura D, 14; Snowmaker, S, 12; Alie D, 10; Dawes, S, 8; Tuxie, S, 3; Nannie, D, 1

[GALCATCHER, Emma. See #10966] *(Note: entry separate from other family groups)*

17425 GALCATCHER, Tom Claremore, OK, 24

[GALCATCHER, Wesley. See #5264]
[GALCATCHER, Maud. See #5264]
[GALCATCHER, Ruthy. See #5264]   *(Note: entries separate*
[GALCATCHER, Lilly. See #5264]   *from other family groups)*
[GALCATCHER, Mollie. See #5264]

  1613 GALLOWAY Dolly E, Vinita, OK, 66
  2839 GALLOWAY, Ruth E Coffeyville, KS, 40; Rogers, Maud E D, 17
  8301 GANN Chas. H Akins, OK, 43; 9435, Nancy J, W, 40; Leo, S, 18; Ventoria D, 14; Bessie D, 11; George, S, 9; Henry, S, 7; Augusta M D, 4; Mary D, 2
  8796 GANN, Elias, Gans, OK, 54; Rabbit, S, 18; Minty D, 16; Lizzie May D, 12; J. Foxey, S, 6
26365 GANN, George, Muldrow, OK, 26; Floyd, S, 2

[GANN, Jim. See #8630]   *(Note: entry separate from other family groups)*

  8629 GANN, Joe, Stilwell, OK, 21; 42185, Kate, W, 22; Cynthia D, ¼
24002 GANN, Mary B, Southwest City, MO, 15
33235 GANN, Robert Akins, OK, 20; Perry, S, 1/12
  8302 GANN, Thos. Bunch, OK, 47; 14272, Nannie, W, 24; George, S, 2

[GANT, William. See #12227]   *(Note: entries separate*
[GANT, Mattie. See #12227]   *from other family groups)*
[GANT Chas. Fount. See #12227]

15933 GARBARINO, Martha L, Vinita, OK, 41
35583 GARDENHIRE, Nellie, Long, OK, 18
  8784 GARDENHIRE, Rhoda Dora AR, 32; Richard, S, 6; Wm. F, S, 2; Geo. M, S, 1

Key: Guion Miller Application Number; Name; Address, Relation (to Head); Age in 1906

2962 GARLAND, Elizabeth M Chelsea, OK, 58; John F, S, 19

24783 GARLAND, Frederick Chelsea, OK, 24

24886 GARLAND, Lottie, Tajique, NM, 34; Harris, William B, S, 16; Thomas Mackeroy, S, 14; John F, S, 8

2960 GARLAND, Sallie Chelsea, OK, 56

16744 GAR-LOR-YE-DER, Tahlequah, OK, 68

752 GARNER, Virgil A, Lowrey, OK, 36; Benjamin F, S, 10; James E, S, 8; Pearly May D, 6; William Hood, S, 3; Gatsie S D, 1

24404 GARRETT Bessie, Gideon, OK, 18; Robert A, S, 1

23981 GARRETT Cherokee D, Pryor Creek, OK, 27; Kathleen Butler D, 1

27534 GARRETT, Margarett[sic], Siloam Springs AR, 29; John, S, 12; Gracie D, 7; Loy D, S, 5; Annie E D, 3; Teddy R, S, 1

27535 GARRETT, Mary C, Siloam Springs, AR, 27; Roy P, S, 8; Earl, S, 6; Millie R D, 3

1607 GARRETT, Rachel C Centralia, OK, 46; Frank P, S, 16; Susan F D, 14; Eva D, 10; Joseph B, S, 7

28832 GARRETT, Robert M Centralia, OK, 20

3300 GARRISON Betsy Choteau, OK, 25

39395 GARROUTT, Etta P, Gideon, OK, 21; Lillian O D, 7; Daisy L D, 5; Edith M D, 3; Eleanor S D, 1

8022 GARVIN Benj. F, Hanson, OK, 45; 9165, Eliza, W, 38; John F, S, 17; Mary E D, 15; Elizabeth C D, 13; Benj. R, S, 11; Mose Edward, S, 9; Elmer C, S, 2

3987 GARVIN, Ernest F, Pryor Creek, OK, 13; By Geo D, Logan, Gdn.

8089 GARVIN, Walter A, Hanson, OK, 21

[GASKEY, John R. See #888]   *(Note: entry separate from other family groups)*

4495 GASSAWAY, Esther L, Hulbert, OK, 25

[GASSAWAY, Henry. See #24364]   *(Note: entries separate*
[GASSAWAY, Neoma. See #24364]   *from other family groups)*

1395 GATES, Margaret Catoosa, OK, 25; Ross Arvil V, S, 8; Oma V D, 6

5139 GATLIN, James E, Sulphur, OK, 35; Ida L D, 11; James A, S, 9

[GATLIN, Samuel. See #9397]   *(Note: entries separate*
[GATLIN, Joel. See #9397]   *from other family groups)*
[GATLIN, William. See #9397]

13545 GAYLOR David H, Wagoner, OK, 22; Emma Fay D, 2; Agnes Elizabeth D, 1/3

[GAYLOR, Elizabeth. See #8668]   *(Note: entry separate from other family groups)*

Key: **Guion Miller Application Number; Name; Address, Relation (to Head); Age in 1906**

16507 GAYLOR, Grover, Wagoner, OK, 18
13545½ GAYLOR, Perry, Wagoner, OK, 16   By William Jackson, Gdn.
16505 GAYLOR, Thos J, Wagoner, OK, 22

[GE-AH-DICK. See #6541]   *(Note: entry separate from other family groups)*

24590 GENTRY Cora F, Grove, OK, 24
30060 GENTRY, Eva Viola, Southwest City, MO, 30; Wayne A, S, 10; Vivian D, 5
 8310 GENTRY, Louisa, Grove, OK, 37
  171 GENY Berly E, Hutchinson, KS, 32; Charles G, S, 9
32000 GEORGE, Nora Ann, Grove, OK, 17
17668 GER-LI-DAH, Watt, Whitmire, OK, 21
13109 GETTINGDOWN, Jesse Bunch, OK, 48
24860 GHORMLEY Don, Tahlequah, OK, 22
12714 GHORMLEY, Ewing C Adair, OK, 49; 27429, Ida N, W, 40; Carrie E D, 18;
       Bulah May, D, 13; Hugh W, S, 10; Lillian J D, 8; Ewing M, S, 6; Janice M D, 1
31604 GHORMLEY, Mattie, Stilwell, OK, 19; Mary D, 2
43292 GHORMLEY, Michael A, Tahlequah, OK, 23; Ah-ni-wake D, 4; Georgia D, 1
10783 GHORMLEY, Michael O, Tahlequah, OK, 59; 10784, Nancy, W, 50; Lorenzo, S,
       20; Rachel C D, 15; Lillie M D, 13; Stephen M, S, 11; 27507, Nancy J D, 16
 1301 GHORMLEY, Sarah C Cove, OK, 74
15954 GHORMLEY, Thos, Stilwell, OK, 31; 1953, John, S, 6
26166 GHORMLEY, Walter S, Moody, OK, 37; Willeah M D, 14; Leola M D, 10;
       Walter F, S, 9
16117 GHORMLEY, William, Tahlequah, OK, 16   By William O. Ghormley, Gdn.
27506 GHORMLEY, William, Tahlequah, OK, 30
32665 Elizabeth, W, 27; Stella D, 5; Maurice, S, 3; Connell R, S, 2
10462 GIBBONY, Sarah J, Texanna, OK, 31; Simmons, Maggie D, 15; Columbus, S,
       12; Gibbony, Laura May D, 9; Russel, S, 7; John William, S, 4; Mary E D, 1
34568 GIBBS, Edith, Westville, OK, 31; Thomas H, S, 11; Virgie D, 6; Nellie D, 4;
       Preston F, S, 1
16870 GIBBS, Eliza Claremore, OK, 33; Charles, S, 12; Joseph S, S, 10
24189 GIBBS, Lizzie Claremore, OK, 23; Mary D D, 3; Edward H, S, ¼

[GIBSON Clausine. See #33207]   *(Note: entry separate from other family groups)*

10776 GIBSON, Frances B, Muskogee, OK, 19

[GIBSON, James. See #25291]

17089 GIBSON, James E, Wagoner, OK, 32
24663 GIBSON, John H, Grove, OK, 46; Quinton B, S, 19; Mattie B D, 18; Mary L D,
       16; John R, S, 7; Jennie C D, 14

Key: Guion Miller Application Number; Name; Address, Relation (to Head); Age in 1906

28691 GIBSON, Lillie B, Foyil, OK, 30; Mary D, 11; James, S, 10; Mallie D, D, 8; John A, S, 3; Maggie D, 1

16511 GIBSON, Marion W, Webbers Falls, OK, 26

16850 GIBSON, Minnie, Texanna, OK, 11; James Bro, 8; Ode Bro, 6; By Gent Gibson, Gdn.

16512 GIBSON, William M, Webbers Falls, OK, 29; Hazel W D, 4

 5526 GIFFORD, Elizabeth E, Hillside, OK, 10; John O B, 8; By James W. Gifford, Gdn.

 9118 GILBERT, Fannie Byers Cookson, OK, 27; Betsy Ann D, 3

16161 GILBERT, George Coffeyville, KS, 27; Florence D, 4; Allen, S, 2

 9183 GILBERT, Vinnie R, Sallisaw, OK, 31; Curtis, Joe W, S, 8; Dave T, S, 6; Gilbert Chas. Lester, S, 1

22022 GILLILAND, Luvena, Vian, OK, 25 [3-27-1907]; By Wm T. Gilliland Adm.

31651 GILLISPIE Della M Coffeyville, KS, 22

 3015 GILLISPIE, William M Afton, OK, 26

[GILLUM, Myrtle. See #18521]   *(Note: entry separate from other family groups)*

 5580 GILMORE, Rachel C Douglas AR, 39; Cyrus, S, 15; Harry W, S, 13; Nancy V D, 10; Donald B, S, 8; Mary Lucile D, 4

 5764 GILSTRAP, Jennie May Bartlesville, OK, 19

14798 GILSTRAP, Louisa Braggs, OK, 34; Petitt, Watie, S, 18; Gilstrap, Louis, S, 14; Horace, S, 11; Carrie L D, 9; Ernest H, S, 6; Clarie O D, 4; Harry, S, 2

30000 GILSTRAP,. Martha F Duenweg, MO, 20

 6229 GILSTRAP, Nora, Hillside, OK, 12; Albert Bro, 10; Robert D Bro, 8; George A Bro, 5; By Artelia Gilstrap, Gdn.

 9492 GIPSON, Margaret L, Hermosa Beach, Box 51, CA, 26; Finnie Dovie D, 4; Fannie Laura, D, 2

 9786 GIRTY Caty, Vian, OK, 26

25488 GIRTY, Eliza, Gritts, OK, 28; McCoy, Sadie D, 4; Girty, Kate D, 2; Red Hawk, S, 1/12

 8999 GIRTY, Esther, Webbers, Falls, OK, 44; Crapo, James, S, 18; Collins, S, 15; Girty Alex, S, 12; Buck, S, 10; Martin, S, 4

11775 GIRTY, Jennie, Webbers Falls, OK, 26; Stan, S, 3

13486 GIRTY, Jennie, Vian, OK, 17

[GIRTY, Maria. See #8911] *(Note: entry separate from other family groups)*

23200 GIRTY, Mary, Webbers Falls, OK, 23

17184 GIRTY, Minty, Webbers Falls, OK, 54

14671 GIRTY, Nancy, Webbers Falls, OK, 21

23199 GIRTY, Peggie, Webbers Falls, OK, 26

17017 GIRTY, Tom, Webbers Falls, OK, 32; 23198, Jennie, W, 20; Katie D, 2

Key: Guion Miller Application Number; Name; Address, Relation (to Head); Age in 1906

22880 GISH, Lula, Lena, OK, 23; Jesse F, S, 5; Earl, S, 3; Ada D, 1

26129 GIVENS, Mary, Gideon, OK, 30; John W, S, 14; David L, S, 13; Bertha L D, 11; Nancy J D, 10; Blanche O, S, 8; George W, S, 6; Jessie I D, 5; Marvin M, S, 3; Martha Lee D, 1

31050 GLADNEY, Elmira, Eureka, OK, 51; Henry S, S, 20; Minnie B D, 17; Charlotte D, 15; Elizabeth D, 13; John R, S, 8

3659 GLADNEY, Joseph B, Tahlequah, OK, 56; 25934, Ellie A, W, 38; Essie D, 6

6617 GLADNEY, Jos. F, Eureka, OK, 27

30828 GLASS Anna, Stilwell, OK, 35; Sanders, James, S, 7; Bearpaw, George, S, 3

30829 GLASS Bettie, Evansville AR, 24; Taylor, S, 3; Frank, S, 1

13227 GLASS, Elizabeth, McLain, OK, 16; Cornelius Bro, 14; Harvey Bro, 12; Dennis Bro, 9; Caswell Bro, 6;   By Mary Jane Tate, Gdn.

14039 GLASS, Ella G Bushyhead, OK, 19

8251 GLASS Charley Cherokee City AR, 24

9478 GLASS, Emma, Stilwell, OK, 20

[GLASS, Hawk. See #2231]   *(Note: entry separate from other family groups)*

17130 GLASS, John, Muldrow, OK, 19

8863 GLASS, John D, Foyil, OK, 15;   By Samantha C. Glass, Gdn.

6451 GLASS, John T, Stilwell, OK, 30; 42225, Emma, W, 20; French, S, 1

9468 GLASS, Joshua, Vian, OK, 49; 25293, Annie, W, 38

5700 GLASS, Lewis, Pryor Creek, OK, 17; Homer Bro, 15; Cloud Bro, 12; By Alice Washam, Gdn.

30830 GLASS, Lizzie, Stilwell, OK, 20

9757 GLASS, Louiza, Stilwell, OK, 42; Mary D, 18; Fanny D, 16; Hester D, 13; Emma D, 8; Ezekiel, S, 11; Nancy D, 5; Mary Jane D, 3

11923 GLASS, Lucy, Stilwell, OK, 19

11920 GLASS, Mary, Stilwell, OK, 18

9170 GLASS, Mary Isabel Braggs, OK, 28; 12574, Charles D, H, 36; Lizzie B D, 3

42826 GLASS, Myrtle M, Southwest City, MO, 17

1004 GLASS, Paul Dragger, OK, 55; 15083, Peggy D, 12; Nancy D, 7

[GLASS, Sallie. See #32745] *(Note: entry separate from other family groups)*

7514 GLASS, Tom, Vian, OK, 65; 7513, Nancy, W, 55

9174 GLASS, William, Hulbert, OK, 22

14167 GLASS, William, Evansville AR, 60; 8647, Chatuseang, W, 66

7006 GLENN Daisy Ella, Vinita, OK, 25; Willis, Jerry D, 8

11413 GLENN, Frank C, Miles, OK, 16; Jesse E Bro, 12   By Charles L. Clapper, Gdn.

[GLENN, Lydia J, See #16432]   *(Note: entry separate from other family groups)*

Key: Guion Miller Application Number; Name; Address, Relation (to Head); Age in 1906

4700 GLENN, Nancy Ann, Grove, OK, 47

1601 GLENN, Richard F, Miles, OK, 53; Charlie R, S, 19; Dot D, 14; Thomas, S, 12; Ross, S, 8

31785 GLENN, Vinnie R, Miles, OK, 21

1683 GLENN, William H, Miles, OK, 26

7032 GLORY Chas Cookson, OK, 24; 30018, Sallie, W, 17; Mose, S, 5

7033 GLORY, Henry Cookson, OK, 21

2440 GLORY, Joe, Tahlequah, OK, 24; 2972, Mary, W, 21; Martin, S, 1

2442 GLORY, Nancy, Tahlequah, OK, 55

1251 GLORY, Richard, Pryor Creek, OK, 39; 32301, Lydia, W, 24

9624 GLORY, Steve, Flint, OK, 47; 9623, Nannie, W, 43; Tinna D, 13; Bluford, S, 3

2441 GLORY, William, Tahlequah, OK, 27; 4913, Fannie, W, 36; Annie D, 1

24883 GLORY, William P Braggs, OK, 13; Richard Bro, 12; Elizabeth, Sis, 8; George W, Bro, 6; By Sarah Glory, Gdn.

23288 GLOVER, Jane, Gans, OK, 44

87134 GOAD, Eliza, Texanna, OK, 34;Jesse J, S, 14; Frank, S, 12; Grover C, S, 10; Alice D, 8; Pearl D, 6; Myrtle D, 2; Arthur, S, 1; Vennie D, 1/6

4073 GOBACK, Jesse, Welling, OK, 34

1413 GOBACK, Lydia, Stilwell, OK, 75

23349 GODDARD Anna M, Tahlequah, OK, 30

11795 GODDARD, Elbert G Chelsea, OK, 11; Stiles H Bro, 8; Irene E, Sis, 6; By James W. Goddard, Gdn.

1826 GODDARD, Henry, Kinnison, OK, 55

29122 GODDARD, Henry M, Kinnison, OK, 53; Lutitia E D, 9; Mary E D, 7; Babe D, 6; James I, S, 4; Walter T, S, 1

1827 GODDARD, James Centralia, OK, 71

31576 GODDARD, James W Catale, OK, 23

23544 GODDARD, Julia, Stilwell, OK, 18

2115 GODDARD, William P Chetopa, KS, R.F.D. #6, 36; Fleming G, S, 10

25078 GOFORTH, Rachel M, Okoee, OK, 31; Eulma D, 14; Eulillie D, 13; Lula B D, 9; Alta D, 7; Mary E D, 1

10967 GOINGSNAKE Arch, Oaks, OK, 50

1882 GOINGSNAKE Betsey, Row, OK, 60

5734 GOINGSNAKE, Lizzie, Southwest City, MO, 83

2139 GOINGSNAKE, Thomas, Rose, OK, 32; 2137, Nancy, W, 22; Nanny D, 5; Roy, S, 3; Lizzie, S[sic], 1

12584 GOING-TO-SLEEP, Looney, Oaks, OK, 35; 12585, Nancy, W, 47

3725 GOINGWOLFE Aaron Baron, OK, 79

6666 GOINGWOLF, Sylvester Baron, OK, 48

30424 GOINS Adam, Vian, OK, 34

16339 GOINS, Riley, Vian, OK, 48

16338 GOINS, Sherman, Vian, OK, 39; 2337, Missouri R, W, 29; Moore, Jessie D of W, 11; Goins, Janette D, 6; Ethel D, 4

Key: Guion Miller Application Number; Name; Address, Relation (to Head); Age in 1906

24803 GOLDEN, Ellen, Siloam Springs AR, 31; John, S, 5; Dee, S, 2; James, S, 1
24107 GOLDEN, Sarah J Chance, OK, 21
846 GOLLIGER, Thomas J Collinsville, OK, 25

[GONZALES Ada. See #36442]
[GONZALES. Dave. See #36442]   *(Note: entries separate*
[GONZALES, John. See #36442]   *from other family groups)*
[GONZALES, Lenora. See #36442]

[GONZALES Ancy. See #4400]   *(Note: entry separate from other family groups)*

11861 GONZALES, Lucinda Braggs, OK, 22; 12815, John, S, 4
2274 GONZALES, Sarah, Stilwell, OK, 34; John, S, 11; Lizzie D, 10; Ollie D, 6; Jack, S, 1
2397 GOOD, Emeline Collinsville, OK, 66
2398 GOODALL Delilah Claremore, OK,39; Caroline D D, 18; Ida O,D, 17; Leora D, 15; Elizabeth,D,13; William E,S,12; Robert J,S,10; Levi F, S, 8;Elisha L, S,5; Samuel O,S,1
5948 GOODEN Dock, Maysville AR, 55; 5555, Quaty, W, 63

[GOLDEN, William. See #28280]   *(Note: entry separate from other family groups)*

43218 GOODMAN Albert A Caney, KS, 23
15748 GOODMAN Barbara C Caney, KS, 46; Robert F, S, 16; Jos. F, S, 13
43217 GOODMAN, Edw. J Caney, KS, 30; Jesse J, S, 8
33457 GOODMAN, Ora M Caney, KS, 25
8090 GOODMAN, Pauline R. C, Vinita, OK, 23; Katharine E D, 2
11966 GOODMONEY Annie, Southwest City, MO, 33; Webster, S, 3
12923 GOODMONEY, Jesse, Maysville AR,   29
16499 GOODMONEY, Rider, Eucha, OK, 36; Phoebe D, 14; Alonzo, S, 7

[GOODRICH, Geo. See #8075]   *(Note: entry separate from other family groups)*

[GOODRICH, Jack. See #24710]   *(Note: entry separate from other family groups)*

2160 GOODRICH, John C, Stilwell, OK, 31; 25126, Minnie L, W, 25 [Died 2-3-1907]; Edith D, 3

[GOODRICH, Lydia. See #36885]   *(Note: entries separate*
[GOODRICH, Martha. See #36885]   *from other family groups)*

5490 GOODWIN Anna M Childress, TX, 35; Jos. F, S, 15
24222 GOODWIN, John, Pagosa Springs CO, 28; 24221, Margie E, W, 20

Key: Guion Miller Application Number; Name; Address, Relation (to Head); Age in 1906

28288 GOODWIN, Rufus,Ft. Gibson, OK,25[Died 6-20-1906]; By Paralie J Alexander,Admr.

26585 GOODYKOONTZ Amanda H, Vinita, OK, 55

33494 GOODYKOONTZ, Frank A, Sapulpa, OK, 28; 13469, Jessie H, W, 21

24853 GORDEN, Ida Ballard, OK, 24

27191 GORDON Callie, Stilwell, OK, 35; Laura D, 15; John B, S, 10; Effie L D, 9; Ella D, D, 3

23899 GORDON Dora A, Stilwell, OK, 31; James C, S, 8; Dora M D, 5; Odie M, S, 3; George F, S, 1/12

23515 GORDON, Mary R, Stilwell, OK, 34; Cora D, 12; Elizabeth D, 7; William F, S, 3

13998 GORDON, Silas, Long, OK, 48; Noah, S, 15; Martha J D, 12; Mary E D, 9; William H, S, 6; Lucy B D, 3; Jas G, S, 11/12

2482 GOSS Benjamin F, Stilwell, OK, 79

25516 GOSS Benjamin F, Pryor Creek, OK,22; 25517, Flora, W, 21

31363 GOSS, George W, Pryor Creek, OK, 46; 3208, Mary A, W, 52

9148 GOSS, Lucretia M, Welch, OK, 23; Otis W, S, 2; Owen, S, 1

22575 GOSS, William P, Stilwell, OK, 32; Mamie J D, 6; Walter F, S, 5; William T, S, 3

31306 GOSSETT, Sterling O, Vinita, OK, 17, Box #12; James U Bro, 15; By James M. Gossett, Gdn.

33869 GOTT Alfonzo, Ft. Gibson, OK, 29; Gott Anna, Evansville AR, 52; Pickens, S, 16; James L, S, 13; Ruth D, 9

28174½ GOTT, Ella, Stilwell, OK, 16; Kennie Bro, 13; Alma, Sis, 7; By William Gott, Gdn.

33868 GOTT, John, Jr, Ft. Gibson, OK, 29; Susan E D, 4; Alice Pauline D, 2

23207 GOTT, John W, Stilwell, OK, 27

22789 GOTT, Pearl, Stilwell, OK, 22

6795 GOTT, Susan E, Ft. Gibson, OK, 49; Gott, Laura D, 20; James, S, 15; Sophia D, 13; Mamie D, 11; William H, S, 8; 5406, Nannie D, 4

8680 GOTT, Susan T, Nowata, OK, 59

[GOTT, William. See #4730]   *(Note: entry separate from other family groups)*

[GOURD, R. See RATTLINGGOURD.]

[GO-YIH-NE-E. See #9946]   *(Note: entry separate from other family groups)*

24643 GRAHAM, Elizabeth M Collinsville, OK, 27; Ellen G D, 9; Mason, Willis J, S, 7

13242 GRAHAM, Kate Chelsea, OK, 20

3973 GRAHAM, Luvada Collinsville, OK, 31; Rowden Amon, S, 14; Emma D, 12; Graham, Joseph Arthur, S, 3

Key: Guion Miller Application Number; Name; Address, Relation (to Head); Age in 1906

[GRAHAM, Mamie. See #4396]   *(Note: entry separate from other family groups)*

84443 GRAHAM, Ora J, Wyandotte, OK, 25
5765 GRANT Donald P, Grove, OK, 24
5610 GRANT, Geo O, Stilwell, OK, 23
25583 GRANT, Lillie M, Stilwell, OK, 28
25111 GRASS Daniel, Locust Grove, OK, 26
25110 GRASS, Jess, Locust Grove, OK, 36; 25556, Sarah, W, 25
25113 GRASS, Joseph, Locust Grove, OK, 38; 2498, Elizabeth, W, 32; Dave, S, 12; Ida D, 10; Thomas W, S, 8; Benjamin E, S, 5; Levi, S, 3
81 GRASS, Rider, Locust Grove, OK, 64; 80, Lucy, W, 61
28236 GRASS, Tom, Spavinaw, OK, 29; 9007, Betsy, W, 31; Tanner, Sequoyah, S, 11; Grass, Levi, S, 7; Daw-yah-nee-sah, S, 4; Jose D, 2
910 GRASS, William, Locust Grove, OK, 53; 452, Tooyennie, W, 48; James, S, 11
17804 GRASSHOPPER, George, Tahlequah, OK, 29
3054 GRASSHOPPER, Jack, Southwest City, MO, 63
768 GRAVITT, James M Catoosa, OK, 67; Oma L D, ¼
25178 GRAVITT, Jefferson M Catoosa, OK, 44
27872 GRAY, Emma J, Vinita, OK, 53
11453 GRAY, Jesse, Tahlequah, OK, 8;   By Horace Gray, Gdn.
5047 GRAY, Josanna Cove, OK, 49
27123 GRAY, Mary F, Ft. Smith AR, 20
4284 GRAY, Susan Cove, OK, 37
4953 GRAY, Susie C Choteau, OK, 53

[GRAY, Thomas J. See #10286]   *(Note: entry separate from other family groups)*

24677 GRAY, William Oce Cove, OK, 22
8911 GRAYSON Cynthia Whale, Porum, OK, 28; James, S, 5; Girty, Maria D, 9; Grayson, Emma D, 5/12

[GRAYSON, Napoleon. See #79]   *(Note: entry separate from other family groups)*

16917 GRAYSON, Samuel, Locust Grove, OK, 37; 6253, Carrie, W, 22; Annie D, 2
25793 GRAZIER, Homer M, Narcissa, OK, 22; Joseph, S, 3; Homer M, Jr, S, 1
1820 GRAZIER, Martha, Narcissa, OK, 56; Elmer, S, 17; Luther, S, 15; Ora D, 12; Alice, D, 10; Bertha D, 8
5516 GREASE Charles, Welling, OK, 44
5805 GREATHOUSE, May, Nowata, OK, 20; George Edward, S, 2
1124 GREECE Betsy, Welling, OK, 56; Carlile, Maggie, GD, 15; Speaker, Samuel, GS, 11; Dick, GS, 9; Joe, GS, 7
34185 GREECE, Edna, Tahlequah, OK, 10;   By John Greece, Gdn.
8094 GREECE, Ella, Welling, OK, 16

CHEROKEE DESCENDANTS RESIDING WEST OF MISSISSIPPI RIVER.
VOLUME II   (A – M)

Key: Guion Miller Application Number; Name; Address, Relation (to Head); Age in 1906

3147 GREECE, George, Tahlequah, OK, 49; 3308, Wuttie, W, 51; Skake, S, 20; Eliza D, 17; Jinnie D, 15

27351 GREECE, Isaac, Tahlequah, OK, 34; 17119, Lillie, W, 31; Lucy D, 4; Bird, S, 2

14046 GREECE, Nannie, Welling, OK, 27

33400 GREECE, Thomas, Tahlequah, OK, 25

11755 GREECE, Will Braggs, OK, 46; 9173, Nancy, W, 41

4018 GREEN Bertha M, Tahlequah, OK, 8;   By Paris Green, father and Gdn.

[GREEN, Ernestine L. See #2479]   *(Note: entries separate*
[GREEN, Ethel R. See #2479]   *from other family groups)*
[GREEN, Herbert L. See #2479]

220 GREEN, Evelyn Victoria, Kelso, OK, 21

24632 GREEN, Francis Chetopa, KS, 31; Lucy D, 5; Wylie R, S, 1

15599 GREEN, Hannah C, Ft. Gibson, OK, 38; Mary P D, 17; Floyd C, S, 10; Florence D, 8; Paul W, S, 6; Fannie A D, 3

8882 GREEN, Jackson Akins, OK, 18;   By Elizabeth Berry, Gdn.

23992 GREEN, Lanora B Akins, OK, 22; Marion F, S, 4; Jas F, S, 2; Benjamin F, S, 1/12

24706 GREEN, Laura B Chelsea, OK, 31; Scruggs, Lincoln, S, 12; Green, William T, S, 7; Emiline E D, 5; Carry M D, 3

26696 GREEN, Lenora Chapel, OK, 23; Lewis F, S, 5; Oscar R, S, 1

24615 GREEN, Louie P, Stilwell, OK, 24; James W, S, 3; John A, S, 2

2292 GREEN, Lowie Mae, Vinita, OK, 26

33799 GREEN, Mamie L, Tiawah, OK, 16; Carle E, S, 1

[GREEN, Mary. See #3151] *(Note: entry separate from other family groups)*

4017 GREEN, Mary J, Tahlequah, OK, 28; Harden H, Jr, S, 2; Marguritte S D, 1

22975 GREEN, Mary Jane Chance, OK, 44; Margaret A D, 15; Jesse, S, 13; Minnie E D, 11; John R, S, 9; Georgia D, 7; Preston D, S, 5

140 GREEN, Rachel D Claremore, OK, 20; Oliver Leo, S, 1

3547 GREEN, Ralph Seymour, St. Louis, 301 Chamber of Commerce, MO, 27

27499 GREENLEAF, Mary W, Kansas City, MO, 52; Martha E D, 15

27500 GREENLEAF, Robt W, Kansas City, MO, 23

31872 GREENWOOD, May B, Ramona, OK, 29; John M, S, 13; Ola C D, 10; Lelia D, 8; D. P, S, 3; Lester, S, 1/12

25688 GREENWOOD, Susie J Dewey, OK, 26; Martha E D, 11; William F, S, 9; Mary R D, 5; Hassie F D, 3

4005 GREER, Eugenia Rogers Chelsea, OK, 47

29290 GREER, Mattie F Chelsea, OK, 28; Vera M D, 6; Rufus P, S, 4

24588 GREER, Mae W, Maysville AR, 26; Jennie F D, 3; Alice Edna D, 1

28334 GREY, Minnie E, Owasso, OK, 30; Bartow, S, 8; Clara L D, 3

Key: Guion Miller Application Number; Name; Address, Relation (to Head); Age in 1906

[GRIBBLE, Ida. See #29730]   ⎤   *(Note: entries separate)*
[GRIBBLE Dollie. See #29730] ⎦   *from other family groups)*

7698 GRIDER, Margarette, Leach, OK, 39; Mary D, 9; Harry, S, 6; Clarence, S, 4
1950 GRIFFIN, Andrew J, Muskogee, OK, 57
19191 GRIFFIN, Chas, Ft. Gibson, OK, 27
28318 GRIFFIN, Eliza L, Muldrow, OK, 26; William H, S, 1
11529 GRIFFIN, Jack, Porum, OK, 29
3644 GRIFFIN, James, Jr, Fawn, OK, 16; Nannie, Sis, 15; Louis Bro, 10; Addie, Sis, 12; John Bro, 4;   By James D. Griffin, Gdn.
26232 GRIFFIN, Jenette, Metory, OK, 45; Cordrey, Willie A D, 8;   Griffin Alice D, 5
18349 GRIFFIN, Mary A, Warner, OK, 31; Lugie D, 13; Eliza D, 11; Tommy, S, 9; Charlie, S, 7; Joe, S, 4
13148 GRIFFITH, Martha J, Sallisaw, OK, 24; Mary F D, 7; Liddy J D, 5; Perry G, S, 3; Bonnie M D, 1
11654 GRIFFITH, Undeen, Sallisaw, OK, 21; William W, S, 2; Mary May, D, 1 [Died 3-7-1907]
19726 GRIGSBY Charlotte, Westville, OK, 12;   By Wm Grigsby, Gdn.
19728 GRIGSBY Dan, Westville, OK, 18;   By Wm Grigsby, Gdn.
19727 GRIGSBY, Emmons, Westville, OK, 16;   By Wm Grigsby, Gdn.
19724 GRIGSBY, Henry C, Westville, OK, 14;   By Wm Grigsby, Gdn.
19725 GRIGSBY, Jas, Westville, OK, 14;   By Wm Grigsby, Gdn.
5707 GRIGSBY, Jennie, Westville, OK,
10595 GRIMET, George, Vian, OK, 25; 10671, Ida, W, 24
11559 GRIMET, Turner, Marble, OK, 21; 14275, Mary, W, 19
10301 GRINNETT, William Cookson, OK, 47;12407, John, S, 14
12136 GRINSTEAD, Mary B Coffeyville, KS, 23
22848 GRISHAM, Susan L, Westville, OK, 26; Beavers, Ellen I D, 9; Grisham Clifford, S, 3; Lucile[sic] D, 1
16722 GRITTS Anderson W, Vian, OK, 56; 12882, Lizzie, W, 51
2339 GRITTS, Franklin, Gritts, OK, 72
5254 GRITTS, George, Whitmire, OK, 35; Crabgrass, S, 4
19721 GRITTS, George, Welling, OK, 25
30432 GRITTS, George A, Vian, OK, 25; 16658, Rachel, W, 26
8313 GRITTS, James, Tahlequah, OK, 13;   By James B. Layne, Gdn.

[GRITTS, James. See #16349]   *(Note: entry separate from other family groups)*

7885 GRITTS, John, Welling, OK, 20
9025 GRITTS, Levi, Tahlequah, OK, 32; Levi, Jr Cou, 9
36484 GRITTS, Levi, Tahlequah, OK, 22
36485 GRITTS, Maggie, Tahlequah, OK, 21; Johnson, Martha, 2
2699 GRITTS, Nancy, Stilwell, OK, 64

Key: Guion Miller Application Number; Name; Address, Relation (to Head); Age in 1906

4079 GRITTS, Nancy Christie, OK, 61

42528 GRITTS, Nannie Christie, OK, 25; Charlotte D, 6; Jennie D, 5; Nicol, S, 3; Nancy, D, 2

9028 GRITTS, Ned, Tahlequah, OK, 29

[GRITTS, Peggy. See #936] *(Note: entry separate from other family groups)*

21141 GRITTS, Sarah, Welling, OK, 38

5320 GRITTS, Stann[sic] Ballard, OK, 28

9026 GRITTS, Susie Q Baptist, OK, 22

12645 GRITTS, Thos, Tahlequah, OK, 56;17120, Agnes, W, 46;36486, Charlotte D, 19; John, S, 16;Bernice D, 14;Steve, S, 12; Lily D, 10; Lizzie D, 7; Thomas, S, 4

1732 GRITTS, Thomas, Jr, Tahlequah, OK, 22; 6057, Lizzie, W, 18

1096 GRITTS, Tom, Tahlequah, OK, 46; 1100, Emma, W, 35; 1125, Bird, S, 16; 1126, Edna, D of W, 10

30431 GRITTS, Wesley W, Vian, OK, 21

11602 GRITTS, William Cookson, OK, 29

42195 GRITTS, William Cookson, OK, 31

25680 GROOMS, Lucile Chetopah, KS, 7; Leota, Sis, 6; By Robert Grooms, Gdn.

25679 GROOMS, Lue Chetopah, KS, 22; Lessie, S, 3; Lethie D, 2

4632 GROUNDHOG, Joanna, Stilwell, OK,23

10389 GROUNDHOG, Joe, Tahlequah, OK, 24; 14697, Nancy, W, 20

12152 GROVE, Evan E, Porum, OK, 28

11806 GROVE, Johnson, Porum, OK, 28

12149 GROVE, Ned, Porum, OK, 24

12145 GROVE, Susie, Porum, OK, 26

12147 GROVE, Fannie, Porum, OK, 17

16551 GROVES, James C, Porum, OK, 28; Lawrence M, S, 6

1583 GROVES, John, Porum, OK, 34; Bird, S, 1/3

23240 GRUBB Charlotte, Gideon, OK, 30; Lillie M D, 13; Ella B D, 11; Lydia J D, 9; Joseph, S, 7; Rosie J D, 4; John, S, 2

33115 GRUBBS, Madenia, Tiawah, OK, 28; Naomi D, 10; Monon D, 9; Marie D, 5

8093 GUESS Addie, Welling, OK, 20

7706 GUESS Albert, Ramona, OK, 17; Eliza, Sis, 13; Susia[sic], Sis, 11; By Frances Haggard, Gdn.

5059 GUESS, George Chloeta, OK, 25; 27244,Jennie, W, 26; High, S, 2

17322 GUESS, Tom, Kansas, OK, 16; Polly, Sis, 15; Maud, Sis, 13; By Alice Beamer, Gdn.

[GUESS, Victoria. See #42978]   *(Note: entry separate from other family groups)*

6676 GUESS, Watie, Welling, OK, 34; Willie, S, 13; Nannie D, 1

CHEROKEE DESCENDANTS RESIDING WEST OF MISSISSIPPI RIVER.
VOLUME II (A – M)

Key: Guion Miller Application Number; Name; Address, Relation (to Head); Age in 1906

[GUINEAHEAD Charley. See #5927] *(Note: entry separate from other family groups)*

12805½ GUINN Alma Lee Chetopah, KS, 19; Charley E Bro, 16; James L, Jr Bro, 14; Willie I Bro, 11; By James L. Guinn, Gdn.

4549 GUINN, James D, Tahlequah, OK, 32; 28393, Luellen, W, 30; Alice Ellen D, 10; James D, Jr, S, 8; Mary Etta D, 7; Anna T D, 4

13183 GUINN, Malinda, Southwest City, MO, 23

23001 GUINN, Mary Christie, OK, 17; Carrie D, 1/12

31770 GUINN, Mayze[sic], Tahlequah, OK, 1; By Amelia Guinn, Gdn.

41007 GUINN, Myrtle, Tahlequah, OK, 16

12805 GUINN, Sarah Chetopa, KS, 32; Roach, Robert George, S, 9; Guinn, Ida G D, 2

33448 GULAGER Christian, Tahlequah, OK, 32

33238 GULAGER, Henry G, Tahlequah, OK, 24

33237 GULAGER, John D, Tahlequah, OK, 18; By Martha L. Gulager, Gdn.

6999 GULAGER, Martha L, Tahlequah, OK, 51

34722 GULAGER, Mary E, Tahlequah, OK, 26

42818 GULAGER, William M, Muskogee, OK, 35

4380 GUNTER, Elba H, Muldrow, OK, 28

4377 GUNTER, Fannie, Muldrow, OK, 27

7423 GUNTER, George, Gans, OK, 33; Okla D, 5; Ola D, 4; Addie D, 2

23594 GUNTER, Geo. W Coffeyville, KS, 31; Lois Fern D, 2½

2004 GUNTER, James M, Redland, OK, 31; Etta D, 5

901 GUNTER, John E, Muldrow, OK, 60; 4378, Marvin J, S, 16

9429 GUNTER, John E, Inola, OK, 37; Fannie R D, 9; Rachel R D, 1/12

23480 GUSTIN Charles E, Hulbert, OK, 24

5340 GUTHRIE Calvin P, Jr, Stilwell, OK, 42; 5796, Ruth, W, 45; Oscar, S, 20; Margaret, D, 17; Florence C D, 15

26683 GUTHRIE Charles, Stilwell, OK, 14; Emerson Bro, 12; By J. W. Kelley, Gdn.

12229 GUTHRIE, Loren P Cookson, OK, 44; Myrtle D, 9; William, S, 6; Maud D, 3; Odie B, S, 1

5307 GUTHRIE, Martha, Evansville, AR, 51;Jesse A, S, 18; Lorenzo L, S,16; Ora Ella, D,11

5338 GUTHRIE, Oscar, Evansville AR, 28; Lora V D, 2

5344 GUTHRIE, Walter D, Stilwell, OK, 36

5339 GUTHRIE, William P, Evansville AR, 41

27479 HABICH, George E, Hudson, OK, 31; Dorothy D, 2; Ethel D, 1/12

12196 HACKER, Frances L Claremore, OK, 25; Almon R, S, 8; William McKinley, S, 5; Alexander G, S, 3; Frank, S, 1 [Died 8-22-'06]

3706 HADDAN, Elizabeth J, Pryor Creek, OK, 26; Thomas E. F, S, 8; Marie S D, 3

28010 HADDOCK Charles W Collinsville, OK, 14; George W Bro, 12; Dewey W Bro, 8; Myrtle M, Sis, 6; By John T. Haddock, Gdn.

28251 HADDOCK, Mollie Collinsville, OK, 15

CHEROKEE DESCENDANTS RESIDING WEST OF MISSISSIPPI RIVER.

VOLUME II   (A – M)

Key: Guion Miller Application Number; Name; Address, Relation (to Head); Age in 1906

13309 HADE, Ruth W Checotah, OK, 58

2736 HADEN Caldona, Knobnoster, MO, 24, Box #133; Juanita D, 4

26390 HAEGERT, Rudolph H, Shawnee, OK, U.S. Recruiting Office, 25

17970 HAIFLICH, Hettie Collinsville, OK, 36; Brady, Etheral D, 10; Edgar, S, 8; Haiflich, Heimean, S, 1

14098 HAGLAND, Fannie E, Tahlequah, OK, 27; Marie M D, 3

33209 HAIKEY, Henrietta, Muskogee, OK, 30

25189 HAIL, Elizabeth, Welch, OK, 20

29992 HAIL, General M Akins, OK, 24; 8129, Ada C, W, 19; Nina M D, ¼

26915 HAIL, George W, Tahlequah, OK, 20; Owen L, S, 1/6

1734 HAIL, Geo. Washington, Hanson,OK,62; Mary E D, 17; Maudie M D, 14; George J, S, 11

6689 HAIL, James M, Welch, OK, 55; Amy D, 17; Kittie M D, 15; Oscar S, S, 9

33324 HAIL, John G, Welch, OK, 25

5633 HAIL, John P, Gideon, OK, 57; John W, S, 16; William L, S, 14; Annie E D, 12; A. Cleo B, S, 9; Lee M, S, 5; Mary Lee D, 2

26298 HAIL, Joseph, Roland, OK, 55; Zula Lee D, 16; George Beely, S, 14; Bessie May D, 10; Alla Luada D, 8; Eliza Lucinda D, 5; Jada James, S, 1

9438 HAILBEAN Betsy, Oaks, OK, 80

4593 HAIR Addie, Tahlequah, OK, 16; Annie, Sis, 14;   By John R. Price, Gdn.

22784 HAIR Alex, Stilwell, OK, 22

5205 HAIR Alex, Peggs, OK, 20

1211 HAIR Amanda, Proctor, OK, 61

3057 HAIR Andy, Rose, OK, 51; Bessie P D, 20; Lucie J D, 19; Nannie D, 17; Jesse J, S, 15; Maud Y D, 13; Frank J, S, 11; Delilah D, 9

9269 HAIR Andy, Melvin, OK, 49; 10426, Lizzie, W, 50

2416 HAIR Annie, Eucha, OK, 26

17790 HAIR Bird, Melvin, OK, 27; 17791, Jennie S, W, 21; Pearl D, 1

24756 HAIR Cherokee N, Rose, OK, 22

4412 HAIR Dave, Spavinaw, OK, 53; 462, Sarah, W, 62

4411 HAIR Dave, Jr, Eucha, OK, 25; 652, Eliza, W, 23; Susie D, 1

4791 HAIR, Frank, Proctor, OK, 21; 24045, Annie, W, 22

1964 HAIR, James, Vian, OK, 59

5622 HAIR, James, Proctor, OK, 23; 10382, Sallie, W, 18

16559 HAIR, James, Locust Grove, OK, 23

[HAIR, Jefferson. See #468]
[HAIR, Jack. See #468]   *(Note: entries separate*
[HAIR, Lizzie. See #468]   *from other family groups)*
[HAIR, George. See #468]
[HAIR Charlotte. See #468]

[HAIR, Jimmie. See #10168]   *(Note: entry separate from other family groups)*

Key: Guion Miller Application Number; Name; Address, Relation (to Head); Age in 1906

7025 HAIR, John, Stilwell, OK, 55; 7027, Lucy, W, 57
13176 HAIR, John, Melvin, OK, 36

[HAIR, John. See #13941]   *(Note: entry separate from other family groups)*

29887 HAIR, Leach, Hulbert, OK, 21
13074 HAIR, Lizzie, Tahlequah, OK, 17;   By Jennie Hair, Gdn.
36150 HAIR, Maggie, Hulbert, OK, 12;   By Andy Hair, Gdn.
 9414 HAIR, Maude, Lometa, OK, 35
 4611 HAIR, Nick, Spavinaw, OK, 21

[HAIR, Oscar. See #9234]   *(Note: entry separate from other family groups)*

22785 HAIR, Sarah, Stilwell, OK, 22; Betsy, (D?), 1
 9172 HAIR, Walter Campbell, OK, 20; Betsy, Sis, 17; Oscar Bro, 15; By Fannie Hair, Gdn.
15606 HAIR, Watson, Lometa, OK, 10; Sarah, Sis, 8; Samuel Bro, 56; By Maud Hair, Gdn.
16966 HAIR, William M, Pryor Creek, OK, 34; 5189, Susie, W, 29; Fields, Walter, S, 12
 9311 HAIR, Wilson, Melvin, OK, 20
37647 HALE, Mattie Claremore, OK, 17
 3891 HALE, Nancy E Brushy, OK, 32; Chulie D, 15; Myrtle D, 12; Emma D, 10; Nannie, D, 5; Thomas, S, 1/6
28874 HALEY, Nellie, Oglesby, OK, 34; Arnee L D, 14; Albert J, S, 12; Emma Q D, 9; William W, S, 6; Emmett C, S, 4

[HALFBREED, Lucy. See #2688]   *(Note: entry separate from other family groups)*

11918 HALFBREED, Webster, Miami, OK, 37; Thomas C, S, 2

[HALL Andrew Z. See #36556]   *(Note: entry separate from other family groups)*

28001 HALL, Edward L, Vinita, OK, 37; Walter L, S, 10; Louis F, S, 7; Beatrice G D, 5; Jessie G D, 2; Mary E D, 1/12
13962 HALL, Esther, Vian, OK, 51; Wattie, S, 14; Floyd, S, 12; Bess D, 9
25860 HALL, Franklin Catale, OK, 39; Ollie D, 11; Webster, S, 10; Call W, S, 5; Frank Hearn, S, 2; Mollie May D, 1
26565 HALL, Frederick, Vera, OK, 33; Martha May D, 9; William Newton, S, 7; Arthur Lee, S, 5; Elsie Marie D, 3
23770 HALL, James Eugene, Vinita, OK, 39; Mae Evelyn D, 13
22558 HALL, Jane E, Wann, OK, 21; Gilbert S, S, 2; Laura E D, ¼
35328 HALL, Jane P, Vinita, OK, 25

Key: Guion Miller Application Number; Name; Address, Relation (to Head); Age in 1906

28000 HALL, Jasper Newton, Bluejacket, OK, R.F.D. #2, 31; Abner, S, 11; Jesse R, S, 5; Joseph N, S, 2; R. Lee, S, 1/12

13113 HALL, John M Catale, OK, 23

10353 HALL, John R Chetopa, KS, 21

9396 HALL, Joseph Ann, Vinita, OK, 61

6525 HALL, Lucy Coffeyville, KS, 24; Luella D, 6; Bessie Stacy D, 4; Kitty D, 1

23379 HALL, Lula P Claremore, OK, 17; Bessie May D, 2

1099 HALL, Martha C Afton, OK, 64; Benjamin, S, 17

24450 HALL, Martha Viola, Fairland, OK, 26; James R, S, 4; Martha E D, 1

[HALL, Mary. See #4802]   *(Note: entry separate from other family groups)*

5150 HALL, Mary E, Vinita, OK, 62

8035 HALL, Maud Chetopa, KS, 21

28002 HALL, Sewell W, Kingsburg CA, 39; 28003, Bessie D, 17

2406 HALL, Susan Big Cabin, OK, 18; Jeff F, S, 1

11105 HALL, William F, Stilwell, OK, 35; Stella E D, 9; John W, S, 6; Gracie D, 2

13112 HALL, William O, Oglesby, OK, 26; Floyd E, S, 2; Charlie O, S, 3

28692 HALLFORD, Ida J, Foyil, OK, 28; William R, S, 10; James W, S, 6; John A, S, 4; Nellie E D, 2

24391 HALLMARK, Nellie, Stilwell, OK, 19; Pleasant, S 2; Allen, S, 1/3

31273 HALLUM, Mamie C Centralia, OK, 20

3302 HALLUM, Mary E, Vinita, OK, 25; Maud D, 5; Eliza May D, 3

23078 HALSELL, Eva,Vinita, OK,20; Clarence, Bro, 17; Mary, Sis, 15; By W E. Halsell,Gdn.

23077 HALSELL, Ewing, Vinita, OK, 29

17163 HALSELL, Josie, Vinita, OK, 31

22646 HALSELL, Pauline P, Muskogee, OK,   43

8007 HAM Betsy, Woodley, OK, 34; David, S, 15; Pearl D, 14; Jennie D, 11; Osie D, 9; Martha D, 7; Wesley, S, 5

23736 HAMBLEN, Modie, Westville, OK, 19

23164 HAMIL, Victoria, Nowata, OK, 27; Elsie Myrtle D, 9; Lester, S, 4; Mable J D, 3; Geo. Edward, S, ½

28791 HAMILTON Alice Bell, Joplin, MO, 25

11509 HAMILTON Alsie Dewey, OK, 33; Hugh M, S, 9; Clarence, S, 7; James R, S, 2; George T, S, 1

29730 HAMILTON Barbara Bartlesville, OK, 27; Gribble, Ida D, 8; Dollie D, 6; Hamilton, Ralph, S, 3; Luster D, 1

29190 HAMILTON, Elizabeth, Parkhill, OK,   25

29484 HAMILTON, Neppie, Muskogee, OK, 106 Kankakee St, 25; Ballard, Jessie D, 7; Timson Agnes D, 4

5863 HAMILTON, Susan C. T. Okmulgee, OK, 38; Mary E D, 11; Waunett D, 8; Jessie E, D, 6

Key: Guion Miller Application Number; Name; Address, Relation (to Head); Age in 1906

5333 HAMMER Adam, Westville, OK, 54

9006 HAMMER Annie, Peggs, OK, 29; Ginseng, S, 5

14695 HAMMER, Eli Braggs, OK, 25

23368 HAMMER, Ellen, Westville, OK, 19

2465 HAMMER, John, Westville, OK, 54; 2464, Margaret, W, 52; Walter, S, 9

11190 HAMMER, Looney Braggs, OK, 39; 6674, Jennie, W, 31; Josie D, 13; Eliza D, 9; Jane D, 11; Mary D, 4; Minnie D, 1

4909 HAMMER, Rider, Kansas, OK, 48; 43938, Ury, S, ¼

23467 HAMMETT, Mary Claremore, OK, 31; Richard, S, 11; Mary E D, 10; Ethel C D, 8; James E, S, 5

30685 HAMPTON Bertha, Needmore, OK, 16

405 HAMPTON, Geo. W, Sallisaw, OK, 52; Charlie S, S, 16; Mary E D, 15; Walter A, S, 13; Sadie D, 10

22863 HAMPTON, Georgie E, Grove, OK, 22; William C, S, 6; George S, S, 4

[HAMPTON, Jennie. See #22594] ⎤   *(Note: entries separate*

[HAMPTON Bert. See #22594] ⎦   *from other family groups)*

13943 HAMPTON, John W, Greenbrier, OK, 35; Charley, S, 12; Nettie D, 8; Walter, S, 5; Henry, S, 4; Oto, S, 1

40440 HAMPTON, Lula, Grove, OK, 25; Maxine D, 2

32287 HAMPTON, Mary, Salina, OK, 11; By R. L. Pack, Gdn.

13633 HAN, Mary E, Vinita, OK, 42; Dail, Mary F D, 15; Mark L, S, 10; Springer, S, 7; Han, Mattie J D, 2; Dora M D, 1

216 HANAN, Margaret L, Talala, OK, 35; Joseph E, S, 19; Newton E, Jr, S, 17; James T, S, 15; Roland H, S, 12; Levi E, S, 10; Wesley D, S, 8; Cherokee Delilah D, 6; Emmet F, S, 4; Lawrence J, S, 1; Florence D, 1

22824 HANCOCK, Viola S, Pryor Creek, OK, 34; Neva M D, 11; Nina M D, 9; William H, S, 6; Mabel F D, 4; Maggie L D, 1

11983 HAND, Tom, Marble City, OK, 21

26662 HANDLE Dave, Zena, OK, 21

29633 HANDLE, Tom, Zena, OK, 23; 13360, Lesra, W, 26; Marie D, 1; Betsy D, 5

1101 HANDLE, William, Zena, OK, 51; Edward, S, 18

13453 HANER, Linnie, Sleeper, OK, 42; 13454, Love, Lizzie D, 18; Richard, S, 15; Haner, Lucinda D, 10; Ton, S, 9; Nancy D, 3

32413 HANEY Annie M Big Cabin, OK, 20

30023 HANEY, Floyd, Welling, OK, 4; Lloyd May, Sis, 2;   By James Haney, Gdn.

11875 HANKS Calvin J, Webbers Falls, OK,   48; Ora May D, 15; James Otto, S, 13; Maud K, D, 12; Grace D, 11; Fannie D, 9; Annie D, 7; Emma D, 2

28029 HANKS Daisy, Sallisaw, OK, 32

2178 HANKS, Robert T, Webbers Falls, OK, 66; 26680, Mary E, W, 42; Roberta I D, 12

20172 HANLIN, Emma H, Turley, OK, 31; Hussey Clyde C, S, 12

Key: Guion Miller Application Number; Name; Address, Relation (to Head); Age in 1906

1736 HANNA Claude, Grove, OK, 12;   By Wiley Hanna, Gdn.

24365 HANNA Cleaveland, Miami, OK, 22

26395 HANNA, Eliza J Dodge, OK, 25; Dennis R, S, 4; John R, S, 1

1739 HANNA, Nancy, Grove, OK, 31; Annie E D, 6; Cora O D, 5

27433 HANNA, Rosa A Dawes, OK, 31; Robert O, S, 7; Mabel L D, 6

13474 HANNAH, Georgia F, Sallisaw, OK, 27

22658 HANNAH, John, Stilwell, OK, 20

5584 HANNAH, Julia, Evansville AR, 35; Lee H, S, 19; William T, S, 16; Stella M D, 13; Samuel A, S, 11; Chuce, S, 8; Hooley Bell, S, 6; Daniel, S, 4

23393 HANNAH, William Stilwell, OK, 25; May E D, 6; Charles B, S, 4; Cherokee D, 2

25992 HANNON, Edward, Nowata, OK, 26

1605 HANNON, Jennie, Nowata, OK, 46; Gertrude D, 16; James, S, 14; Frank, S, 12; Wadie, S, 8

1686 HANSON, Pigeon, Estella, OK, 29; Rosie Lee D, 3

21094 HARCHO, John Christie, OK, 54

14195 HARDBARGER, John Bunch, OK, 60; 9704, Peggie, W, 25; John, Jr, S, 8; Sam, S, 5; Annie D, 2; Lewis, S, 16; Johnson, S, 13   [Died 11-'06]

[HARDER, William H. See #30363]   *(Note: entry separate from other family groups)*

6466 HARDIN Caldona C, Oolagah, OK, 49; Delta L D, 17; Jack, S, 15; Mattie D, 13; Maggie D, 10; George D, S, 8

23553 HARDY Anna, Grove, OK, 27; Jennie Ethel D, 9; Howard Lee, S, 6;   Claud, S, 4; John R, S, 1

3914 HARDY Dudley R, Grove, OK, 21; Jennie M D, 1

4372 HARDY, Henry W, Southwest City, MO, 16; Mary Alice, Sis, 13; Lee Bro, 11; Della, Sis, 9; Opal Polson, Sis, 5;   By Josiah T. Hardy, Gdn.

7575 HARDY, John Davis, Dodge, OK, 23; Earl S, S, 2

4282 HARDY, Myrtie M, Southwest City, MO, 19

2050 HARLAN Albert W, Fairland, OK, 60

8000 HARLAN Andrew O Big Cabin, OK, 38; Myrtle B D, 12; Nina E D, 9

7999 HARLAN Clifford, Vinita, OK, 25; Homer R, S, 3; Opal A D, 1

7998 HARLAN, George W, White Oak, OK, 50

4386 HARLAN, John Henry, Holly CO, 28; Harry W, S, 6; Clifton A, S, 4; Frances L D, 1

4390 HARLAN, Nathan L, Vinita, OK, 58

2650 HARLAN, Ruba V, Fairland, OK, 7; Daisy, Sis, 11; Bessie M, Sis, 14; By Myrtle Harlan, Gdn.

4239 HARLAN, William, Ft. Gibson, OK, 37

24545 HARLAN, William L, WhiteOak,OK,32; 24546, Lucinda, W, 26; Grace L D, 1

10929 HARLAND, Geo. Alex. Westville, OK, 51

Key: Guion Miller Application Number; Name; Address, Relation (to Head); Age in 1906

29772 HARLEN, Huey, Proctor, OK, 12; Ellis Bro, 10; Annie B, Sis, 6; By Johnson Mayes, Gdn.

11016 HARLESS, Lola, Siloam Springs AR, 25; Carr C, S, 2; Luster L Bro, 10

12390 HARLESS, Louisa, Pryor Creek, OK, 15; Reed Warren Bro, 17; Rufus Bro, 19; By Annie L. Abbott, Gdn.

597 HARLESS, Ophela J, Peggs, OK, 31; Guy, S, 17; Trenton, S, 13; Elizabeth D, 8; Robert, S, 2

27660 HARLIN Alviso V, Grove, OK, 28

3658 HARLIN Callie D, Welch, OK, 18

28394 HARLIN Charles, Grove, OK, 12;   By W. E. Ross, Gdn.

2051 HARLIN David L, Fairland, OK, 63; David L, Jr, S, 5

23134 HARLIN Delbert, Fairland, OK, 27; Cecil W, S, 7

31397 HARLIN, Edgar C, Welch, OK, 34; Claude, S, 12; Esther V D, 10; Luther A, S, 8; Edgar L, S, 4; Mary E D, 2

26508 HARLIN, Edna E, Summers AR, 21

2694 HARLIN, Eli, Tahlequah, OK, 28

31906 HARLIN, Ellis C, 32; John R, S, 8; Nannie C D, 5; Ellis S, S, 3

6490 HARLIN, George,Christie, OK,18; Caleb Bro, 16; Eliza J, Sis,13; By Silas Harlin,Gdn.

24370 HARLIN, James Dutch Mills AR, 26

2682 HARLIN, James E, Grove, OK, 76; 2681, Nancy A, W, 64

27661 HARLIN, Jarrett B, Grove, OK, 22

5882 HARLIN, Jesse C, Welch, OK, 23

4636 HARLIN, John, Summers AR, 62; 4862, Eliza, W, 56; 26510, Cherokee D, 20; 26509, Sarah E D, 17; Eli, S, 15

12426 HARLIN, John H, Welch, OK, 31; Miriam Louise D, 5

[HARLIN, Maria. See #5720]   *(Note: entry separate from other family groups)*

26511 HARLIN, Nannie J, Summers AR, 22 [Died 8-1906]; By John Harlin, Gdn.

[HARLIN, Ned. See #5721]   *(Note: entry separate from other family groups)*

43488 HARLIN, Richard G Baxter Springs, KS, 2;   By Lewis S. Harlin, Gdn.

32785 HARLIN, Ridge H, San Luis Obispo, CA, 50

5880 HARLIN, Ruth E, Welch, OK, 35 [Non compos.] By Edward D. Ballard, Gdn.

6491 HARLIN, Silas Christie, OK, 51; 17023, Ellis, S, 11

12602 HARLIS, Harrison Choteau, OK, 14;   By William Harlis, Gdn.

13694 HARLOW Alabama Dawson, OK, 53; Samuel T, S, 16; Rosa I D, 11

13025 HARLOW Annie, Hominy, OK, 31; Crittenden Albert C, S, 12

31375 HARLOW, John, Owasso, OK, 23

2399 HARLOW, Peggy A Chetopa, KS, 42; Alice D, 20; James, S, 19; Joseph, S, 16; Elick, S, 13; Beulah M D, 10

Key: Guion Miller Application Number; Name; Address, Relation (to Head); Age in 1906

27010 HARLOW, Walter, Hollow, OK, 21

31376 HARLOW, William S, Owasso, OK, 21

42971 HARMER, Katie, Gritts, OK, 24; Emmer M D, 6; Jessie D, 5; Charley, S, 3; Olin, S, 2

24616 HARMON Benjamin, Webbers Falls, OK, 25

6310 HARMON Charles, Texanna, OK, 62; Maggie D, 9; Edward, S, 7; Manda D, 4; Annie D, 2

1688 HARMON Cynthia P, Webbers Falls, OK, 62

24593 HARMON, Elizabeth, Webbers Falls, OK, 29

29858 HARMON, Henrietta, Webbers Falls, OK, 39

24594 HARMON, Lena, Webbers Falls, OK, 21

24617 HARMON, McGilbra D, Webbers Falls, OK, 27

6720 HARMON, Nancy Brent, OK, 51; Jack, S, 19; Whitsett, S, 17; Jim, S, 14

31592 HARMON, Willoughby Brent, OK, 26

422 HARNAGE Custis[sic], Talala, OK, 39; 25957, Fannie C, W, 32; Emma Ruth, D, 6; James Hall, S, 4; Nannie Pauline D, 3

25830 HARNAGE, Jesse L, Tulsa, OK, 35

26667 HARNAGE, John G, Tahlequah, OK, 30; 23529, Jane S, W, 20

22905 HARNAGE, Lena, Tahlequah, OK, 20

24684 HARNAGE, Rosana, Tahlequah, OK, 20

27491 HARNAGE, William C, Tahlequah, OK, 24

6432 HARNAGE, William T, Tahlequah, OK, 59; Ruth B D, 16

5522 HARNAGE, William W, Muskogee, OK, 54; 8167 Richard, S, 17; 8168 Charles, S, 14

10899 HARNAR, Nellie M Bluejacket, OK, 27, R.F.D. #1; Eulailiah D, 7; Ralph R, S, 5; Claud R, S, 4; Randall D, S, 2; Clyde, S, 1/6

12241 HARP, Ellis Cookson, OK, 30

5794 HARP, Ruth M, Porum, OK, 18

30014 HARP, Thomas L, Tulsa, OK, 23

6961 HARPER, Elsie Surrat, Foyil, OK, 23; Cherokee D, 2 [Died 1-24-1907]

10736 HARPER, Polly, Texanna, OK, 18

27158 HARPER, Sarah C, Red Rock, NM, 36; Olive M D, 15; Elroy L, S, 14; Lelie J D, 13; Madison T, S, 10; William E, S, 1

28831 HARRELL, Louise H, Miles, OK, 25; Mary T D, ¼

3151 HARREN, Mattie C, Proctor, OK, 48; Green, Mary D, 17; Sanders, Nannie D, 15; Sherley[sic], Mattie D, 6

17891 HARRIS Alice R, Pantano AR, 26

22651 HARRIS Bessie L Collinsville, OK, 23; George R, S, 4; Violet S D, 2

38557 HARRIS Bettie V Catoosa, OK, 15; By Jos. W Bridges, Gdn.

24058 HARRIS Bird, Patton CA, 22

[HARRIS Bonnie. See #28727]   *(Note: entry separate from other family groups)*

Key: Guion Miller Application Number; Name; Address, Relation (to Head); Age in 1906

23608 HARRIS C. Parker, Muskogee, OK, 21
 1219 HARRIS Callie, Tahlequah, OK, 10;   By Colonel J. Harris, Gdn.
  686 HARRIS Charles, Muskogee, OK, 64; Charles D, S, 18; William B, S, 15
29452 HARRIS Charles Collinsville, OK, 24
 1220 HARRIS Charles H, Tahlequah, OK, 7;   By Colonel J. Harris, Gdn.
38558 HARRIS Adeline Catoosa, OK, 6;   By Jos. W. Bridges, Gdn.
28728 HARRIS Chester H, Muskogee, OK, 24; William C, S, ¾
 8148 HARRIS Claude, Gritts, OK, 18
  968 HARRIS Colonel J, Tahlequah, OK, 50
24057 HARRIS Daisy, Yuma AZ, 31
11735 HARRIS Daisy V, Longmont CO, 25, 320 Emery St.
 8212 HARRIS David, Gritts, OK, 21
15988 HARRIS Dennis B, Muskogee, OK, 25; Claude, S, 3; De Witt, S, 3/6
11887 HARRIS, Emily Coffeyville, KS, 51; Fred A, S, 20; Minnie D, 18; Charles J, S,
        15
11722 HARRIS, Eva M, Pryor Creek, OK, 13;   By Mary S. Gwartney, Gdn.
   28 HARRIS, Flora J, Long View, TX, 55
 1132 HARRIS, Ida Josephine Big Cabin, OK, 36; 23932, Flora May D, 19; 3924,
        Gertie N, D, 17; Ulalah S D, 15; Roy C, S, 14; John W, Jr, S, 9
 1299 HARRIS, James, Ketchum, OK, 71
11718 HARRIS, James H Collbran CO, 43
 1218 HARRIS, Joel A, Tahlequah, OK, 12;   By Colonel J. Harris, Gdn.
29090 HARRIS, John E, Pryor Creek, OK, 18; Bessie M, Sis, 15;   By John H. Harris,
        Gdn.
 5762 HARRIS, John R, Muskogee, OK, 32
 1845 HARRIS, Johnson, Greenbrier, OK, 24
  921 HARRIS, Joseph Alluwe, OK, 32; James S, S, 8; Othello, S, 6; Roy, S, 3; Troy,
        S, 3

[HARRIS, Joseph A. See #24910]   *(Note: entry separate from other family groups)*

17266 HARRIS, Lucy, Porum, OK, 11;   By William Harris, Gdn.
41516 HARRIS, Malinda Checotah, OK, 11; Frank M Bro, 14; Nila, Sis, 10;
        By A. J. Shostid, Gdn.
30111 HARRIS, Margaret C Claremore, OK, 21
 7586 HARRIS, Martha A, Vinita, OK, 51; Richard, S, 16; Willie, S, 15
11817 HARRIS, Martha L Collinsville, OK, 41; Johnnie A, S, 16; Robert P, S, 13;
        Nellie M, D, 9; William M, S, 6
23905 HARRIS, Mary C, Gideon, OK, 22
 8894 HARRIS, Mary J, Vinita, OK, 54
10923 HARRIS, Mary J, Foyil, OK, 20
30375 HARRIS, Olive M Afton, OK, 22

1392 HARRIS, Parker Collins, Muskogee, OK, 61; 23609, Emily D, 19; James G, S, 17; Sue L D, 16; Mary U D, 13; George, S, 11; Martha D, 7; Ida D, 5; Kate D, 3

820 HARRIS, Philo, Lynch, OK, 58

23610 HARRIS, Robert, Muskogee, OK, 24

7505 HARRIS, Thomas, Muskogee, OK, 29; 35268, Nancy J, W, 21; James, S, 11; Frank, S, 2; Jesse, S, 1

16864 HARRIS, Thomas J Claremore, OK, 26

16091 HARRIS, William, Porum, OK, 30; 23440, Annie, W, 19; Walter, S, 3; Martha D, 1

29091 HARRIS, William H, Pryor Creek, OK, 23

1923 HARRIS, William R, Greenbrier, OK, 26

[HARRIS, Wyley B. See #5009]   *(Note: entries separate*
[HARRIS, Ward B. See #5009]   *from other family groups)*
[HARRIS, Elizabeth. See #5009]

26175 HARRISON Andrew P Bluejacket, OK, 36; Marguerite E D, 3

9209 HARRISON, Edgarrena, Nowata, OK, 42; Allison, Laura Bell D, 16; Paten, S, 14; Clara D, 11; Edith D, 9; Harrison, Mary D, 4

24968 HARRISON, Florence Adair, OK, 21;   Vivian M, S, 1/3

[HARRISON, Jessie J. See #41543]   *(Note: entry separate from other family groups)*

36505 HARRISON, Josie, Wetumka, OK, 21

9215 HARRISON, Lella, Muskogee, OK, 26; Ray, S, 4; Hazel L D, 3; Lloyd C, S, 5/12

11768 HARRISON, Mary A Afton, OK, 69

4804 HARRISON, Nannie D, Oktaha, OK, 28; N. Rector, S, 9; Bertha M D, 6; Johnnie, S, 4; Harrie[sic], S, 2

24500 HARRISON, Nathan E Bluejacket, OK, 27

24430 HARRISON, Pearl, Sallisaw, OK, 15

24020 HARRISON, Robbie J Collyer, KS, 22; Harold P, S, 1

23404 HARROLD, Rebecca M, Needmore, OK, 26; William, S, 10; Maggie D, 8; Tredetta, D, 6; Jay L, S, 4

42154 HARRY, Offie E, Kansas, OK, 1; May O, Sis, 4;   By Lewis Horner, Gdn.

1985 HART, Joanna, Manard, OK, 30; Robert, S, 5; John H, S, 4; Helen D, 2

4183 HART, John, Locust Grove, OK, 25; 6527, Kate, W, 24; Charlie, S, 1

[HART, Maggie I. See #27809]   *(Note: entry separate from other family groups)*

25258 HART, Ollie E, Edmond, OK, 34; Francis, S, 10; Eula D, 5; Carl, S, 3

4012 HART, Sarah, Ft. Gibson, OK, 58

Key: Guion Miller Application Number; Name; Address, Relation (to Head); Age in 1906

9654 HART, William, Oaks, OK, 22; 2213, Susie, W, 22; Russell Annie D of W, 4

[HARTGRAVES, William. See #100]   *(Note: entry separate from other family groups)*

[HARTMAN, Louis L. See #4056]   *(Note: entry separate from other family groups)*

24287 HARTNESS Allie, Tahlequah, OK, 20
24286 HARTNESS David, Tahlequah, OK, 22
24283 HARTNESS, Edward, Tahlequah,OK,33
28379 HARTNESS, Erastus Wm Talala, OK, 35; George W, S, 12; Albert J, S, 10; Indianola, D, 6; Mineola D, 4; Buster, S, 1; Allie May D, 1/12
24284 HARTNESS, John, Tahlequah, OK, 25
24285 HARTNESS, Octavia, Tahlequah,OK,53
25845 HARTSOCK, Lizzie Chetopa, KS, 24, R.F.D. #4;   John Louis, S, 5; Teddie, S, 2
31814 HASKIN Beulah Colville, WA, 21
41209 HASTINGS, John R, Needmore, OK, 41; 7418, Elizabeth V, W, 34; William W, Jr, S, 4; Suewayne D, 3; John R, S, ¼
  823 HASTINGS, Louisa J, Maysville AR, 60?

[HASTINGS, Rosa. See #2046]   *(Note: entry separate from other family groups)*

23624 HASTINGS, William W, Tahlequah, OK, 40; 10768, Lulu S, W, 33; Lucille D, 7; Mayme Starr D, 4
  6309 HATFIELD, Margaret, Warner, OK, 35;   Isaac, S, 11; Hannah D, 8
  5180 HATFIELD, Nannie L, Whitmore, OK, 36; Winnie D, 16; Rollin, S, 11
27498 HATHCOAT, Josie A, Valeda, KS, 22; Oma L D, 6; Nonie L D, 4; Horace C, S, 2; Harold D, S, 1/3
18476 HATHCOCK, Maud B, Ray, OK, 26;Thomas Roy,S,11; Charles M, S, 8; Edward T,S,5
  6785 HATHCOAT, Susan E, Parkhill, OK, 22; Floyd E, S, 3; Thadeus L, S, 1
35040 HATTON Agnes E, Narcissa, OK, 27; Monroe N, S, 10; Samuel B, S, 5; Maud J D, 3; Bessie E D, 2
    74 HAUSE Daniel M Claremore, OK, 49
12158 HAUSE, George W Claremore, OK, 18;   Sarah R, Sis, 16; Joseph M Bro, 15; Caleb W, Bro, 14; Ruth E, Sis, 13; Thomas Oliver Bro, 11; Mabel E, Sis, 9; Daniel M, Jr Bro, 7; Maria V, Sis, 6; Benjamin F Bro, 1;   By Daniel M, Hause, Gdn.
12669 HAUX, Nanie, Kinnison, OK, 19
30826 HAVING, Sarah, Evansville AR, 22; Snow, S, 1
29013 HAWK Adam, Gritts, OK, 49
39473 HAWK Benjamin C Afton, OK, 33
43252 HAWK, George, Muldrow, OK, 26
  2231 HAWK, John, Melvin, OK, 50; 2230, Susan, W, 52; Charley, S, 17; Annie D, 15

Key: Guion Miller Application Number; Name; Address, Relation (to Head); Age in 1906

[HAWK, Lucy. See #13062] *(Note: entry separate from other family groups)*

1341 HAWK, Noah Afton, OK, 27
2861 HAWK, Richard, Stilwell, OK, 25; Lucy D, 4; Martha D, 1
8149 HAWKINS Alex, Tahlequah, OK, 53; 8299, Eve, W, 55; Lucy D, 16
24922 HAWKINS Biddy, Oglesby, OK, 32; Adda Opal D, 3
29081 HAWKINS, Eleanor, Edna, KS, 42; Ralph, S, 20; Maude D, 18; Samuel O, S, 16; Edith D, 14; Ruby D, 11
27480 HAWKINS, Glendwyn[sic] E, Fredalba, CA, 20
8644 HAWKINS, Jack, Peggs, OK, 45; Lizzie D, 12; Susie D, 10

[HAWKINS, John. See #6770]   *(Note: entry separate from other family groups)*

10625 HAWKINS, Joseph, Locust Grove, OK, 40
41207 HAWKINS, Josiah, Tahlequah, OK, 26; 8142, Belle, W, 27; Mima D, 7; Eliza Jane, D, 6; George, S, 3; Peggy D, 1
30452 HAWKINS, Linnie S Dewey, OK, 19
24455 HAWKINS, Lundy C, Narcissa, OK, 22
8643 HAWKINS, Nancy, Peggs, OK, 46 [Died 3-1907]

[HAWKINS, Nancy. See #13258]
[HAWKINS, Jesse. See #13258]   *(Note: entries separate
[HAWKINS, Jim. See #13258]   from other family groups)*
[HAWKINS, Nannie. See #13258]

999 HAWKINS, Peggy, Tahlequah, OK, 73
245 HAWKINS, Ruth J, White Oak, OK, 36; Katie E D, 16; Pearl D, S, 12; Emma Lee,D,9
1084 HAWKINS, Ruth K, Vinita, OK, 40; Roswell Drake, S, 15; Charles G, S, 13; Thomas, S, 11; Willie J D, 4
31548 HAWKINS, Walter H, Kansas, OK, 22
33371 HAWLEY, Susan B Canyon City, TX, 28; James Dee, S, 1/12
31062 HAWORTH, Ida L, Tulsa, OK, 41; Perry E, S, 13; Edgar M, S, 11; Claude W, S, 9; Grace D, 8; Owen H, S, 5

[HAYES Charles J. See #22776]   *(Note: entry separate from other family groups)*

9906 HAYES, Eliza, Porum, OK, 45

[HAYES, Ethel. See #27906]   *(Note: entry separate from other family groups)*

14108 HAYES, Luella J, Tahlequah, OK, 20; Roy R, S, 3; Thomas F, S, ¼
3143 HAYES, Martha, Tahlequah, OK, 21; Nellie Ruth D, 1

Key: Guion Miller Application Number; Name; Address, Relation (to Head); Age in 1906

4314 HAYES, Sabra R, Pryor Creek, OK, 46; Holt, John W, S, 16; Charles W, S, 14; Hayes Bryan, S, 11; Craig C, S, 4

26203 HAYES, Serenear, Webbers Falls,OK,22; Padgett, George, S, 5

12157 HAYHURST, Mary Jane Douglas AZ, 30

23830 HAYMES, Nora Claremore, OK, 22

6803 HAYNES, Oliver M, White Oak, OK, 19

6802 HAYNES, Willie P, White Oak, OK, 22

8158 HAYS, Hugh McElrath, Stilwell, OK,37; Curtis E, S, 12

8048 HAYS, James E, San Francisco CA, 28

22477 HAYS, Mary, Ochelata, OK, 19

9427 HAYS, Tilden, Lometa, OK, 46

23186 HAYS, Tinsey Chance, OK, 22; Clyde, S, 2

5009 HEAD, Lucy A, Muskogee, OK, 46; Harris, Wyley B, S, 19; Ward B, S, 15; Elizabeth, D, 12; Head, Etta Lee D, 10; Roosevelt, S, 8

40071 HEADLEY, Elsie Bluejacket, OK, 14; By Lottie Bluejacket, Gdn.

13524 HEADRICK, Lucy, Tulsa, OK, 34; Watie, S, 15

13494 HEADRICK, Michael P, Tulsa, OK, 19; By Chas. Headrick, Gdn.

11166 *HENDRICKS David, Ochelata, OK, 55; Cynthia, W, 48; Mike, S, 19
*(*NOTE: Possibly Headricks)*

16555 HEADRICKS, Joe, Ft. Gibson, OK, 32; 21702, Mary, W, 32; William, S, 5; Mark, S, 3

5856 HEAPE, Lenora, Ft. Gibson, OK, 25; Flora B D, 10; Hiram L, S, 6; Lizzie M D, 7/12

9485 HEAPE, Serena Alluwe, OK, 29; Walter A, S, 12; Clara E D, 11; George W, S, 9; Richard E, S, 6

9489 HEARD, Lula, Keefeton, OK, 22; Willie, S, 5; Clifton, S, 2

16459 HEART, Ollie Christie, OK, 15

24162 HEATH, Emma E, Wagoner, OK, 21; Eva E D, 2; Henry Franklin

8675 HEATON, Ester, Webbers Falls, OK, 56; Charley, S, 19; David, S, 17; Calvin, S, 10; Maggie D, 8

[HEAVEN Aggie. See #1440]   *(Note: entry separate from other family groups)*

[HEAVEN, Steve. See #2709]   *(Note: entry separate from other family groups)*

[HEAVEN, Lucy. See #2708]   *(Note: entry separate from other family groups)*

[HEAVEN, Jim. See #2707]   *(Note: entry separate from other family groups)*

14091 HEDERICK, Rebecca, Edna, KS, 32; Minnie E D, 1; Joanna D, 9; Morgan, S, 7; Asa E, S, 5; Ida A D, 3; Lena E D, 2; David N, S, 1/3

16911 HEDGEPATH, Nellie, Tulsa, OK, 21

17165 HEDRICKS, Mary J, Webbers Falls, OK, 21

Key: Guion Miller Application Number; Name; Address, Relation (to Head); Age in 1906

13166 HEDRICKS, Samuel, Webbers Falls, OK, 48; Claude, S, 11; Saphrona D, 9; Jack, S, 7

11262 HEFFLEFINGER, Elizabeth Dawson, OK, 54

23239 HEFFLEFINGER, Joseph E Dawson, OK, 33; Pace Gerald, S, 6; Veva Josephine D, 4

 9397 HEFLEY, Jennie Y, Webbers Falls, OK, 32; Bessie D, 6; May D, 4; Kate D, 2; James, S, 1; Gatlin, Samuel Bro, 19; Joel O Bro, 15; William L Bro, 12

17250 HEIM, Fannie E, Tulsa, OK, 21

11472 HEINDSELMAN, Sarah E Chelsea, OK,33; Ada E D, 13; William R, S,9; Leon E, S,2

 5390 HEINRICKS, Henry, Tahlequah, OK, 23

 6444 HEISTAND Carrie A, Keefeton, OK, 26; Palone Clarence, S, 10; Heistand, Millard, S, 9; Bluford, S, 7; Adam, S, 5; Osker, S, 2

 4374 HELVENSTON, Lucy A Checotah, OK, 48; Charles E, S, 16; Ruth L D, 15; Claude, S, 13; Ethel D, 9

23614 HELVENSTON, Mary E Checotah, OK, 24

 1267 HENDERSON Ada Catoosa, OK, 28; Albert L, S, 8; Ophelia M D, 5

24892 HENDERSON, Louella, Lenapah, OK, 19

33418 HENDERSON, Lula V,Tahlequah,OK,30

14779 HENDERSON, Maud F Claremore, OK, 20

 6626 HENDREN, Josephine, Row, OK, 20; Lonie O D, 1

23420 HENDREX Annie Adair, OK, 23; Virgil F, , 5; William H, S, 2

 7432 HENDRICKS Adam, Vian, OK, 38; Tom, S, 6; Jones, S, 4; William, S, 2

13320 HENDRICKS Alexander, Ochelata, OK, 32; 13318, Mary, W, 24; George, S, 4; Albert, S, 2

 2065 HENDRICKS Bettie, Vinita, OK, 23; Lorena D, 3

17260 HENDRICKS Charley, Ochelata, OK, 28

 4246 HENDRICKS Coss Claremore, OK, 25

13504 HENDRICKS Daniel, Vian, OK, 28

29011 HENDRICKS, Elmore E. J, Vinita, OK, 24; Zilph H, S, 5; Lonnie C D, 3; Mamie E, D, 2

 2105 HENDRICKS, Eliza J, Tahlequah, OK, 62

33941 HENDRICKS, Jesse L Claremore, OK, 11; Ruby E, Sis, 9;   By Rosa Foster, Gdn.

 9585 HENDRICKS, John Blackgum, OK, 30; 9586, Nancy, W, 27; Starr, Florence D of W, 8 [Died, 1908]

[HENDRICKS, Katharine. See #27727] *(Note: entry separate from other family groups)*

29062 HENDRICKS, Laura E Bluejacket, OK, 19

25464 HENDRICKS, Levi Ahniwake, OK, 27

[HENDRICKS, Louisa. See #27727] *(Note: entry separate from other family groups)*

Key: Guion Miller Application Number; Name; Address, Relation (to Head); Age in 1906

23437 HENDRICKS, Mary A.F, Tahlequah, OK, 19

870 HENDRICKS, Nellie, Metory, OK, 67

24250 HENDRICKS, Nelson L Ahniwake, OK, 24

671 HENDRICKS, Robert M, Ochelata, OK, 33; Anitta[sic] M D, 1

27315 HENDRICKS, Rufus, Tahlequah, OK, 37; Joseph, S, 10; James K, S, 9; Wildie A , D, 7; Marcus A, S, 5; Harvey S, S, 3

7416 HENDRICKS, Sam Dutch Mills AR, 44; 7419, Susan, W, 35

[HENDRICKS, Sarah. See #13500] ⎤   *(Note: entries separate*
[HENDRICKS, Sam. See #13500]   ⎦   *from other family groups)*

42952 HENDRICKS, Susie Bartlesville, OK, 21

18634 HENDRICKS, Teece Claremore, OK, 22

27316 HENDRICKS, Thomas, Metory, OK, 29; Robert R, S, 7; Clara E D, 5; Viola D, 4; Thelma G D, 2; Wirt, S, 1/12

25487 HENDRICKS, Thomas J Ahniwake, OK, 29; 24996, Susie, W, 28; Nelson L, S, ½

9312 HENDRICKS, White McC Coffeyville, KS, 34; Cora M D, 1/6

6034 HENDRICKS, William, Hulbert, OK, 39; James R, S, 10; Sarah H D, 8; Isaac J, S, 5; Charley, S, 2

12447 HE~~N~~DRICKS*, William, Texanna, OK, 63; Rosy D, 9; Ruthy D, 7; Susie D, 5; Annie D, 3; Charlie, S, 1;
(*NOTE: "N" marked out and HEDRICKS written at top of page.]

17174 HE~~N~~DRICKS*, William, Webbers Falls, OK, 32
(*NOTE: "N" marked out and HEDRICKS written at top of page.]

12245 HENDRIX, Susie, Vian, OK, 59

12607 HENDRON, Eula B, Row, OK, 24; Beulah D, 3; Nina D, 1

3163 HENDRYX, Eva M, Vinita, OK, 22

23559 HENEGER, Leona, Eucha, OK, 32; Charles A, S, 2

23779 HENRY Albert G, Sequoyah, OK, 32

4148 HENRY Amelia D, Pryor Creek, OK, 46; William Mark, S, 17; Agnes Blythe D, 14; Viola Beatrice D, 10; Alvin Ware, S, 8

5284 HENRY Ben, Locust Grove, OK, 50; 6514, Sarah, W, 58

15591 HENRY Charlotte J, Pryor Creek, OK, 20; Clemmie, S, 5/6

8123 HENRY, Hugh M Adair, OK, 16; Wilbur W Bro, 13; By Spencer W. Cannon, Gdn.

8125 HENRY, Jesse Claremore, OK, 31; Josiah, S, 8; William E, S, 5

10612 HENRY, John W, Longmont CO, 33; Almel D, 12

138 HENRY, Laura A Claremore, OK, 54

13367 HENRY, Levi J Claremore, OK, 48

9134 HENRY, Mary B Campbell, OK, 28; Jesse J, S, 8; Oscar E, S, 6

22964 HENRY, Maybello, Pryor Creek, OK, 20

CHEROKEE DESCENDANTS RESIDING WEST OF MISSISSIPPI RIVER.
VOLUME II   (A – M)

Key: Guion Miller Application Number; Name; Address, Relation (to Head); Age in 1906

[HENRY, Opal Lee. See #25762]   *(Note: entry separate from other family groups)*

4422 HENRY, Patrick, San Antonio, TX, 71; Bessie L D, 15; Clarence Roy, S, 13; Catherine D, 8; Ada Bell D, 5

24639 HENRY, Patrick D, Joplin, MO, 42; Odeyne D, 15; Archie L, S, 12; Warren D, S, 4

25853 HENRY Pollie Campbell, OK, 20

14227 HENRY, Polly Claremore, OK, 75

2931 HENRY, Thomas J, Locust Grove, OK, 27; Ida, W, 28; Ben, Jr, S, 6; Martin, S, 2

23249 HENRY, Wallace G Chelsea, OK, 34; 1181, Myrtle, W, 33; Dewitt C, S, 14; Roy W, S, 9; Myra D, 2

24230 HENRY, Walter N, Pawhuska, OK, 26

1530 HENRY, William A Bartlesville, OK,56

3630 HENSLEY Clara E, Ray AZ, 40; Eddie, S, 19; Walter, S, 17; Lella M D, 14; Ruth J, D, 11; Nannie E D, 4; Archie, S, 7; Rachel E D, 2

4530 HENSLEY Daisy Bakersfield CA, 29; Lee, John F, S, 7; Hensley, Ethel L D, 4; William L, Jr, S, 1

17096 HENSLEY, Houston, Tahlequah, OK, 18; Jim Bro, 14; Joe Bro, 14; By Samuel Hensley, Gdn.

17095 HENSLEY, Samuel, Tahlequah, OK, 20

32434 HENSLEY, Serena E Collinsville, OK, 18

42924 HENSON Alice, Muskogee, OK, 27

10611 HENSON Andrew J, Owasso, OK, 40; Chili, S, 17; Joseph, S, 1/12

17683 HENSON Bettie, Tahlequah, OK, 32; William, S, 7; Vena D, 1

26535 HENSON Charley, Melvin, OK, 55; 9799, Peggie, W, 40; Pearl D, 13; Charley, S, 11; Nancy, D, 10; Dora D, 3

28869 HENSON, George L, Owasso, OK, 36; George E, S, 6; [S. R. Lewis, Gdn of George E]

12230 HENSON, James Cookson, OK, 39; Pearlie D, 13; Dulcomore D, 10; Vestie D, 6; Hugh, S, 5; Eliza D, 3

764 HENSON, Jennie, Stilwell, OK, 56; John, S, 26[Died 5-1907]; Johanna D, 16; Charlotte D, 14

2502 HENSON, Jesse, Locust Grove, OK, 48; 30365, Nellie, W, 38; 16522, Loonie, S, 19; Laura D, 17; Levi, S, 5

30370 HENSON, Joseph, Foyil, OK, 29

12232 HENSON, May Cookson, OK, 17;   By James Henson, Gdn.

24589 HENSON, Mollie E, Grove, OK, 32

3934 HENSON, Myrta, Vian, OK, 16; Lee Bro, 13; Mary, Sis, 11; James McK Bro, 8; Tatum, Sitting Bull Cou, 17; Thomas Cou, 15; Jay Cou, 12; Dock Cou, 9; Earl Cou, 3;   By Jay Tatum, Gdn.

11174 HENSON, Poss, Evansville AR, 52

11763 HENSON, Powhatan, Skiatook, OK, 33; 17439, Mariah, W, 34; Jack, S, 16

Key: Guion Miller Application Number; Name; Address, Relation (to Head); Age in 1906

1490 HENSON, Richard, Foyil, OK, 38; Hattie M D, 9; Pearl J D, 7; Martha I D, 6; Ella E, D, 5

28231 HENSON, Richard, Hulbert, OK, 21; 10191, Caline, W, 20; Enoch, S, 1

21089 HENSON, Sam, Melvin, OK, 39; 9303, Nancy, W, 32; Ada D, 16; James, S, 5

42929 HENSON, Sarah Jane, Ketchum, OK, 9;   By Thomas F. Baker, Gdn.

4301 HENSON, Sixkiller, Locust Grove, OK, 33; 24852, Nancy, W, 26; 4301, Casa May, D, 12; Jesse T, S, 6; Grover, S, 4

2744 HENSON, Susannah, Melvin, OK, 82

11298 HENSON, Taylor, Tahlequah, OK, 37

17024 HENSON, Thomas, Stilwell, OK, 24

12231 HENSON, Wash Cookson, OK, 21

23243 HEPLIN Ada, Tahlequah, OK, 22; Dennis G, S, 1/12

24208 HERBERGER Annie Collinsville, OK, 18

4524 HERBERGER, Polly Collinsville, OK, 39 [Died 10-1907]; Wm. Martin, S, 13; Francis, S, 11; Sally D, 9; Hiram A, S, 7; Joe, Jr, S, 1/6

[HEREFORD Blanch. See #25291]   *(Note: entry separate from other family groups)*

29947 HEREFORD, James, Webbers Falls, OK, 24

29946 HEREFORD, Joseph, Webbers Falls, OK, 28

29948 HEREFORD, Linnie B, Webbers Falls, OK, 25; Goldie D, 4

12427 HEREFORD, Sophronia, Webbers Falls, OK, 47; Robert, S, 16; Jessie, S, 16; Burk, S, 12; Ross B, S, 8

15669 HERNDON, Maggie B Caney, KS, 19

32716 HERR Carrie B, Vinita, OK, 27; J. Michael, S, 1/12

[HERROD, Julian. See #27180]   *(Note: entry separate from other family groups)*

40008 HERRON, John H, Proctor, OK, 29

27011 HERRON, Richard F Centralia, OK, 28

33034 HESS, Maud G Ballard, OK, 19

29277 HESTER, Hettie Chelsea, OK, 33; Alfred W, S, 6; Russell P, S, 1

13270 HEWIN, Spade, Stilwell, OK, 22; Nancy D, 2

11177 HEWING, Levy, Stilwell, OK, 24

[HEWING, Ruth. See #32745]   *(Note: entry separate from other family groups)*

[HEWING, Sarah and son, Snow. See #30826]
    (Note: entry separate from other family groups)

29745 HIBBS Dennis B Centralia, OK, 22

22632 HIBBS, Emma M, Muskogee, OK, 18

22631 HIBBS, John A, Muskogee, OK, 24

Key: Guion Miller Application Number; Name; Address, Relation (to Head); Age in 1906

16243 HIBBS, Mary A Centralia, OK, 53
   14 HIBBS, Nancy M. J, Muskogee, OK, 48; David A, S, 19; Carl C, S, 15; Viola D, 13; Ollie D, 10

[HICK, Walter. See #25392] *(Note: entry separate from other family groups)*

[HICKERY, Jennie. See #2143]   *(Note: entry separate from other family groups)*

23626 HICKEY, George H, Pryor Creek, OK, 26; 4528, Sallie, W, 26; Miller, Benjamin, S of W, 6; Hickey, Lula D, 2

[HICKEY, Lawrence. See #23945]   *(Note: entry separate from other family groups)*

24669 HICKEY, Nellie M, Wagoner, OK, 25
37446 HICKEY, Rachel C, Wagoner, OK, 19
 6725 HICKEY, Thomas Preston, Wagoner, OK, 53; William, S, 18; John, S, 15; Richard, S, 12; Mary Lou D, 10
 3255 HICKLE, Mary Ann, Sallisaw, OK, 54; William R, S, 17
10630 HICKORY, John, Locust Grove, OK, 29
24458 HICKOX, Henry, Fairland, OK, 37; Pauline D, 10
13502 HICKS Aaron, Vian, OK, 35; 42214, Mary, W, 21; Richard, S, ¼
17435 HICKS Andy Campbell, OK, 24
22179 HICKS Austin Chloeta, OK, 23
11699 HICKS Beatrice, Tahlequah, OK, 21; Mary Bell D, 3
19250 HICKS, Claud J,Skiatook,OK,15; Mary Magdeline,Sis, 12; By Emma Dora Rogers,Gdn
11892 HICKS, Eddie Chelsea, OK, 29
  103 HICKS, Edward D, Tahlequah, OK, 40; Joseph D, S, 18; Clara E D, 16; William P, S, 11; Edward, S, 8; Margaret E D, 5
  789 HICKS, Emma I, Ft. Gibson, OK, 52
 2706 HICKS, Eugene Ross Claremore, OK, 23
12844 HICKS, Frank Chelsea, OK, 23
 7482 HICKS, George, Gans, OK, 43; David H, S, 12; George C, S, 9; Squirrel, S, 6; Aaron, S, 4; Mary D, 2

[HICKS, George. See #12630]   *(Note: entry separate from other family groups)*

13511 HICKS, George, Vian, OK, 33; 13503, Ida, W, 25; 13511, Lydia D, 1
 6742 HICKS, George W, Hobart, OK, 48; Almon, S, 17; Ruth D, 13; Grace D, 11
 4326 HICKS, Hubert W Bluejacket, OK, 45; Ethel I D, 17; Homer W, S, 15;Clifton A, S, 12; Ralph C, S, 3
34278 HICKS, Jennie L, Vinita, OK, 22

CHEROKEE DESCENDANTS RESIDING WEST OF MISSISSIPPI RIVER.
VOLUME II   (A – M)

Key: Guion Miller Application Number; Name; Address, Relation (to Head); Age in 1906

1082 HICKS, John, Lynch, OK, 43; John H, S, 20; Guy, S, 18; Arlie B D, 16; Owen, S, 13; Claud, S, 11; Nina A D, 8; Etta M D, 5

4927 HICKS, John, Locust Grove, OK, 57; Emma D, 9; Maggie D, 4; Jessie D, 4

8856 HICKS, Levia L Collinsville, OK, 26

11466 HICKS, Lillie, Tahlequah, OK, 26; Jennie M D, 5; Beatrice I D, 3; George E, S, 2

11891 HICKS, Lonnie Chelsea, OK, 25

3085 HICKS, Lucy K, Lodgegrass, MT, 26

8970 HICKS, Mary, Locust Grove, OK, 19

12577 HICKS, Mary, Vian, OK, 66

4668 HICKS, Millard F Chelsea, OK, 58; 10961, Sallie E, W, 39; Ada L D, 18; Maggie A, D, 13; Emmit S, S, 11; Viola D, 7; Daniel Arthur, S, 3

4234 HICKS, Nancy E, Manard, OK, 75

3767 HICKS, Nannie, Melvin, OK, 14;   By Thomas J. Johnson, Jr, Gdn.

27258 HICKS, Nellie, Pryor Creek, OK, 38; Arch, S, 16; Fisher David, S, 18

1221 HICKS, Nelson, Moodys, OK, 58; Jeff, S, 18; Henry, S, 16; Ellen D, 14; George, S, 8; Rhoda D, 4

1582 HICKS, Percy W, Ft. Gibson, OK, 54

3544 HICKS, Ranzia, Melvin, OK, 39; Rosey Lee D, 10; Henry T, S, 8; Nancy Jane D, 6; Dovey D, 3

7990 HICKS, Robert L, Pryor Creek, OK, 37; 7991, Jennie I, W, 38; William S, S, 11; Robert F, S, 9; Harvey I, S, 5; Fay C D, 3; Vivian A D, 5/12; Bowman Clara D D of W, 14; Delilah D D of W, 14

33258 HICKS, Susie J Caney, KS, 18; Floyd, S, 2

736 HICKS, Taylor Choteau, OK, 59; Lee M, S, 18; Mary M D, 15; Annie L D, 12; Z. Taylor, S, 8; Eliza V D, 4

8432 HICKS, Tony, Sallisaw, OK, 52

[HICKS, Walter. See #25392]   *(Note: entry separate from other family groups)*

11890 HICKS, William C Chelsea, OK, 15;   By Eddie Hicks, Gdn.

1083 HICKS, William H, Spavinaw, OK, 53

14207 HIDER, Joel, Spavinaw, OK, 35; 26061, Jennie, W, 37; Ned, S, 7; Daniel, S, 3

[HIDER, Rachel. See #10272]   *(Note: entry separate from other family groups)*

[HIDER, Treakie. See #4730]   *(Note: entry separate from other family groups)*

2835½ HIGGINS, Isabell, Porum, OK, 12; Paul Bro, 9;   By Mary E. Robbs, Gdn.

23284 HIGGINS, Lillie O Collinsville, OK, 30; Nettie M D, 6; Robert J, S, 4; Vinita D, 2; William L, S, ½

14147 HIGH, Oce, Spavinaw, OK, 24

13189 HIGH, Sarah E Chetopa, KS, 48; Eddie C, S, 20; William J, S, 14

Key: Guion Miller Application Number; Name; Address, Relation (to Head); Age in 1906

[HIGHLAND, Lucy. See #7572]   *(Note: entry separate from other family groups)*

24975 HIGHSMITH, Mary F, Welch, OK, 39; Myrtle A D, 18; Roy B. L, S, 14; Cora E D, 12; Stella H D, 11; Viola D, 9; Minta Z D, 7; Georgia M D, 2

5386 HIGHTMAN, Henry Claremore, OK, 22

14145 HILDERBRAND Ah-diah, Locust Grove, OK, 25 [Died 9-1907]

5383 HILDERBRAND Arch, Locust Grove, OK, 26; 2208, Lucy D, 18

7571 HILDERBRAND Betsy, Tahlequah, OK, 51; 7639, Lucy D, 18; Joe, S, 11; Maggie, D, 12

8984 HILDERBRAND Charles, Zena, OK, 57

10341 HILDERBRAND Cherokee, Pawhuska, OK, 34

31415 HILDERBRAND Daniel, Webbers Falls, OK, 27

6462 HILDERBRAND, Elijah, Zena, OK, 51; 7576, Nancy, W, 50

2186 HILDERBRAND, Ezra, White Oak, OK, 21

1913 HILDERBRAND, George, Webbers Falls, OK, 59; Emma D, 9

16874 HILDERBRAND, Hoolie Braggs, OK,   16

4283 HILDERBRAND, James, Zena, OK, 48; 8983, Ida, W, 49   Susie D, 15

5031 HILDERBRAND, James, Southwest City, MO, 16; By Waitie Old Kingfisher, Gdn.

6797 HILDERBRAND, James, Proctor, OK,   36; John William, S, 6

8102 HILDERBRAND, James F, Vinita, OK, 23

1920 HILDERBRAND, Joe, Estella, OK, 32; 11027, Elizabeth, W, 24; Francis J, S, 4; Cherokee D D, 1

2 HILDERBRAND, John Bartlesville, OK, 70

8253 HILDERBRAND, John, Zena, OK, 31; 8252, Flora, W, 47; Fannie D, 3; Elic, S, 1

8262 HILDERBRAND, John, Muldrow, OK, 48; 8263, Maggie, W, 25; Joe, S 15; Riley, S, 8; Jesse, S, 6; Sissie D, 5

12701 HILDERBRAND, John, Pryor Creek, OK, 18 By Geo. W. Mayes, Gdn.

8378 HILDERBRAND, John B, Vian, OK, 9   By James Hair, Gdn.

15598 HILDERBRAND, John H, Jr Braggs, OK, 26

12699 HILDERBRAND, Joseph, Muskogee, OK, 36; Tookah D, 15; Josie D, 14; Mary D, 10; Thomas, S, 8; Mike, S, 6; William, S, 3

11224 HILDERBRAND, Julia E, Remy, OK, 13;   By Margaret E Moton, Gdn.

[HILDERBRAND, Karlardee. See #42978]

(Note: entry separate from other family groups)

2290 HILDERBRAND, Laura, Vinita, OK, 33; Rosa D, 16; Cicero, S, 13; Laura Mae D, 10; Benjamin D, S, 7; Gracie L D, 4; Dennis D, S, 1

22529 HILDERBRAND, Lilia, Webbers Falls, OK, 23; Earl, Susie D, 4; Reece, S, 2

28603 HILDERBRAND, Lem Braggs, OK, 39

Key: Guion Miller Application Number; Name; Address, Relation (to Head); Age in 1906

2187 HILDERBRAND, Lucinda, Estella, OK, 24
16701 HILDERBRAND, Maggie Braggs, OK, 5;   By Katie Brown, Gdn.
11697 HILDERBRAND, S. Mary Braggs, OK, 13;   By Geo. Meeker, Gdn.
28281 HILDERBRAND, Mose, Webbers Falls, OK, 22
11441 HILDERBRAND, Na-ke Cove, OK, 28

[HILDERBRAND, Nettie. See #16642]   *(Note: entry separate from other family groups)*

9596 HILDERBRAND, Reese, Webbers Falls, OK, 55; Thomas, S, 16; John, S, 14; Annie, D, 11; William, S, 19
2185 HILDERBRAND, Samuel, Estella, OK, 26; 11026, Fannie, W, 27; Lillian A D, 4; Lura Pixie D, 2; Edward E, S, 1/12
2291 HILDERBRAND, Wallace, Vinita, OK,   29; Mary E D, 4; Samuel J, S, 3; Wallace A, S, 1
16286 HILDERBRAND, William Cripple Creek CO, 46,   333 Irene Ave.
9305 HILL Arley, Melvin, OK, 18   By Alsey Flying, Gdn.
13142 HILL Daisy, Fawn, OK, 23
36763 HILL Davis, Vinita, OK, 43; 4137, Frances E, W, 35; George R, S, 16; James J, S, 14; William T, S, 11; Rachel,D, 9; John R,S, 7; Maria A,D,5; Francis E, S, 3; Mary D, D, 3
3240 HILL Donzolean Adair, OK, 30; Helen A D, 6; John E, S, 4; Pauline D, 2
3531 HILL, Eliza A, Fairland, OK, 73

[HILL, Hattie. See #22798]   *(Note: entry separate from other family groups)*

27846 HILL, John H, Oseuma, OK, 41; Minta E D, 9; Mamie E D, 7; Dessa D, 3
31579 HILL, Margaret E, Mountain Park, OK, 34
28047 HILL, Martha, Moodys, OK, 40
26682 HILL, Matilda A, Stilwell, OK, 30; Waunita D, 4; Mary A D, 2; Eva D, 1/6
28477 HILL, Oliver M, Oseuma, OK, 34; Elmer M, S, 7; Paul E, S, 5
4132 HILL, Rachel, Vinita, OK, 64
35325 HILL, Robert L Claremore, OK, 38; Rachel B D, 11
28478 HILL, Roland, Oseuma, OK, 31; Clara M D, 8
2052 HILLEN, Samantha, Fairland, OK, 60
29113 HILLIN Carrie L, Trawick, TX, 21
29111 HILLIN, Garfield, Pinehill, TX, 25; Robert, S, 1
11733 HILLIN, James B, Rusk, TX, 75
29108 HILLIN, James T, Rusk, TX, 43; Ben T, S, 19; Henry T, S, 17; James H, S, 14; Rosa L, D, 9; Franklin M, S, 4; Joe, S, 1
29112 HILLIN, Jesse, Pinehill, TX, 31
29078 HILLIN, Joe A, Pinehill, TX, 14; Samuel B Bro, 11; Lorine, Sis, 7; Finnis Lee Bro, 4; By Samuel R. Hillin, Gdn.
11727 HILLIN, Joseph L, Pryor Creek, OK, 37

Key: Guion Miller Application Number; Name; Address, Relation (to Head); Age in 1906

11734 HILLIN, Pinkney H, Hereford, TX, 39
11732 HILLIN, William, Sapulpa, OK, 56
16311 HINDS, Sarah C, Westville, OK, 30; Bushyhead, Louis, S, 8; Hinds, Caralyn[sic] Ruth, D, 2
23677 HINEM, James P, Wauhillau, OK, 24
22106 HINES, Henry W, Wann, OK, 18; Dowell Claud E, ½ Bro, 14;   By Frank T. H. Higgins, Gdn.
24581 HINES, Jennie, Westville, OK, 23; Letha D, 3; Mose, S, 1
15969 HINMAN Anna B, Las Animas CO, 27
 6570 HINTON, Henriette J, Parkhill, OK, 51; Emma A D, 18; Herbert T, S, 16; Hattie F, D, 15; William C, S, 12; Gulielma D, 9
27511 HINTON, Henry R, Parkhill, OK, 20
24247 HITCHCOCK Charles D, Proctor, OK, 24; 24246, Callie, W, 18

[HITCHCOCK, Edward O. See #3207] *(Note: entry separate from other family groups)*

24422 HITCHCOCK, Lucy J, Welling, OK, 24; Zoe Dimple D, 5;   Clayburn M, S, 3
23551 HITCHCOCK, William I, Proctor, OK, 22
 2862 HITCHER, John, Stilwell, OK, 22
13059 HITCHER, Lewis, Southwest City, MO, 5;   By Nancy Hitcher, Gdn.
 4899 HITCHER, Ned, Westville, OK, 31; 15974, Peggie, W, 34; Sallie D, 12; Charley, S, 10; Annie D, 6; Cora D, 5
13181 HITCHER, Sarah, Southwest City, MO, 7;   By Nancy Hitcher, Gdn.
26359 HITCHER, Sarah, Stilwell, OK, 19; Redbird, Hoolie Bell, S, 1
13086 HITCHER, William, Southwest City, MO, 15;   By Nancy Hitcher, Gdn.

[HITCHER, Wilson. See #20321]   *(Note: entry separate from other family groups)*

34260 HOBBS Belle Collinsville, OK, 32; Voet, S, 10; Hista D, 5
 1130 HOBBS, Malzerine Collinsville, OK, 31; Blackman, Lou D, 15; Jesse L, S, 10; Hobbs, Thomas A, S, 7; Walter J, S, 4
 5315 HODGE Annie, Talala, OK, 21; Ernest, S, 6; Richard, S, 4; George, S, 2
29200 HOFFMAN, Ellen Collinsville, OK, 30; James C, S, 8; John W, S, 3; Lilie[sic] L D, 1
13713 HOFFMAN, Ruth Coffeyville, KS, 36; James, S, 17; Allen, S, 15; Minnie D, 13; Charles, S, 10; Ralph, S, 8; Christine D, 1
31450 HOGAN, John Z, Pryor Creek, OK, 30; 22921, Eva M, W, 29
30369 HOGAN, Laura A, Pryor Creek, OK, 30; Ruth M D, 10; John C, Jr, S, 8; Karl H, S, 5; James P, S, 3
 3860 HOGAN, Margaret M, Pryor Creek, OK, 56; Graham, S, 20; Mabel D, 16
12205 HOGG, Oliver, Sallisaw, OK, 59; John, S, 9

[HOGNER Chennasse. See #1191]   *(Note: entry separate from other family groups)*

Key: Guion Miller Application Number; Name; Address, Relation (to Head); Age in 1906

5897 HOGNER Clem, Welling, OK, 21; 15663, Jennie, W, 20

16114 HOGNER, George Baron, OK, 26

22781 HOGNER, George, Stilwell, OK, 30; 5280, Annie, W, 26; 22781, Lucy D, 8; May B, D, ½

16596 HOGNER, John, Stilwell, OK, 34; 25353, Nannie, W, 2

23986 HOGNER, Joseph, Stilwell, OK, 38; Mary D, 11; Aggie D, 9; Levi, S, 2

22780 HOGNER, Lizzie, Stilwell OK, 28

6912 HOGNER, Nellie, Tahlequah, OK, 60

16592 HOGNER, William, Stilwell, OK, 35; 25352, Ora, W, 26; Ella D, ¼

1294 HOGNER, Writer, Stilwell, OK, 63; 1244, Charlotte, W, 61; Adam, 8[sic], 18

27658 HOGSHOOTER Charley, Maysville, AR, 27; 12924, Susie, W, 24

5721 HOGSHOOTER Dock, Oaks, OK, 64; 5720, Maria, W, 59

7465 HOGSHOOTER, Gus Chance, OK, 33; Willie, S, 3

23632 HOGSHOOTER, James, Oaks, OK, 32; 5814, Mary, W, 39; Martha D, 9; Sarah D, 7; Andy, S, 5; Marcissa D, 3

5944 HOGSHOOTER, Jesse, Maysville AR, 49; 5974, Rebecca, W, 49; Polly D, 15

27800 HOGSHOOTER, Osie, Oaks, OK, 40; Emma D, 14; Joe, S, 11; Ida D, 8; Ada D, 6

7889 HOGSHOOTER, William, Oaks, OK, 21

10380 HOGSHOOTER, Youngbeaver, Maysville AR, 39; 1908, Sarah, W, 41; 10380, Watt, S, 12; Ed, S, 7; Turner Annie D of W, 14

1447 HOGTOTER, Sunday, Vian, OK, 66

3750 HOGUE, Laura, Warner, OK, 40; Cherry, Lenora D, 17; Jesse, S, 14; Mamie D, 8; Angie D, 6

29145 HOGUE, Mary Erskine, Rogers, OK, 26; Joseph C, S, 6; Condray Lea, S, 3; Sarah Erskin D, 1/12

42176 HOLCOMB Betsey Bunch, OK, 18

13204 HOLCOMB Charlie Bunch, OK, 13; By Richard Holcomb, Gdn.

13294 HOLCOMB, George Bunch, OK, 21

13205 HOLCOMB, Mary Bunch, OK, 6; By Richard Holcomb, Gdn.

9710 HOLCOMB, Richard Bunch, OK, 50

29632 HOLDEN Delilah Alluwe, OK, 26; Verdie F D, 4; Ethel G D, 3

29808 HOLDERMAN Curtis E, Muskogee, OK, 35; Dorothy L D, 10; Theodore G. E, S, 8; Hilda M D, 4; Lena Violet D, 2

28011 HOLDERMAN, Henry C, Vinita, OK, 32; Mary A D, 5; Marion S, S, 4; Covel S, S, 1

16016 HOLDERMAN, Mary E Chetopa, KS, 62

28012 HOLDERMAN, Pearl Chetopa, KS, 23

27250 HOLLAND Arthur E, Wann, OK, 23

23761½ HOLLAND Dennis P Centralia,OK,1;   By Nola Holland, Gdn.

23760 HOLLAND Dennis W, Ruby, OK, 22; 1486, Nellie E, W, 19

22949 HOLLAND, Felix N,Stilwell, OK, 24; 22947, Nannie C,W, 26;Gladys,D,3; Clarice, D, ¼

CHEROKEE DESCENDANTS RESIDING WEST OF MISSISSIPPI RIVER.
VOLUME II (A – M)

Key: Guion Miller Application Number; Name; Address, Relation (to Head); Age in 1906

23367 HOLLAND, Henry S, Stilwell, OK, 36; Mary L D, 6; Mabel A D, 5; Beulah B D, 3; Albert J, S, 7/12

8283 HOLLAND, Isaac Bartlesville, OK, 14; By Noah S, Holland, Gdn.

[HOLLAND, James B. See #22967]
[HOLLAND, Robert H. F, See #22967]   *(Note: entries separate*
[HOLLAND, Henry Dean. See #22967]   *from other family groups)*
[HOLLAND, Thos Reed, See #22967]

31297 HOLLAND, James D, Foyil, OK, 33; Ada F D, 12; Fox, S, 9; James C, S, 7; Minnie B, D, 5; Daisy A D, 1

23127 HOLLAND, John Centralia, OK, 32

22779 HOLLAND, John A, Stilwell, OK, 18; Mary C, Sis, 15; By America A Holland, Gdn.

30526 HOLLAND, John A, Foyil, OK, 42

23597 HOLLAND, John W, Wann, OK, 52; Robert, S, 16; Maggie D, 14; Carrie D, 11; Dora A, D, 8; Nancy M D, 5

30117 HOLLAND, Laura C, Foyil, OK, 29

26976 HOLLAND, Leonard, Wann, OK, 22

23045 HOLLAND, Lugie Centralia, OK, 20

5234 HOLLAND, Ludia, Stilwell, OK, 57; Florey S D, 13

22609 HOLLAND, Manuel J, Manard, OK, 49; 22617, Fannie E D, 20; Robert B, S, 18; Horace S, S, 12; Grace G D, 10

6953 HOLLAND, Margaret E, Grove, OK, 43; Walter, S, 17; Henry, S, 13; Ruth D, 16; Lelah D, 8; Elizabeth D, 3

106 HOLLAND, Mary E, Foyil, OK, 70

1367 HOLLAND, Nancy, Westville, OK, 73

24369 HOLLAND, Noah S Bartlesville, OK, 39; Isaac J, S, 15; Noah S, Jr, S, 11; Charles B, S, 8; Lizzie D, 10; Loretta D, 5; Birdie D, 3; Vivian, S, 1/12

23761 HOLLAND, Pleasant, Jr Centralia, OK, 27

334 HOLLAND, Pleasant H Centralia, OK, 56; 1626, Nancy, W, 55; Anna D, 17

31405 HOLLAND, Richard S, Wann, OK, 33; 31406, Laura, W, 33; Flora L D, 6; Grace D, 4; Franklin H, S, ¼

6663 HOLLAND, Robert J Baxter Springs, KS, 23

23043 HOLLAND, Thomas A, Ruby, OK, 25; 23042, Ella, W, 36; Nelson, Ruby D of W, 17; Pollie A D of W, 15; Effie D of W, 13; James, S of W, 9

22783 HOLLAND, Thomas E, Stilwell, OK, 22

22608 HOLLAND, Virgil C, Manard, OK, 26; Bertha D, 2; Clyde V, S, 1

9759 HOLLAND, Walter A, Welch, OK, 33; Francis L, S, 9

33143 HOLLAND, William, Westville, OK, 25; 33144, Lou, W, 21

24769 HOLLAND, William G, Wann, OK, 38; 12198, Rachel, W, 29; Jesse W, S, 19; Robert L, S, 16; Charles T, S, 4; Florence M D, 2; Claude J, S, 1/12

28840 HOLLAND, William H, Foyil, OK, 25; 1650, Minnie B, W, 24

161

Key: Guion Miller Application Number; Name; Address, Relation (to Head); Age in 1906

29410 HOLLEMAN, Martha S Bellvue CO, 41; Charles J, S, 19; Harvey M, S, 16; Henry C, S, 15; Claude, S, 11

29410 Holleman, Jesse D Bellvue CO, 9; Lena M D, 5

22603 HOLLIS, Elzorah, Miami, OK, 41; Perry D, S, 1; Lawrence P, S, 3; Edna L D, 8; Effie E, D, 13

23386 HOLLOWAY Alice A, Stilwell, OK, 27; Lelia E D, 6; Floyd E, S, 4; Cleburne A, S, 2

22791 HOLLOWAY, Ena Collinsville, OK, 20

13761 HOLMES, James Cookson, OK, 46; 13141, Alsie, W, 43

2700½ HOLMES, Simon, Wauhillau, OK, 12;   By Jesse Sittingdown, Gdn.

12172 HOLMES. Susie Collinsville, OK, 22; Patrick, S, 2

 7424 HOLMES, William, Sallisaw, OK, 53; William S, S, 7

 8303 HOLSON, Sallie, Gans, OK, 52

25731 HOLT Ala, Lincoln AR, 6; Mark Bro, 3; Delina, Sis, 1; By Deba[sic] Holt, Gdn.

23671 HOLT Allie B Chelsea, OK, 21; William H, S, 3; Lucy D D, 1

25024 HOLT Amanda Adair, OK, 23; Sylvia R D, 3

 1892 HOLT Annie, Long, OK, 57; 12905, Frances D, 15

[HOLT, Emma. See #10279] *(Note: entry separate from other family groups)*

[HOLT, John W. See #4314]   ⎤   *(Note: entries separate*
[HOLT Charles W. See #4314]   ⎦   *from other family groups)*

27827 HOLT, London Pearl, Westville, OK, 9; Thomas B Bro, 6; Preston Reed Bro, 3; Ella Blanche, Sis, 1/3;   By Parker Holt, Gdn.

12904 HOLT, Mary E, Long, OK, 12; Tuxie T, Sis, 10; Jacob D,Bro, 8; By Sarah H. Holt,Gdn

 8919 HOLT, Mary M, Westville, OK, 59

13681 HOLT, Nancy, Vian, OK, 20; Vann, Lillie D, 3

17240 HOLT, Norah, Pryor Creek, OK, 20

10280 HOLT, William, Muldrow, OK, 23

 6536 HOMAN, Maggie, Evansville AR, 23; James E, S, 2

 5090 HONEYSUCKLE, Martha, Warner, OK, 44; Samuel D, S, 1

23641 HOOD Bessie L, Peggs, OK, 12;   By B. C. Timmons, Gdn.

16650 HOOD Dave, Fawn, OK, 32; Ida W D, 1

10793 HOOD Dennis Brushy, OK, 32; Lizzie D, 8; Hattie E D, 6; Tokay E, S, 4

11577 HOOD, John, Warner. OK, 51; 11574, Mary, W, 46; Charley, S, 19; Lizzie D, 15; Jennie D, 13; Jimmie, S, 10; Kitty D, 7; Steve, S, 5

13146 HOOD, Sterling P Checotah, OK, 40

23601 HOOD, Susan Afton, OK, 36; Radford Gay, S, 18; Benjamin H, S, 17; Lenettie D, 13; Cyrus Caleb, S, 12; Oscar, S, 8; Dollie D, 5; Ida May D, 2; Gladis P D, 1

Key: Guion Miller Application Number; Name; Address, Relation (to Head); Age in 1906

[HOOD, Susie. See #31599]   *(Note: entry separate from other family groups)*

23640 HOOD, Willie D, Peggs, OK, 14;   By B. C. Timmons, Gdn.
16591 HOOPER Charlie, Westville, OK, 43
43361 HOOPER Cynthia A, Etta, OK, 22; Christie, Wilson, S, 3
13324 HOOPER, George Cookson, OK, 24
7690 HOOPER, Jack Cookson, OK, 29
13325 HOOPER, James Cookson, OK, 26; 12412, Nancy, W, 22
2863 HOOPER, John Christie, OK, 29; 5132, Mary, W, 25; Ellis, S, 1
13322 HOOPER, John Cookson, OK, 33; 13306, Lizzie, W, 32; George, S, 3
13326 HOOPER, Lewis Cookson, OK, 21
13149 HOOPER, Lucy Cookson, OK, 29

[HOOPER, Rabbit. See #4402]   *(Note: entry separate from other family groups)*

4441 HOOPER, Robert A, Moodys, OK, 17; Roxie, Sis, 13; Dewey Bro, 7; By Jesse Shearer, Gdn
4406 HOOPER, Turkeystand, Stilwell, OK, 32; 4404, Alie, W, 38; Frog, Lizzie D of W, 15; Silk, Sarah D of W, 12; 4406, Hooper, Caroline, D, 7; Cornelius, S, 4; Jincy D, ½
28312 HOOVERMALE, Mary A, Pryor Creek, OK, 50; 28313, Stella D, 18; 28312, Maude, D, 16; Wiley, S, 13; Pearl D, 13
28314 HOOVERMALE, Robert, Pryor Creek, OK, 23
28315 HOOVERMALE, Walter, Pryor Creek, OK, 27; 23674, Carrie, W, 19
5092 HOPE Delbert, Muldrow, OK, 23
23351 HOPKINS, Emma M, Grove, OK, 19; Virgil A, S, 4; Opal M D, 3
9708 HOPPER, Lucy Bunch, OK, 48
603 HOPPER, Martin, Stilwell, OK, 49; Mary D, 14; Dick, S, 12; George, S, 10; Tom, S, 8; Nancy D, 4; Gussie D, 2

[HOPPER, Martin. See #5766]   *(Note: entry separate from other family groups)*

4325 HOPSON Clara A Bluejacket, OK, 48
13640 HORN Callie, McKay, OK, 16;   By Tennessee Ridgway, Gdn.
21703 HORN David, Ft. Gibson, OK, 17;   By J. C. Humberd, Gdn.
8004 HORN, Eliza J, Vinita, OK, 50; Charles T, S, 17; George H, S, 13

[HORN, Florence. See #6487]   *(Note: entry separate from other family groups)*

[HORN, George. See #22525]   *(Note: entry separate from other family groups)*

8967 HORN, John L, Vian, OK, 34
15017 HORN, Lafayette R, McKey, OK, 29; Samuel B, S, 6; Laura E D, 3

Key: Guion Miller Application Number; Name; Address, Relation (to Head); Age in 1906

13689 HORN, Maud, McKey, OK, 13;   By Tennessee Ridgway, Gdn.

8966 HORN, Robert L, Vian, OK, 32; Andy, S, 3; Ophelia D, 2; Jess, S, ¼; Louisa J, Mother, 69 [Unsound mind]

5915 HORN, Thomas, Stilwell, OK, 49; 10676, Fannie M, W, 27; Clyde, S, 17; John, S, 16; Thomas M, S, 5; Violet D, 1/12

9390 HORN, Thomas, Lometa, OK, 62; 9391, Mary, W, 40

25277 HORN, Thomas W, McKey OK, 22; 26373, Rosa, W,18; Florence L, D,1[Died 8-1906]

18160 HORN, William, Webbers Falls, OK, 26; 23326, Rachel, W, 31; John, S, 4; Lizzie D, 1; Lee, Lafayette, S of W, 13; Leola D of W, 10

1355 HORNBUCKLE, Lucinda, Inola, OK, 23; Mamie F D, 6; Nellie E D, 4; Andy C, S, 2; Tressie L D, 1/6

1345 HORNBUCKLE, Mabelle Claremore, OK, 30; Lydia M D, 12; William L, S, 9; Isaac, S, 2; Pocahontas D, 1

3068 HORNBUCKLE, Rebecca J, Inola, OK, 27; Nancy G D, 13; Lee M, S, 9; Viola E D, 6; Stella M D, 3; Curtis, S, 1

22860 HORNER, Laura, Tahlequah, OK, 33; Lillie D, 6;   Willie, S, 4

2268 HORNER, Nannie (Ahquas), Kansas, OK, 19

3803 HORNET Daniel, Moodys, OK, 35; 5619, Jennie, W, 30; 3803, Charlie, S, 9; Sarah, D, 6; Lucinda D, 4

3805 HORNET, Thompson, Tahlequah, OK, 27; 26285, Janenna, W, 25; Nannie B D, 2

3804 HORNET, Wilson, Tahlequah, OK, 32; 6061, Lucy, W, 26

3305 HORSEFLY, James, Vinita, OK, 66; 3306, Arie, W, 52

7978 HORSEFLY, John, Row, OK, 34

9219 HORSEKIN, John Afton, OK, 68

[HORSEKIN, Mary Ann. See #1593]   *(Note: entry separate from other family groups)*

1340 HORSLEY, Martha E, Maysville AR, 68

1943 HOSEA, Katy, Locust Grove, OK, 44; Alsie D, 16; Dan, S, 7; Dick, S, 1

2495 HOSEA, Nicer, Locust Grove, OK, 25; Ellen D, 4 ?

29532 HOSEY Charles A, Webbers Falls, OK, 15; Cora J, Sis, 14; By Robert A. Hosey, Gdn.

7026 HOSKINS, Jennie, Stilwell, OK, 62

24161 HOSKINS, Ned, Vinita, OK, 39; 2156, Nellie, W, 39; Christie Alice, GD of W, 5; 24161, Hoskins,, John, S, 16; Ned, S, 13; Lodge, S, 10; Dennis, S, 8; Neal, S, 1

10168 HOTHOUSE Blue, Hulbert, OK, 52; 8151, Jinnie, W, 39; 10168, Lucinda D, 16; Lydia D, 13; John, S, 6; Hair, Maggie D of W, 11; Chester, S of W, 7; Wallace, S of W, 2

10167 HOTHOUSE, Oce, Gideon, OK, 25

13500 HOTHOUSE, Sarah, Vian, OK, 24; Sam, S, 6

Key: Guion Miller Application Number; Name; Address, Relation (to Head); Age in 1906

1538 HOUSE, Martha Allewe, OK, 31; Robert L, S, 9; Ettie M D, 6; Ethal M D, 1/12

[HOUSEBERG, Lydia. See #9263]
[HOUSEBERG Dora. See #9263]   *(Note: entries separate*
[HOUSEBERG, Jack. See #9263]   *from other family groups)*

13763 HOUSEBUG, Ellen Cookson, OK, 16;   By Henry Housebug, Gdn.
4488 HOUSEBUG, Henry Cookson, OK, 45; 13665, Callie, W, 29
4516 HOUSEBUG, John, Stilwell, OK, 46; Johnson, S, 18; Robert, S, 14; Annie D, 10; Cullin, S, 5
27082 HOUSEN, Maud B, Maple, OK, 21; William T, S, 5; Andrew D, S, 4; Lee Roy, S, 2; Loy H D, 1/3
43254 HOUSLEY, Myrtle I Choteau, OK, 19
17552 HOUSLEY, Ruth Choteau, OK, 6;   By N.H. Housley, Gdn.
31396 HOUSLEY, Sidney Elizabeth, Vinita, OK, 39; Mary E D, 17; Louisa R D, 15; John M, S, 12; Kennie C D, 9; William M, S, 4; Jessie E D, 1
8444 HOUSTON Annie, Tahlequah, OK, 67

[HOUSTON Bread. See #17504]   *(Note: entry separate from other family groups)*

8159 HOUSTON, Isaac, Hulbert, OK, 34; 10175, Annie, W, 27; Nellie D, 8; Sarah D, 6; Jesse, S, 4; Jason, S, 1
5207 HOUSTON, Mack, Gideon, OK, 19; Jackson Bro, 16; Alex Bro, 15; George Bro, 12; By Mary Hicks, Gdn.
90 HOWARD Alice Ross, Ft. Gibson, OK, 48
13577 HOWARD Bernice M, Ft. Gibson, OK, 28
23161 HOWARD Bessie B, Ft. Gibson, OK, 23
24553 HOWARD Charles P, Porum, OK, 29; Charles F, S, 4; Pearl May D, 3; Eva Nell D, 2
16781 HOWARD Cicero J, Rose, OK, 27
41542 HOWARD, Emily, Porum, OK, 30; Corbett, S, 7; Pearl D, 5; Charlie, S, 1
9123 HOWARD, Emma, Muskogee, OK, 26
17427 HOWARD, George A, Rose, OK, 54
36625 HOWARD, George A, Muldrow, OK, 26; Theodore R, S, 2
13695 HOWARD, Josephine L Claremore, OK, 27
16785 HOWARD, Lewis A, Rose, OK, 24
1366 HOWARD, Mollie, Ft. Gibson, OK, 30
25256 HOWARD, Rebecca E, Muldrow, OK, 42; William W, S, 19; Lillie M D, 17; Enos Q, S, 16; Josephine D, 10; John, S, 14; Arthur Roosevelt, S, 1
26734 HOWARD, Russell R, Fawn, OK, 31; Della May D, 2
34527 HOWARD, Walter L, Muldrow, OK, 22; Wretha May D, 2/3
8671 HOWDESHELL Dewitt C, Muskogee, OK, 29; 8672, Dewitt, S, 7; Minnie D, 5

Key: Guion Miller Application Number; Name; Address, Relation (to Head); Age in 1906

1331 HOWDESHELL, William L Catoosa, OK, 41; William H, S, 13; Ralph, S, 11; James F, S, 9; Grace D, 7; Mary D, 4; Annie D, 1

4417 HOWELL Bertha A, Spavinaw, OK, 20; Ora Lee D, 1

1370 HOWELL, Eliza, Oseuma, OK, 60; Laboyteaux, Willie Gray, GS, 13; Hutton, GS, 11

25647 HOWELL, Lou G, Nowata, OK, 20; Sue D, 1/12

4037 HOWELL, Mary I, Long, OK, 35; Bessie D, 17; Carrie D, 13; Prudie D, 12; Lillie D, 10; Herbert F, S, 4; Hazel D, 1

1397 HOWELL, Sena, Vinita, OK, 19, R.F.D. #3

13046 HOWERTON Didd, Row, OK, 18

6624 HOWERTON, Leava , Row, OK, 17

6625 HOWERTON, Sabra A, Row, OK, 15

5687 HOWERTON, Sarah J, Row, OK, 23; Erva O, S, 6

1682 HOWIE, Mary T, Vinita, OK, 75

26654 HOWLAND, John, Warner, OK, 38; Ira Lee, S, 3

17148 HOWLAND, Susan E, Warner, OK, 62

26684 HOWLAND, William R, Warner, OK, 24

11762 HOYT, Sue Claremore, OK, 14;   By Sue G. Williams, Gdn.

13562 HUBBARD Ada, Eureka, OK, 22

3175 HUBBARD Charlotte, Proctor, OK, 39;   William, S, 11; Nancy J D, 9; Thomas, S, 7

17215 HUBBARD Daniel, Eureka, OK, 21

29 868 HUBBARD, Lola, Porum, OK, 18; Bessie D, 1/4

8153 HUBBARD, Moses, Eureka, OK, 47; 17214, Thomas, S, 17; Gracie D, 9; Nevermore, S, 7; Beulah D, 1/3

8152 HUBBARD, Thomas, Tahlequah, OK, 41; Allen, S, 16; Corrilla D, 12; Stella I D, 8; Craig T, S, 4

9626 HUBBARD, Thomas, Metory, OK, 54

34877 HUCKLEBERRY, Margaret, Muskogee, OK, 32; Margaret C D, 6; Florence D, 4; Louise D, 2

24587 HUDDLESTON, Etta, Maysville AR, 10;   By H. H. Huddleston, Gdn.

5459 HUDGPETCH Bertha Collinsville, OK, 22; D. Floyd, S, 5; Nellie L D, 3

32250 HUDSON, Etta M, Grove, OK, 15; Alpha B Bro, 9;   By John Wickizer, Gdn.

565 HUDSON, James S. P, Fairland, OK, 44

1065 HUDSON, Lewis B Chelsea, OK, 65

978 HUDSON, Lucy Ann, Miami, OK, 40; 22887, HUDSON, Mabel R, Tahlequah, OK, 10;   By Waddie Hudson, Gdn.

25339 HUDSON, Mandy Chelsea, OK, 24

25338 HUDSON, Samuel W Chelsea, OK, 33;   Katie C D, 7; Nancy M D, 5

313 HUDSON, Sylvanus B, Fairland, OK,37; 1837, Cherokee, Westville, OK, W, 36; Sylvanus B, S, 1; Morton, Edna A D of W, 14; Maud M D of W, 11; Lock, S of W, 9; George, S of W, 6

20210 HUELSENKAMP Cherokee, Vinita, OK, 14

Key: Guion Miller Application Number; Name; Address, Relation (to Head); Age in 1906

32564 HUGGINS, Lula B, Fairland, OK, 25; Shink, S, 4; Robert L, S, 2

23540 HUGHES Benjamin F, Roland, OK, 23

[HUGHS Alice. See #38795] ⎤   *(Note: entries separate*
[HUGHS Arthur. See #38795] ⎬   *from other family groups)*
[HUGHS, Emma. See #38795] ⎦

2456 HUGHES Bryant, Hulbert, OK, 49; Louis, S, 11; Clifford, S, 9; Ada D, 5; May D, 3

28730 HUGHES Carrie, Rose, OK, 29

13033 HUGHES Dave, Hulbert, OK, 20

2959 HUGHES, Ellen, Rose, OK, 57; Rachel D, 17; John, S, 15

10790 HUGHES, George M, Tahlequah, OK, 34; 11885, Sue A, W, 38

25071 HUGHES, Ida Adair, OK, 26; Henry L, S, 3; Carrie B D, 5/6

28729 HUGHES, James, Rose, OK, 21

2721 HUGHES, Jane, Melvin, OK, 44

5778 HUGHES, Jane, Kansas, OK, 45; George, S, 19; William P, S, 15; Annie M D, 12; Eliza J D, 17

24403 HUGHES, Lizzie, Gideon, OK, 32; Willis Charles, S, 12; Hughes, Jesse A, S, 3; Maude E D, 1

[HUGHES, Maggie. See #13034] ⎤   *(Note: entries separate*
[HUGHES, Mattie See #13034] ⎦   *from other family groups)*

30168 HUGHES, Mary A, Kansas, OK, 35; Charley, S, 12; Bessie D, 9; George, S, 7

23878 HUGHES, Mary, Nowata, OK, 19

23539 HUGHES, Mary J, Roland, OK, 36

32078 HUGHES, Mattie, Vian, OK, 20

8114 HUGHES, Nancy Ann, Roland, OK, 58;   Monie, S, 18

28607 HUGHES, Nathaniel, Rose, OK, 25

23538 HUGHES, Richard Taylor, Roland, OK, 25

23518 HUGHES, Theodocia, Stilwell, OK, 24; William F, S, 2

26791 HUGHES, William, Roland, OK, 28

29699 HUGHES, William, Rose, OK, 23

2843 HUGHES, William M, Lometa, OK, 55

1665 HUGHGIN Charlotte, Peggs, OK, 58

1665½ HUGHINS Dickrie, Peggs, OK, 12;   By Charlotte, Hughins, Gdn.

3202 HUITT, Susanna, Vinita, OK, 60

4662 HULBERT, Susie E, Hulbert, OK, 34; Clarence E, S, 11; Nannie R D, 8; Norris B, S, 6; Carlton M, S, 4

[HULLY, Jalum. See #2968]   *(Note: entry separate from other family groups)*

VOLUME II (A – M)

Key: Guion Miller Application Number; Name; Address, Relation (to Head); Age in 1906

1429 HULSEY, Josephine, Needmore, OK, 53

4938 HUMANSTRIKER, Jennie, Evansville, AR, 56

27196 HUMANSTRIKER, Mary, Evansville, AR, 30; Kate D, 12; Robert, S, 3

4734 HUMANSTRIKER, William, Evansville AR, 52; 1689, Nellie, W, 67; Lizzie D, 14; Margaret D, 11; Joe, S, 6

8645 HUMMINGBIRD Daniel, Stilwell, OK, 23; Dick, S, 3; Charley, S, 1

4867 HUMMINGBIRD Dick, Spavinaw, OK, 54

4869 HUMMINGBIRD, Flint, Spavinaw, OK, 54; 4866, Susannah, W, 58

7657 HUMMINGBIRD, Isaac, Stilwell, OK, 54; 7696, Amanda, W, 45; Stand, S, 17; Rogers, S, 15; Lizzie D, 9; Isaac, S, 6; Eliza D, 2

6618 HUMMINGBIRD, Jacob Baron, OK, 43; 6665, Jennie, W, 57; 33146, Emma D, 17

14204 HUMMINGBIRD, Jacob, Locust Grove, OK, 28; 16916, Ada, W, 16

8651 HUMMINGBIRD, James, Stilwell, OK, 21

6542 HUMMINGBIRD, Joshua, Stilwell, OK, 46; 25802, Lizzie, W, 34; George, S, 17; Wilson, S, 12; Gus, S, 4

16982 HUMMINGBIRD, Nancy, Kansas, OK, 49

4868 HUMMINGBIRD, Randolph Dragger, OK, 44; Walter, S, 12; George, S, 10; Henry, S, 8; Homer, S, 7; Chester, S, 5; Sister D, 5; Dennis, S, 3; Eugene D, S, 1

12504 HUMMINGBIRD, Thomas, Stilwell, OK, 51; 15961, Nancy, W, 25; Drunker, S, 8; Annie D, 5; William, S, 1

3695 HUMMINGBIRD, Walter, LocustGrove, OK, 54; 2948, Charlotte, W, 46; Maggie D, 18; Stann, S, 15; Jessie D, 13

5960 HUMPHREY David, Vinita, OK, 50; Andrew, S, 18; A.G, S, 15; Sadie D, 12

43243 HUMPHREY, Joseph, Muskogee, OK, 28

40446 HUMPHREY, William, Hollow, OK, 23

826 HUMPHREYS, John Collinsville, OK, 57; Perry, S, 10; Eddie, S, 8; Roy, S, 6; Dora, D, 4; Jessie E D, 1

24009 HUNAN, Elizabeth, Muskogee, OK, 17

8743 HUNGRY Ben, Locust Grove, OK, 41; 3578, Jennie, W, 45; Car-wa-he-yor-der D, 10

6541 HUNGRY, Ge-as-dick, Hulbert, OK, 81; 8748, Jennie, W, 58; Bean, Ella AdD, 5

10149 HUNGRY, Sallie, Locust Grove, OK, 58

4815 HUNGRY, Soldier, Locust Grove, OK, 58; 4188, Cahweyhawca, W, 44; Quatie D, 12

25952 HUNT Charles J, Vinita, OK, 30; Bates J, S, 6

9217 HUNT Daisy B, Estella, OK, 24; Evan R, S, 6; Helen E D, 5; Nettie L D, 4; Annie Ruth D, 2; Henry L, S, 1/12

25953 HUNT, Joseph, Jr, Vinita, OK, 23

2348 HUNT, Laura M Coffeyville, KS, 30; Lucille D, 4; Roy Edwin, S, 2; Roberts Alex L, S, 10; Paul W, S, 7

25954 HUNT, Nathaniel G, Vinita, OK, 26

4995 HUNT, Ruth J, Vinita, OK, 59; 25956, Lucille D, 19

Key: Guion Miller Application Number; Name; Address, Relation (to Head); Age in 1906

12601 HUNT, Sallie G, Ft Smith AR, 18

 1488 HUNTER Charles, Estella, OK, 46

 2485 HUNTER, Lizzie, Evansville AR, 61

12686 HUNTER, Maud, So. McAlester, OK, 30; Florence I D, 9; Grace D, 1

33639 HURLBUT Beulah, Pryor Creek AR, 28; Anna May D, 8

29202 HURLEY, Emma C, Maysville AR, 35; Parham Claude C, S, 13; Clarence W, S, 11; Ada E D, 9

  268 HURST, John R Chetopa, KS, 53; Rachel D, 15; Albert J, S, 13

 5804 HURST, Sylvester Chetopa, KS, R.F.D. #4, 49; John W, S, 19; Maggie E D, 15; Gracie A D, 13; Sarah E D, 11; Nellie G D, 6; James C, S, 3; Emma S D, 4; 40279, Annie M D, 17

40278 HURST, Walter E Chetopa, KS, R.F.D. #4, 21; 7704, Elizabeth, W, 21; Clifton, S, 1

[HUSSEY Clyde C. See #20172]   *(Note: entry separate from other family groups)*

 3643 HUSTON Charlie, Locust Grove, OK, 33

[HUSTON, Ola. See #14735]   *(Note: entry separate from other family groups)*

11987 HUTCHINS, Nettie Claremore, OK, 34; Lou W D, 14; Ralph B, S, 13; Uhal R, S, 11; Ethel D D, 9; Willard B, S, 3

 6029 HUTCHINSON, Edith F, St Louis, MO, 8; Henry R Bro, 9; By W. C. Hutchinson, Gdn

 6492 HYATTE, Martha, Peggs, OK, 34; Lorena D, 10; Erastier, Peggs, OK, S, 9; Edwin, S, 8; John V, S, 5; Lillie M D, 4; Clifford A, S, 2

26127 HYATTE, Martha L, Peggs, OK, 26; Walker, Willard L, S, 6; Hyatte Bertha M D, 3; Clara E D, 1

16689 HYDE Charley, Tahlequah, OK, 31

 1709 HYDER, Joseph, Eucha, OK, 29

 1825 HYDER, Nancy, Eucha, OK, 47; Levi, S, 13

 8360 HYDER, Sallie, Eucha, OK, 32

10378 HYDER, Tom, Maysville AR, 28; Daniel, S, 6; Lewis, S, 4; Jesse, S, 2; Grace D, 1/6

17153 HYSEL, Thomas J, Warner, OK, 21

13659 ICE, Lewis Bunch, OK, 37

 9919 INGLIS Cora, Welch, OK, 25; Burl D, S, 1

17421 INGRAM Albert T, England AR, 33

 4022 INGRAM Clue, Tahlequah, OK, 6; Horner Anna, Sis, 5; By Betsey Parris, Gdn.

21684 INGRAM David M, San Antonio, TX, 817 San Pedro Ave.   38?

15920 INGRAM, Emma E.L, Ft. Gibson, OK, 31

Key: Guion Miller Application Number; Name; Address, Relation (to Head); Age in 1906

10896 INGRAM, John M Dawson, OK, 37; 21830, Mattie B, W, 25; Georgia L D, 13; Roy B, S, 11; John M, Jr, S, 9; Anna L D, 7; Waunita D, 3

8122 INLOW, Thomas J, Grove, OK, 40; Susan D, 15; Myrtle D, 12; William S, S, 9; Carrie D, 7; Laura J D, ½

8658 INLOW, William H, Grove, OK, 38; Edgar, S, 12; Sylvester, S, 10; Henry H, S, 7; Nancy D, 5; George O, S, 2

13999 IRELAND, Eliza, Warner, OK, 36; Vowell, Eva C D, 4

24425 IRONSIDE, Zula G, Miami, OK, 26

36841 IRVIN Carrie, Muldrow, OK, 27; Sedalia D, 5; Essie D, 3; Bessie D, 3; Otis, S, 1/3

13568 IRVING, Emory Braggs, OK, 16; Stella, Sis, 14; William Bro, 11; By Henrietta E. Irving, Gdn.

10601 IRVING, Joe Braggs, OK, 43; Watie, S, 16; Roy, S, 10; Grover, S, 8; Samuel, S, 6; Renie D, 4; Venie D, 2

1277 ISAAC, William, Locust Grove, OK, 21; 5036, Jennie, W, 21

17230 ISBELL, Jennie L, Vinita, OK, 20; Olive M, Sis, 18;   By L. P. Isbell, Gdn.

17228 ISBELL, Morris F, Vinita, OK, 24

17229 ISBELL, Thomas J, Vinita, OK, 31; Thomas Pascal, S, 1

2047 ISRAEL David, Oaks, OK, 31; 2037, Minnie, W, 20; Bessie M D, 7; Toy R, S, 1

12814 ISRAEL, John Braggs, OK, 32

[ISRAEL, Loyd. See #35917]   *(Note: entry separate from other family groups)*

28382 ISRAEL, Margaret, Porum, OK, 33; Walter, S, 12; Della D, 11; Ada D, 4; Minnie,D,2

10682 ISRAEL, Roy, Oaks, OK, 25

6936 ISRAEL, Will Baron, OK, 18

2048 ISRAEL, William, Oaks, OK, 50; 6885, Chester E, S, 14; Ella D, 7

1182 IVEY Augustus E, Stilwell, OK, 48; Augustus E, Jr, S, 2; Paul, S, 1/12

28595 JACK, Lide, Gans, OK, 47

2850 JACK, Nancy, Gans, OK, 55

44692 JACK, William, Porum, OK, 30; Clifford, S, 12; Leo, S, 6; Katie D, 1

33754 JACKSON Albert J Buck, TX, 28; Glenn, S, 4; Eunice D, 1

28717 JACKSON Andrew, Wagoner, OK, 39; Mattie D, 8; Ruth D, 5

32650 JACKSON Ariminta J, Zena, OK, 33; Hugh E, S, 14; Bomma L, S, 11; Otto R, S, 9; Leona E D, 6; Mattie C D, 4; Winnie I D, ½

1687 JACKSON Caroline, Ochelata, OK, 23

23653 JACKSON Charles C, Greenbrier, OK, 21

12727 JACKSON Cherrie B, Muskogee, OK, 39

21704 JACKSON Clara, Vian, OK, 27; Dora D, 5; James Cleo, S, 3; William B, S, 2; John Bryant, S, ½

Key: Guion Miller Application Number; Name; Address, Relation (to Head); Age in 1906

2046 JACKSON, Emma, Kansas, OK, 33; Hastings, Rose D, 15; Jackson, Joe V, S, 7; John F, S, 3; Henry D, S, 1

7883 JACKSON, Emma L Brent, OK, 26

9330 JACKSON, Flora, Southwest City, MO, 26; White, James, S, 9; Jackson, Swimmer, S, 5; Minnie D, 2

14773 JACKSON, Hannah E, Porum, OK, 22; 41543, Harrison, Jessie J D, 6

11685 JACKSON, Henrietta, McLain, OK, 51; Wilson, S, 17; Anna May D, 17; Susan Ethel, D, 15

14253 JACKSON, Ice J Cookson, OK, 23; 13686, Sarah, W, 26; Rattlinggourd, Betha, D of W, 6

25177 JACKSON, Jesse C Catoosa, OK, 21

16984 JACKSON, Jessie, Kansas, OK, 18

40687 JACKSON, Joe Boxelder, TX, 32; Virgie D, 1

16639 JACKSON, John, Pryor Creek, OK, 32; Viola D, 11; Bertha D, 9; Allen, S, 7; Mary, D, 4; Reese, S, 1; Musie D, 1/6

16986 JACKSON, John, Kansas, OK, 9;   By Annie Nellie, Gdn.

33753 JACKSON, John C, Leesville, LA, 50; Fred L, S, 18; Addie B D, 15; Arthur D, S, 10

24897 JACKSON, Lillie M, Ketchum, OK, 26; Lee R, S, 9; Edith S D, 7; Cleo A, S, 4; Mary J, D, 1

822 JACKSON, Lizzie Bartlesville, OK, 54; Thompson, Newton, S, 14

22742 JACKSON, Louisa Catoosa, OK, 37

14777½ JACKSON, Mary, Porum, OK, 48; Henry, S, 14;   Cornelius, S, 12; 29930, Lula M, D, 17

29989 JACKSON, Mary M Coffeyville, KS, 26; George W, S, 10; Edwin W, S, 6

9763 JACKSON, Maud M, Muldrow, OK, 20; Gussie F D, 2

25176 JACKSON, Minnie L Catoosa, OK, 15;   By Jefferson M, Gravitt, Gdn.

27804 JACKSON, Sarah, Oaks, OK, 28; Vera, D,7; Mollie V,D, 5; Tom, S, 3; Emmett D, S, 1

22775 JACKSON, Sarah A. E Collinsville, OK, 22; Zella M D, 4; John E, S, 2

872 JACKSON, Sarah L, Greenbrier, OK, 51; George A, S, 15; Jesse T, S, 11

16925 JACKSON, Susie, Kansas, OK, 7;   By Annie Nellie, Gdn.

16985 JACKSON, Tom, Kansas, OK, 16;   By Annie Nellie, Gdn.

16987 JACKSON, Walter, Kansas, OK, 5;   By Annie Nellie, Gdn.

12727½ JACKSON, Walter, Muskogee, OK, 5;   By Cherrie Jackson, Gdn.

33755 JACKSON, William H, Thurber, TX, 24; Earnest C, S, 4

4247 JACOBS, Jennie, Muskogee, OK, 725 S. Cherokee St, 36

7994 JACOBS, Lizzie M, Muldrow, OK, 34; Beulah M D, 11; Isaac W, S, 5

3220 JADEN, Laura, Ft. Gibson, OK, 51

32932 JAMES Albert B, Fairland, OK, 28; 1092, Lucinda, W, 36; Cherokee M D, 7; Opal T, D, 6; Calvin D, S, 4; Mildred D D, 3; Eillena A D, ¼

23767 JAMES Beuna J Boerne, TX, 21

30017 JAMES Calvin G, Fairland, OK, 39

Key: Guion Miller Application Number; Name; Address, Relation (to Head); Age in 1906

31089 JAMES Clara D, Fairland, OK, 32

24708 JAMES Dora, Gritts, OK, 19; Ella M D, ¼

[JAMES Duke. See #8332]   *(Note: entry separate from other family groups)*

4389 JAMES, Homer, Vinita, OK, 31 [Insane];   By O. L. Conner, Gdn.

32563 JAMES, Houston W, Fairland, OK, 25; Houston R, S, 3

35456 JAMES, Irvin, Fairland, OK, 28; Euchalata, S, 4

30803 JAMES, Jesse P, Fairland, OK, 21

8330 JAMES, Joe, Eucha, OK, 41; 8331, Dirttrack, Mary, W, 37

31305 JAMES, John J, Fayetteville AR, 21

30802 JAMES, Lorenzo D, Fairland, OK, 36; Flora L D, 14; Clara B D, 13

1532 JAMES, Martha E Boerne, TX, 47; Leland D, S, 19; Louisa Matha D, 17; Frank W, S, 14

312 JAMES, Mary A. E, Fairland, OK, 50

8361 JAMES, Peter, Eucha, OK, 39; 8332, Jennie, W, 20; Falling Blossom D, 6; Dew or Duke, S, 1

29187 JAMES, Sarah A Chieftain, OK, 21; Jesse L D, 5; Clara E D, 2

8327 JAMES, Silas, Eucha, OK, 39

10660 JAMES, Sabrina L, Fayetteville AR, 41; Rex E, S, 19; Ray B, S, 17; Ethel N D, 15; Max A, S, 13; Ruth G D, 10; Fairy F D, 9; Harold F, S, 4

2053 JAMES, Tennessee A, Fairland, OK, 57; Claud F, S, 16; Jesse L, S, 19

4621½ JAMES, William R, Gideon, OK, 20; Thomas L. Noah, S, 1/6

[JAMISON, Vida E. See #12885]   *(Note: entry separate from other family groups)*

7407 JEFFERY, Samantha, Sleeper, OK, 25

8700 JENKINS, Henry W, Vinita, OK, 35; Mandie M D, 12; Ollie A D, 10

22599 JENKINS, Ida, Wann, OK, 23; Grover, S, 2

10583 JENKINS, Mauda, Vinita, OK, 38; Walter, S, 19; Fannie D, 17; Johnnie, S, 14; Levi, S, 12; Lizzie D, 11; Rufus, S, 10; Lulu D, 9; Dolly D, 7; Otis, S, 5; Theodore, S, 2

15047 JENNINGS, Eloise B, McKey, OK, 17

7915 JENNINGS, Jane A, Keefeton, OK, 25; Little, Lucile D, 9; Jennings, Clara M, D, 6; Caroline C D, 4; Loui W, S, 2

1766 JEREMIAH, Orchard, Moody, OK, 14;   By Clark L. Collins, Gdn.

16064 JERNIGAN Drusilla A Durant, OK, 42

[JESSE, Goodmoney. See #12923]   *(Note: entry separate from other family groups)*

16633 JESSE, Lewis, Whitmire, OK, 51; Annie D, 15; Willie, S, 9; Frank, S, 5

12919 JESSE, Tasting, Maysville AR, 49; 12921, Jennie, W, 26; Nancy D, 16; Fannie D, 12; Robert, S, 4; Annie D, 1/6

Key: Guion Miller Application Number; Name; Address, Relation (to Head); Age in 1906

4917 JEW-LE-OH-WAH, Elsie, Locust Grove, OK, 44; Bigacorn, Ollie D, 14

23620 JILES, Mary A, Tipp, OK, 22; Alvin Guy, S, 2; Lenna Opal D, 1

11849 JOE, Willie, Oaks, OK, 39; 9946, Go-yih-ne-e, W, 47; Bluebird, Charlie, S of W, 18; Lomon, Jackson, S of W, 15; Joe, S-qua-ny, S, 12

17973 JOOSON Coo-wee-scoo-wee, Eucha, OK, 18

17974 JOHN, Josiah, Whitmire, OK, 18

3840 JOHN, Jennie Chelsea, OK, 48

16039 JOHNS, Mary, Muskogee, OK, 32

28042 JOHNS, Sidney, Fawn, OK, 30; Thomas L, S, 14; Ollie D, 11; Joseph B, S, 10; Ella, D, 8; Richard G, S, 4; Delora D, 2

2997 JOHNSON Alcy A, Stilwell, OK, 65

7692 JOHNSON Alec, Hulbert, OK, 29; 11293, Peggie, W, 25; Elizabeth D, 1

27643 JOHNSON Alice, Siloam Springs AR, 19

25824 JOHNSON Allen, Tahlequah, OK, 27

24681 JOHNSON Alonzo, Tahlequah, OK, 20; Josie D, ½

40900 JOHNSON Alta L, Tahlequah, OK, 21

13226 JOHNSON Annie, McLain, OK, 33; John A, S, 11; Grace M D, 8; Lafayette L, S, 5

15970 JOHNSON Annie, Westville, OK, 26

13071 JOHNSON Annie B, Spavinaw, OK, 22; Bertha M D, 7; Andrew A, S, 5; Roy C, S, 3; Robert L, S, 2; Truly V D, 1/6

9582 JOHNSON Benjamin,Tahlequah,OK,52; 33937, Maggie, W, 29

28233 JOHNSON Berry H Afton, OK, 23

1328 JOHNSON Betsey, Stilwell, OK, 30; Sanders Benjamin, S, 8

1153 JOHNSON Betsey, Porum, OK, 53

3766 JOHNSON Betsey, Melvin, OK, 9;   By Thomas J, Johnson, Gdn.

2149 JOHNSON Charlotte F Afton, OK, 56; 28234, Charlotte T D, 18

1379 JOHNSON Cicero, Tahlequah, OK, 63;   Belle D, 13

15625 JOHNSON Clint, Westville, OK, 13; Hugh Bro, 7; John T Bro, 5; Ray Bro, 3; By Thomas B. Johnson, Gdn.

16543 JOHNSON Clem, Rose, OK, 9;   By David E. Smallwood, Gdn.

16420 JOHNSON Cloud Cookson, OK, 45; 13488, Nellie, W, 61

27487 JOHNSON Cora E, Stilwell, OK, 39

7872 JOHNSON Dave, Tahlequah, OK, 19; Andrew Bro, 16; Levi Bro, 14; By James Waterfallen, Gdn.

42222 JOHNSON David, Lenapah, OK, 12; Viola, Sis, 10; By Peter C. Suagee, Gdn.

16715 JOHNSON Davis, Hulbert, OK, 33; 16716, Annie, W, 26; Mandy D, 4; Sampson, S, 1

2884 JOHNSON Dudley, Tahlequah, OK, 31

27382 JOHNSON, Edmond F Claremore, OK, 21

1319 JOHNSON, Everett H, Edna, KS, 31

28372 JOHNSON, Florence E, Nowata, OK, 23

28522 JOHNSON, Francis C Dawes, OK, 33; Ross, S, 4; Truman, S, 2

Key: Guion Miller Application Number; Name; Address, Relation (to Head); Age in 1906

27485 JOHNSON, Frank, Stilwell, OK, 12;   By Eliza Smith, Gdn.

5816 JOHNSON, George, Oaks, OK, 22

14261 JOHNSON, George Bunch, OK, 13;   By Hunter Poorbear, Gdn.

28613 JOHNSON, George H, Rose, OK, 21

26807 JOHNSON, George J, Tahlequah, OK, 22

1888 JOHNSON, George W, Uniontown AR, 34; Dasey Pear D, 9; James Dewey, S, 7; Georgia Lee, S, 6; John Doss, S, 3; Tribble Byrum, S, 1

7474 JOHNSON, George W, Tahlequah, OK, 43; 8282, Cherokee C, W, 35; Bulah M D, 14; Bessie,D, 13; Samuel M, S,11; Robert E, S, 9; Cherrie D, 7; Louis C, S, 5; Percy L, S,1

12648 JOHNSON, Henry, Stilwell, OK, 18;   By Johnson Simmons, Gdn.

2886 JOHNSON, Isaac, Tahlequah, OK, 23

14107 JOHNSON, Jacob E, Tahlequah, OK, 23

3534 JOHNSON, James, Melvin, OK, 49

25124 JOHNSON, James B, Stilwell, OK, 26

23208 JOHNSON, James M, Stilwell, OK, 33

9699 JOHNSON, Jennie Catoosa, OK, 39; Tom, S, 7;   Susie D, 5

26274 JOHNSON, Jennie Dewey, OK, 37; Frank M, S, 15; Edith M D, 12; Roy R, S, 10; Flora D D, 8; Annie E D, 5; Paul, S, 2

5598 JOHNSON, Jesse, Locust Grove, OK, 49; 5353, Bigacorn, Nancy J, W, 26; Buckskin, Josie D of W, 7; Susie D of W, 5; Zeke, S of W, 3; Bigacorn, Maud D of W, 1/12

28871 JOHNSON, Jessie Collinsville, OK, 15; Edward Bro, 14; Fannie, Sis, 12; By F. M Bussy, Gdn.

5518 JOHNSON, Jessie M, Muskogee, OK, 5; Norris, Florence, Sis, 2; By William L. Miller, Gdn.

[JOHNSON, John. See #16369]   *(Note: entry separate from other family groups)*

9439 JOHNSON, John, Locust Grove, OK, 35; Si-wi D, 5; Susi D, 3

16719 JOHNSON, John, Hulbert, OK, 41; 8305, Lucy, W, 41; Ella D, 16; Peggy D, 14; Alice D, 6; Redbird, S, 4; Joe, S, 2

14106 JOHNSON, John B, Tahlequah, OK, 23

5012 JOHNSON, John H, Tahlequah, OK, 20; Carl F, S, ¼

11783 JOHNSON, John W Claremore, OK, 46

34651 JOHNSON, Joseph Bristow, OK, 21

18320 JOHNSON, Joseph, Jr, Sallisaw, OK, 22

25128 JOHNSON, Joseph R, Stilwell, OK, 28

25748 JOHNSON, Joseph T, Nowata, OK, 41; 25747, Maud, W, 33; Winnie V D, 14; Lillie E, D, 13; Grady, S, 11; Callie M D, 9; John W, S, 5; Bettie D, 2

1899 JOHNSON, Joseph W,Uniontown,AR,54; 17712, Mary, W, 34; Minnie D, 16; Lanetta, D, 14; Charley, S, 6; Lillie D, 4; Rosevelt, S, 1

291 JOHNSON, Josephine B, Nowata, OK, 49; Ada L D, 19; Howard B, S, 15

Key: Guion Miller Application Number; Name; Address, Relation (to Head); Age in 1906

5976 JOHNSON, Kadie, Southwest City, MO, 56
16775 JOHNSON, Leonidas R Dora AR, 28   [Died 1907]
5679 JOHNSON, Lizzie, Stilwell, OK, 19
11781 JOHNSON, Lucinda, Verdegris, OK, 33; Moore, Daniel E, S, 19; David, S, 16;
     Charlie, S, 10; Lizzie D, 4; Johnson Cordelia D, 1
5686 JOHNSON, Lula, Stilwell, OK, 17
23256 JOHNSON, Maggie Roach, Gideon, OK, 20
27359 JOHNSON, Mamie A Big Cabin, OK, 21
26387 JOHNSON, Margaret, Proctor, OK, 26; James Ralph, S, 1/12

[JOHNSON, Martha. See #36485]   *(Note: entry separate from other family groups)*

25124 JOHNSON, Martha A, Stilwell, OK, 53; Jesse, S, 18; Anna B D, 16; Lura M, D,
     13
11638 JOHNSON, Martha E Centralia, OK, 29
** JOHNSON, Martha E Caddo, OK, 17;   John W Bro, 20; Oscar E Bro, 15;
     Dannie L, Bro, 9; Roy W Bro, 7; By Elijah Johnson, Gdn.
     (**NOTE: No Application number(s) given. Only Roll #'s 15501 - 15505)
11531 JOHNSON, Martin, Porum, OK, 18
10746 JOHNSON, Mary B, Porum, OK, 18; L. W, S, 2
30833 JOHNSON, Mary B, Pryor Creek,OK,23
2887 JOHNSON, Miah [or Myer], Tahlequah, OK, 25
7917 JOHNSON, Mike, Gideon, OK, 25; 25580, Lucy, W, 23; Wilda D, 3; Polly D, 1
16541 JOHNSON, Nancy, Rose, OK, 12;   By David E, Smallwood, Gdn.
29278 JOHNSON, Nellie Chelsea, OK, 35; Claude V, S, 14; Minnie M D, 12; Ernest
     E, S, 10; William R, S, 8; Mary B D, 1
11867 JOHNSON, Nettie, Ft. Gibson, OK, 22
14104 JOHNSON, Oliver W, Tahlequah, OK, 18;   By John B. Johnson, Gdn.
16542 JOHNSON, Ora, Rose, OK, 6; By David E. Smallwood, Gdn.
25826 JOHNSON, Oscar, Tahlequah, OK, 13; Myrtle, Sis, 10; Frank Bro, 8; By
     Cicero Johnson, Gdn.

[JOHNSON, Ottis. See #42149]   *(Note: entry separate from other family groups)*

182 JOHNSON, Patsy, Locust Grove, OK, 76 [Died 7-12-1907]
16581 JOHNSON, Peggie Baptist, OK, 87
7443 JOHNSON, Rachel Chelsea, OK, 62
22612 JOHNSON, Rebecca A, Tahlequah, OK, 48; James Z, S, 19; Marth[sic] J D, 17
27530 JOHNSON, Rebecca Catherine, Siloam Springs,AR, 40; Calvin, S, 15; Margaret,
     D,13; Emma D, 11; Henry, S, 8; Viola D, 4; Lafayette, S, 1
31987 JOHNSON, Robert E, Tahlequah, OK, 23

[JOHNSON, Ross. See #34081]   *(Note: entry separate from other family groups)*

Key: Guion Miller Application Number; Name; Address, Relation (to Head); Age in 1906

11009 JOHNSON, Samuel, Vian, OK, 35; 3926, Jennie, W, 26; Nannie D, 9; Rachel D, 7; Albert, S, 4; Elcy D, 1

[JOHNSON, Samuel. See #14097]   *(Note: entry separate from other family groups)*

17463 JOHNSON, Stephen Blackgum, OK, 26
9661 JOHNSON, Stonewall J, Akin, OK, 31; Mary J D, 9; Thomas W, S, 7; Lizzie D, 4; Flora L D, 3; Carrie L D, 1
25825 JOHNSON, Tom, Tahlequah, OK, 23
10451 JOHNSON, Thomas Afton, OK, 15;   By George Johnson, Gdn.
30834 JOHNSON, Thomas E, Pryor Creek, OK, 26
25923 JOHNSON, Thomas J, Melvin, OK, 35; Betsie D, 9
39162 JOHNSON, White Bunch, OK, 29; 6709, Jennie, W, 38; Smith, Wilson, S of W, 17
15975 JOHNSON, Will, Westville, OK, 26
1941 JOHNSON, William Cookson, OK, 28; 5954, Quatie, W, 29
24723 JOHNSON, William Collinsville, OK, 27
25812 JOHNSON, William I, Metory, OK, 35; 25718, Cyntha, W, 29; Ellis R, S, 4; Thomas F, S, 2

[JOHNSON, William. See #44692]
[JOHNSON Clifford. See #44692]   *(Note: entries separate*
[JOHNSON, Leo. See #44692]   *from other family groups)*
[JOHNSON, Katie. See #44692]

22746 JOHNSON, William A Centralia, OK, 25; Ethel May D, 1/12
5793 JOHNSON, William E, Rose, OK, 51; 3156, Lucy, W, 49; William M, S, 19; Cicero L, S, 17; Venie D, 14; Samuel M, S, 11; Lewis, S, 7; David L, S, 4
25209 JOHNSON, William O, Stilwell, OK, 28; 25210, Ella L, W, 28
825 JOHNSTON, Eliza E, Tahlequah, OK, 56
9634 JOHNSTON, Frances Brent, OK, 29; Albert, S, 12; Charley, S, 7; Miller, Jennie D, 2
8032 JOHNSTON, George H, Sallisaw, OK, 54
8334 JOHNSTON, John E, Muldrow, OK, 25
31768 JOHNSTON, Lula B Afton, OK, 22; Winnie E D, 3
8333 JOHNSTON, Sallie, Muldrow, OK, 24
31767 JOHNSTON, Samuel L, Sallisaw, OK, 33; 5953, Mary L, W, 33; Horace, S, 11; Sarah O, D, 10; Johnsie D. A D, 7; Samuel, S, 5
27381 JOHNSTON, William P Claremore, OK, 30; Ouita D, 7; William L, S, 5
5263 JOHNSTONE, Julia, Tahlequah, OK, 42; Mary L D, 16; Vivian W D, 13; William P, S, 11; Jimmie B, S, 6
1571 JONES Agnes Cleora, OK, 28

CHEROKEE DESCENDANTS RESIDING WEST OF MISSISSIPPI RIVER.
VOLUME II   (A – M)

Key: Guion Miller Application Number; Name; Address, Relation (to Head); Age in 1906

28302 JONES Annie Bushyhead, OK, 29; Hattie D, 11; Thomas, S, 10; Cherokee D, 8; Everet, S, 6; William Herbert, S, 4; Louis, S, 3

24912 JONES Annie O Big Cabin, OK, 19

5775 JONES Bird, Rose, OK, 65; 33432, Lizzie D, 19; 33435, Jinnie, D, 17; 10499, Tom, S, 9

7677 JONES Carrie [or Caroline] Claremore, OK, 51

25494 JONES Catherine, Narcissa, OK, 17

2288 JONES Charner M Cleora, OK, 24

24386 JONES Clara, Ft. Gibson, OK, 31; Everett Walter, S, 6; Laura Daylight D, 3

16368 JONES Cobb, Stilwell, OK, 22

13083 JONES Cowie, Webbers Falls, OK, 19

4407 JONES, Ella, Stilwell, OK, 48

24554 JONES, Ella, Porum, OK, 33; Jerry, S, 10; Helen D, 8; Gracie D, 4; Patsy R, S(?), 3; Francis, S, 2

35554 JONES, Francis, Sallisaw, OK, 20; Ellen M D, 3

13085 JONES, Franklin P, Porum, OK, 22

3074 JONES, James, Ft. Sill, OK, 28; Estelle D, 6

17173 JONES, Jesse, Webbers Falls, OK, 17;   By Oscar Jones, Gdn.

39187 JONES, Joe Bunch, OK, 25

937 JONES, Johanna, Miami, OK, 50; Myrtle J D, 17; James W, S, 14

24497 JONES, John E Chelsea, OK, 21

4508 JONES, Johnson, Stilwell, OK, 30

8247 JONES, Joseph, Southwest City, MO, 24

275 JONES, Judge, Grove, OK, 27; Jennie, W, 21; Roy, S, 1

26124 JONES, Laura A, Grove, OK, 30; Rogers, Tipton, S, 9

33805 JONES, Levi, Vinita, OK, 30; Archie, S, 3

2278 JONES, Lossie or Rose, Stilwell, OK, 49; Mariah D, 14; Jessie D, 11; Seven Starr, S, 8; Ellis, S, 6

16367 JONES, Maggie, Stilwell, OK, 17

6963 JONES, Magnolia Chelsea, OK, 34

13165 JONES, Margaret B, Webbers Falls, OK, 19

8957 JONES, Mary, Westville, OK, 59

29264 JONES, Mary C, Hillside, OK, 27; William M, S, 8; Sarah F D, 7; Caddie D, 5; Charles E, S, 3; Claborne E, S, 1/12

24364 JONES, Mary E, Owasso, OK, 37; Gassaway, Henry, S, 19; Neoma D,15; Jones, Tommie C, S, 9; Frank, S, 7; Ramon B, S, 5; Fredie, S, 4; Pearlie I D, 2

6501 JONES, Mary F, Southwest City, MO, 20; Willard, S, 3

99 JONES, Mary Ross Chelsea, OK, 40; George O, S, 20; Perry, S, 14; William Andrew, S, 10; Alma J D, 7; Mora D, 5; Thomas R, S, 1

29998 JONES, Mattie, Kansas, OK, 30; James B, S, 9; Claude W, S, 6; Clide[sic] H, S, 6; Flossie M D, 3

3142 JONES, Minerva Dewey, OK, 44; 16135,Zinn Beulah M D, 19; Lyman, Savola R, D, 17; Jones, Ethel G D, 10

Key: Guion Miller Application Number; Name; Address, Relation (to Head); Age in 1906

23166 JONES, Myrtle, Nowata, OK, 24; Mabel D, 5; Harry, S, 4; Arthur, S, 1

22503 JONES, Nancy, Grove, OK, 35; Jessie Pearl D, 5

24711 JONES, Nancy J Baron, OK, 25; Flora D, 4

23479 JONES, Nellie E, Hulbert, OK, 26; Tipton, Ruffus, S, 6

7003 JONES, Oo-loo-che, Southwest City, MO, 57; James, S, 19; Celia D, 13

5614 JONES, Oscar, Webbers Falls, OK, 22

3930 JONES, Polly Campbell, OK, 26

23940 JONES, Quatie, Vera, OK, 22; Mead B. S, S, 5; Mollie R D, 2

14158 JONES, Rachel B, Tip, OK, 32; Bryan, S, 9; Poke, S, 8; Granvil, S, 6; Nancy
Lenora, D, 4; Margaretta D, 2; Ruth D, 1/6

16366 JONES, Sam, Stilwell, OK, 24

4506 JONES, Smith, Stilwell, OK, 26

27841 JONES, Susan, Fairland, OK, 23; Maggie A D, 1

22010 JONES, Swimmer, Oaks, OK, 19;   By Sarah Oo-yar-sat-tah, Gdn.

4075 JONES, Will, Stilwell, OK, 26

29406 JONES, Willie, Tyler, TX, 24

[JONES, Willie E. See #34485]   *(Note: entry separate from other family groups)*

15666 JONES, Zona Caney, KS, 28; James A, S, 5; Ray E, S, 3; Warren, S, 1/3

24033 JORDAN Alice, Westville, OK, 32; Bert, S, 15; Henry, S, 13; Bruce, S, 11;
Fannie D, 8; Fairy D, 6; Claud, S, 4; Mabel D, 2; Savola D, 1/12

998 JORDAN Delia P, Vinita, OK, 49; John D, S, 19; Watie B, S, 17

24753 JORDAN, Ellen Chelsea, OK, 27; Clara D, 7; Walter B, S, 4

28252 JORDAN, Felix R Collinsville, OK, 17

1442 JORDAN, John W Cleveland, OK, 63; 35597, Tennessee J, W, 44; John B, S,
15; Dixie M, S, 18; Daisy L D, 12; Robert Owen, S, 6; Winnie Davis D, 3

38302 JORDAN, Madison Denison, TX, 23

23047 JORDAN, Vannie Centralia, OK, 21

32929 JORDAN, Robert E. Lee, Vera, OK, 39; Lee, Owen, S, 15; William P. A, S, 14;
Dennis B, S, 12

693 JORDAN, Samantha I Akins, OK, 28;   David W, S, 1

225 JORDAN, Susie, Kansas, OK, 34; Lola E D, 14; Lester L, S, 12; Stella B D, 10;
Gertrude M D, 8; Martin M, S, 6; Mary E D, 3

8433 JORDAN, Taky or Jennie, Sallisaw, OK, 50; 36933, John, S, 17; Bell D, 15;
Amelia, D, 13

36166 JORDAN, Thomas J Collinsville, OK, 37; Felix W, S, 17; Mollie D, 15; Sallie
D, 5; George W, S, 4; Bright D, S, 1

5071 JORDAN, Victory, Big Cabin, OK, 26; Myrtle M D, 3; William L, S, 2

1442½ JORDAN, William Owen, Tulsa, OK, 13; Ruthey May, Sis, 11; Mary, Sis, 6; By
Nancy E. Downs, Gdn.

2950 JOURNEYCAKE, Eliza, Nowata, OK, 46; Jesse D, S, 16;Isaac N,S, 14; Buster
B, S,11

Key: Guion Miller Application Number; Name; Address, Relation (to Head); Age in 1906

17209 JUDGE Charles, Wauhillau, OK, 36

8747 JUDGE, One, Locust Grove, OK, 66

43198 JUDGE, William, Ft. Leavenworth, KS, 36; Bety[sic], Peggs, OK, Sis, 16; Katy, Sis, 10;   By One Judge, Gdn.

4608 JULIAN, Edwin Clinton Checotah, OK, 40

4607 JULIAN, Etta Pearl Checotah, OK, 23

4819 JULIAN, Robert W, Porum, OK, 35

43354 JUMPER Clun-des-ta [Pleasant], Southwest City, MO, 39; 7002, Fanny, W, 35; Young, S, 4

8375 JUMPER De-tla-da-ke Cherokee City, AR, 48; 8374, Ge-la-na-che, W, 47; Si-jin-ni [Sargent], S, 15; E-si, S, 8; A-ke D, 3

15086 JUMPER Dora, Moodys, OK, 20

14782 JUMPER, Hunter Campbell, OK, 20

4905 JUMPER, Jesse, Rose, OK, 25; Sarah, W, 27; Betsy D, 1; Downing, Nannie D of W, 6

8340 JUMPER, Mollie Campbell, OK, 56

[JUMPER, Nick. See #9005]
[JUMPER, Nannie. See #9005] (Died 4-1907)   *(Note: entries separate*
[JUMPER, Lucy. See #9005]   *from other family groups)*
[JUMPER, Lizzie. See #9005]

43353 JUMPER, Oo-yah-skah, Southwest City, MO, 25

[JUNE-KA-LI-DA. See #8373]   *(Note: entry separate from other family groups)*

10642 JUNE-STOOT, Quatie, Locust Grove, OK, 66

1059 JUSTICE Betsy Cookson, OK, 62

12406 JUSTICE Dick Cookson, OK, 21

4369 JUSTICE, Eliza B, Tahlequah, OK, 26; William R, S, 5; Claud R, S, 2; Wayne B, S,1/6

16579 JUSTICE, Freddie Dunawas, Stilwell, OK, 15

6486 JUSTICE, Walter [Watt], Westville, OK, 18

22930 JUSTUS, Ella J, Owasso, OK, 27; William I, S, 1

2034 KAH-KA=WEE Dick, Oaks, OK, 59; 2035, Katie [Darkey], W, 46; 6884, Blackfox David, S of W, 18; 4903, Wilson, S of W, 16

22562 KAISER Alcie, Needmore, OK, 17

9813 KAMEY Annie, Marks, OK, 39; Austin L, S, 17; Maggie D, 14; Frank O, S, 11; William V, S, 5

22990 KARNS, Susan E, Westville, OK, 23

1610 KATES, Nancy E, Hulbert, OK, 26; Mandy M D, 7; Jasper W, S, 4; Nathaniel, S, 2

Key: Guion Miller Application Number; Name; Address, Relation (to Head); Age in 1906

23289 KAY Angie, Ramona, OK, 45; Ora D, 17; William E, S, 15; Lulu May D, 10; Emma B, D, 6; Elizabeth D, 3

27131 KAY, Stella M Adair, OK, 22

16103 KEARNS, Susan V, Vera, OK, 32; Reynolds, Eva A D, 15; McCauley Bertha D, 11; Kearns, Rutha J D, 7; Pearlie D, 4; John W, S, 2/3

3179 KECK, Eva, Sallisaw, OK, 35; Dora D, 16; Clarence, S, 13; Ethel D, 11; Bonnie D, 7

24111 KEEFER, Maggie V Bartlesville,OK,21; Louis Jay, S, ½

29497 KEELER Albert, Ramona, OK, 26; Dixie Joe, S, 2; Alberta D, 5/12

5275 KEELER Charles R, Melrose, OR, 32; Marjora D, 4

24383 KEELER, Frank Bartlesville, OK, 28

24382 KEELER, Fred Bartlesville, OK, 24

22667 KEELER, Joseph Cathern Bartlesville, OK, 49

22669 KEELER, Lillie A Bartlesville, OK, 19

22668 KEELER, Maud Bartlesville, OK, 21

22595 KEELER, Pearl Bartlesville, OK, 17 [Died 6-9-1906]; (By) George B. Keeler Admr.

13421 KEELER, William Bartlesville, OK, 30; 26051, Lula, W, 26; Lela Blanch D, 7

25762 KEELING, May E, Miami, OK, 23; Henry, Opal L D, 3; Keeling, Louis M, S, 2/3

24959 KEEN Albert F Coffeyville, KS, 25; Albert, S, 3; Wiley A, S, 1

23922 KEEN, Arnold Perry Coffeyville, KS,22

31953 KEEN, James Hooly Coffeyville, KS, 19; 31954, Rosa B, W, 18

484 KEEN, Nannie A Coffeyville, KS, 47; Cora S D, 16; John R, S, 12; Ross K, S, 10; John Lindsey, S, 6

23921 KEEN, William A Coffeyville, KS, 28; Wilmia P, D, 7; Dora Olive D, 5; Hazel Fern, D, 2

13414 KEENER Aggie Choteau, OK, 54

9336 KEENER Betsy, Melvin, OK, 56

24295 KEENER Betsy, Hulbert, OK, 20

9279 KEENER Charley, Tahlequah, OK, 38; 9282, Lucinda, W, 35; 9279, Louise D, 17; Austin, S, 12; Walter, S, 9; Rufus, S, 6; Alsey D, 2; Coleman, S, 1

4296 KEENER, George, Melvin, OK, 47; 9803, Sarah, W, 39; 4296, Lettie D 16; Jeff, S, 14; Nick, S, 12; Richard, S, 10; Evans, S, 6; Ben, S, 3

[KEENER, Heavy. See #9234]   *(Note: entries separate*
[KEENER, Hattie. See #9234]   *from other family groups)*

9801 KEENER, Jack, Melvin, OK, 32; Chow-we-yu-ke [Susie] D, 6; Gah-naw-hau-nuh [Hominy], S, 1

4295 KEENER, Johnson, Hulbert, OK, 22

9258 KEENER, Johnson, Melvin, OK, 23; 13832, Sarah, W, 23; 9258, Lucy D, 1

CHEROKEE DESCENDANTS RESIDING WEST OF MISSISSIPPI RIVER.
VOLUME II   (A – M)

Key: Guion Miller Application Number; Name; Address, Relation (to Head); Age in 1906

3884 KEENER, Joseph, Locust Grove, OK, 39; 18101, Jennie, W, 25; 3884, Henry, S, 16; Lila D, 2

1381 KEENER, Levi Ahniwake, OK, 35; 1236, Annie, W, 35; 1381, Robert, S, 13; Samuel, S, 12; Ella D, 9; Myrtle D, 6; Joe W, S, 4; William R. R, S, 2

43421 Carrie, Hulbert, OK D, 18

5355 KEENER, Lewis, Locust Grove, OK, 35; 5350, Alice, W, 27; 5355, Daniel, S, 14; White, S, 13

10187 KEENER, Lula, Hulbert, OK, 17

8800 KEENER, Thomas W, Hulbert, OK, 41; 9810, Jennie, W, 39; 8800, Laura [Lila] D, 18; Maggie [Mary] D, 12; Emily D, 4; Aggie D, 2

9280 KEENER, William, Melvin, OK, 27; 9310, Lizzie, W, 22; 9280, Sampson, S, 3; Andrew, S, 1 [Died since 5-28-1906]

5134 KEITH Annie, Stilwell, OK, 29

7992 KEITH, James G, Pryor Creek, OK, 32; Joe A, S, 5; Viola R D, 3; James R, S, 1

4820 KEITH, Johnson, Stilwell, OK, 23; 43250, Wallie, W, 17

1342 KEITH, Nina I, Maysville AR, 25; Hugh Y, S, 2

5601 KEITH, Ollie, Wahhiyah, OK, 31

9406 KEITH, Soldier, Stilwell, OK, 20

10799 KEITH, William F, Porum, OK, 35; Albert M, S, 13; Paul, S, 10; Pearlie L D, 8; Reuben M, S, 6; Veror Azzeleen D, 4; William, Jr, S, 2; Beulah B, S, ¼

12832 KELL Charles L Cherokee City AR, 35; Perry C.L, S, 6; Edith E D, 3

1352 KELL, James L Chelsea, OK, 31; 22938, Susan C, W, 30; Lewis P, S, 7; Emma E D, 5; Kermit K, S, 1

4058 KELL, Louisa, Ft. Gibson, OK, 55

7878 KELLER Annie D Coffeyville, KS, 23; George, S, 3

33236 KELLER, Nora, Hansom, OK, 31

[KELLEY Claude. See #9221]   *(Note: entry separate from other family groups)*

1812 KELLEY, Laura Z Centralia, OK, 38; Mary I D, 11; Louie A, S, 2

5199 KELLEY, Lulu N, Vinita, OK, 44; Pauline G D, 17; Fred L, Jr, S, 13; George S, S, 11

24845 KELLEY, Margaret E, Fairland,OK, 36; Clyde B, S, 6; Clara M D, 13; Earnest H, S,17

23788 KELLEY, Mary, Ketchum, OK, 27; Downing Caldonia D, 10

4898 KELLEY, Nellie, Westville, OK, 87

22577 KELLY, Sarah A, Stilwell, OK, 38; George W, S, 20; Valentine [Viola] D, 17; Addie R, D, 13; Lillie M D, 11; Floyd, S, 10; Gertie D, 8; Homer, S, 7; Flora D, 4; Grace D, 2; Norma D, 1

4691 KELLEY, Susan Chance OK, 53; Joel, S, 19; Mary D, 12; Maud D, 9

2847 KELLEY, Theodore E Afton, OK, 24

32035 KELLOGG Albert L, Red Bluff CA, 37

4420 KELLOGG, Sarah, Red Bluff CA, 57

Key: Guion Miller Application Number; Name; Address, Relation (to Head); Age in 1906

23187 KELLY Charley Chance, OK, 26; Lee W, S, 1

37202 KELLY Cherokee, Waco, TX, 34; Ben T, S, 11; John C, S, 7; William P, S, 1;
Odella, S, 13

26123 KELLY Cora, Echo, OK, 23

[KELLY, Edna. See #13946] *(Note: entry separate from other family groups)*

11860 KELLY, Ellen, Manard, OK, 34

22922 KELLY, Elsie A, Pryor Creek, OK, 25; Norval Ray, S, 1

23148 KELLY, James L Chance, OK, 22

2649 KELLY, Myrtle A, Fairland, OK, 16; William Howell Bro, 13; Mamie Delilah,
Sis, 7; By William Kelly, Gdn.

1469 KELLY, Susan E, Grove, OK, 43; Minnie M D, 12; Nainah D, 9; Joseph E, S,
7; Laura M D, 2

12843 KENNEDY, Ermina V, Roswell, NM, 21

13513 KENNEDY, Maggie, Vian, OK, 33

7664 KENNEDY, Peggie, McKey, OK, 23; William Riley, S, 3; John Lee, S, 1

2976 KENNEY Charles D, Vinita, OK, 52; Amanda Caroline D, 14; Emmett H D, 10

14105 KENT, Nancy R, Tahlequah, OK, 31; Buse, Onie M D, 13; Charles F, S, 11; Ada
E, D, 9; Samuel T, S, 6; Sherman B, S, 4; Kent, Margaret C D, 1

2977 KENWORTHY, Mary E, Vinita, OK, 58; Summers, Frederick, S, 19

18521 KEPLER Cynthia E, Sherman CA, 34; Gillum, Myrtle D, 14; Kepler, Howard
[Andrew H], S, 10; Neva W D, 2

22972 KERKENDALL, Sidney E Chance, OK, 18

22786 KERNS Cora, Westville, OK, 27

29485 KERR Albert S, Warner, OK, 20

4215 KERR Cynthia [Lucinda], Warner, OK, 56; George L, S, 18

30677 KERR, Gussie B, Pryor Creek, OK, 21

29784 KERR, John L, Warner, OK, 30; Mamie E D, 6; Nannie D, 5; Ellen D, 5;
Edmond B, S, 3; Edgar D, S, 3; Earl S, S, 1

24878 KERR, Susan T, Vinita, OK, 33; Ollie M D, 11

28699 KERR, William W, Warner, OK, 28

24150 KESSLER, Zora W Claremore, OK, 34; Evers Avrin B, S, 10; Jesse B, S, 7;
Kessler, Emina E D, 4; Libren M, S, 2 [Died since 5-1906]; Ochaleta F, S, 1/12

[KETCHER. See CATCHER.]

13710 KETCHER Aaron, Sleeper, OK, 23; Susie D, 16; Jesse A, S, 4; Frank, S, 3;
Mabel D, 1/12

[KETCHER Anderson. See #4512]   *(Note: entry separate from other family groups)*

[KETCHER, Rachel. See #4513]   *(Note: entry separate from other family groups)*

CHEROKEE DESCENDANTS RESIDING WEST OF MISSISSIPPI RIVER.

VOLUME II   (A – M)

Key: Guion Miller Application Number; Name; Address, Relation (to Head); Age in 1906

[KETCHER, Nancy. See #26715]
[KETCHER, Robert E. See #26715]   *(Note: entries separate*
[KETCHER, Lena. See #26715]   *from other family groups)*
[KETCHER, Elmira. See #26715]

[KETCHER Andrew. See #24561]   *(Note: entry separate from other family groups)*

[KETCHER Carrie. See #16713]   *(Note: entry separate from other family groups)*

4626 KETCHER Charles, Evansville AR, 58; 1917, Annie, W, 56; 4626, Tom, S, 9
14188 KETCHER Charlie, Locust Grove, OK, 62; 8749, Sallie, W, 38
11967 KETCHER Cornelius, Eucha, OK, 35; 640, Lydia, W, 29; Lula D, 7; Sarah D, 4; Davis, S, 2
25739 KETCHER Dennis, Tahlequah, OK, 26
8761 KETCHER, Ellis, Muldrow, OK, 34; Harvey E, S, 11; Minnie M D, 7; Faloney D, 1; Ruth M D, 9

[KETCHER, Ellis. See #34243]   *(Note: entry separate from other family groups)*

24712 KETCHER, Ezekiel Baron, OK, 22
228 KETCHER, George Baptist, OK, 45; 572, Martha, W, 36; Lee, S, 19; Henry, S, 16; Willie, S, 13; Cornelius, S, 9; Bettie D, 3
8236 KETCHER, George, Westville, OK, 22; Floid[sic], D, 1/6
38486 KETCHER, George, Hulbert, OK, 20
4202 KETCHER, Green, Flint, OK, 52
1402 KETCHER, James Christie, OK, 25; Fred L, S, 2
1432 KETCHER, John, Westville, OK, 29; Levi, S, 5/6
3646 KETCHER, John, Grove, OK, 24
4850 KETCHER, Johnson, Grove, OK, 37 [Died 3-17-1907]; Alice D, 15; Susie D, 14; Lee, S, 12; Nancy D, 10; Celia D, 8; Isaac, S, 7; Cora D, 3
1314 KETCHER, Key, Tahlequah, OK, 61; 1473, Betsy, W, 53; 1314, Henry, S, 18; John, S, 16; Lucinda D, 12
3647 KETCHER, Levi, Grove, OK, 35; 23335, Rowena, W, 24; B_rt, S, 3; Davis, S, 1
8738 KETCHER, Levi, Salina, OK, 35; 8917, Sis, W, 28 [Died 8-11-1907]
2795 KETCHER, Lizzie, Flint, OK, 54
13451 KETCHER, Richard Choteau, OK, 38; 13531, Hattie, W, 31; Ollie D, 15; Carrie D, 13; Dollie V D, 4; Flossie B D, 3; Ned Roosevelt, S, 1½
13836 KETCHER, Richard, Melvin, OK, 18; Josie, Sis, 15;   By Andrew Hair, Gdn.
24696 KETCHER, Richard Baron, OK, 24
7483 KETCHER, Ruth V, Gans, OK, 3; Leonard L Bro, ½ ;   By Benjamin F. Doyle, Gdn.
1430 KETCHER, Sarah, Westville, OK, 26
1741 KETCHER, Sarah, Grove, OK, 54

Key: Guion Miller Application Number; Name; Address, Relation (to Head); Age in 1906

27677 KETCHER, Susie Baron, OK, 33

26716 KETCHER, Thomas J Baron, OK, 23

1715 KETTLE, Jennie, Porum, OK, 42 [Deceased]

1716 KETTLE, John, Porum, OK, 69;   By Wm Smallwood Admr.

25924 KEY, Minnie M, Uniontown AR, 16

11042 KEYS Betty Coffeyville, KS, 45; Campbell L, S, 18

28207 KEYS Bluford A Choteau, OK, 24

27910 KEYS Charles, Pauls Valley, OK, 30; 5688, Caroline, W, 38; 27910, Jananthy
D, 6; Dick, S, 4; Hazel D, 1; 12589, Scott, Nancy D of W, 15; 12588, Jennie D
of W, 19

12631 KEYS Charles L, Wauhillau, OK, 55; Theodore S, S, 19; Wilson, S, 16

31617 KEYS Dennis B Choteau, OK, 29; 36659, Nannie E, W, 23; Gorden L, S, 1

13526 KEYS, George Checotah, OK, 12; Jesse Bro, 7; Henry Bro, 6;
By Martha Ashley, Gdn.

25019 KEYS, James M Cookson, OK, 22; 25018, Eliza V, W, 16

16186 KEYS, James T Cookson, OK, 53; 1412, Margaret E, W, 51; John D, S, 18;
Walter S, S, 15; Levi H, S, 12

8269 KEYS, Joanna, Locust Grove, OK, 19

22830 KEYS, John A, Wauhillau, OK, 28; Stuart, S, 4; John R, S, 1

16160 KEYS, Levi Cookson, OK, 54; 1080, Elizabeth, W, 71

3177 KEYS, Lewis K, Sallisaw, OK, 13; Lawrence T, Bro, 12; David H, Bro, 11
By Maggie J. Keys, Mother

28208 KEYS, Lizzie C, Pryor Creek, OK, 21

9015 KEYS, Lorenzo D, Wauhillau, OK, 49

6584 KEYS, Lucinda J, Wauhillau, OK, 75

253 KEYS, Lucy L, Vinita, OK, 75

23861 KEYS, M. T. W, Muldrow, OK, 22

27943 KEYS, Maggie, Cookson, OK, 23; Lovett, Rodgers, S, 3

12626 KEYS, Manda C Ballard, OK, 33; Lorenzo D, S, 22

1205 KEYS, Mary J Childers, OK, 42; Spencer Allen, S, 19; Keys Carrie D, 17;
Minnie, D, 17; Charles C, S, 9

9014 KEYS, Mary O, Wauhillau, OK, 36

9012 KEYS, Mike G, Stilwell, OK, 39; Willie M D, 11; Neoma D, 7; Mary E D, 4;
Verlie, D, 2; Paul, S, 1/6

30133 KEYS, Monroe A Bluejacket, OK, 36; 30134, Mattie A, W, 32

9934 KEYS, Nancy J, Pryor Creek, OK, 56

23860 KEYS, R. W. M, Muldrow, OK, 24

9208 KEYS, Riley, Welling, OK, 47; William H, S, 19; Addie R D, 17; Fannie L D,
15; George M, S, 11; Riley V, S, 7; Alfred C, S, 1

23336 KEYS, Robert L, Owasso, OK, 21

12228 KEYS, Sam Cookson, OK, 33; 5618, Mollie, W, 23; Jesse, S, 2

1133 KEYS, Samuel J, Owasso, OK, 50; William F, S, 18; Nettie M D, 13; James M,
S, 9; Colbert E, S, 5; Tolbert M, S, 5

Key: Guion Miller Application Number; Name; Address, Relation (to Head); Age in 1906

28532 KEYS, Samuel L, Owasso, OK, 24

6045 KEYS, Williamson R. W. C, Muldrow, OK, 59; George A. L, S, 20; Lorenzo D, S, 18; Walter C, S, 14; Otta G D, 12; Cleo M, GD, 2

25037 KIDD, Felix Chelsea, OK, 33; Oscar, S, 10; Richard, S, 9; Blanchia D, 7; Lester, S, 2; Captain, S, 1

34112 KIDD, Garfield Ashland, OR, 25

[KIDD, James C. See #24288]   ⎤   *(Note: entries separate*
[KIDD, Roxey. See #24288]   ⎦   *from other family groups)*

32558 KIDD, Martha, Kiefer, OK, 20

23949 KIDD, Wilburn, Salina, OK, 36; James C, S, 11; Rocksy D, 5

10463 KIDWELL, Rosa Chant, OK, 28; Nora D, 10; Clella D, 1

4799 KIEFER, Sarah C, Fairland, OK,52; 24454, Emma,D, 19; 31595, Mary Elizabeth, D,18

[KIE-SKA, Jennie. See #15962]   *(Note: entry separate from other family groups)*

4400 KILLER Alice, Evansville AR, 36; Gonzales Ancy, S, 12; Vann, Ida D, 6

3871 KILLER, Ellen, Stilwell, OK, 55; Nancy D, 17; Georgian D, 9

36442 KILLER, Maggie, Stilwell, OK, 33; Gonzales Ada D, 10; Dave, S, 8; John, S, 6; Senora D, 5; Killer, James, S, 1

7414 KILLER, Rolland, Stilwell, OK, 38

12534 KILLER, Starr Bunch, OK, 34; 42197, Kate, W, 30; 12534, Betsey D, 8; Crawfish, S, 6; Lawler D, 4; Ga-yo-he D, 2

13252 KILLINEGER, Jennie Bunch, OK, 52; 13250, Sarah D, 19; 13251, Tom, S, 15; 13252, Aggy D, 12

9614 KIMBROUGH, John, Ketchum, OK, 34; John L, S, 9; William A, S, 6; Woodie R, S, 4; Gladys I D, 1

8037 KIMMONS Annie Chetopa, KS, 23

31388 KINCAIDE Andrew M Adair, OK, 21

31386 KINCAIDE Charles W Adair, OK, 23

31385 KINCAIDE, Edward C Adair, OK, 30

30243 KINCAIDE, Francis N Adair, OK, 27

31387 KINCAIDE, James L Adair, OK, 20

30245 KINCAIDE, Martha L Adair, OK, 17

23918 KINCAIDE, Robert L, Stilwell, OK, 33; Samuel L, S, 8; Batie E, S, 2

30244 KINCAIDE, William R Adair, OK, 25; Leona A D, 1/6

1975 KING Abbie, Tahlequah, OK, 68

16612 KING Annie, Eucha, OK, 58

165 KING Cathron H, Maple, OK, 54

8871 KING Charlie, Locust Grove, OK, 55; Tom, S, 28; Susie D, 12; John, S, 10

Key: Guion Miller Application Number; Name; Address, Relation (to Head); Age in 1906

28870 KING, Edward C Collinsville, OK, 32; 20093, Aggie, W, 24; 28870, Benjamin W, S, 5; Richard J, S, 1/24

22621 KING, Etta, Hollow, OK, 26; George W, S, 3; Pauline M D, ¼

21831 KING, George, Muldrow, OK, 26; 10279, Mary, W, 32; Holt, Emma D of W, 11

116½ KING, Jackson J, Maple, OK, 28; Fredie, S, 1

10252 KING, James Dragger, OK, 25; 26080, Susie, W, 19; West, S, 3; Maggie D, 1/12

3861 KING, Jennie Choteau, OK, 41; Carrie M D, 19; Alma Etta D, 16; Joel B, S, 12; Jessie F D, 10; Lydia [Lillie] P D, 8; Henry, S, 4; Essie A D, 2

21832 KING, John W, Muldrow, OK, 27

30174 KING, Mary E, Vian, OK, 33; McKinley, S, 9; Stanley, S, 7; Jocie D, 4; Maggie D, 1

4813 KING, Nancy, Locust Grove, OK, 18; Leaf, Sarah D, 1

28199 KING, Parker, Long, OK, 22

29387 KING, Richard W, Tahlequah, OK, 35; 29386, Melvina, W, 35; Benjamin C, S, 15; James W, S, 10; Clifford W, S, 4

30454 KING, Sam Dragger, OK, 21

1608 KING, Sophie, McKey, OK, 54

24043 KING, Susie Braggs, OK, 27

712 KINGFISHER, Blackfox, Peggs, OK, 55; 2938, Wal-leas-cie, W, 35; Going Snake, S, 19; Susan D, 5; Nancy D, 3

18498 KINGFISHER Clark, Peggs, OK, 14;   By Polly Kingfisher, Gdn.

[KINGFISHER Doo-na-ge or Tooniah. See #5286]
(Note: entry separate from other family groups)

2930 KINGFISHER, Israel, Locust Grove, OK, 23

742 KINGFISHER, James Bartlesville, OK, 35; 705, Lizzie, W, 34; Mack, S, 13; Cumming, S, 8

[KINGFISHER, James. See #9257]   *(Note: entry separate from other family groups)*

[KINGFISHER, Joe. See #4311]   *(Note: entry separate from other family groups)*

[KINGFISHER, John. See #43405]   *(Note: entry separate from other family groups)*

4109 KINGFISHER, John W, Oaks, OK, 38; 2282, Cora, W, 39; 4109, Fannie D, 17; Maggie D, 15; Willis, S, 8; Ida D, 6; Susie D, 4; Jesse, S, 2

4305 KINGFISHER, Josiah, Peggs, OK, 38; 4307, Lizzie, W, 36; Stella D, 3

25584 KINGFISHER, Katie, Peggs, OK, 17

4309 KINGFISHER, Minnie, Locust Grove, OK, 21

[KINGFISHER, Philip. See #4851]   *(Note: entry separate from other family groups)*

Key: Guion Miller Application Number; Name; Address, Relation (to Head); Age in 1906

[KINGFISHER, Polly. See #4304]   *(Note: entry separate from other family groups)*

[KINGFISHER, Skake. See #1288]   *(Note: entry separate from other family groups)*

[KINGFISHER, Susan O. See #4859]   *(Note: entry separate from other family groups)*

4306 KINGFISHER, Tom, Peggs, OK, 31; 25634, Margaret, W, 31; Luella D, 9; Wofford, George, Neph, 4

[KINGFISHER, Watie. See #4870]   *(Note: entry separate from other family groups)*

10266 KINGFISHER, West, Gideon, OK, 54; 10219, Ah-lee, W, 27; 10220, Oo-lo-gu-la [or Chullo], S, 16; 10219, Williams Charley, S of W, 13; Betsy D of W, 6
10238 KINGHORN, Jennie Albany, OK, 55
22528 KINNISON, Mary V, Welch, OK, 32; Arthur B, S, 5; Amanda N D, 4; Lieura N D, 2
23266 KINZER, Ethelynne Afton, OK, 19; Willie C, S, 2
23973 KIPER Charlotte, Locust Grove, OK, 29; Jennie May D, 11; Hester D, 9; Cassie D, 5
29861 KIRK Annie Braggs, OK, 16
5704 KIRK Bertha, Westville, OK, 17
24789 KIRK, John, Westville, OK, 22
28222 KIRK, Julia, Eureka, OK, 24; George E, S, 2½
28380 KIRK, Luvinia Rider, Porum, OK, 19
13116 KIRK, Mary, Rose, OK, 26; Adair Bluie, S, 9; Kirk, Susie D, 5; Jane D, 3; Minnie D, 2; Benjamin, S, 1

[KIRK, Ora Ethel. See #2848]   *(Note: entry separate from other family groups)*

40822 KIRK, Robert, Tahlequah, OK, 19; Lee, S, 1/6
8268 KIRK, Sarah, Rose, OK, 27; Downing, Lewis, S, 5½; Murphy, Verna D, 3
2885 KIRK, Susanna, Tahlequah, OK, 44; Samuel, S, 17; Asberry, S, 13; Ezekiel, S, 9; Albert, S, 7; Susan M D, 3; Lottie A D, 2
24790 KIRK, William, Westville, OK, 21

[KIRKPATRICK, Lillian. See #2233]   *(Note: entry separate from other family groups)*

1302 KIRKSEY, Irene, Owasso, OK, 27
21033 KISER, Rosa Choteau, OK, 19; Carver, Emma D, 2
8765 KITE, Florence Bartlesville, OK, 18
31585 KITTERMAN, Fannie P Dewey, OK, 20
28126 KIZER, Henry, Row, OK, 21

Key: Guion Miller Application Number; Name; Address, Relation (to Head); Age in 1906

1694 KIZER, Katy, Row, OK, 49; Catherine D, 16; William, S, 14; 28127, Mary L D, 19; 1694, Lila D, 12; Jeanetta D, 10; Charles Ira, S, 8

28125 KIZER, Milton, Row, OK, 22

5051 KLAUS Annie Afton, OK, 20

3856 KLAUS Betty Afton, OK, 49

6946 KLAUS, Robert, Jr, Zena, OK, 24; Everett Arlos, S, 2

5171 KLAUS, William H, Woodley, OK, 32; 26952, Carlotta, W, 29; Jesse H, S, 9; Anna Mae, D, 1

30097 KNAPP, Mary Ann Camas, WA, 39; Maud May D, 20; Flora Jane D, 18; Agnes Belle, D, 13

93 KNEELAND, Fannie R, Ft. Gibson, OK, 44; Harry Ross, S, 15; Louis G, S, 12; Herbert, S, 10; Ross M, S, 1

7023 KNIGHT Ben, Westville, OK, 67; 7024, Ollie, W, 39; Cochran, John D, 14; Knight, Mary D, 14; Charlotte D, 9; Willie, S, 4; Peggie D, 1; 15973, Starr, S, 17

16651 KNIGHT Ben Baron, OK, 29; 1782, Aggie, W, 30; Thornton, Johnson, S of W, 10; Knight Ada D, 6; Laura D, 2; Mary L D, 1

[KNIGHT Betsy. See #41529]   *(Note: entry separate from other family groups)*

28035 KNIGHT, E. Goldie, Welch, OK, 23; Reunnis D, 1 2/3

26580 KNIGHT, Fannie M, Vinita, OK, 26

26579 KNIGHT, Henry S, Vinita, OK, 28

26582 KNIGHT, Joseph Dewey, OK, 34

26581 KNIGHT, Morris F, Vinita, OK, 32

11636 KNIGHT, Polly Christie, OK, 46

[KNIGHT, Sarah. See #41529]   *(Note: entry separate from other family groups)*

30869 KNIGHT, Sarah D, Paw Paw, OK, 33; Ida D, 8; Willie, S, 7; Floid, S, 5; Claudy, S, 2

24011 KNIGHT, Thomas M Bartlesville, OK, 30

8949 KNIGHTKILLER Bird, Westville, OK, 26; 8954, Mary, W, 27; Gertrude D, 5

8118 KNIGHTKILLER, William, Westville,   OK, 30; 6489, Lydia, W, 42; Knight, Mintie, D of W, 12; Knight, Henry, S of W, 1

13099 KNIGHTKILLER, Zeke, Lometa, OK, 35

5172 KNIGHTON Cornelia J, Tahlequah, OK, 28; William C, S, 8; Telitha L D, 7; Elsie J, D, 4; Susie A D, 3

3916 KOLPIN, Eliza A, Tahlequah, OK, 48; Augusta D, 9

29323 KOLPIN, John P, Tahlequah, OK, 30

28324 KOLPIN, Leon, Tahlequah, OK, 25

37062 KRIGBAUM, James A Coweta, OK, 7;   By James E. Krigbaum, father

Key: Guion Miller Application Number; Name; Address, Relation (to Head); Age in 1906

33796 KUDER Corah M Afton, OK, 28; Winrow E, S, 7; Cora B D, 5; James A, S, 3; Charles F, S, 1

1818 KUHN, Malinda J Chelsea, OK, 59

12920 KUL-STOO-HER-SKY, Elizabeth, Southwest City, MO, 41

5173 KYLE, Eleanor, Sallisaw, OK, 30; Morris, Susie I D, 9; Ronnie T, S, 6; Kyle, Kittie E, D, 3

[LABOYTEAUX, Willie Gray. See #1370]   *(Note: entries separate*
[LABOYTEAUX, Hutton. See #1370]   *from other family groups)*

16882 LACEY Annie, Oaks, OK, 13;   By Sam Lacey, Gdn.

9340 LACEY, Henry, Warner, OK, 25

9337 LACEY, James, Warner, OK, 26

14135 LACEY, Samuel, Locust Grove, OK, 35; 9437, Nannie, W, 25; Mary D, 9; Emma D, 4; Jennie D, 2

9339 LACEY, Susan F, Warner, OK, 16

16996 LACIE, Lottie E, Westville, OK, 10; By Jennie Grigsby, Gdn. and Mother

16995 LACIE, Ona, Westville, OK, 8;   By Jennie Grigsby, Gdn.

16997 LACIE, Rufus, Westville, OK, 20; 6488, Lydia Ann, W, 29

16994 LACIE, Silas, Westville, OK, 20; 16992, Katie, W, 18

5750 LACKEY Carrie, Southwest City, MO, 29; Walters, Jas, S, 13; Lee Clarence Earl, S, 4; Lackey, Harvey Hutchinson, S, 2

461 LACY Ancy, Spavinaw, OK, 49

7886 LACY, Jane, Muldrow, OK, 19; Hershel V, S, 1

8850 LACY, Joseph or Josiah, Locust Grove, OK, 33; 8912, Jennie, W, 20; Sut-tur-way-ki, D, 1/12

9338 LACY, Lizzie, Warner, OK, 52

5551 LACY, Mattie, Vinita, OK, 18

9299 LACY, Nel-se-ne Cherokee City AR, 64

35272 LADD Burnett A, Narcissa, OK, 22

33259 LADD Burris O Caney, KS, 27

[LADD Delmar. See #22865]   *(Note: entries separate*
[LADD Clifford. See #22865]   *from other family groups)*

5174 LADD, Mary J, Narcissa, OK, 52; Henry E, S, 20; James David, S, 20; Tula Mary D, 17; Clara L D, 13; Mattie P D, 10

13032 LADD, Nettie, Wann, OK, 35; Percy H, S, 13; Sadie D, S, 11; Roy, S, 9; Essie May D, 7; Ethel D, 2

11824 LAFON, Sarah Bartlett, KS, 37; Amos, S, 18; Claude, S, 18; Flossy D, 15; Essie D, 13; Mayes, S, 11; Clark, S, 8; Ambrose, S, 6; Beverly, S, 6

8874 LaHAY, Joseph M Claremore, OK, 41; John F, S, 19; Maggie D, 16; Helen M D, 12

Key: Guion Miller Application Number; Name; Address, Relation (to Head); Age in 1906

27438 LAHLEY Dayke, Vian, OK, 20
14682 LAHLEY, Mose, Vian, OK, 45
31892 LAIN, Lydia M Coffeyville, KS, 25; Delphia O D, 6; Rean, S, 5; Ida M D, 2
17842 LAMAR Charles E Afton, OK, 34; Ada Marie D, 3
5105 LAMAR, Edward, Fairland, OK, 27
13955 LAMAR, Florence E, Skiatook, OK, 18
31402 LAMAR, Franklin Taylor, Hillside, OK, 19
4816 LAMAR, James E Afton, OK, 37
5106 LAMAR, James R, Fairland, OK, 31; Essie D D, 2
5175 LAMAR, Jesse S, Wynnewood, OK, 41; 23780, Vivian U, S, 17; Paden M, S, 16; J. Sims, S, 3

[LAMAR, Maudie. See #31403]   *(Note: entry separate from other family groups)*

4798 LAMAR, Maud, Fairland, OK, 17; Lucius Bro, 19; Nettie, Sis, 15; Mildred, Sis, 12; Franklin Bro, 10;   By Henry Kiefer, Gdn.
31404 LAMAR, Jas R, Hillside, OK, 13;   By Sarah J. Birdsong, Gdn.
27093 LAMASCAS Annetta, McLain, OK, 26; Bertha Ella D, 4; Roby M D, 2

[LAMBERT. John. See #8215]   *(Note: entry separate from other family groups)*

23338 LAMBERT, Fannie Collinsville, OK, 18
16359 LAMM, Florence, Pryor Creek, OK, 20
23740 LAMON, Mattie E, Wagoner, OK, 32; Mary E D, 7; Malvina D, 5; Katharine W D, 4; Helen D, 2
24630 LAND, Pearl M, Neosho, MO, 26; Stewart M, S, 5
19059 LANDERS Callie Porum, OK, 30; Bertha D, 10; William II, S, 7; Gracie D, 6; George, S, 2; Ruth D, 1/12
4225 LANDRUM Ada Cleora, OK, 32
3500 LANDRUM Benjamin C, Pryor Creek, OK, 45; Roxie May D, 12; Thomas E, S, 10; Bailey B, S, 7; Ocie L, S, 4; Morya C D, 2
4221 LANDRUM Charles F, Cleora, OK, 37
5646 LANDRUM Charlotte J, Cleora, OK, 46; 11897, Alice W D, 15
4220 LANDRUM Cicero M Cleora, OK, 48
5176 LANDRUM, E. M. Tahlequah, OK, 40; David S, S, 11; Elias M, S, 9; Margaret D, D, 7; Lois S D, 5
4365 LANDRUM, Edward, Vinita, OK, 36
2726 LANDRUM, Hiram T, Echo, OK, 12; Jesse Van Bro, 10; Roxie Ann, Sis, 8; By Dine Bowman, Gdn.
13072 LANDRUM, Hiram T Cleora, OK, 24
265 LANDRUM, James K, Echo, OK, 29; Hiram W, S, 7; Arkansas C D, 5; Pearl M D, 1
12704 LANDRUM, James P Cleora, OK, 28; Alice J D, 2

Key: Guion Miller Application Number; Name; Address, Relation (to Head); Age in 1906

17805 LANDRUM, John A Cleora, OK, 26

4363 LANDRUM, Johnson,Big Cabin, OK, 47; 31291, Catherine, W, 38[Died 11-19-1906]; Nellie J D, 17; Clifton L, S, 14; Stephen E, S, 12; Mary I D, 10; Ada M D, 8; Wannetta T D, 5; Helena B D, 2

4223 LANDRUM, Lonia Cleora, OK, 16; Margaret E, Sis, 14; Benjamin Bro, 11; Cherokee, Sis, 8; Allison Bro, 6;   By Charles F. Landrum, Gdn.

456 LANDRUM, Nellie, Vinita, OK, 70

4224 LANDRUM, Pansy Cleora, OK, 19

4364 LANDRUM, Samuel, Vinita, OK, 40

1399 LANDRUM, Thos. L, Foyil, OK, 43

2683 LANDRUM, William, Iola, KS, 29

3207 LANE Annie L, Proctor, OK, 41; Hitchcock, Edward Owen, S, 19; Craig Buell, D, 14; Leonard, S, 11; Anie May D, 9; Burley, S, 4

40062 LANE, Henry, Muldrow, OK, 26

22565 LANE, Martha E, Oglesby, OK, 43; Henry K, S, 12; Goldie Myrtle D, 8; Geo. Floyd, S, 4½; Preston, Willie M, S, 16

2379 LANE, Maud Chelsea, OK, 39; Estelle D, 13; Ethel L D, 11; Gunter, S, 10; Lasca, S, 11/12

23357 LANE, Rachel, Vinita, OK, 33; Alfred C, S, 13; Debora D, 12; Lenora D, 9; Rosa M, D, 6; William V, S, 4

11756 LANGLEY Andrew J, Westville, OK, 42; John J, S, 15; Robert E, S, 15; Rena Ellen, D, 12

9181 LANGLEY Bayless M, Ft. Gibson, OK, 41; J. Oscar, S, 20; Mary Gladys D, 14 Andrew E, S, 12

16616 LANGLEY Charles, Verdigris, OK, 29; 15029, Anna, W, 26; 16616, William C, S, 3;

16674 LANGLEY, James E, Lometa, OK, 47; 4241, Sallie, W, 45; Susie D, 12; George, S, 8; Ella D, 5

25978 LANGLEY, Jimmie A Afton, OK, 27

11741 LANGLEY, Joseph H, Westville, OK, 23

33460 LANGLEY, John W. D Catoosa, OK, 38; 33461, Sarah R. L,D,?; Joseph O, S, 13; Minnie E D, 11; Jesse R. W, S, 7; Audie E D, 5; Maud L. P D, 2

15028 LANGLEY, Lock Claremore, OK, 32; 12155, Catherine, W, 32; Catherine D, 3

10262 LANGLEY, Maggie, Nowata, OK, 18;   By J. K. Lowry, Gdn.

33459 LANGLEY, Marion J Catoosa, OK, 26;   Charles O, S, 8; Eva E D, 6; Zachariah F, S, 5; Homer L, S, 3

27671 LANGLEY, Martha A Baptist, OK, 20

27670 LANGLEY, Mary J Baptist, OK, 24

10669 LANGLEY, Noah Big Cabin, OK, 29; Hattie Lee D, 6; Noah R, S, 3

27669 LANGLEY, Robert R Baptist, OK, 36; Charles B, S, 8; Western T, S, 6; Mary E D, 4; Joseph A, S, 2; Francis E, S, 5/12

11912 LANGLEY, Samuel B, Westville, OK, 29; Clarence B, S, 5; Fannie L D, 3; Manerva L, D, 1

Key: Guion Miller Application Number; Name; Address, Relation (to Head); Age in 1906

11740 LANGLEY, Sidney J Baptist, OK, 36; Joseph B, S, 15; Alice L D, 14; Lock, S, 14; Ollie H, S, 12; William J, S, 8; Lillie J D, 6; John C, S, 4; Katie E D, 1/6

13968 LANGLEY, William F, Wauhillau, OK, 32; 8974, Ophelia, W, 31; Clarence F, S, 10; Jesse H, S, 8; William H, S, 6; Mary J, E D, 4; Gladys d D, 2

11666 LANGLEY, William J Alluwe, OK, 32; Andrew J, S, 1

10267 LANGLEY, Zachariah T Chelsea, OK, 57; Charley O, S, 19

1901 LANGLY Amos, Long, OK, 55; Levi, S, 13

9002 LANING, Ida May Afton, OK, 31; Lelia D, 6

24070 LANSFORD, Nannie E, Warner, OK, 24; Rastie, S, 7; Luola D, 3; Eugene, S, 1

14276 LANGTON, Ellen Braggs, OK, 25; Bertha D, 4; Mary D, 1

3180 LARGE Benjamin F, Vinita, OK, 46; Birt F, S, 17

13269 LARGE, John W Cliff, NM, 55

3181 LARGE, Oceola Q, Knobbs CA, 42; Vernon Adair, S, 10; Earle Wayne, S, 8

4421 LARGE, Robert Dedrick CA, 59; Zima D, 16; Annie S D, 14

3182 LARGER, William C, Vinita, OK, 40; Eunice M D, 13; Grace Lee D, 10; William C, S, 3

15010 LARGEN, Mary E, Sallisaw, OK, 12; William J Bro, 16; John T Bro, 7; By Wm W. Wheeler, Gdn.

6928 LARMAN, Martha A, Row, OK, 21

1120 LASLEY, Joseph V Catoosa, OK, 19

[LASSLEY Cecil M. See #9972]   *(Note: entry separate from other family groups)*

[LASSLEY, Sarah. See #8111]   *(Note: entry separate from other family groups)*

17788 LASTER, Nancy, Inola, OK, 52

5252 LATTA Annie, Muskogee, OK, 37

10748 LATTA, Felix, Porum, OK, 68

29089 LATTY, Mary E, Etta, OK, 27; Alice D, 6; Susie L D, 1/6

13696 LAUGHLIN, Nancy J, Ramona, OK, 22; James G, S, 5; Betty M D, 2; Mary Lee D, 1

31190 LAWHEAD Celia, Eucha, OK, 30; Downing, George, S, 13; On-the-hill, John, S, 9; Lawhead, Ollie D, 3

[LAWLAH, Mose. See #14682]   *(Note: entry separate from other family groups)*

4494 LAWRENCE Bluie, Tahlequah, OK, 31; Augustus Adair, S, 6; Gilbert Shelton, S, 3

26186 LAWRENCE, Mary C, Tahlequah, OK, 27

24874 LAWRENCE, Rebecca J, Vinita, OK, 42; Cox, J. D, S 19; Elvy D, 14; Lawrence, Forest L, S, 12; Elbert R, S, 6

23944 LAWSON, Maggie R, Muskogee, OK, 20

16993 LAZIE Charlotte, Westville, OK, 17;   By Jennie Grigsby, Mother

Key: Guion Miller Application Number; Name; Address, Relation (to Head); Age in 1906

205 LEACH Annie, Leach, OK, 72

[LEACH Che-arke. See #179]   *(Note: entries separate*
[LEACH Ar-ne-la. See #179]   *from other family groups)*

3146 LEACH Dave, Tahlequah, OK, 27; 1742, Ella, W, 28
33686 LEACH, Elizabeth Jane Catoosa, OK, 45 [Died 6-1906]; Ethel J. M D, 19; Robert, S, 17; Lolie M D, 16; Minnie D, 14; Hartsel, S, 10; Marcus, S, 8; By Marcus Y. Leach, Husband and Father
9139 LEACH, Felix, Stilwell, OK, 42
6252 LEACH, French, Leach, OK, 49; 6251, Peggie, W, 43; Ar-le-tsa, S, 18; Sampson, S, 16; Take D, 14; Betsy D, 11; Pheasant, S, 6; Kee-too-wa-kie, S, 4; Lucy D, 2
29182 LEACH, John Alfred, Gilliam, LA, 21
2900 LEACH, John W Claremore, OK, 48
23534 LEACH, John R, Leach, OK, 44; John Annie D, 12; Wm McKinley, S, 10; Lee Emmit, S, 8
970 LEACH, Mary, Tahlequah, OK, 60
17025 LEACH, Sam, Stilwell, OK, 21
10305 LEACH, Thompson Cookson, OK, 40; 10322, Wakee, W, 31; Henry, S, 17; Thomas, S, 15; Wat, S, 13
28381 LEACH, William, Porum, OK, 20
26517 LEACH, Worcester, Oaks, OK, 21
31555 LEADER Andrew, Porum, OK, 18; Charles Bro, 15;   By J. J. Leader, Gdn.
16136 LEADER, Jesse J, Porum, OK, 34; Claud J, S, 9; John, S, 7; Joseph M, S, 5; Nancy R, D, 3; Ed, S, 2; Ozie, S, 1/6
8181 LEADER, Lucinda, Texanna, OK, 29; Joseph, S, 11; David, S, 6
11030 LEADER, Polly, Texanna, OK, 54
5674 LEAF Dave Constitution Chloeta, OK, 51; 5675, Jennie, W, 33; Six, Groundhog, S of W, 17; Leaf, Lizzie D, 15; Six, McLaughlin, S of W, 13; Leaf, Oo-le-skia-te, S, 11; Six, Handcup [Tincup], S of W, 8; Leaf, Leaf, S, 4

[LEAF, Elizabeth. See #12920]   *(Note: entry separate from other family groups)*

14185 LEAF, James, Vian, OK, 30; 9264, Nellie, W, 37; Vann, Lee, S of W, 5; 14263, Silk, Lizzie D of W, 14
16349 LEAF, James Cookson, OK, 10;   By Sally Vann, Gdn.
5672 LEAF, Ja-si-yu-law-ge Chloeta, OK, 47

[LEAF, Jesse. See #7655]
[LEAF, Sallie. See #7656]   *(Note: entries separate*
[LEAF, Nannie. See #7656]   *from other family groups)*
[LEAF, Jennie. See #7656]
[LEAF, Mary. See #7656]

Key: Guion Miller Application Number; Name; Address, Relation (to Head); Age in 1906

13399 LEAF, John, Muskogee, OK, 14;   By Belle Bush, Gdn.

6566 LEAF, Lydia Joseph Cherokee City, AR, 58

7670 LEAF, Maggie, Vian, OK, 54

[LEAF, Mary. See #1453]   *(Note: entry separate from other family groups)*

13672 LEAF, Nancy Cookson, OK, 28; Lizzie D, 7; Eli, S, 5; Lucy D, 3; Charley, S, 1

12402 LEAF, Nellie Cookson, OK, 57; Mary D,16; Adam, S, 15

[LEAF, Sarah. See #4813]   *(Note: entry separate from other family groups)*

[LEAF, Tom. See #16376]   *(Note: entry separate from other family groups)*

[LEAF, Nancy. See #10387]   *(Note: entry separate from other family groups)*

28489 LEAFER, Florence, Moodys, OK, 24; Johnnie, S, 2; Lawrence, S, 1

6962 LEAHERMAN, Loretta Coffeyville, KS, 31; Susan D, 12; Bessie O D, 9; Blanche M, D, 7; Wilbur A, S, 4

23681 LEATHERS Callie, Sallisaw, OK, 22; Lillian T D, 3; Irene B D, 5/6

36152 LEATHERS, Tooka A, Tahlequah, OK, 20; Flint, S, 2; Roy L, S, 1

23383 LEATHERWOOD, James L, Stilwell, OK, 34; Tory S, S, 12; Arthur K, S, 9; Ralph W, S, 3

23385 LEATHERWOOD, Lear C, Stilwell, OK, 22

23384 LEATHERWOOD, Louis N, Stilwell, OK, 32

1548 LEATHERWOOD, Martha E, Stilwell,   OK, 56

23176 LEATHERWOOD, Ruth, Stilwell, OK, 19

30528 LEE Ada, Foyil, OK, 17

17404 LEE Addie, Marble City, OK, 13

1175 LEE Ah-ley, Evansville AR, 76

29294 LEE Allie B Chelsea, OK, 20; Lois Lodema D, 1/12

4057 LEE Amelia, Ft. Gibson, OK, 38; Etha Mayo D, 11; Lawson, S, 8; Tommie Edna D, 5; Aubrey D, 3; Audrian, S, 3

1451 LEE Calvin, Sallisaw, OK, 41; 17529, Martha, W, 36; Hannah D, 13; John A, S, 9; Robert, S, 7; Walter, S, 7; Albert, S, 4; William P, S, 1

16012 LEE Carl E Campbell, OK, 10; Ola J, Sis, 9;   By Henry E. Lee, Gdn.

[LEE Clarence E. See #5750]   *(Note: entry separate from other family groups)*

7929 LEE David M, Muldrow, OK, 45; Francis E, S, 15; 26824, Flora E D, 18; 26823, Lou Emma D, 20

3983 LEE, Esther, Vian, OK, 56

17403 LEE, Felix, Marble City, OK, 31; Lucille Lillian D, 4; Myrtle D, 3; Felix Helen D, 1

Key: Guion Miller Application Number; Name; Address, Relation (to Head); Age in 1906

12656 LEE, Frances E Ahniwake, OK, 41; Almon, S, 9
11539 LEE, Isaac Dutch Mills AR, 19
7655 LEE, Jesse Christie, OK, 53; 7656, Sallie, W, 52; Nannie D, 19; Jennie D, 16; Mary, D, 14; Lucy D, 11
9169 LEE, John, Webbers Falls, OK, 55
23322 LEE, John, Jr, Webbers Falls, OK, 26

[LEE, John F. See #4530]   *(Note: entry separate from other family groups)*

[LEE, Julius P. See #23189]   *(Note: entry separate from other family groups)*

[LEE, Lafayette. See #23326] ⎤   *(Note: entries separate
[LEE, Leola. See #23326]   ⎦   from other family groups)*

1058 LEE, Laphila, Wimer, OK, 31; Petiett Andrew, S, 9; Lee, Robert, S, 3
24421 LEE, Levi, Westville, OK, 33; Carl, S, ¾
8767 LEE, Lucy, Vian, OK, 34
1113 LEE, Lula R, Needmore, OK, 26; Everett R, S, 5
25531 LEE, Mattie Campbell, OK, 22; Oral Evaline D, 3; Spy James, S, 1
16590 LEE, Narcissa, Marble City, OK, 11;   By Nellie Christie, Gdn.
23324 LEE, Robert E, Webbers Falls, OK, 29; Bertha E D, 2; David M, S, 1
8025 LEE, Robert E Cottonwood, OK, 38; Maud D, 13; Edna D, 10; Jewel D, 7; Fred, S, 5; Louvenia D, 17
8762 LEE, Roy E, Muldrow, OK, 18; William S Bro, 16;   By Sallie E. Bethel, Gdn.
16376 LEE, Tom Christie, OK, 54; 10387, Nancy, W, 50
23323 LEE, Walter, Webbers Falls, OK, 23; Daisy D, 2
8128 LEE, Wash Cottonwood, OK, 23; Mary Marie D, 2; Chas. Herbert, S, 1/3
31611 LEECH, Jemima, Porum, OK, 39; Jefferson Franklin, S, 18; Katie D, 14; John Allen, S, 11; Peggie D, 4
30838 LEEMASTER, Mary E, Okoee, OK, 19
11872 LEFEW, Henry, McLain, OK, 31
27848 LEFORCE, Emma G Centralia, OK, 25; Ora B D, 3
27847 LEFORCE, Fannie Keys, Vinita, OK, 44; Flossie May D, 13; James Lowrey, S, 11; Sarah Lottie D, 9; Rachel Amanda D, 6; Charles William, S, 1
23776 LEFORCE, Sarah A, Vinita, OK, 40
5873 LEMASTER, Mary Jane, Fairland, OK, 33; Frederick G, S, 9; Leo A, S, 6; John A, S, 4
6262 LEMASTER, Victoria E, Stilwell, OK, 27; George E, S, 9; Oatha P, S, 6; Narcissa B, D, 4; Robert Sylvester, S, 1
29657 LEMASTER, Wollie P, Fairland, OK, 19; Mildred I D, 1/6
6423 LEMONS, Grace V, McLain, OK, 23; Eunice V D, 5; Wallace E, S, 3
9812 LEMONS, Leslie W, Marks, OK, 15;   By Annie Cloud Karney, Gdn.
9811 LEMONS, Roy, Marks, OK, 12;   By Annie Cloud Karney, Gdn.

Key: Guion Miller Application Number; Name; Address, Relation (to Head); Age in 1906

4678 LENOIR, Mary O Chelsea, OK, 63

5373 LEON Amelia Claremore, OK, 24

26923 LEOSER Callie, Tahlequah, OK, 35

26921 LEOSER, John H, Tahlequah, OK, 52

8291 LEOSER, Susan, Tahlequah, OK, 76

26922 LEOSER, Walter S, Tahlequah, OK, 48

7676 LEPHEW, Robert E, Warner, OK, 26

695 LESSLEY, Sarotha A Akins, OK, 33; Iantha P D, 15; William E, S, 13; James B, S, 10; Bewna V D, 8; Samuel C, S, 5; Icie R D, 1

3458 LESTER, Julia B Claremore, OK, 36; Dick, William E, S, 15; Ellis, S, 12; Lester Alfred L, S, 8

[LEVI Adam. See #13642]   *(Note: entry separate from other family groups)*

1990 LEVI Charlie, Leach, OK, 36; 4289, Nannie, W, 33; Miller, Jennie D of W, 10; Katie, D of W, 8; Levi, Fred, S, 2

4184 LEVI, John, Leach, OK, 39; 10650, Dianna, W, 27; William, S, 6; Redbird, S, 2

11895 LEVIN, May Dallas, TX, 20

36360 LEWELLEN, Sallie Belle, Sallisaw, OK, 18

4052 LEWIS Amanda M, Wagoner, OK, 65

28303 LEWIS, Esther, Foyil, OK, 27; Richard, S, 6; Edward E, S, 5; Charles W, S, 4; William H, S, 1

23623 LEWIS, George M Choteau, OK, 23; 9467, Charlotte, W, 17; Dollie Caroline D, 1/6

22967 LEWIS, Hattie Chance, OK, 30; Holland, James B, S, 11; Robert H. F, S, 9; Henry Dean, S, 7; Thos. Reed, S, 5; Lewis Arthur G, S, 1

25533 LEWIS, Ida Campbell, OK, 19

1329 LEWIS, Joanna Ruth Afton, OK, 45; Nidiffer, John R, S, 20; George W, S, 17; Freeman E, S, 13; M_mie Lucile D, 11 (Letter marked out); Lewis, Lorena D, 6; Nellie May D, 1

29346 LEWIS, Lula E Chester AR, 19; David H, S, 1/12

9374 LEWIS, Nellie Braggs, OK, 32; Ka-ho-ga D, 9; Lizzie D, 2

[LEWIS, Polly. See #5784]   *(Note: entry separate from other family groups)*

[LEWIS Dick. See #5770]   *(Note: entries separate*
[LEWIS Dave. See #5770]   *from other family groups)*

33749 LIGON Charles C, Snyder, TX, 29; Jessie L D, 5; William A, S, 1

33751 LIGON, Gracie, Pryor Creek, OK, 17; Claud G Bro, 16; Thomas H Bro, 12; By Julia Ligon, Mother.

11736 LIGON, Louisa J, Snyder, TX, 68

Key: Guion Miller Application Number; Name; Address, Relation (to Head); Age in 1906

33748 LIGON, William, Longmont CO, 811 Emery St, 37; Norma R D, 9; Edgar R, S, 7; Joseph R, S, 4; Ora D, 2; William C, S, 1

7489 LILLARD Andrew J, Tahlequah,OK,62

25848 LILLARD, William Cookson, OK, 22; 41509, Elizabeth, W, 19

4367 LILLARD, Zacariah[sic] T Cookson, OK, 58; 15993, Ellen, W, 51; Charles, S, 18

27902 LINCOLN, Lelia Adah, Fairland, OK, 37; Kathleen D, 13

8870 LINCOLN, Robert A, Spavinaw, OK, 37; 8869, Aggie, W, 29; Nannie D, 9; Arcinie, D, 7

9150 LINDER, Hiram D Campbell, OK, 47; 27754, Fannie B, W, 30; Ira A, S, 4

4237 LINDER, John, Melvin, OK, 70; Hiram, S, 19; Annie D, 15; Ross, S, 13; Cinderella, D, 9; Johnnie, S, 6; Carl, S, 4; Rocco B, S, 2

27764 LINDER, Julius C, Melvin, OK, 23

9151 LINDER, Martha A Campbell, OK, 72

5552 LINDER, Minnie, Parson, KS, 18

18105 LINDER, Owen L Black Gum, OK, 9;   By W. J. Bailey, Gdn.

18104 LINDER, Prean Black Gum, OK, 11;   By W. J. Bailey, Gdn.

15718 LINDER, Richard, Ft. Gibson, OK, 26; Inez D, 4; Jenevia D, 3; Aline D, 1

2177 LINDSEY Bettie J, Texanna, OK, 72

5265 LINDSEY, Jennie, Melvin, OK, 45

133 LINDSEY, Margaret A, Westville, OK, 57; Manar, Jessie D, 17; Annie M D, 15

8163 LINDSAY[sic], Rachel Snow, St. Louis, MO, 2962 Morgan St, 32

26552 LINDSEY, William A, Vinita, OK, 35; Elizabeth R D, 7

5492 LINES, Lucy B, Jacksonville, TX, 50

2785 LINN Arie [Ora], Row, OK, 22

2794 LINN, Lucinda Cherokee City AR, 25; John Wyley, S, 3; Goldie M D, 2

2806 LINN, Lydia, Row, OK, 23; James R, S, 2

26564 LINSCOTT, Ellen, Pryor Creek, OK, 39; Odeller D, 12; Joseph A, S, 10; Callie J D, 9; John W, S, 8; Walter T, S, 4; Frank E, S, 4; Beatrice J D, 3

1206 LINT, Lillie W, Muskogee, OK, 49; Wallace, Jennie D, 18; Florence D, 10

13018 LIPE Clarence, Oologah, OK, 15;   By Maggie E. Lipe, Gdn.

13021 LIPE Clark C, Oologah, OK, 19

12495 LIPE De Witt Claremore, OK, 66

1632 LIPE, Herman V, Oologah, OK, 32; Mattie D D, 7

13016 LIPE, John C, Oologah, OK, 28

32593 LIPE, John G, Talala, OK, 42; 10391, Sarah L, W, 31; Flora F D, 7; Ada C D, 5; De Witte, S, 2

31499 LIPE, Lola V Claremore, OK, 29

31500 LIPE, Nannie E Claremore, OK, 34

5267 LITTLE, Elizabeth, Vinita, OK, 23

7429 LITTLE, Frank H, Ramona, OK, 33

7427 LITTLE, Joe C, Ramona, OK, 27; 29275, Myrtle A, ?, 22; Ramona D, D, 1

Key: Guion Miller Application Number; Name; Address, Relation (to Head); Age in 1906

[LITTLE, Lucile. See #7915] *(Note: entry separate from other family groups)*

23233 LITTLE, Mary, Lenapa, OK, 34; George, S, 19
 9491 LITTLE, Mary L Claremore, OK, 31; Flippin, Mary T D, 10; Ruth A D, 4; Rebecca L, D, 1
 7428 LITTLE, William M, Jr, Ramona, OK, 29
16381 LITTLEBIRD, John Black Gum, OK, 26; 13673, Eliza M, W, 25; Bark, Willia, S, 8

[LITTLEBIRD, Katie. See #181]   *(Note: entry separate from other family groups)*

17211 LITTLEDAVE, (No other name given), Spavinaw, OK, 30; John, S, 6; Ollie, S, 5; Jeff, S, 1
   82 LITTLEDAVE Betsey, Locust Grove, OK, 41; Alex, S, 18; Dick, S, 11; Eliza D, 8; Betsey D, 3
 3701 LITTLEDAVE Dave, Locust Grove, OK, 23; 10332, Ella, W, 24; Andrew, S, 2; Maria, D, 1/6
11404 LITTLEDAVE, Elizabeth, Southwest City, MO, 28
  521 LITTLEDAVE, Frank, Locust Grove, OK, 40
17083 LITTLEDAVE, Isaac, Locust Grove, OK, 20; 516, Minnie, W, 28; Cochran, Mariah, D of W, 7; Jessie D of W, 4; Alex, S of W, 2

[LITTLEDAVE, John. See #17211]
[LITTLEDAVE, Ollie. See #17211]   *(Note: entries separate*
[LITTLEDAVE, Jeff. See #17211]   *from other family groups)*

 3172 LITTLEDAVE, William, Locust Grove, OK, 34; 2501, Nancy, W, 36; Charlie, S, 8; Emma D, 6; Miner, S, 2
 3886 LITTLEJOHN, Catharine, Brushy, OK, 50
 3887 LITTLEJOHN, Charles P, Brushy, OK, 34; William J, S, 8; Charles J, S, 6; Thomas F, S, 3; James S, S, 1
29192 LITTLEJOHN, Goliath, Eucha, OK, 35; A-ge D, 1
16920 LITTLEJOHN, John, Long, OK, 22; 24954, Jennie, W, 21
 5604 LITTLEJOHN, Levi, Hulbert, OK, 29
22542 LITTLEJOHN, Narcena A, Stilwell, OK, 54; Felix E, S, 12
23406 LITTRELL Cora Collinsville, OK, 20; Alfred J, S, 1
 5643 LIVER Blair, Locust Grove, OK, 22
12525 LIVER, Eliza Brushy, OK, 31; Lizzie D, 14; Felix, S, 12; Susie D, 9; Martha D, 6; Lydia D, 2
42203 LIVER, George, Stilwell, OK, 36; 42087, Emma, W, 23; Theodore R, S, 2
 2832 LIVER, John, Stilwell, OK, 47; 2831, Lyd-da, W, 46; Ben, S, 19; Lula D, 16; Lizzie, D, 15; John, S, 12
 5324 LIVERS Chulio, Stilwell, OK, 62

Key: Guion Miller Application Number; Name; Address, Relation (to Head); Age in 1906

42178 LIVERS, Jackson, Stilwell, OK, 36; 8324, Bettie, W, 25; Joe M, S, 6; Eliza D, 4; John L, S, 1

42090 LIVERS, John C, Stilwell, OK, 26

39158 LIVERS, Jennie, Stilwell, OK, 29; Chulio, John W, S, 2

42177 LIVERS, Taylor, Stilwell, OK, 24

143 LIVINGSTON, Sarah Choteau, OK, 56; Alfred, S, 19; Lonnie, S, 18; Robert, S, 14

4664 LIZZARD, Samuel Catale, OK, 79

27891 LLOYD, Albert L, Tulsa, OK, 26

27892 LLOYD, Eliza J, Tulsa, OK, 51; 27889, Maggie E D, 19; Nannie A D, 17; Hazel G, D, 10

27887 LLOYD, Rachel M, Tulsa, OK, 39; Clarence L, S, 18; Laura B D, 14; Rosa B D, 11; Pansy B D, 7; James E, S, ¾

30015 LLOYD, Robert L, Tulsa, OK, 24

27890 LLOYD, William T, Tulsa, OK, 21

11561 LOCKER, Richard, Talala, OK, 39; Lola R D, 10; Dallas C, S, 8; John S, S, 6; Edward B, S, 3

10698 LOCUST, George, Vian, OK, 26

2198 LOCUST, Ida, Stilwell, OK, 55; 9475, Minnie D, 17

9750 LOCUST, Jackson, Stilwell, OK, 48; 4723, Susie, W, 35; Abraham, S, 17; Ross, S, 9; Luke, S, 5; Peter H, S, 1

316 LOCUST, Jesse, Porum, OK, 56; Frank, S, 15; Martha E D, 13; William, S, 9; Mike, S, 5; May D, 3

13247 LOCUST, John, Wauhillau, OK, 33; 13248, Maggie, W, 26

16082 LOCUST, Johnson, Gideon, OK, 26; 8216, Sallie, W, 21; Thomas J, S, 1

5639 LOCUST, Lewis, Vian, OK, 26; 15585, Kate, W, 23; Esther D, 1

9474 LOCUST, Lizzie [Ruthie], Vian, OK, 20

24362 LOCUST, Ocie, Wagoner, OK, 25

9631 LOCUST, Sandy, Stilwell, OK, 35; Henry, S, 13; Katie D, 10

5803 LOCUT, Fish, Vian, OK, 50; 9377, Peggy, W, 52

35982 LOCUT, Ned, Vian, OK, 23

9382 LOCUT, Willie, Vian, OK, 33

7517 LOFTON, Nannie, Muskogee, OK, 24

41512 LOGAN, Clara Adams, Talihila, OK, 35; Mabel O D, 11; Hugh A, S, 6

11 LOGAN, Lena L, Pryor Creek, OK, 53; Garvin, Frances H, N, 15 [Died 6-1906]

27504 LOGSDON Bessie B, Owasso, OK, 26; Albert Izen, S, 8; Everett Ed, S, 3; Nora May, D, 1

[LOMON, Jackson. See #9946]   *(Note: entry separate from other family groups)*

23271 LONDAGIN, Kate, Foyil, OK, 24; Pasha, S, 4; Robert B, S, 1

5128 LONG Akey, Tahlequah, OK, 25; Minnie D, 9; Jackson A, S, 7

Key: Guion Miller Application Number; Name; Address, Relation (to Head); Age in 1906

18959 LONG, Katie, Wauhillau, OK, 23; Columbus, Jr, S, 6; Eugene, S, 4; Cornelius, S, 2

10654 LONG, Eliza Caney, OK, 57

11728 LONG, Ida L, Pawnee, OK, 25

8922 LONG, Maud P, Pagoda CO, 31

3588 LONG, Ned, Stilwell, OK, 30; John, S, 4; Betsy D, 2

[LONGBIRD, Edward. See #3588]
[LONGBIRD, John. See #3588]   *(Note: entries separate*
[LONGBIRD Betsy. See #3588]   *from other family groups)*

16638 LONGBIRD, Fannie, Stilwell, OK, 24

2381 LONGBIRD, Jennie Bunch, OK, 64; 2375, Annie D, 19

6303 LONGBIRD, Samuel Bunch, OK, 21

2393 LONGBIRD, Smith Bunch, OK, 35

23274 LONGBRIER, Frances, Mark, OK, 26; William B, S, 9; Rosa B D, 7; Minnie D, 4; Henry B, S, 3; Howard, S, 1

5745 LOOKABOUT, George, Welling, OK, 21

993 LOOKIN Arch Claremore, OK, 56

1786 LOONEY, John, Westville, OK, 68; John, Jr, S, 7

25951 LOOPER, Mary E, Sallisaw, OK, 20

10355 LOUTHER, Eugene W, Keefeton, OK, 36; Jennie Lee,D, 8;Willie E, S, 4; Clifford, S,2

29912 LOUTHER, Grover L Claremore, OK, 21

12846 LOUTHER, Joanna Claremore, OK, 50; William A, S, 15

26694 LOUX, Lura Ward, Maysville, AR, 25; John Raymond, S, 2

15071 LOVE, Alexander, Hadley, OK, 27

[LOVE, Lizzie. See #13454]   *(Note: entries separate*
[LOVE, Richard. See #13454]   *from other family groups)*

1422 LOVETT, John, Gans, OK, 27

2377 LOVETT, John J, Cookson, OK, 28

13173 LOVETT, John J, Braggs, OK, 31

7572 LOVETT, Lydia, Braggs, OK, 28; Highland, Lucy, D, 9

2167 LOVETT, Richard, Cookson, OK, 40; 3215, Rachel, W, 45

[LOVETT, Rodgers. See #27943]   *(Note: entry separate from other family groups)*

10603 LOVITT, James, Braggs, OK, 32; Irene, D, 5; Ina Bell, D, 3

16873 LOVITT, William, Jr, Braggs, OK, 18; Elmira, Sis, 16; Rosa, Sis, 14; By William Lovitt, Gdn.

29095 LOVING, David L, Waco, TX, 1527 N. 5th St, 22

CHEROKEE DESCENDANTS RESIDING WEST OF MISSISSIPPI RIVER.
VOLUME II   (A – M)

Key: Guion Miller Application Number; Name; Address, Relation (to Head); Age in 1906

29094 LOVING, Joseph J, Cleburne, TX, 24
29092 LOVING, Nancy C, Waco, TX, 1527 N. 5th St, 45
29093 LOVING, William M, Welsh, LA, 27
39470* LOWE, Mary, Afton, OK, 35; William S, S, 19; Ralph, S, 14; Louis, S, 10;
      James, S, 5; Nina, D, 2; Nellie, D, 1/6;   *(*NOTE: number difficult to read)*
23591 LOWE, Rachel, Estella, OK, 24; Carroll, Henry L, S, 8

[LOWE, Sadie (or Sada). See #24880] *(Note: entry separate from other family groups)*

11029 LOWERY, Anderson, Muskogee, OK, 29; 11028, Lucy B, W, 30; Wanetta, D, 4;
      Raymond, S, 2
 1321 LOWERY, Andrew, Tahlequah, OK, 53; Daniel V, S, 17; Charley A, S, 15;
      Janette S, D, 13; Andrew, Jr, S, 9; George H, S, 8; Lucy, D, 6; Silas C, S, 1
 5103 LOWERY, Charlotte E, Manard, OK, 23
  935 LOWERY, Daniel W, Lenapah, OK, 46; George, S, 19; Richard, S, 15; James, S,
      13; John, S, 12; Dora, D, 7
12529 LOWERY, Eliza, Muskogee, OK, 27
  562 LOWERY, Henry, Wann, OK, 33; Joanna, D, 9; John A, S, 7; Eugene, S, 2;
      Gladist[sic], D, 1/12

[LOWERY (or LOWREY), Henry C. See #254]
                 (Note: entry separate from other family groups)

25817 LOWERY, James B, Tahlequah, OK, 23; 25818, Fannie E, W, 21; Johnnie B, S,
      ¾
13431 LOWERY, Jas. M, Jr, Muskogee, OK, 22; Jas. Fite, S, ½
23168 LOWERY, Nannie, Nowata, OK, 20

[LOWERY, Oma (or Omer). See #29157]
                 (Note: entry separate from other family groups)

[LOWERY, Jeter (or Peter) B, See #29154]
                 (Note: entry separate from other family groups)

[LOWERY, Charles. See #29159]   *(Note: entry separate from other family groups)*

16658 LOWERY, Randolph, Childers, OK, 19;   By Richard Downing, Gdn.
12531 LOWERY, Raphael, Muskogee, OK, 31; Henry C, S, 2
17253 LOWERY, Return J, Briartown, OK, 39; Jack, S, 9; Charles, S, 4; Emett[sic], S,
      1
 5102 LOWERY, Sarah, Manard, OK, 20
12530 LOWERY, Susie, Muskogee, OK, 17; Elsie J, Sis, 14; Andrew, Bro, 12; Henry C,
      Bro, 7;   By Susie Lowery, Gdn.

Key: Guion Miller Application Number; Name; Address, Relation (to Head); Age in 1906

23165 LOWERY, Thos. J, Braggs, OK, 26; 29860, Laura, W, 24; Vance, S, 1; Owen, S, 1/6

16660 LOWERY, William A, Childers, OK, 22

23167 LOWERY, William P, Nowata, OK, 28; 16365, Mary, W, 26; Katie E, D, 8; Paul, S, 6

8636 LOWERY. William W, Wann, OK, 28; 27170, Lou V, W, 25; Fannie Pauline, D, 5; Cora Lee, D, 3; Floridan Haridan, S, 1

4561 LOWREY, Ellis, Muskogee, OK, 48

32087 LOWREY, Ellis, Texanna, OK, 20

32086 LOWREY, George, Texanna, OK, 22

[LOWREY, Carrie. See #254]   *(Note: entries separate*
[LOWREY, Mose. See #254]   *from other family groups)*

4187 LOWREY, Ida, Lowery, OK, 18

5049 LOWREY, John, Chapel, OK, 34; Gladys, D, ½

17411 LOWREY, Johnson, Muskogee, OK, 28

14139 LOWREY, Ned, Jr, Peggs, OK, 21

12533 LOWREY, Susie, Muskogee, OK, 48; Susie, D, 17; Jennie, D, 14; Andrew, S, 11; Henry, S, 7

5048 LOWREY, William, Ft. Gibson, OK, 36; Howard R, S, 1½

13457 LOWRIMORE, Bessie, Briartown, OK, 22; J. Arley, S, 4; Vera L, D, 3

5959 LOWRIMORE, Flora M, Big Cabin, OK, 5; William H, Bro, 3; By Perry S. Lowrimore, Gdn.

6264 LOWRY, Bettie, Southwest City, MO, 30; Samuel C, S, 9; Minnie O, D, 6; Maggie N, D, 4; John W, S, 1

10910 LOWRY, George, Stilwell, OK, 55; 3870,Lizzie, W, 57; Killie, D, 9; Joe, S, 7; Eagle, Adam, AdS, 8

324 LOWRY, John, Nowata, OK, 61; John, Jr, S, 16; Willia, D, 11

17205 LOWRY, John J, Claremore, OK, 28

37648 LOWRY, Josephine E, Claremore, OK, 24; Beulah M, D, 4

31786 LOWTHER, Katie Lee, Inola, OK, 25

10608 LOWTHER, Leroy G, Inola, OK, 53; Wayne S, S, 13; Lem M, S, 10; Laura E, D, 4; Viola F, D, 2/3; Lewis, Lorena, D, 6; Nellie May, D, 1

29753 LOWTHER, Matthew, Inola, OK, 21

39584 LOWTHER, Watson B, Inola, OK, 30

2823 LUCAS, John, Flint, OK, 34; 2825, Sarah, W, 44; Silcox, Eliza, D of W, 17; Lucas, Frank, S, 11

13145 LUKE, Mary J, Texanna, OK, 38; Wells, Joseph J, S, 16; Bessie, D, 14; Joeson, S, 9; Elzora, D, 4; Elmer, S, 1

5178 LUCKY, Jackie M, Vinita, OK, 27

5176 LUCKY, Sarah F, Vinita, OK, 36

26496 LUNSFORD, Ellen, Wagoner, OK, 20

Key: Guion Miller Application Number; Name; Address, Relation (to Head); Age in 1906

6067 LUNSFORD, Jesse, Wagoner, OK, 19; 26495, Lucy, Sis, 15; Mary, Sis, 14; By Ed Lunsford, Gdn.

30217 LUSK, Lorenzo J, Wauhillau, OK, 26

30218 LUSK, James S, Wauhillau, OK, 24

5909 LUTZ, Mary T, Ft. Smith, AR, 30; Herman A, S, 4; Frederick A, S, 7

5550 LUTZ, Rachel, Wagoner, OK, 23

1177 LYMAN, James, Moodys, OK, 52

2982 LYMAN, Johnson, Chelsea, OK, 47; Joseph, S, 19; Martha, D, 17; Callie, D, 13

12819 LYMAN, Lewis, Talala, OK, 88; Elmira, D, 14; Levi, S, 13; Lewis A, S, 7

209 LYMAN, Mary P, Talala, OK, 57

5195 LYMAN, Nancy J, Hulbert, OK, 57

12162 LYMAN, Patrick, Talala, OK, 26

[LYMAN, Savola R. See #16135]   *(Note: entry separate from other family groups)*

13492 LYMAN, Susie, Braggs, OK, 46; Lucy, D, 11; Nancy, D, 8

12161 LYMAN, William, Ramona, OK, 29

23790 LYNCH, Andrew, Bluejacket, OK, 29; Josephine, D, 8; Roosevelt, S, 3

23789 LYNCH, Bert, Bluejacket, OK, 29

1599 LYNCH, Cynthia, Ketchum, OK, 56; Emma O, D, 16

42149 LYNCH, Cynthy, Vinita, OK, 17; Johnson, Ottis, S, 2

25181 LYNCH, Earl C, Vinita, OK, 25

25180 LYNCH, Edward B, Vinita, OK, 35

35243 LYNCH, Fannie Bell, Tulsa, OK, 30; Pricie Golding, S, 10; Isla Marie, D, 8; Herbert L, S, 4

16887 LYNCH, Jeter, Webbers Falls, OK, 26

12893 LYNCH, John B, Bunch, OK, 38; 12892, Cicero L, Jr, S, 12; Nancy Esther, D, 1

10742 LYNCH, Joseph J, Woodville, OK, 32

9646 LYNCH, Joseph M, Stilwell, OK, 25; 9645, McEnery, Ruth, N, 7

9687 LYNCH, Leonidas, Bunch, OK, 65

2223 LYNCH, Lucy, Muskogee, OK, 58

28387 LYNCH, Mariah, Sallisaw, OK, 26; Nancy E, D, 2

9493 LYNCH, Ruth B, Vinita, OK, 52; 42147, John, S, 20; 9493, Claud, S, 15; Rose M, D, 13; Willis, S, 11

9401 LYNCH, Susan F, Webbers Falls, OK, 60

31529 LYNCH, Zula, Glen Oak, OK, 36; Alice F, D, ½

16015 LYONS, Anna E, Ft. Gibson, OK, 33

25551 McADOO, Margaret E, Springfield, 533 S. Campbell St, MO, 27

9366 McAFEE, Mary J, Muldrow, OK, 36; Johnie E, S, 7; Frances, D, 4; Robert W, S, 3

9912 McAFFREY, Fannie, Afton, OK, 53; Napoleon, S, 19; Walter, S, 16; Rhoda, D, 11

Key: Guion Miller Application Number; Name; Address, Relation (to Head); Age in 1906

29139 McAFFREY, Hugh, Jr, Afton, OK, 23

29138 McAFFREY, James, Afton, OK, 26; Roscoe, S, 6; Beulah, D, 3

29141 McAFFREY, John, Cleora, OK, 30; William M, S, 10; Joseph L, S, 5; Katie O, D, 2

29140 McAFFREY, Andrew, Afton, OK, 32; Ollie C, D, 9; Aldona, D, 6; William H, S, 3; Cleora I, D, 2

905 McALISTER, John W, Choteau, OK, 60

22462 McALISTER, John W, Jr, Choteau, OK, 24; Joe W, S, 4; Mary E, D, 1

25658 McALLISTER, Josephene, Ft. Gibson, OK, 28; Ellis, Harvey M, S, 2

32783 McALISTER, Susie, Tahlequah, OK, 24; Lawrence S, S, 1

10945 McANDREWS, E. Eleanor A, Oolagah, OK, 34; Nora E, D, 10; Mike C, S, 7; David R, S, 5; John F, S, 3; Mary M, D, 1

31600 McBEE, Susie, Alderson, OK, 22; Carrie, D, 3; Leona, D, 2

33262 McBRIDE, Mary J, Ft. Gibson, OK, 41

4053 McBROOM, Ida G, Melvin, OK, 49

17892 McCABE, Elizabeth, Ft. Smith, AR, 621 S. 12th St, 53

11301 McCAFFREE, Georgia C, Vera, OK, 41; Brice, Charles M, S, 19; Annie L, D, 17; Walter J, S, 12; Louis A, S, 5

11287 McCAFFREE, Czarina V, Vera, OK, 22

9615 McCALEB, Addison F, Bartlesville, OK, 45; Charles G, S, 10

1049 McCULLOUGH, Rachel Janes, Fairland, OK, 62

2125 McCAMISH, Eliza A, Vinita, OK, 32; Dodson, Alma Pearl, D, 11

3184 McCAMPBELL, Birdie, Hay Fork, CA, 39; Stella V, D, 14; William A, S, 12; Maibell R, D, 9; Robert L, S, 7; Ronald A, S, 6; Mavis A, D, 1

6544 McCARTER, Clem, Proctor, OK, 28; 6616, Susie, W, 26; Charlotte, D, 4; Sampson, S, 3; Nancy, D, ¼

[McCARTER, Joe. See #12612] ⎤   *(Note: entries separate*
[McCARTER, Watt. See #12612] ⎦   *from other family groups)*

[McCARTER (or McKARTY), Lula. See #10310]
        (Note: entry separate from other family groups)

[McCAULEY, Bertha. See #16103]   *(Note: entry separate from other family groups)*

11670 McCAUSLAND, Mary M, Rose, OK, 26 Fannie Bell, D, 2

5542 McCAY, Alfred, McAlester, OK, Stone Wall Ave, 58; John B, S, 16; Evelyn D, D, 13; Alfred A, S, 11; William C, S, 7; Charles B, S, 1

6545 McCAY, Charles C, Inola, OK, 14; Jessey F, Bro, 11; Ivera G, Sis, 2; Benjamin F, Bro, 1/8;   By Ida B. McCay, Gdn.

14804 McCAY, Dick, Jr, Campbell, OK, 26

22750 McCAY, James J, North McAlester, OK, 20; Florence J, D, ½

28279 McCAY, Jennie, Melvin, OK, 18

Key: **Guion Miller Application Number; Name; Address, Relation (to Head); Age in 1906**

10607 McCAY, John S, Inola, OK, 31; William L, S, 9; Claude R, S, 7; Watson B, S, 5; Ruth, D, 2

 5902 McCAY, Looney, Sallisaw, OK, 35; 7668, Cherokee, S, 1

12222 McCAY, William H, Claremore, OK, 28

[McCLAIN, Mattie M. See #22776] ⎤   *(Note: entries separate*
[McCLAIN, Mollie A. See #22776] ⎬   *from other family groups)*
[McCLAIN, Maudie L. See #22776] ⎦

12507 McCLAIN, Myra, Claremore, OK, 34

12424 McCLAIN, William H, Claremore, OK, 36; Robert, S, 9; Addie, D, 8; William E, S, 4

11103 McCLANAHAN, Zoe, Vian, OK, 11; Leonard, Bro, 7; By T. B. Cornelius, Gdn.

 9341 McCLELLAN, Jennie L, Claremore, OK, 56; Lela G, D, 17

34172 McCLELLAN, John F, Claremore, OK, 34

 2176 McCLELLAN, Margaret P, Webbers Falls, OK, 66

13363 McCLELLAN, Rachel L, Claremore,OK, 39; Edward W,S, 25[Insane]; Charles T, S,18

34175 McCLELLAN, Steve F, Claremore, OK, 22

34174 McCLELLAN, Susan, Claremore, OK,   25

25165 McCLELLAN, William A, Claremore,   OK, 23

 4596 McLEMORE, Robert, Tahlequah, OK, 30

12133 McCLURE, Charles J, Porum, OK, 42; Francis, S, 19; Della, D, 16; Hattie, D, 14; Douglas, S, 10

23205 McCLURE, Edwin, Porum, OK, 22

27242 McCLURE, Fannie F, Vinita, OK, 45; Hugh C, S, 18; Marguerite J, D, 14; Elizabeth L, D, 11; Eulala, D, 8; Eva P, D, 5

12885 McCLURE, Henry B, Porum, OK, 50; Kathryn, Briertown, OK, D, 18; Thomas, S, 16; Minnie F, S, 9; Hazel, D, 5; Ella, D, 3; Jamison, Vida E, GD, 6

23123 McCLURE, James E, Briertown, OK, 23

23436 McCLURE, John, Texanna, OK, 24

10755 McCLURE, Katy, Porum, OK, 55

13418 McCLURE, Robert L, Porum, OK, 40

27243 McCLURE, Roy M, Vinita, OK, 23

25838 McCLURE, Slater L, Vinita, OK, 25; 17136, Laura E, W, 25

26469 McCLURE, Susan T, Coffeyville, KS,   23

12134 McCLURE, William J, Porum, OK, 60

27745 McCLURE, William L, Hartshorn, OK, 20

19189 McCOLLUM, Annie, Vian, OK, 19; Floren, D, 1

22560 McCOMBS, Elizabeth, Big Cabin, OK, 35; John Wesley, S, 10; Birdie, D, 8; Clara V, D, 5; Charles H, S, 3; William Felix, S, 1/12

20171 McCONNELL, Lizzie, Talala, OK, 36; 25943, Benge, Cornelius C, S, 18; 20171, McConnell, Ida, D, 10; Jerry, S, 6; Lillie May, D, 4

Key: Guion Miller Application Number; Name; Address, Relation (to Head); Age in 1906

8996 McCONNELL, Mary, Vian, OK, 46; Short, Joe, S, 19; Hugh [Houston], S, 20

43255 McCOY, Albert T, Choteau, OK, 25

6546 McCOY, Alex, Vian, OK, 52; 3984, Saphronia, W, 35; 16348, George, S, 17;

14194, Ezekiel, S, 17; 6546, Lila, D, 11; Sam, S, 9; Cherokee, D, 8; Ellen, D, 6; Lee, S, 5; Levi, S, 5; Emma, D, 4; Sadie, D, 1/3

10904 McCOY, Alex, Jr, Vian, OK, 29; 7658, Eyarne, W, 26; Levi, S, 8; Jack, S, 2

563 McCOY, Archibald B, Claremore, OK, 47; Archibald C, S, 16; Claude S, S, 12

18554 McCOY, Bettie, Vian, OK, 24

[McCOY, Charley. See #5957]   *(Note: entry separate from other family groups)*

10935 McCOY, Charles, Sallisaw, OK, 33; Edward E, S, 11; Peachie, D, 7

8365 McCOY, Charles R, Claremore, OK, 48

6032 McCOY, Chester F, Centralia, OK, 47; John M, S, 11; Minnie V, D, 9; Robert L, S, 8; Fredonia I, D, 7; Lucy J, D, 4; Pauline A, D, 1/3

11502 McCOY, Edward, Sadie, OK, 35; Orlbie[sic], S, 2

13507 McCOY, Ester, Vian, OK, 24

24854 McCOY, George, Flint, OK, 48; William B, S, 16;   Ida R. V, D, 13

7463 McCOY, James L, Bartlesville, OK, 30

26835 McCOY, James W, Ballard, OK, 40; William Memory, S, 19; Lela F, D, 15; Sina Alma, D, 13; Bula H, D, 2; Raymond Hugh, S, 1

17261 McCOY, Jeff D, McKey, OK, 45; Mayes, S, 16; Grover, S, 14; Mary, D, 11; Laura, D, 5; Jessie L, D, ¼

23816 McCOY, John W, Jr, Pryor Creek, OK, 25; Vernon, S, 3; Chester C, S, 1

238 McCOY, John W, Sr, Pryor Creek, OK, 47; 23820, Annie Lillie, D, 19; Lem L, S, 17; Vina, D, 15; George, S, 11

6715 McCOY, Lester, Vian, OK, 58

9787 McCOY, Lucy, Vian, OK, 58; Richard, S, 19; Robin [Robert], S, 17

5045 McCOY, Mary A, Claremore, OK, 76

13202 McCOY, Ned, Vian, OK, 29; 10884, Hester, W, 29

5499 McCOY, Rosanna, Ballard, OK, 66

[McCOY, Sadie. See #25488]   *(Note: entry separate from other family groups)*

16965 McCOY, Sam, Vian, OK, 21

11752 McCOY, Stand W, Stilwell, OK, 11; By Nancy Sixkiller, Gdn.

11104 McCOY, Thomas, Vian, OK, 21

26836 McCOY, Tom, Siloam Springs, AR, 33; Hattie, D, 5; Fannie, D, 3; Walter, S, 1

2952 McCOY, Waddie T, Kansas, OK, 50; Watt W, S, 15

10249 McCRACKEN, James T, Nowata,OK,13;   By J. K. Lowery, Gdn.

12582 McCRACKEN, Mary E, Braggs, OK, 34

27739 McCRACKEN, William E, Braggs, OK, 20

12831 McCRADY, Beulah, Sallisaw, OK, 10;   By L. L. McCrady, Gdn.

CHEROKEE DESCENDANTS RESIDING WEST OF MISSISSIPPI RIVER.
VOLUME II (A – M)

Key: Guion Miller Application Number; Name; Address, Relation (to Head); Age in 1906

12834 McCRADY, Foster, Sallisaw, OK, 12; By L. L. McCrady, Gdn.

12833 McCRADY, Mack, Sallisaw, OK, 18; By L. L. McCrady, Gdn.

10893 McCRARY, Jack W, Vinita, OK, 11; By Laura Whittington, Gdn.

17152 McCRARY, Lizzie, Warner, OK, 23; Ella May, D, 2

11848 McCRARY, William, Kansas, OK, 15; By Louisa McCrary, Gdn.

10374 McCRARY, William C, Denver, CO, 30; Willie A, D, 10; David E, S, 8

24665 McCREADY, Viella, Zena, OK, 16

2822 McCUEN, George, Akin, OK, 49 [Dead]; 12417, Akey, W, 45; Virgie E, D, 12; William B, S, 9; Sarah, D, 6

25640 McCUEN, Katie, Akin, OK, 19

25641 McCUEN, Lewis, Akin, OK, 22

31091 McCULLOUGH, Charles H, Afton, OK, 24

31577 McCULLOUGH, George E, Afton, OK, 28; Milton H, S, 7; Luther A, S, 6; George E, Jr, S, 4; Bernice L, D, 2

30807 McCULLOUGH, James F, Ketchum, OK, 33; Lelia H, D, 10; Ardath E, D, 6; James W, S, 3

30801 McCULLOUGH, John N, Fairland, OK, 37; Rachel J, D, 16; Milton J, S, 13; Ora, D, 11; Oma, D, 9; Venie, D, 6; Esta Z, D, 1

30664 McCULLOUGH, Joseph H, Afton, OK, 27; Eva C, D, 5; Cleva O, D, 4; Reba O, D, 2; John H, S, 1/3

762 McCULLOUGH, Kiamitia C, Coffeyville, KS, 26; Zelma C, D, 2

31088 McCULLOUGH, Pete, Miami, OK, 34; 31086, Magino J [Maggie], W, 35; Winnie D, D, 7; Rex J, S, 5; Gladys M, D, 2

[McCULLOUGH, Rachel Jane. See #1049]
(Note: entry separate from other family groups)

31087 McCULLOUGH, William P, Fairland, OK, 36; Lillian M, D, 8; Milton M, S, 7; William E, S, 4; Peter C, S, 1

22647 McCUTCHEN, Florence E, Claremore, OK, 30; Gracie J, D, 6

24072 McDANIEL, Cal, Locust Grove, OK, 23

37447 McDANIEL, David, Pryor Creek, OK, 14; Kim, Bro, 5; Robert, Bro, 17; By P. E. Sadler, Gdn.

12840 McDANIEL, Eliza, Warner, OK, 50

36043 McDANIEL, Jeff, Hulbert, OK, 19

27015 McDANIEL, Joseph T, Tahlequah, OK, 28; 5515, Kate E, W, 28; Joseph J, S, 3

3675 McDANIEL, Lewis, Melvin, OK, 46; William, S, 14; Leonard, S, 12; Albert, S, 10; Etta F, D, 8; Sarah M, D, 6; Anna L, D, 3

3672 McDANIEL, Martha H, Tahlequah, OK, 57; Susan A, D, 15

1104 McDANIEL, Martin, Catoosa, OK, 43; Willie, S, 15; Bessie, D, 11; Clifford, S, 2

1489 McDANIEL, Nancy, Muskogee, OK, 72

33734 McDANIEL, Nelson, Pryor Creek, OK, 41

Key: Guion Miller Application Number; Name; Address, Relation (to Head); Age in 1906

12851 McDANIEL, Thomas, Warner, OK, 30; Willis, S, 8; Louie T, S, 5; Noah, S, 3; Susie, D, 1

9286 McDANIEL, Wilson, Melvin, OK, 28; 34243, Sarah, W, 28; Ketcher, Ellis, S of W, 11; McDaniel, Ida, D, 4; Mona, D, 2

27024 McDANIELS, Looney M, Tahlequah, OK, 26

8611 McDONALD, Charley C, Wagoner, OK, 37

9999 McDONALD, George W, Porum, OK, 67; Edward L, S, 16

35466 McDONALD, Isaac M, Bluejacket, OK, 48; Ray, S, 14; Ralph, S, 4

36595 McDONALD, John O, Knobnoster, MO, 47

9791 McDONALD, Maggie, Muskogee, OK, 44

26560 McDONALD, Margaret, Metory, OK,19

17458 McDONALD, Margaret, Granada, CO, 26; Tomy[sic] Jack, S, 3

2857 McDONALD, Mary A, Watova, OK, 35; Charles Vaughn, S, 17; Winnie May, D, 13

23935 McDONALD, Mattie C, Adair, OK, 10; Garland, Bro, 12; By John F, Warren, Gdn.

29922 McDONALD, Narcina, Porum, OK, 23

36596 McDONALD, Newton, Knobnoster, MO, 22

35467 McDONALD, Roy, Bluejacket, OK, 21

24831 McDONALD, Sidney M, Westville, OK, 21

30180 McDANIEL, Susie E, Muskogee, OK, 21

[McDONALD, Theodore. See #21095] *(Note: entry separate from other family groups)*

29639 McDONALD, Virgil T, Ramona, OK, 37; Robert Roy, S, 12; Essie Viola, D, 8; Ernest Clyde, S, 6; Afton Claude, S, 2

22793 McDOWELL, Joe, Talala, OK, 40; Jessie M, S, 13; Dewey R, S, 6; Dora K, D, 1

16003 McDOWELL, Martha, Campbell, OK, 22; Ivy Myrtle, D, 5

11776 McEACHIN, Margaret, Sallisaw, OK, 39; Martha, D, 12

13400 McELHANEY, Myrtle, Manard, OK, 24; Faye, D, 3

31113 McELRATH, Ann Ed, Oakland, CA, 5101 Dover St, 24

31371 McELRATH, Hilda, Oakland, CA, 5101 Dover St, 20

10467 McELRATH, John Edgar, Oakland, CA,5101 Dover St,62; Alden, S, 17; Clifford, S,15

31112 McELRATH, John Edgar, Jr, Oakland, 5101 Dover St, CA, 23

31111 McELRATH, Katharine, Oakland, CA, 5101 Dover St. 19

31114 McELRATH, Marion, Oakland, CA, 5101 Dover St, 27

31370 McELRATH, Phoebe, Oakland, CA, 5101 Dover St, 26

37057 McELREATH, Daisy, Adair, OK, 1;   By John F. Warren, Gdn.

32556 McELREATH, Thomas M, Pryor Creek, OK, 19

[McENERY, Fred B. See #4013]   *(Note: entries separate*
[McENERY, Hazel. See #4013]   *from other family groups)*

Key: Guion Miller Application Number; Name; Address, Relation (to Head); Age in 1906

[McENERY, Ruth. See #9645]   *(Note: entry separate from other family groups)*

4610 McFALL, Eugenie, Seattle, WA, 2117½ 1st Ave, 46; 31160, Frank, S, 19; Eddie M, S, 17; Webbie, S, 10; Jessie, D, 8

17971 McFARLAND, Lucy, Collinsville, OK, 33

1047 McFARLAND, Mary L, Fairland, OK, 25; Jessie, D, 10; Willie, D, 4; Homer G, S, 1

5868 McGHEE, Albert V, Welch, OK, 47; Nellie, D, 18; Sarah A, D, 16; Claretta, D, 11; Rosa M, D, 8; Blueford, S, 7; James A, S, 4

5182 McGHEE, Ambrose H, Kinnison, OK, 26

11411 McGHEE, David A, Southwest City, MO, 57; Florence E, D, 14; Ambrose, S, 12

33122 McGHEE, David A, Dawes, OK, 29; Warren A, S, 6; Pauline, D, 4; Lucile, D, 2

26397 McGHEE, Dennis B, Dodge, OK, 28

25428 McGHEE, Elizabeth, Dodge, OK, 21

25429 McGHEE, Esther L, Dodge, OK, 18

26955 McGHEE, James M, Miami, OK, 33; 26956, Martha A, W, 34; Robert J, S, 13; Thomas O, S, 11; Walter C, S, 8; Martha E, D, 5; Lorena M, D, 2

2999 McGHEE, John H, Kinnison, OK, 50; Jasper H, S, 17; Byrl H, D, 15

25430 McGHEE, John R, Dawes, OK, 23

26272 McGHEE, Joseph F, Afton, OK, 21

30704 McGHEE, Nannie M, Vian, OK, 17

26273 McGHEE, Saladin C, Dawes, OK, 23; Mabel C, D, ¼

24772 McGHEE, Samuel B, Dawes, OK, 34; 24773, Belle, W, 31; Bertie O, D, 14; Buena Vista, D, 10; Richard J, S, 8; Edith Irene, D, 5

918 McGHEE, Susan, Grove, OK, 76

390 McGHEE, Thomas J, Afton, OK, 62; Quilliki, S, 20

32774 McGHEE, Thomas J, Jr, Miami, OK, 30; Rondal E, S, 8; Eula Bell, D, 6; Lionel Boone, S, 3; Hazel Marie, D, ½

13403 McGERRY, Francis, Las Vegas, NV, 24

4551 McGINNIS, Cleveland C, Turley, OK,   21

4102 McGINNIS, William T, Turley, OK, 26; Christine G, D, 2

23140 McGLOUTHLIN, Mary Ellen, Ballard, OK, 17

23328 McINERNEY, Pinkie, Vian, OK, 23; Mary, D, 2; George, S, 1/12

8963 McINTOSH, Frank, Locust Grove, OK, 39; 16521, Mary, D, 12; Richard, S, 10

23465 McINTOSH, James, Bartlesville, OK, 21

22564 McINTOSH, John, Bartlesville, OK, 24; 22563, Mayhauka, W, 22; Huling, S, 5; Bertha, D, 2

14037 McINTOSH, John R, Chelsea, OK, 40; 4686, Maria L, W, 40; N. Beatrice, D, 15; Ethel R, D, 4

30109 McINTOSH, Myrtle S, Checotah, OK, 23

10310 McKARTY, Lula, Tahlequah, OK, 21

5530 McKAY, Charlotte, Melvin, OK, 71

9189 McKAY, Eliza, Melvin, OK, 51

Key: Guion Miller Application Number; Name; Address, Relation (to Head); Age in 1906

13241 McKAY, Nellie, Hulbert, OK, 56

13308 McKEE, Alfred C, Parkhill, OK, 28

13307 McKEE, George D, Parkhill, OK, 25

10190 McKEE, John T, Parkhill, OK, 23

10191 McKEE, Joseph R, Parkhill, OK, 30; 8667, Lizzie, W, 27; Alphonso, S, 9; Theodore C, S, 7; Joseph R, Jr, S, 4

27442 McKEE, Lillie C, Valeda, OK, 20

30792 McKEE, Margaret A, Stilwell, OK, 17

10189 McKEE, Pearlie A, Parkhill, OK, 21

 2446 McKEE, Sabra, Hulbert, OK, 47; 5626, Butler, James, S, 17; 2446, Cochran, Landon, GS, 1

10956 McKEE, William J, Tahlequah, OK, 65

13838 McKEE, William R, Parkhill, OK, 36; 13837, Mary Jane, W, 24; Florian M, S, 4; Freeman, S, 3; Pearlie E, D, 1

 928 McKEEHAN, Minnie M, Catoosa, OK, 30; Laura Victoria, D, 11; Verna B, D, 5; Norean J, D, 1

30061 McKELLOP, Ira Arthur, Muskogee, OK, 22

27789 McKELVEY, Johnsanna D, Welch,OK,   33; Purkey, Effie, D, 11; McKelvey, Edna, D,7

28232 McKEY, Joe, Hulbert, OK, 23

 6690 McKINNEY, Annie, Hulbert, OK, 34; John, S, 2

27907 McKINNEY, Effie L, Porter, OK, 29

27906 McKINNEY, Elmira J, Wagoner, OK, 36; Hayes, Ethel, D, 12; McKinney, Amanda E, D, 6; John Inlow, S, 2

[McKINSEY, Annie. See #9649]   *(Note: entry separate from other family groups)*

 8024 McKINSTER, Letha A, Copan, OK, 48

 1880 McKNIGHT, Susie, Al-lu-wee, OK, 30; Jessie, D, 10; Joe, S, 9; George, S, 7; Cora L, D, 4; Lola State, D, 2

28339 McLAIN, Austin, Owasso, OK, 46; Ellen C, D, 17; Jessie H, D, 15; Sarah F, D, 14; John A, S, 11; Clyde, S, 8; Rachel, D, 5; Mary S. L, D, 3

32015 McLAIN, Dee [Delilah], Muskogee, OK, 540 N 11th St.   21

11660 McLAIN, Edward, Braggs, OK, 34

26115 McLAIN, Floyd, Braggs, OK, 28

35856 McLAIN, Henry, Valeda, KS, 35; 14778, Ella M, W, 28; Earl, S, 5; Elmer, S, 3; Arthur, S, 1

13574 McLAIN, James, Braggs, OK, 25; Harley M, S, 3

 9790 McLAIN, John, Campbell, OK, 41; 26312, Ella N, W, 34; Cynthia, D, 16; Henry, S, 12; George B, S, 9; Edward, S, 7

 5669 McLAIN, Jesse, Ft. Gibson, OK, 51; 7899, Maggie, W, 36; Sam H, S, 18; Calvin C, S, 16; Eliza J, D, 14; George W, S, 11; Charlotte, D, 6

11663 McLAIN, Jesse, Braggs, OK, 29

Key: Guion Miller Application Number; Name; Address, Relation (to Head); Age in 1906

12436 McLAIN, Jesse J, McLain, OK, 26

15597 McLAIN, Joseph, Braggs, OK, 63; Myra M, D, 4; Susie, D, 3; Isaac, S, 2; Oda B, D, ½

185 McLAIN, Luney, Locust Grove, OK, 33; 3883, Rachel, W, 34; Ellis, S, 11; Calvin, S, 9; Lillie, D, 6; Lewis, S, 3

9955 McLAIN, Martha, Pryor Creek, OK, 33; Lloyd L, S, 12; Cora N, D, 10; Nannie R, D, 7; Wat M, S, 1

4054 McLAIN, William, Muskogee, OK, 57; Josie, D, 17; William F, S, 14; Ethel, D, 7

16951 McLAUGHLIN, Annie, Southwest City, MO, 6;   By Sally England, Gdn.

7958 McLAUGHLIN, Anna E, Afton, OK, 26

16949 McLAUGHLIN, Frank, Southwest City, MO, 5;   By Sally England, Gdn.

28957 McLAUGHLIN, George, Rose, OK, 40

25270 McLAUGHLIN, Ila, Adair, OK, 26

4567 McLAUGHLIN, Joshua E, Pensacola,OK,55; 4566, Margaret C,W, 35;William C, S,11

4362 McLAUGHLIN, Joseph F, Estella, OK, 53; Carrie E, D, 16; George F, S, 13

9001 McLAUGHLIN, Louisa I, Afton, OK, 23

6791 McLAUGHLIN, Sanfrancisco, Ft. Gibson, OK, 59

9003 McLAUGHLIN, Susie, Afton, OK, 19

16950 McLAUGHLIN, Turner, Southwest City, MO, 8; 16948, Neal, Bro, 3; By Sally England, Gdn.

9643 McLEMORE, Chester, Bunch, OK, 22; 14278, Luggie, W, 19; Cicero L, S, 1

9686 McLEMORE, George, Bunch, OK, 38; 15627, Elizabeth, W, 31; Lucinda, D, 11; Gussie, D, 9; Emmet, S, 7

9737 McLEMORE, Lizzie, Bunch, OK, 17;   By George McLemore, Gdn.

9685 McLEMORE, John, Bunch, OK, 15;   By George McLemore, Gdn.

9705 McLEMORE, Thomas, Stilwell, OK, 31; 42181, Ollie, W, 24; Louisa J, D, 4

9701 McLEMORE, Robert, Bunch, OK, 20;   By George McLemore, Gdn.

4596 McLEMORE, Robert, Tahlequah, OK, 30; 6691, Peggie, W, 18

130f75 McLEMORE, Thomas, Welling, OK, 30

9670 McLEMORE, Samuel, Bunch, OK, 34; 42189, Margaret, W, 27; Robert, S, 10; Gussie, D, 4; Jessie P, D, 2

1297 McLEMORE, William, Stilwell, OK, 56; 9480, Ah-lee, W, 49; Lee, S, 19; Dick, S, 14

25734 McMAKIN, Andrew J,Muskogee,OK,26

25485 McMAKIN, Charles, Muskogee, OK, 23

25949 McMAKIN, Kennie, Muskogee, OK, 31

1055 McMAKIN, Savannah, Muskogee, OK, 59

[McMULLENS, Minnie M. See #25310]

(Note: entry separate from other family groups)

11804 McMURTY, Louisie, Porum, OK, 61

CHEROKEE DESCENDANTS RESIDING WEST OF MISSISSIPPI RIVER.
VOLUME II   (A – M)

Key: Guion Miller Application Number; Name; Address, Relation (to Head); Age in 1906

24823 McMURTRY, Louisie, Sallisaw, OK, 27; Birtie B, D, 7; Jessie E, D, 5

21672 McNAIR, Clem, Choteau, OK, 25

7430 McNAIR, Clement A, La Colorado, Mexico, 50

15600 McNAIR, Dennis, Tahlequah, OK, 23

1369 McNAIR, Edward B, Tahlequah, OK, 31

6504 McNAIR, Etta, Pryor Creek, OK, 24

5227 McNAIR, Nancy S, Tahlequah, OK, 63

282 McNAIR, Nicholas B, Pryor Creek, OK, 47; Nannie, D, 11; William G, S, 9; Benjamin F, S, 7; James P, S, 5; Phillip P, S, 1

16685 McNAIR, Oscar, Tahlequah, OK, 27 [Insane];   By Nancy S. McNair, Gdn.

878½ McNAIR, Owen F, Tahlequah, OK, 25

33392 McNEIL, Lizzie, Tahlequah, OK, 17

8166 McNEIR, Emily A. P, Smith's Point, TX, 59

30029 McNEIR, Forest W, Houston, TX, 2603 Chartres St, 31

30186 McNEIR, George Paschal, Chambers, TX, 29

11676 McPHERSON, Beatrice, Pryor Creek, OK, 8;   By Ida McPherson, Gdn.

11678 McPHERSON, C. Verner, Pryor Creek, OK, 20

[McPHERSON, David. See #1890]   *(Note: entry separate from other family groups)*

6461 McPHERSON, Jackson, Pryor Creek, OK, 26; 10082, Ada, W, 27; Ayline, D, 1/12

9203 McPHERSON, Joanna, Tahlequah, OK, 16; 9204, Jennie, Sis, 18; By Julia McPherson, Gdn.

1657 McPHERSON, John T, Warner, OK, 34; 5091, Mary W, W, 22; Herbert D, S, 4

5197 McPHERSON, John V, Stilwell, OK, 71

11675 McPHERSON, John W, Pryor Creek, OK, 6;   By Ida McPherson, Gdn.

11677 McPHERSON, Lewis L, Pryor Creek, OK, 18;   By George W. Mays, Gdn.

5600 McPHERSON, William R, Stilwell, OK, 36

10312 McPHERSON, Willis, Braggs, OK, 24

5262 McSPADDEN, Capitola V, Tahlequah, OK, 40; Madeline, D, 13

14100 McSPADDEN, Cora, Tahlequah, OK, 32; Theodore B, S, 11; Nellie, D, 9; Gertrude, D, 7

4839 McSPADDEN, Ellen, Tahlequah, OK, 42; Cherrie A, D, 11

2858 McSPADDEN, Florence E, Chelsea, OK, 48; Theodore, S, 18; Oscar L, S, 14

8169 McSPADDEN, James W, Tahlequah, OK, 23; 5652, Callie Q, W, 21

8682 McSPADDEN, Richard V, Vinita, OK, 27; 28809, Ermina E, W, 25

2380 McSPADDEN, Sallie C, Chelsea, OK, 43; Clement W, S, 20; May, D, 14; Herbert T, S, 12; Maud I, D, 11; Helen, D, 8; Pauline, D, 4; Maurice R, S, 1

97 McSPADDEN, Serena C, Chelsea, OK, 36; Zoe, D, 17; Floyd C, S, 15; Roscoe C, S, 13; Zella C, D, 9; Alma, D, 6; William Fair, S, 4; Clinton, S, 1

37709 McSPADDEN, Thomas B, Chelsea, OK, 36

Key: Guion Miller Application Number; Name; Address, Relation (to Head); Age in 1906

13701 MABRY, Sallie B, Briertown, OK, 47

10592 MADDEN, Clarence T, Braggs, OK, 6; Jack J, Bro, 4; Joseph Howard, Bro, 1; By William Ballard, Gdn.

 1320 MADDEN, Constance, Edna, KS, 14

13576 MADDEN, Emily, Braggs, OK, 36; Victor, S, 15; Leo B, S, 12; Thomas R, S, 7; Mamie M, D, 4; George E, S, 1/6

 1318 MADDEN, Eunice M, Edna, KS, 19

 2458 MADDEN, Ora, Coffeyville, KS, 26; Vera B, D, 2

 9375 MADDEN, Thomas R, Edna, KS, 16

23136 MADDOX, Lucian B, 16; Eliza Bell, Sis, 15; Robert, Bro, 11; By Marian C. Maddox, Gdn.

 4708 MAHER, Elvira, Keefeton, OK, 41; Jessie, D, 17; Frank, S, 15; Jennie, D, 8; Mary, D, 6; James T, S, 3

25162 MAHER, Henry, Keefeton, OK, 22

 6910 MAHER, William, Talala, OK, 30; Minnie A, D, 6

31589 MAINE, Florence E, Wann, OK, 29; William O, S, 5; Sigsbee F, S, 3

 2120 MAJORS, Nellie, Vinita, OK, 20; Robert R, S, 3; Forrest, S, 1

40521 MANAHAN, Henry A, Coffeyville, KS, 23

38352 MANAHAN, Samuel C, Nowata, OK, 21

23373 MANAR, Laura J, Westville, OK, 26; Burl, S, 1

24830 MANER, Jessie M, Westville, OK, 17; Walter J, S, 1

17803 MANIES, Richard, Braggs, OK, 16;   By Jackson Locust, Gdn.

 7808 MANIFEE, Victoria B, Chelsea, OK, 25; Leah, D, 5; George M, S, 2

11998 MANKILLER, Arch, Stilwell, OK, 52; 11917, Polly, W, 50

[MANKILLER, George. See #6581]   *(Note: entries separate*
[MANKILLER, Mary. See #6581]   *from other family groups)*

[MANKILLER, Jack. See #17439]   *(Note: entry separate from other family groups)*

12662 MANKILLER, Jacob, Stilwell, OK, 53; 13678, Susan, W, 38; John, S, 17; Lizzie, D, 15; Jennie, D, 13; Maggie, D, 11; Calson, S, 9; Richard, S, 6; Mary, D, 4

16895 MANKILLER, Maud, Wauhillau, OK, 18

 5602 MANKILLER, Sallie, Wauhillau, OK, 16

[MANKILLER, Thomas H. See #11533]   *(Note: entries separate*
[MANKILLER, Beecher. See #11533]   *from other family groups)*

11991 MANKILLER, William, Stilwell, OK, 51; 11916, Nancy, W, 43; Synthia[sic], C, 16; Bessie, D, 13; Hester, D, 8; William, Jr, S, 5

 571 MANLEY, Phenia, Muskogee, OK, 23; Bezonia, Delitha M, D, 5

28075 MANN, Annie B, Wagoner, OK, 18; Robert F, S, 1

25619 MANN, Bertha C, Oaks, OK, 27; Getha E, D, 1/12   [Died 1907]

Key: Guion Miller Application Number; Name; Address, Relation (to Head); Age in 1906

4787 MANN, Elizabeth, Oaks, OK, 63

25617 MANN, Henderson, Oaks, OK, 25; Sarah E, D, 6; Homer E, S, 4

4728 MANN, Pauline J, Muskogee, OK, 52; 30853, Lola, D, 20

25618 MANN, Pleasanton, Oaks, OK, 23

25620 MANN, Richard C, Oaks, OK, 34; Henderson L, S, 7; Ida L, D, 4; William H, S, 2

5726 MANNING, John, Oaks, OK, 61; 5719, Jennie, W, 48; Curl, D, 15; Mary, D, 13; Nannie, D, 8; Johnson, S, 6; White Lady, D, 3

1909 MANNING, Johnson, Tahlequah, OK, 47; 26112, Nancy, W, 31; Ellis, S, 12; Polly or Sally, D, 8

10196 MANNING, Johnson, Porum, OK, 18

1854 MANNING, Sarah Jane, Braggs, OK, 40

8790 MANNING, Wilson, Bushyhead, OK, 31; Jessie, D, 5

14753 MANTOOTH, Mary E, Vinita, OK, 43; Edna E, D, 13; Catherine G, D, 12; Sarah W, D, 10; Susan E, D, 6; Mary E, D, 5

4711 MANUS, Aggie, Stilwell, OK, 53

16374 MANUS, Annie, Stilwell, OK, 17; William, Bro, 15; Jesse, Bro, 14; George, Bro, 11; Simon, Bro, 9;   By Agen Watt, Gdn.

1939 MANUS, Clabran, Peggs, OK, 57; 1881, Polly, W, 45

34561 MANUS, Della, Peggs, OK, 18; Richard, Bro, 11;   By Clabran Manus, Gdn.

24423 MANUS, John, Welling, OK, 32; Annie, D, 8

29480 MANUS, Joseph Lewis, Tahlequah, OK, 35; Edna M, D, 9; Dorothy I, D, 7; Allison, S, 5; Celestia E, D, 1; Vivian E, D, 1

5268 MANUS, Mary, Tahlequah, OK, 49; 22594, Hampton, Jennie, D, 19; Bert, S, 17; 5857, Manus, Maggie, D, 8

[MANUS, Maggie. See #26515]   *(Note: entry separate from other family groups)*

2734 MANUS, Sallie, Welling, OK, 56

28048 MARCUS, Lucius, Moodys, OK, 21

30985 MARION, James S, Pryor Creek, OK, 31; John Franklin, S, ½

27778 MARKER, Laura A, Welch, OK, 35; Grace A, D, 11

12359 MARKHAM, Allen M, Kansas City, MO, 23

14096 MARKHAM, Carter D, Tahlequah, OK, 61; 14097, Eliza A, W, 52; Fortner, S, 20; Beatrice, D, 18; De Witt, S, 17; Hogan, S, 15; Earl, S, 15; Lucile, D, 12; Johnson, Samuel, GS, 14

10285 MARKHAM, Charlotte, Vinita, OK, 15; By L.S. Parks, Gdn.

22207 MARKHAM, CiceroW, Black Diamond, CA, 26

11523 MARKHAM, Clarence B, Locust Grove, OK, 21

11522 MARKHAM, Ewing, Locust Grove, OK, 23

10283 MARKHAM, James B, Locust Grove, OK, 17; By Ewing Markham, Gdn.

14243 MARKHAM, John, Warner, OK, 30

14228 MARKHAM, Lonzo B, Warner, OK, 15

Key: Guion Miller Application Number; Name; Address, Relation (to Head); Age in 1906

12385 MARKHAM, Ray P, Muskogee, OK, 21

13299 MARKHAM, Walter A, Locust Grove, OK, 27; 36598, Ella V, W, 29; Mary M, D, 1

26584 MARKS, Albert B, Vinita, OK, 21

26583 MARKS, Fannie E, Vinita, OK, 43; Walker R, S, 17; Marjora M, D, 14

10704 MARLOW, Carrie E, Braggs, OK, 31; Minnie, D, 9; Edna, D, 7; Ruby, D, 2

15981 MARRS, Arkansas D, Westville, OK, 32; Ivey N, D, 14

2235 MARRS, Charles, Welling, OK, 32; 2234, Jennie, W, 24

9594 MARRS, Harrison, Dora, AR, 34; Ruth M, D, 3; Marvin, S, 1/12

4396 MARSH, Rosa, Braggs, OK, 33; Graham, Mamie, D, 17; Marsh, Clarence, S, 5

2718 MARSHALL, Martha J. R, Temple, TX, R.F.D. #7, 40; William B, S, 20; Ethel, D, 17; Paul, S, 16; Fannie, D, 14; Myrtle, D, 12; Charles E, S, 10; Hazel M, D, 5

6257 MARTIN, Abraham, Cherokee City, AR, 29; Roxy B, D, 10; John B, S,5; Dottie B, D,1

13993 MARTIN, Allmon, Claremore, OK, 64; Olive, D, 19; Ira, D, 15; William P, S, 10

25264 MARTIN, Allmon, Jr, Claremore, OK, 22

1039 MARTIN, Amanda, Ruby, OK, 64; Sarah Edith, GD, 2

9694 MARTIN, Andrew J, Centralia, OK, 39; Myrtle B, D, 17; Hassie I, D, 15; Idus A, D, 13; Cassie L, D, 11; Opal R, D, 7; Harney C, S, 3; Finney E, S, 1

27806 MARTIN, Anna, Ft. Gibson, OK, 21

16113 MARTIN, Anna L, Manard, OK, 18

25505 MARTIN, Austin, Childers, OK, 25; Mamie, D, 6; Andy, S, 4; Edward, S, 2; Joseph C, S, ½

10714 MARTIN, Caledona, Claremore, OK, 23; Jessie S, D, 4; William E, S, 2

13530 MARTIN, Callie, Choteau, OK, 24

499 MARTIN, Caroline, Leach, OK, 38; Still, General, S, 11; Martin, George A, S, 6; Mack McK, S, 4; Jesse R, S, 2

21683 MARTIN, Charlie R, Vinita, OK, 33

2002 MARTIN, Charlotte C, Vinita, OK, 44; John S, Jr, S, 13

31722 MARTIN, Chorena C, Muskogee, OK, 19

254 MARTIN, Cleranda, Texanna, OK, 47; Lowrey, Henry C, S, 16; Carrie, D, 15; Mose, S, 13; Martin, Elmer, S, 6

11612 MARTIN, Cora, Porum, OK, 33; John A, Jr, S, 15; George D, S, 13; Ada B, D, 12; Charles J, S, 10; Lilla May, D, 4; Fay, D, 1

25506 MARTIN, Cora, Childers, OK, 19

255 MARTIN, Cora D, Welch, OK, 25; George M, S, 9; Ingram C, S, 7; Lottie L, D, 5; Nell B, D, 3

3168 MARTIN, De Witt, Greenbrier, OK, 18;   By Louise T. Thompson, Gdn.

2174 MARTIN, Dollie E, Manard, OK, 44; Matilda, D, 20; Edgar, S, 17; Calvin, S, 15

22550 MARTIN, Eugene W, Manard, OK, 20

23787 MARTIN, Florence, Bluejacket, OK, 38; Lycergus, S, 19; Allen J, S, 17; Frazier D, S, 12; Howard P, S, 10; Robert McC, S, 8

25599 MARTIN, Frank G, Independence, KS, 22

Key: Guion Miller Application Number; Name; Address, Relation (to Head); Age in 1906

27879 MARTIN, George W, Childers, OK, 32; Eben C, S, 5

32986 MARTIN, George W, Ruby, OK, 32; James N, S, 12; Paul R, S, ½

 1417 MARTIN, Grandville, Greenbrier, OK, 30; 37448, Lola, W, 26; Clarence, S, 3; Marie, D, 2

24229 MARTIN, Henry C, Claremore, OK, 26; 22482, Leona L, W, 24

28602 MARTIN, Hercules, Braggs, OK, 25

 3167 MARTIN, Hernando, Greenbrier, OK, 24

27880 MARTIN, James R, Childers, OK, 28

10754 MARTIN, Jennie, Porum, OK, 23

14725 MARTIN, Jennie E, Pryor Creek, OK, 28

22747 MARTIN, Joel T, Centralia, OK, 30; William A, S, 9

 3067 MARTIN, Johana R, Greenbrier, OK, 20

31766 MARTIN, John D, Vinita, OK, 13; Dora M, Sis, 12;   By W. J. Hendricks, Gdn.

13529 MARTIN, John W, Choteau, OK, 26; 9411, Lucy, W, 18

29855 MARTIN, Josephus, Alluwe, OK, 17

 1695 MARTIN, Lucinda, Cherokee, City, AR, 64

24987 MARTIN, Mary, Pryor Creek, OK, 39; 24988, Harriet, D, 18; Clare May, D, 16; Grover, S, 14; William R, S,12; Richard T, S, 10; Lizzie, D, 8; Rosa, D, 6; Felix A, S,3

 6568 MARTIN, Mary A, Siloam Springs, AR, 39; Hurman[sic] S, S, 17; Ilo Loreta, D, 16; Martha Ann, D, 11; Mary Elize, D, 9; Frederick, S, 7; Rhoda May, D, 4; Elvira, D, 1

26095 MARTIN, Mary G, Flint, OK, 54

 1691 MARTIN, Mary J, Gans, OK, 36; Roy, S, 14

44080 MARTIN, Monta May, San Bernardino,   CA, 14; Ferrill A, Bro, 11; By William W. Martin Gdn.

25846 MARTIN, Nannie, Vinita, OK, 21

18b79 MARTIN, Richard L, Pensacola, OK, 59

 6294 MARTIN, Sarah E, Childers, OK, 50

 2171 MARTIN, Sarah Jane, Manard, OK, 48; Henry, S, 18; Susie L, D, 17; Josephine, D, 14; Cordelia, D, 13; Jennie, D, 11; Sequoyah R, S, 7

  256 MARTIN, Susie J, Leach, OK, 34; Susie, J, D, 13; Minnie, D, 11; Annie M, D, 9; John S, S, 8; Charles D, S, 6; Walter E, S, 4; Nettie B, D, 1

15640 MARTIN, Tom, Campbell, OK, 20

40909 MARTIN, Viola H, Muskogee, OK, 20; Ouida Rae, D, 1

 6260 MARTIN, William, Cherokee City, AR, 36; Ivy M, D, 12; Zella, D, 10; Margarett J, D, 7; Samuel B, S, 4; Cynthia, D, 6; Nora V, D, 2

17812 MARTIN, William Vinita, OK, 36; Peter, S, 13; Lawrence W, S, 7; Wayne H, S, 2

36506 MARTIN, William A, Miami, OK, 46

26697 MARTIN, William H, Southwest City, MO, 31; Henry A, S, 11; Nora A, D, 8; Pearly Emiline, D, 4; Mary M, D, 2/3

Key: Guion Miller Application Number; Name; Address, Relation (to Head); Age in 1906

29086 MARTIN, William H, Afton, OK, 15; Rebecca E, Sis, 13; Anna E, Sis, 9;   By
Mary Gillespie, Gdn.

25507 MARTIN, William P, Centralia, OK, 23

10369 MARTIN, Willie V, Greenbrier, OK, 14

25347 MARYFIELD, Ella, Talala, OK, 21; Ora, D, 3; Lucinda, D, 1

42099 MASON, Ava C, Afton, OK, 9; Charles L, Bro, 8;   By O. F. Mason, Gdn.

[MASON, Willis J. See #24643]   *(Note: entry separate from other family groups)*

8753 MASTERSON, Minnie E, Akins, OK, 18

28039 MASTERSON, Ruby L, Adair, OK, 30; Mildred C, D, 7; Aldon M, S, 5

26460 MATHERSON, Maud, Coffeyville, KS, 208 W. 4th St, 34; Floyd, S, 13; Richard,
S, 10; Alexander R, S, 8; Ida McKinley, D, 4

29072 MATHEWS, Alma, Hamlin, TX, 25; Othel, S, 5; Annie, D, 3

11724 MATHEWS, Dorothy M, Nubra, TX, 47; Morda, D, 15; Herles, S, 12

[MATHEWS, Madaline. See #5866]   *(Note: entry separate from other family groups)*

29103 MATHEWS, Willie, Nubra, TX, 23

142 MATNEY, Martha, Pryor Creek, OK, 61; French, Joel B, S, 19

25 MATTHEWS, Addie, Claremore, OK, 34; Mary L, D, 15; William L, S, 14;
Joseph T, S, 10; Jessie M, D, 8

17201 MATTOX, Alice, Sallisaw, OK, 36; Claudie, S, 12; Maudie M, D, 8; William A,
S, 6; Gracie B, D, 4; Ruby, D, 2

8084 MATTOY, Lewis, Stilwell, OK, 31; Sarah, D, 6

5635 MAUCK, Sarah E, Lenapah, OK, 35; Jacob T, S, 16; Bessie Lee, D, 8

24086 MAUPIN, Carry Lee, Westville, OK, 30; Bessie B, D, 11; May, D, 10; James W,
S, 4; Claud, S, 1

25260 MAUPIN, Lena, Ruby, OK, 30; Walter G, S, 8; Flossie M, D, 6; Joe Shelby, S, 3

33750 MAURY, Mary, Snyder, TX, 39; Lillian, D, 15

17093 MAXFIELD, Albert, Tulsa, OK, 40

7947 MAXFIELD, Stephen, Owasso, OK, 36; Gracie, D, 7; Cora, D, 3; Pauline, D, 1/3

34484 MAY, Fannie M, Hollow, OK, 20

24451 MAY, Myrtle, Fairland, OK, 25; Vera, D, 1

5387 MAYBERRY, Beatras, Claremore, OK, 29; Maude, D, 11; Perry, S, 7; Floyd, S,
5; Marie, D, 2

8277 MAYES, Adair, Mark, OK, 21

9931 MAYES, Beatrice, Pryor Creek, OK, 12; Julia, Sis, 10; Isabel, Sis, 10;   By Sallie
A. Mayes, Gdn.

816 MAYES, Charles F, Pryor Creek, OK, 31; Jack, S, 7; Cherry N, D, 5; Wanda, D,
2

4817 MAYES, Cherokee C, Sallisaw, OK, 58

2113 MAYES, Edward T, Pryor Creek, OK,   22

Key: Guion Miller Application Number; Name; Address, Relation (to Head); Age in 1906

2238 MAYES, Ermina C, Pryor Creek, OK, 53

9933 MAYES, George W, Sr, Pryor Creek, OK, 60; 9935, Susie E, W, 52; Richard C, S, 18; George W, Jr, S, 16

28510 MAYES, Joe F, St. Louis, MO, 1801 Olive St, 29

13527 MAYES, Joel, Pryor Creek, OK, 13;   By Samuel H. Mayes, Gdn.

819 MAYES, Joel B, Pryor Creek, OK, 25

29244 MAYES, Joel B, Grove, OK, 22

3169 MAYES, John T, Pryor Creek, OK, 31

4802 MAYES, Johnson, Proctor, OK, 54; Jesse, S, 19; George, S, 16; John H, S, 13

8637 MAYES, Lindsey, Mark, OK, 19

28512 MAYES, M. Carrie, Pryor Creek, OK, 26

16506 MAYES, Mary, Wagoner, OK, 32; Georgia, D, 11; Gladys, D, 4; Theodore, S, 1/12

13528 MAYES, Mary Adeline, Pryor Creek, OK, 15;   By Samuel H. Mayes, Gdn.

4024 MAYES, Mary D, Pryor Creek, OK, 68

28513 MAYES, Mary T, Pryor Creek, OK, 12;   Cooie D, Bro, 9; By C. W. Binns, Gdn.

15917 MAYES, Mike, Tahlequah, OK, 22

23112 MAYES, Pixie A, Pryor Creek, OK, 28

9926 MAYES, Samuel H, Pryor Creek, OK, 61; 4035, Martha E, W, 54

257 MAYES, Samuel H, Jr, Pryor Creek, OK, 40; Charlotte E, D, 14; Pearl C, D, 12; Ruth, D, 9; Sarah, D, 6

29910 MAYS[sic], Sallie, Welling, OK, 18;   By Sallie Manus, Gdn.

27715 MAYES, Simon B, Tip, OK, 31

7995 MAYES, Soggie, Mark, OK, 23

2221 MAYES, Susie, Afton, OK, 36; 24059, William L, S, 20; Joel, S, 17; Josie, D, 16; Gertie, D, 14; Bertha, D, 12; Jessie, D, 9; Lee Roy, S, 5; Freddie, S, ¼ [Died 8-15-1906]; Robert A, S, 1

23111 MAYES, Tip C, Pryor Creek, OK, 23

9929 MAYES, Walter A, Jr, Pryor Creek, OK, 46; 9927, Nannie R, W, 41; Paul, S, 16; Washington, S, 13; Mamie, D, 9; Jesse L, S, 6; Joseph M, S, 3

4603 MAYES, Wiley N. B, Tip, OK, 58

20198 MAYES, William, Chapel, OK, 34; 9928, Eliza, W, 38

832 MAYES, William H. H, Tip, OK, 66

28511 MAYES, William L, Pryor Creek, OK, 32; Martha L, D, 4

31602 MAYES, William Penn, Grove, OK, 50; 5645, Annie H, W, 43; Ridge P, S, 17; Mary H, D, 12

31513 MAYFIELD, Ella, Muskogee, OK, 19

6465 MAYFIELD, Francis M, Oologah, OK, 42; John T, S, 17; Elizabeth, D, 15; Fred, S, 13; Julia, D, 14; Frank, S, 10; Leonard, S, 5; Nettie, D, 3

4620 MAYFIELD, Isaac H, Lenapah, OK, 34; Ray, S, 12

11696 MAYFIELD, John B, Rowland, OK, 10; Trixie V, Sis, 9; By Amanda Mayfield, Gdn.

Key: Guion Miller Application Number; Name; Address, Relation (to Head); Age in 1906

17113 MAYFIELD, John R, Vian, OK, 50; Ross G, S, 17; Gretchen, D, 18; Blanch, D, 6; Noah, S, 17

778 MAYFIELD, Joseph M, Lenapah, OK,   38; Charles H, S, 12; Orlando, S, 9; Mary, D, 5; Ruth Francis, D, 2

16724 MAYFIELD, Lena E, Chetopa, KS, 36; Ellison L, S, 18; Alma W, D, 17; Lether C, S, 16; Orley B, S, 12; Edna P, D, 9; Carl R, S, 5; Beulah V, D, 4

3035 MAYFIELD, Michael, Lenapah, OK, 56

32867 MAYFIELD, Nannie M, Garfield, AR, 25

254 MAYFIELD, Sarah, Oologah, OK, 70

3281 MAYFIELD, Thomas, Lenapah, OK, 22

13468 MAYFIELD, Watie L, Muskogee, OK, 17;   By Euretta Norman, Gdn.

5617 MAYFIELD, William R, Lenapah, OK, 27

24748 MAYOR, Ida, Pryor Creek, OK, 36; William, S, 20;Ida, D, 17; Lee, S, 15; Samuel H, S, 11; Joseph H, S, 9; Oliver D, S, 9; Helen M, D, 6; Mable C, D, 4

24522 MAYTUM, Minnie E, Bushyhead, OK, 22; Amos, S, 4; Minerva, D, 2

23650 MEADOWS, Laura May, Montoya, MN, 27; Lola May, D, 6; Emma E, D, 4; Leonard P, S, 2; Russell M, S, 1

28038 MEAGHER, Bessie E, Bluejacket, OK, 16

4437 MEANS, Amanda, Copan, OK, 31; Mary E, D, 5; Alex V, S, 3; Lelia M, D, 3

[MEED, Sarah. See #9120]   *(Note: entry separate from other family groups)*

24056 MEEDEN, Suenette, Yuma, AZ, 20; Charles S, S, 2

31142 MEEK, Ethel R, Vinita, OK, 12;   By W. A. Meek, Gdn.

3556 MEEK, Mary J, Kinnison, OK, 51

11698 MEEKER, George O, Braggs, OK, 28; 23227, Bertha, W, 23

13314 MEEKS, Charles, Webbers Falls, OK, 24; 17497, Mary A, W, 25;Polly, D, 5; William, S, 4; Charles, S, 3

8284 MEEKS, Willie, Adair, OK, 25; Norman Warren, S, 5; Clyde Ledrew, S, 3; Galuga Morgan, D, 1

4186 MEGG, Anderson, Locust Grove, OK,   40; 2840, Annie, W, 37; Doublehead, Jennie, D of W, 15

23507 MEHLIN, Charles H, Alluwe, OK, 32; Wadie Lee, D, 4; Elizabeth K, D, 2; Edna May, D, 1

278 MEHLIN, Elizabeth, Alluwe, OK, 57

31610 MEIGS, Alice Maud, Ft. Gibson, OK, 23

12409 MEIGS, Benjamin F, Park Hill, OK, 32; 9462, John W, S, 7; Elizabeth G, D, 5; Jane E, D, 3; Mary A, D, 1

12410 MEIGS, Cooie, Park Hill, OK, 23

7578 MEIGS, Daniel B, Park Hill, OK, 32

12411 MEIGS, Florein N, Cookson, OK, 39; 10188, Mollie C, W, 39; Brown, Mary E, D of W, 15; Meigs, Josephine E, D, 7; George McKee, S, 4; 26029, Brown, Addie V, D of W, 19; 26030, Bertha E, D of W, 17

Key: Guion Miller Application Number; Name; Address, Relation (to Head); Age in 1906

1363 MEIGS, Henry C, Ft. Gibson, OK, 65

30700 MEIGS, James McD, Ft. Gibson, OK, 26

11274 MEIGS, John H, Hulbert, OK, 47; 11275, Elinor M, W, 44; Carrie M, D, 13; Charles R, S, 12; Elinor B, D, 7; John H, S, 5; Return J, S, 3

31620 MEIGS, Josephine I, Ft. Gibson, OK, 21

7579 MEIGS, Return J, Park Hill, OK, 29

7580 MEIGS, Return F, Park Hill, OK, 60; Silas D, S, 19; Robert E, S, 17; Fannie J, D, 13; Elizabeth G, D, 8

31618 MEIGS, Robert H, Ft. Gibson, OK, 30

8781 MELLOWBUG, Dick, Oaks, OK, 37; 8106, Carrie, W, 33; Dalton, S, 6; 16990, Spade,Rachel, D of W, 13; Spade, Nellie, D of W, 11

9162 MELLOWBUG, Joe, Oaks, OK, 49; 12612, Lydia, W, 29; McCarter, Joe, S of W, 11; Watt, S of W, 7

13235 MELLOWBUG, Smith, Leach, OK, 51

9161 MELLOWBUG, Wilson, Oaks, OK, 35

38484 MELTON, Anna, Ray, OK, 31; Raper, Luella, D, 12; Teehee, Rosie, D, 8; Charboneau, Mary M, D, 6; John H, S, 4

3811 MELTON, Charley F, Afton, OK, 51; Charles W. E, S, 11

25200 MELTON, George A, Vinita, OK, 21; 25201, Martha V, W, 16

23252 MELTON, Gertrude, Echo, OK, 24; Emma B, D, 5; Hubert S, S, 3; Graydon D, S, ½

[MELTON, James. See #167]   *(Note: entry separate from other family groups)*

23119 MELTON, John H, Afton, OK, 22

22864 MELTON, Mattie J, Grove, OK, 25; Opal May, D, 4; Ora N, D, 3; Essa, D, 1

23399 MELTON, Mollie, Afton, OK, 20

3280 MELTON, Simpson F, Vinita, OK, 55; Maudy M, D, 13; Simpson, Jr, S, 11

6708 MELTON, Wiley J, Afton, OK, 47; Lucien, S, 16; Elizabeth, D, 14; Florence, D, 12

2158 MELTON, William T, Grove, OK, 44; Cora M, D, 17; Clara E, D, 15; Annie M, D, 13; Ethel E, D, 11; Otto V, S, 9; Louisa B, D, 7; John Q, S, 5

24787 MERRELL, Dollie, Chelsea, OK, 28; Ethel, D, 9; Fay M, S, 5

31652 MERRELL, John T, Kinnison, OK, 12; Joe, Bro, 7;   By Josie C, McCann, Gdn.

6436 MERRILL, William P, Watova, OK, 23

26917 MERRITT, Hope E, Pryor Creek, OK, 19

26953 MESSER, George P, Dutch Mills, AR, 25; 26056, Lizzie, W, 17

5392 MESSER, Nancy, Dutch Mills, AR, 53; 26954, Ruth, D, 19; 5392, Charles, S, 19; Lizzie, D, 17; Lucinda, D, 13

[MICCO, Jim. See #11197]   *(Note: entries separate*
[MICCO, Bessie. See #11197]   *from other family groups)*

Key: Guion Miller Application Number; Name; Address, Relation (to Head); Age in 1906

11760 MICKLE, Florence, Claremore, OK, 21; Hoyt, S, 2

1993 MIDDLESTRIKER, Jack, Uniontown, AR, 54

13563 MIDDLESTRIKER, John, Uniontown, AR, 27

36494 MIDDLESTRIKER, Moses, Uniontown, AR, 22; 1890, Julia, W, 31; McPherson, David, S of W, 10

15070 MIDDLESTRIKER, Nancy, Hadley, OK, 17;   By Alexander Love, Gdn.

6994 MIKE, Bob, Southwest City, MO, 35; 5945, Susan, W, 29; Peggie, D, 12; Scott, S, 10; Ah-ya-nu, S, 7; Lah-we, S, 4

29292 MILAM, James E, Chelsea, OK, 23

29293 MILAM, Jesse B, Nowata, OK, 22; 33822, Elizabeth, W, 23

5052 MILAM, Sarah E, Chelsea, OK, 42; Noolie, D, 17; Viola, D, 15; Charles, S, 12; William W, S, 9; Annie W, D, 7; Gladys M, D, 4

44638 MILBERAN, Mary E, Remy, OK, 22

10880 MILES, Annie E, Nowata, OK, 8;   By William E. Miles, Gdn.

24496 MILES, Ella E, Vinita, OK, 16

10881 MILES, Jessie, Nowata, OK, 5;   By William E. Miles, Gdn.

8036 MILES, Josephine, Chetopah, KS, 25

26269 MILES, Lucy K, Centralia, OK, 35; Benedict F, S, 11; Elizabeth, D, 9; Guy, S, 2; Lydia E, D, 1/12

30054 MILLARD, Henrietta, Foyil, OK, 19; Byron E, S, ¼

14997 MILLHOLLAND, John D, Chelsea, OK, 22

7422 MILLER, Ah-le, Braggs, OK, 52; Willie, S, 18

11730 MILLER, Alex A, Pryor Creek, OK, 39; Charles E, S, 7; Carrie E, D, 4; Ed, S, 1

6567 MILLER, Alford, Oaks, OK, 49; 6602, Aggie, W, 51; Nancy, D, 13

24962 MILLER, Allie E, Tahlequah, OK, 33; Dora Edna, D, 14; James W, S, 11; Florence, D, 9; May Belle, D, 6; John, S, 3; Clarence, S, 1

24637 MILLER, Alta R, Bartlesville, OK, 23

10879 MILLER, Andrew J, Tahlequah, OK, 33; Mattie E, D, 12

6563 MILLER, Andy, Oaks, OK, 42; 9443, Sallie, W, 38; Lee, S, 19; Henry, S, 17; Dave, S, 10; Lily, D, 7; Lucy, D, 3

8235 MILLER, Arch, Muskogee, OK, 57

43300 MILLER, Avery M, Needmore, OK, 34; Virgil A, S, 8; Calvin T, S, 6; James R, S, 3; Edith E, D, 1

[MILLER, Benjamin. See #4528]   *(Note: entry separate from other family groups)*

[MILLER, Bertha. See #11442] ⎤   *(Note: entries separate*
[MILLER, Emma. See #11442] ⎦   *from other family groups)*

8107 MILLER, Betsy, Oaks, OK, 40

22657 MILLER, Charles W, Claremore, OK, 22

24380 MILLER, Charlie, Long, OK, 29; 36885, Julia, W, 37; Ida, D, 8; Henry, S, 3; Thomas, S, 2; Goodrich, Lydia, D of W, 14; Martha, D of W, 13

Key: Guion Miller Application Number; Name; Address, Relation (to Head); Age in 1906

4056 MILLER, Cora, Ft. Gibson, OK, 32; Blythe, Jack, S, 13; Miller, Chuti, S, 11; Charles, S, 6; Hartman, Louis L, S, 3; Miller, Theodore R, S, 1

3292 MILLER, Cornelius, Stilwell, OK, 48; 22666, Nora, D, 18; George, S, 13; Oatha, D, 11

22561 MILLER, Daniel D, Zena, OK, 27; Nannie G, D, 9; Cassie B, D, 5; Dovie O, D, 3; Ida, D, 1/6   [Died 9-'06]

28327 MILLER, Dave, Vian, OK, 22; Sarah F, D, 2

1987 MILLER, Delilah, Tahlequah, OK, 28; Clara K, D, 6; Ruthie M, D, 4; Bluie, D, 2; Mary Ellen, D, ¼

11729 MILLER, Domitilia, Pryor Creek, OK, 6; Isabela[sic] L, Sis, 4; Lucy O, Sis, 2; By Alex. A. Miller, Gdn.

24631 MILLER, Ellen H, Bartlesville, OK, 44; Lester R, S, 4; Olin F, S, 1/12

12907 MILLER, Florence Sanders, Hanson, OK, 36; Hettie L, D, 15; William J. J, S, 12; Thomas F, S, 10; Ida J, D, 7; Grayson N, S, 4; Waitie H, D, 2

[MILLER, George. See #4806] ⎱   *(Note: entries separate*
[MILLER, Christina. See #4806] ⎰   *from other family groups)*

8779 MILLER, George, Oaks, OK, 47

14259 MILLER, George, Vian, OK, 35; William H, S, 12; Richard, S, 10; Sarah F, D, 8; Lena M, D, 6; John A, S, 2; Bessie Z, D, 1/6

32201 MILLER, Gracie, Wagoner, OK, 23; Alma L, D, 3; Clarence R, S, 1

24568 MILLER, Homer, Dawson, OK, 23

11196 MILLER, Ida, Cookson, OK, 20

23310 MILLER, Ida M, Kiefer, OK, 22

8380 MILLER, James J, Claremore, OK, 46

14669 MILLER, Jane, Akins, OK, 30; Hettie M, D, 12; Peggie B, D, 10; Maud S, D, 6; Finey S, D, 4

[MILLER, Jennie. See #9634]   *(Note: entry separate from other family groups)*

[MILLER, Jennie. See #4289] ⎱   *(Note: entries separate*
[MILLER, Katie. See #4289] ⎰   *from other family groups)*

22805 MILLER, Jesse, Grove, OK, 27

22645 MILLER, John, Gans, OK, 23; Edna, D, 1; Oral, S, 1/12

16360 MILLER, John H, Warner, OK, 26; 24614, Cherokee, W, 17

32249 MILLER, John H, Centralia, OK, 26; Noma A, D, 6; Mamie L, D, 3; Margarette J, D, 2

402 MILLER, John Lewis, Wimer, OK, 40; 3633, Cynthia, W, 34; Annis, S, 12

1359 MILLER, John M, Needmore, OK, 64; 1351, Lucy, W, 60; John J, S, 20; Joseph, S, 17

CHEROKEE DESCENDANTS RESIDING WEST OF MISSISSIPPI RIVER.
VOLUME II   (A – M)

Key: Guion Miller Application Number; Name; Address, Relation (to Head); Age in 1906

3294 MILLER, John W, Stilwell, OK, 51?; 4727, Louvina, W, 44; 22652, Joseph S, S, 20; Newt, S, 16; Franklin F, S, 14; Mary A, D, 11; Raymond, S, 5; Susan, D, 1

41227 MILLER, Lizzie, Houston, TX, 1416 McKinney Ave, 23; Porter, Edward, S, 7; Miller, Lillian, D, 3

[MILLER (or MILLS), Lizzie. See #5690]
(Note: entry separate from other family groups)

25755 MILLER, Lizzie B, Grove, OK, 20

[MILLER, Martha. See #24434]   *(Note: entry separate from other family groups)*

907 MILLER, Martin, Zena, OK, 58

11874 MILLER, Martin, Ft. Gibson, OK, 39; 32557, Alice, W, 24

29658 MILLER, Mary, Marquez, TX, R.F.D. #3, Box 81, 38; Theresa, D, 16; Leroy, S, 14; Velma, D, 12; Oscar, S, 7; Roscoe, S, 5; Bettie, D, 2; Lewis, S, 1/6

23444 MILLER, Mary A, Keefeton, OK, 22; Myrtle, D, 4; Clifford, S, 2

543 MILLER, Mary E, Grove, OK, 56; James C, S, 17; William E, S, 15

[MILLER, Mary J. See #6784]   *(Note: entries separate*
[MILLER, William J. See #6784]   *from other family groups)*
[MILLER, Thomas H. See #6784]

25816 MILLER, Maude, Tahlequah, OK, 25

24567 MILLER, Monnie, Dawson, OK, 25

18857 MILLER, Mose, Cookson, OK, 30

13163 MILLER, Nannie, Tahlequah, OK, 14; Dick, Bro, 11;   By Lucy Sunshine, Gdn.

23978 MILLER, Nannie, Maysville, AR, 35; 11550, Josie, D, 15; 11547, Maria, D, 11; 11548, Ella, D, 5; 11549, Birdie, D, 8

24931 MILLER, Narcissa, Vinita, OK, 23

9964 MILLER, Nellie, Inola, OK, 22; Tip Blueford, S, ½

3461 MILLER, Noah, Wimer, OK, 54; Mattie, D, 16; Edith, D, 14; Elizabeth, D, 11; Admiral Dewey, S, 9; Johnie, S, 5

[MILLER, Pearl L. See #28345]   *(Note: entry separate from other family groups)*

38322 MILLER, Peggy, Texanna, OK, 19

5073 MILLER, Penelope A. Dawson, OK, 49; 24566, Nela, D, 20; Thomas, S, 18; Beryel, S, 16; Rose, D, 15

10699 MILLER, Ples Henry, Webbers Falls, OK, 37; Francis E, S, 16; Effie M, D, 14; George W, S, 12; Eliza P, D, 8; John T, S, 6; Belmont, S, 4; Ollie B, D, 2

[MILLER, Ray F. See #6027]*(Note: entry separate from other family groups)*

Key: Guion Miller Application Number; Name; Address, Relation (to Head); Age in 1906

29457 MILLER, Rebecca, Pryor Creek, OK, 14

1089 MILLER, Robert L, Fairland, OK, 19; Mamie J, Sis, 17; Sarah E, Sis, 15; Andrew J, Jr, Bro, 14; Myrtie T, Sis, 12; Pearl, Sis, 7; Dawes, Bro, 6;   By Martha Miller, Gdn.

24899 MILLER, Robert L, Fairland, OK, 29

5951 MILLER, Rozella, St. Louis, MO, 6815 Magnolia Ave, 25; Everett, S, 4

163 MILLER, Rufus, Centralia, OK, 55; Joshua D, S, 20; Sarah A, D, 17; Lizzie, D, 14; William, S, 9

38561 MILLER, Rufus, Muskogee, OK, 27; 17234, Nannie, W, 27; Mary, D, 7; Ida, D, 5; Julia, D, 1

4392 MILLER, Stan, Ketchem OK, 41; Charlie M, S, 18; Dana E, S, 16; Manervia C, D, 12; John E, S, 14; Lily M, D, 10; Seavola B, D, 5

10422 MILLER, Suake L, Tahlequah, OK, 37; 26666, Minnie L, W, 35; Dicie G, D, 12; Henry S, S, 9

10613 MILLER, Thomas, Verdigris, OK, 28; Sarah, D, 7

24128 MILLER, Thomas H, Wimer, OK, 21

876 MILLER, Warren A, Hudson, OK, 35; 31788, Lillie L, W, 36; Birdie M, D, 1

21834 MILLER, Wash, Lodi, CA, 61

[MILLER, William. See #4209]
[MILLER, Martha. See #4209]   *(Note: entries separate*
[MILLER, Lizzie. See #4209]   *from other family groups)*
[MILLER, Andrew. See #4209]

1895 MILLER, William, Long, OK, 52; 3210, Nancy, W, 54

26109 MILLER, William, Dutch Mills, AR, 34; Ray, Ellis, S, 11

828 MILLER, William H, Wimer, OK, 59; 24749, George W, S, 20; Charles H, S, 19; Joe P, S, 17; William E, S, 14; Stand W, S, 12; Elizabeth, D, 11; Richard A, S, 8; Osa C, S, 6; Cherokee, D, 3

22652 MILLER, William H, Stilwell, OK, 26

10889 MILLER, William L, Muskogee, OK, 45; 5520, America, W, 37; Milo L, S, 19

43301 MILLER, William P, Vinita, OK, 29; 43302, Elizabeth, W, 26; Willie L, D, 4; Wade S, S, 2

24635 MILLER, William R, Ramona, OK, 25; 8091, Florence M, W, 25

1336 MILLER, William W, Claremore, OK, 53; Henry M, S, 19; Joseph G, S, 18; David A, S, 13; Matilda A, D, 10; John B, S, 6

8258 MILLER, William W, Maple, OK, 68

43834 MILLER, Willis L, Sageeyah, OK, 18; Nannie J, Sis, 16; Mary L, Sis, 14; Chloe, Sis, 13; Marion A, Bro, 11; Joe L, Bro, 9;   By Marion Miller, Gdn.

8635 MILLIGAN, Caleb H, McLain, OK, 29

6424 MILLIGAN, Franklyn G, McLain, OK, 19

1358 MILLIGAN, Sophronia, Maysville, AR,   58

6608 MILLS, George, Tulsa, OK, 65; 5904, Elizabeth, W, 19; 5958, Looney, S, 15

Key: Guion Miller Application Number; Name; Address, Relation (to Head); Age in 1906

23298 MILLS, James E, Pryor Creek, OK, 20; 23305,Minnie (No other information given.)

3258 MILLS, James L, Pryor Creek, OK, 38

10687 MILLS, Jessie L, Muskogee, OK, 16; Cynthia E, Sis, 14; Samuel H, Bro, 12; By T. H. Martin, Gdn.

[MILLS, Lizzie [Lee-see]. See #25754]
(Note: entry separate from other family groups)

[MINK, Sar-da-gah. See #2275]   *(Note: entry separate from other family groups)*

3257 MILLS, William R, Pryor Creek, OK, 49; William S, S, 3

43838 MILNER, John G, Claremore, OK, 27; James B, S, 1

8355 MINK, Candy, Stilwell, OK, 53; 5279, Sallie, W, 45; Eve, D, 17; Lizzie, D, 15; Linda, D, 13; Manda, D, 10; Ella, D, 7; Still, Margaret, GD, 4

8356 MINK, Sallie, Stilwell, OK, 60

23044 MINOR, Margarett A, Centralia, OK, 42; Woodward, Albert, S, 17; Bert, S, 16; Minor, Robert E, S, 3

22611 MINOR, Minnie L, Centralia, OK, 28; Delbert L, S, 8; Bulah A, D, 6; Clara B, D, 3; Ray C, S, 1

14037 MISER, Lelia V, Chelsea, OK, 16; John W, Bro, 15; Cora E, Sis, 10; By John R. McIntosh, Gdn.

8098 MISWHACKER, Uniontown,AR, 33; Allen, Susie, D, 13; Vann, Arcene [or Icene], D, 6; Robber, Leona, D, ¼

2720 MITCHELL, Dan, Fairland, OK, 46

2417 MITCHEL, Walker, Southwest City, MO, 44

7495 MITCHELL, Claude S, Bluejacket, OK, 23

29640 MITCHELL, Franklin Bruce, Oolagah, OK, 21

9430 MITCHELL, Frank P, Oolagah, OK, 49; Reese Burch, S, 9

5109 MITCHELL, John M, Flint, OK, 54

24096 MITCHELL, Lucy, Chelsea, OK, 22

2155 MITCHELL, Martha J, Bluejacket, OK, 44; Lee R, S, 18; Joe F, S, 14; Clay A, S, 12; Beulah V, D, 10; George W, S, 7; Ross Benge, S, 5; Foreman D, S, 2

32865 MITCHELL, Mary, Pryor Creek, OK, 19; Inez, D, 2; Bessie L, D, 1/3

24917 MITCHELL, Mary E, Pryor Creek, OK, 31; Mary Josephine, D, 5

30120 MITCHELL, Mattie J, Afton, OK, 27; Opal May, D, 1; Claud O, S, 4; Lee Amos, S, 6; Ott Wilburn, S, 9

5107 MITCHELL, Michel H, Chance, OK, 56; Arvel, S, 18; Dovie, D, 11; Floyd, S, 5; Lovel, S, 3

8857 MITCHELL, Robert Lee, Dow, OK, 30

7469 MITCHELL, Savola L, Bluejacket, OK, 25

14187 MITCHELL, Susie R, Locust Grove, OK 31; Toy, D, 8; Joe, S, 6; Esther, D, 5; Mary, D, 3; Chloede, D, 1

CHEROKEE DESCENDANTS RESIDING WEST OF MISSISSIPPI RIVER.
VOLUME II   (A – M)

Key: Guion Miller Application Number; Name; Address, Relation (to Head); Age in 1906

9431 MITCHELL, William D, Collinsville, OK, 52

16351 MIXEDWATER, Alexander, Baptist, OK, 84

17490 MIXEDWATER, Betsy, Wauhillau, OK, 49; Oo-was-tee-you-lah [or Daniel], S, 17; Cay-hu-ga [or Mary], D, 13

11710 MIXEDWATER, George, Bartlesville, OK, 36; 18490, Nellie, W, 23

39436 MIZER, Jane, Sallisaw OK, 25; Crigbin, James R, S, 7; Mattie O, D, 1 [Died 3-'07]

24520 MIZER, Mary Elizabeth, Bushyhead, OK, 24; Nellie R, D, 5; Ada B, D, 3

711 MIZER, Sarah, Coffeyville, KS, 51; Morris, Jumbo, S, 19; Mizer, Sheridan, S, 8

16189 MOBLEY, Minnie, Sebree, TX, 34; Lender, S, 16; Claud, S, 13; Trula, D, 11

5780½ MOCCASIN, Joe M, Dragger, OK, 12;   By Lewis Dragger, Gdn.

5661 MOCKER, Ben, Oaks, OK, 57; 5660, Polly, W, 54

25589 MOCKER, Mary, Oaks, OK, 27; Sapsucker, Josie, D, 2

457 MOCKSON, Bird, Spavinaw, OK, 19

24532 MODE, John R, Zena, OK, 27; 24533, Etta, W, 21; Bernice, D, 2

4517 MODE, Sarah Elizabeth, Vinita, OK, 51; William E, S, 15; Henry D, S, 12; Georgia, D, 10; Viola, D, 6; Maude May, D, 19

3499 MOHR, Lucinda, Braggs, OK, 64; Cookson, Levi, S, 18; Andrew, S, 16

1959 MONGRAIN, Mary A, Springfield, MO, Loretta Academy, 56

28695 MONROE, Charles S, Cleora, OK, 23

23263 MONROE, Dora A, Pryor Creek, OK, 31; By William A. Fish, Gdn.

4838 MONROE, Grover Cleveland, Afton, OK, 18

28697 MONROE, Nola A, Cleora, OK, 18

6707 MONROE, Thomas J, Afton, OK, 47; Bertha F, D, 15

34488 MONTGOMERY, Clara P, Vinita, OK,   26; Sylvia V, D, 8; Frederick O, S, 6; Andretta I, D, 3; Mary M, D, 1

9433 MONTGOMERY, Kate, Tiawah, OK, 24; Mildred, D, 2; Vera, D, 1; Ethel D, 1/12

39105 MONTGOMERY, Minnie, Hulbert, OK, 23; James W, S, 5

20199 MOODY, Emma V, Tahlequah, OK, 19

24555 MOONEY, Helen, Porum, OK, 27; William B, S, 1/8

25432 MOORE, Albert S, Tahlequah, OK, 21

3712 MOORE, Alice, Pryor Creek, OK, 20; Eddie [or Chas. E], Bro, 18; Jesse, Bro, 15; Dora, Sis, 13; Clarence, Bro, 10;   By C. F. Moore, Gdn.

23178 MOORE, Bessie, Osage, OK, 32; Howard W, S, 4; Malcolm, S, 2

36628 MOORE, Carrie B, Kansas City, MO, 31; Campbell, Flora, D, 12

4493 MOORE, Cherokee Cornelia, Tahlequah, OK, 25;   William A, S, 2

4939 MOORE, Elijah, Vinita, OK, 24

27675 MOORE, Eliza, Moodys, OK, 26; Annie, D, 5; Florence, D, 3; Mary Ola, D, 1

28021 MOORE, Etta, Claremore, OK, 23; Bertie L, S, 2; Ada P, D, 1

848 MOORE, Fannie, Tahlequah, OK, 50; 5433, Kate E, D, 19; Edwin C, S, 17; Callie A, D, 15; Grover C, S, 13; Sallie F, D, 10

226

Key: Guion Miller Application Number; Name; Address, Relation (to Head); Age in 1906

 9693 MOORE, Henry W, Sallisaw, OK, 28; 27122, Ina,W,22; Horace A, S, 3; Emmett T, S,1

 5754 MOORE, Isabelle U, Stilwell, OK, 26

21106 MOORE, Jesse A, Valeda, KS, 8; Evangeline, Sis, 4;   By Milton Moore, Gdn.

 7445 MOORE, Jesse J, Chelsea, OK, 18; Fannie L, Sis, 14; Shaw, Bertha M, Sis, 9; Bessie B, Sis, 9;   By David I. Brown, Gdn.

[MOORE, Jessie. See #2337] *(Note: entry separate from other family groups)*

 4940 MOORE, John, Pryor Creek, OK, 27

31639 MOORE, Katie, Muskogee, OK, 18

 4941 MOORE, Lee R, Fairland, OK: 30; Robert Lee, S, 5/6

 1745 MOORE, Lizzie, Estella, OK, 43; Wood, Rollin M, S, 17

22763 MOORE, Maggie, Muskogee, OK, 23

  964 MOORE, Mary, Fairland, OK, 76

27252 MOORE, Mary E, Dewey, OK, 31; Pearl M, D, 7; Monsieur, S, 3; Clarke S, S, ¼

23435 MOORE, Melvina S, Ray, OK, 21

11814 MOORE, Peggie A, Braggs, OK, 18

 5177 MOORE, Sabrina L, Vinita, OK, 32

16700 MOORE, Tennessee, McKey, OK, 37; Albert, S, 15; Troy, S, 13; Loony, S, 12; Charles, S, 11

 8088 MOORE, Thomas D, Stilwell, OK, 12;   By Charles W Moore, Gdn.

   50 MOORE, Thomas J, Verdigris, OK, 26

 1179 MOORE, William, Lometa, OK, 33; Susie, D, 16; John, S, 14; Eli, S, 4; Willie, S, 1

25431 MOORE, William A, Tahlequah, OK, 29; James Robert, S, 1

 5495 MOREHOUSE, Nora, Vinita, OK, 31; Helen, D, 12; Clarence A, S, 9; Katie M, D, 5

23214 MORELAND, Collins M, Stilwell, OK, 23; Ray H, S, ½

 4937 MORELAND, Ella L, Chelsea, OK, 33; Robert H, S, 10; Thomas M, S, 7; William R, S, 5; Joe Wade, S, 3; Mary E, S, ¼

23215 MORELAND, Martha J, Stilwell, OK,   29

 5594 MORELAND, Sarah J, Stilwell, OK, 63; 23213, Jessie M, D, 20

28166 MORGAN, Amanda P, Pryor Creek, OK, 21

31791 MORGAN, Annie M, Long, OK, 17

14772 MORGAN, Eli, Warner, OK, 20; Betty, Sis, 17;   By James Morgan, Gdn.

 3561 MORGAN, Elizabeth, Sallisaw, OK, 21

25476 MORGAN, Flora A, Eureka, OK, 22

 2759 MORGAN, Frank M, Ft. Smith, AR, 53

   18 MORGAN, Gideon, Pryor Creek, OK, 55; 27878, Sallie Mayo, D, 18; 18, Ellen P. M, D, 10

24821 MORGAN, Houston M, Muskogee, OK,   31; 40540, Birtha[sic] B, W, 28; Gideon I, S, 4; Houston L, S, 1

Key: Guion Miller Application Number; Name; Address, Relation (to Head); Age in 1906

25478 MORGAN, Jessie E, Eureka, OK, 21

20175 MORGAN, Julius W, Tahlequah, OK, 41; Elizabeth A, D, 8; Albert C, S, 6; Julius O, S, 4

14764 MORGAN, Llewellyn H, Tahlequah, OK, 21

27365 MORGAN, Lutitia, Braggs, OK, 21; George F, S, 3; Mary C, D, 1

27877 MORGAN, Margarett E. A, Pryor Creek, OK, 24

3726 MORGAN, Minnie F, Ft. Smith, AR, 18

7909 MORGAN, Olney S, Ft. Gibson, OK, 60; Samuel S, S, 15

1974 MORGAN, Ruth, Eureka, OK, 41; 25477, Elmira, D, 20; 6055, James, S, 18; Leslie Nichols, S, 14; John, S, 12; Mayes, S, 11; Josie, D, 9; Louis, S, 5; Florence, D, 3; Etta Mae, D, 1/12

4949 MORGAN, Sarah, Grove, OK, 54; Blevins, Ollie, D, 16

11928 MORGAN, Ellen, Oolagah, OK, 19

36597 MORLEY, Velma E, Green Ridge, MO, 26; Ella M, D, 1

30870 MORRIS, Augusta, Glenoak, OK, 27; Clarence E, S, 5; Lena J, D, 3

5382 MORRIS, Bessie R, Nowata, OK, 18

17 MORRIS, Charles L, Baptist, OK, 55; James L, S, 15; Bessie, D, 14; Benjamin A, S, 12; Grace P, D, 10; Goldie, S, 6; Lowen B, S, 2

25512 MORRIS, Cora, Pryor Creek, OK, 20; Oscar D, S, 1

4519 MORRIS, Dallas T, Nowata, OK, 6;   By Jennie E. Morris, Gdn.

17426 MORRIS, David, Vian, OK, 27

9920 MORRIS, E. Loyd, Stilwell, OK, 37; John, S, 16; William, S, 14; Noley, D, 11; Mollie, D, 8; Ella, D, 5; Gertrude, D, 2; James, S, 1/12

11884 MORRIS, Edna, Stilwell, OK, 18

1704 MORRIS, Eliza, Vinita, OK, 41; Colston, Cynthia, D, 16; Fannie, D, 11; Morris, William, S, 7

7948 MORRIS, Ella Moore, Oktaha, OK, 35; Stand Watie, S, 18; Harry, S, 15; Carrie, D, 13; Loyal, S, 10; Rebecca L, D, 8; Charles T, S, 6; Lincoln, S, 4

5636 MORRIS, Ellen F, Tahlequah, OK, 59

11753 MORRIS, Enoley, Stilwell, OK, 33; Thomas P, S, ¼

352 MORRIS, Frances E, Ballard, OK, 69

23147 MORRIS, Fred, Ballard, OK, 21

3538 MORRIS, George, Sallisaw, OK, 26

23139 MORRIS, Glove, Ballard, OK, 40; 23138, Gatsey, W, 37; 5318, Nick B, S, 18; Artie, D, 8; Roxie, D, 7; Sarah, D, 5

23184 MORRIS, Henry, Chance, OK, 42; 2218, Polly, W, 45; George, S, 19; Jeff, S, 17; Stella, D, 10

12804 MORRIS, Horra H, Tulsa, OK, 26

25289 MORRIS, Houston, Vian, OK, 8;   By Joseph Morris, Gdn.

40016 MORRIS, Hugh McElrath, Tahlequah, OK, 31

12510 MORRIS, Jennie, Muskogee, OK, 20

38556 MORRIS, Jennie, Vian, OK, 25; Phillips, Caroline, D, 8; Morris, Lulu, D, 2

Key: Guion Miller Application Number; Name; Address, Relation (to Head); Age in 1906

4520 MORRIS, Jennie E, Nowata, OK, 32; Nichols, Frank, S, 11; Morris, Dallas, S, 6; Oweda, D, 3

3539 MORRIS, John, Sallisaw, OK, 58; Lizzie, D, 8

11425 MORRIS, John, Edna, KS, 40; William O, S, 15; Rosa A, D, 11; Bessie J, D, 9; Ruby, D, 6

23146 MORRIS, John B, Ballard, OK, 47; 2229, Fannie, W, 39; Ben, S, 18; Burt, S, 15; Sadie B, D, 13; Kate, D, 11; Francis, S, 9; Olewa, D, 7; Clide, S, 3

7589 MORRIS, Jordan, Edna, KS, 33; Fay, D, 12; Irene, D, 10; Don, S, 8; Dallas, S, 5; Earl, S, 3; Lucile, D, ¼

3540 MORRIS, Joseph, Sallisaw, OK, 26

2070 MORRIS, Joseph, Stilwell, OK, 51; Marcus D. L, S, 19; Minnie E, D, 16; William A, S, 12; Cornelia Ann, D, 10; John A, S, 4; Theodore R, S, 1

[MORRIS, Jumbo. See #711] *(Note: entry separate from other family groups)*

4793 MORRIS, Katie, Tahlequah, OK, 18

2071 MORRIS, Land, Stilwell, OK, 40

8345 MORRIS, Lucy, Vian, OK, 26

539 MORRIS, Margaret, Wann, OK, 65

8344 MORRIS, Mary, Vian, OK, 23; 25290, Carl, S, 4; Justice, S, 2; Annie E, D, 1

9915 MORRIS, Mary John, Stilwell, OK, 15;   By E. Loyd Morris, Gdn.

32706 MORRIS, Mary T, Tahlequah, OK, 25

35267 MORRIS, Moses L, Keefeton, OK, 50; John W. S, 18; Charles T, S, 15; Delie M, D, 13; Myrtle M, D, 12; Jessie M, D, 11; Bertha L, D, 6; Annie L, D, 9; Claud D, S, 4; Maud C, D, 4; Pearl L, D, 2

23471 MORRIS, Osceola E, Ballard, OK, 23

23470 MORRIS, Pearl M, Ballard, OK, 19; Buster A, S, 1

11661 MORRIS, Richard, Braggs, OK, 24

23469 MORRIS, Robert L, Ballard, OK, 25

4808 MORRIS, Sallie, Tahlequah, OK, 15

36467 MORRIS, Savannah, Nowata, OK, 45; Rhodes, Edward, S, 17

[MORRIS, Susie I. See #4041]   *(Note: entries separate*
[MORRIS, Bonnie T. See #4041]   *from other family groups)*

2071 MORRIS, Thaddeus M, Row, OK, 49; Dee, S, 21; Minnie, D, 12; Myrtle, D, 16; Eliza, D, 8; John, S, 6; Cecil, S, 2

32705 MORRIS, Thomas F, Tahlequah, OK, 21

24393 MORRIS, Thomas R, Ballard, OK, 28;   Charley G, S, 1

3183 MORRIS, Victoria, Hay Fork, CA, 36; John Reginald, S, 7; Marion Adrien, S, 2

24034 MORRIS, Virge C, Ballard, OK, 36; Lou, D, 17; Minnie, D, 15; Willie, S, 15; Arthur, S, 13; Richard, S, 11; Sophia, D, 9; Gabe, S, 7; Dennis, S, 6; John, S, 4; Claud, S, ½

Key: Guion Miller Application Number; Name; Address, Relation (to Head); Age in 1906

[MORRIS, Watt. See #12552]   ⎤   *(Note: entries separate*
[MORRIS, Emma Yahola. See #12552]   ⎦   *from other family groups)*

18527 MORRIS, William G, Ashmeadows, NV, Longstreet's Ranch, 41

2072 MORRIS, Wilson E, Ballard, OK, 54; 1616, Polly, W, 47; Johnny, S, 17; Jesse E, S, 15; Margaret A, D, 11

17147 MORRISON, Annie E, Vinita, OK, 47; Elsie, D, 17; Ruth, D, 15; Bessie, D, 12; Henry Clinton, S, 10; LeRoy C, S, 7

24276 MORRISON, Blanche E. H, LosAngeles, 1570 W. Jefferson St, CA, 33

33824 MORRISON, Ella B, Chelsea, OK, 25

25914 MORRISON, Julia, Southwest City, MO, 21; Minnie C, D, 2

708 MORRISON, Susan K, Ochelata, OK, 40; Robert T, Jr, S, 19; Delila L, D, 18; Ellen C, D, 15; Claud A, S, 14; Angie L, D, 11; Dora V, D, 9; John O, S, 7; Cherry O, D, 2; Sherman W, S, 1

27714 MORROW, Bertha, Chetopa, KS, 29; Ruby Lee, D, 1/3

30005 MORROW, Maggie Lene, Centralia, OK, 26; James C, S, 9; Frederick L, S, 6; Leo, S, 5; Otto, S, 3; Roscoe, S, 1

6591 MORROW, Nancy, Muskogee, OK, 70

13426 MORTON, Drew, Long, OK, 22; William H, S, 1

[MORTON, Edna A. See #1837]   ⎤
[MORTON, Maud M. See #1837]   ⎟   *(Note: entries separate*
[MORTON, Lock. See #1837]   ⎟   *from other family groups)*
[MORTON, George. See #1837]   ⎦

13428 MORTON, Edward, Long, OK, 33; Mary E, D, 3

24461 MORTON, Jennie Olive, Bartlesville, Box 957, OK, 28; Catherine, D, 6

11978 MORTON, Joel J, Sallisaw, OK, 54; Robert L, S, 15; Grover C, S, 14; William H, S, 12; Mary B, D, 11; Flossie, D, 5; Junia C, D, 3; Maudie A, D, 1

28192 MORTON, John W, Long, OK, 30; Bessie B, D, 5; Dorothy M, D, 4; Walter E, S, 1

[MORTON, Louis and family. See #8758]
          (Note: entry separate from other family groups)

3864 MORTON, Mary A, Uniontown, AR, 35; Clara D, D, 12; Edna F, D, 5; John E, S, 2

8760 MORTON, Newton, Muldrow, OK, 51; George, S, 17; Rebecca, D, 16

28187 MORTON, Noah, Long, OK, 30; Bessie A, D, 4; Sterling L, S, 3; Willie, S, 1/12

15626 MORTON, Takey, Westville, OK, 60

5533 MOSE, September, Tahlequah, OK, 52

27881 MOSIER, Neva, Centralia, OK, 32; Grace M, D, 11; Iva L, D, 9; Chester S, S, 6; Esther, D, 4; John A, Jr, S, 1

Key: Guion Miller Application Number; Name; Address, Relation (to Head); Age in 1906

4150 MOSSER, Calidona, Pryor Creek, OK, 46; 25514, Emma, D, 19; 25513, Della, D, 18;4150, Minnie, D, 16; Roy, S, 14; Clinton, S, 10; Mamie, D, 6

25515 MOSSER, Eddie W, Pryor Creek, OK, 22

10689 MOTON, Clem C, Long, OK, 48; Andy M, S, 18; Bert E, S, 17

28191 MOTON, Jesse E, Long, OK, 20; Edgar M, S, 2; Golden O, D, 1

8758 MOTON, John H, Remy, OK, 52; Gatsey, D, 14; Frank, S, 12; Fred, S, 11

31793 MOTON, John W, Maple, OK, 31; Milan, S, 6; Clara E, D, 4; Zard, S, 1; Frank, S, ½

17604 MOTON, Robert P, Webbers Falls, OK, 28

23270 MOUNT, Alice, Hollow, OK, 19; Grace A, D, 1/3

24141 MOUNT, Emma L, Hollow, OK, 29; Mike, S, 8; Leta P, D, 5; John R, S, 3

766 MOUNTS, Ruth, Dewey, OK, 60?; Robert E. L, S, 15

7005 MOUSE, Abraham, Southwest City, MO, 33; 6992, Ol-ki-ni, W, 26; Emma, D, 8; Lila, D, 5; Mary, D, 3

[MOUSE, Blossom. See #1907]   *(Note: entries separate*
[MOUSE, Johnson. See #1907]   *from other family groups)*
[MOUSE, Sapsucker. See #1907]

646 MOUSE, Cornelius, Eucha, OK, 51; 606, Darkey, W, 57

660 MOUSE, John R, Spavinaw, OK, 21; 4291, Annie, W, 19

645 MOUSE, Lewis, Spavinaw, OK, 28; 5978, Mollie, W, 29; Jefferson, S, 3; John, S, 1

1713 MOUSE, Mary, Eucha, OK, 18

607 MOUSE, Peggy, Eucha, OK, 70

1184 MOUSE, Price, Eucha, OK, 20; 28060, Nancy, W, 20

9619 MOUSE, Sallie, Leach, OK, 28; Young Beaver, Katie, D, 3

8362 MOUSE, Sam, Eucha, OK, 48

627 MOUSE, Toney, Eucha, OK, 48; 605, Annie, W, 26; 608, Roll, S, 19; 1183, Sallie, D, 9; 605, Fencer, Nancy [Dakie], D of W, 5; 1185, Mouse, Lucy, D, 5; Baby, D, 1

649 MOUSE, Watt, Eucha, OK, 29; 16340, Nancy, W, 27; Aggie, D, 5; Lydia, D, 2

7983 MULCARE, Frederick E. R, Pensacola, OK, 32

7985 MULCARE, Nora, Pensacola, OK, 18; Sterling P, Bro, 14; Ella, Sis, 11;   By Mike Mulcare, Gdn.

7986 MULCARE, Thomas E, Mayes, OK, 33;   George F, S, 3

16547 MULKEY, Alonzo S, Warner, OK, 32; Cora W, D, 3; Nina Inez, D, 1

16546 MULKEY, Charles A, Warner, OK, 30; Clara E, D, 4; Ruby, D, 3

22810 MULKEY, James D, Ramona, OK, 45; James E, S, 20; Ernest, S, 17; Nat, S, 15; Eva E, D, 11; Eunis, S, 8; John R, S, 4; Mannon, S, 2; Mary S, D, 2

22811 MULKEY, John Ross, Ramona, OK, 25

16548 MULKEY, Jonathan D, Warner, OK, 25; 24361, Sallie, W, 22; Vann, Daisy, D of W, 6; Mulkey, Dennis E, S, 1

277 MULKEY, Lewis A, Fawn, OK, 72; Bulah Belle, GD, 5

16549 MULKEY, Lewis W, Warner, OK, 28

22808 MULKEY, Richard J, Ramona, OK, 29

17269 MULKEY, Rose E. C, Warner, OK, 20

2124 MULKEY, Wiley R, Warner, OK, 37; Lettie V, D, 8

239 MULKEY, William R, Ramona, OK, 69

12217 MULLEY, Ella T, Braggs, OK, 30

16858 MULLEY, Fannie, Braggs, OK, 19; Katie, D, 1

36463 MURPHY, Alva M, Big Cabin, OK, 22; Charles T, S, 3

1192 MURPHY, Anna, Sapulpa, OK, 33

31498 MURPHY, Augustus, Claremore, OK, 24; Mattie Louise, D, ¼

6564 MURPHY, Bird, Cherokee City, AR, 48; 6562, Jinny, W, 29; Mike, S, 13; Lila, D, 7; John, S, 2

193 MURPHY, Blue, Locust Grove, OK, 24; 42535, Louisa, W, 17;

30383 MURPHY, Byna, Claremore, OK, 20

42579 MURPHY, Charles, Long, OK, 24

21828 MURPHY, David C, Vinita, OK, 13; Gertrude O, Sis, 13; Joel, Bro, 10; William, Bro, 8;   By Robert Murphy, Gdn.

[MURPHY, Ellen. See #8916] ⎱   *(Note: entries separate*
[MURPHY, Eva. See #8916]   ⎰   *from other family groups)*

30382 MURPHY, Iris, Claremore, OK, 22

14061 MURPHY, Jackson, Locust Grove, OK, 51; 13259, Lizzie, D, 17

9692 MURPHY, Jenanna, Proctor, OK, 23; Pologne, Nancy, D, 2

1928 MURPHY, Jennie, Oaks, OK, 44; 9652, Robert, S, 14; 9653, Maria, D, 18; 9683, Sophie, D, 16

14193 MURPHY, Jennie, Bunch, OK, 27; Esther, D, 1

3261 MURPHY, Jessie C, Claremore, OK, 46; Oliver, S, 16; Wyche, S, 14; Sue, D, 11; Robert H, S, 3

30384 MURPHY,. Lillie, Claremore, OK, 18

9392 MURPHY, Ned, Bunch, OK, 20

2497 MURPHY, Nelson, Locust Grove, OK, 54; 13302, Lydia, W, 41; Canoe, Ben, S of W, 6; Louisa, D of W, 4

43903 MURPHY, Pearl, Coweta, OK, 20; Minnie, Sis, 17; Edna, Sis, 14;   By James B, White, Gdn.

28476 MURPHY, Sallie, Lowrey, OK, 27; Martha M, D, 8; Maggie F, D, 5; Willie C, S, 3; James H, S, 1

17800 MURPHY, Sarah R, Coweta, OK, 45

Key: Guion Miller Application Number; Name; Address, Relation (to Head); Age in 1906

[MURPHY, Watt. See #14271]   *(Note: entries separate*
[MURPHY, Emma (or Amy). See #14271]   *from other family groups)*

10225 MURPHY, William, Locust Grove, OK, 24
29218 MURRAY, Bertha, Chelsea, OK, 19
24354 MURRAY, Catherine, Welling, OK, 37; Robert N, S, 17; Lindley L, S, 14;
Mildred L, D, 8
16910 MURRAY, Elmo, Catoosa, OK, 26
37208 MURRAY, James, Muskogee, OK, 32; Jennie, D, 10; Lizzie, D, 7; Myrtle Belle,
D, 4
35108 MURRAY, John, Muskogee, OK, 28; Cleona, D, 3
17128 MURRAY, Lee, Catoosa, OK, 20; Ross, Bro, 16;   By Elmo Murray, Gdn.
37209 MURRAY, Malcolm, Muskogee, OK, 26; Zora, D, 3
11575 MURRAY, Nannie, Muskogee, OK, 54
13178 MURRAY, Sarah, Wagoner, OK, 28; Annie, D, 5; Charlie W, S, 3; John W, S, 1
12845 MURRELL, George Ross, Bayou Goula, LA, 45; Sarah G, D, 6; Amanda R, D, 1;
Margaret G, D, 1
11800 MURRELL, Jennie Ross, Bayou Goula,   LA, 69
11799 MURRELL, Lewis E, Bayou Goula, LA, 33; George M, S, 8; Richard C, S, 6
24894 MURRELL, Nora, Lenapah, OK, 22

[MUSGROVE, Cassie V. See #13366] *(Note: entry separate from other family groups)*

 7653 MUSH, Cicero, Stilwell, OK, 23; 7663, Eva, W, 37
12632 MUSH, Lucy, Wauhillau, OK, 20
11717 MUSH, Nannie, Rose, OK, 26
17548 MUSKRAT, Annie, Webbers Falls, OK, 12; Georgie, Sis, 10; Dawson [Dawes],
Bro, 6; Steve, Bro, 3;   By Susie Muskrat, Gdn.
12888 MUSKRAT, Arch, Warner, OK, 18; Narcie, Sis, 16; By Stephen M. McDaniel,
Gdn.
 8176 MUSKRAT, Daniel, Grove, OK, 36
 4735 MUSKRAT, Darkie, Evansville, AR, 75
 4945 MUSKRAT, David, Evansville, AR, 62; 16353, Polly, W, 62; Sawney, Anna,
GD, 8; Colonay, GD, 3
 1573 MUSKRAT, Henry, Kansas, OK, 20
16470 MUSKRAT, Jake Jackson, Southwest City, MO, 20
22051 MUSKRAT, James, Sacramento, CA, 49
 4327 MUSKRAT, James E, Grove, OK, 46; Maud, D, 15; Claud, S, 13; Arba A, S, 11;
Ruth, D, 9; Jewel, D, 7; Thelma, D, 5; Truman, S, 2
36099 MUSKRAT, John, Evansville, AR, 32; 16352, Mary, W, 33; Charlotte, D, 11
 5760 MUSKRAT, Joseph, Afton, OK, 55; Ira D, S, 9; Ruby, E, D, 8; Frank R, S, 4

Key: Guion Miller Application Number; Name; Address, Relation (to Head); Age in 1906

22051 MUSKRAT, Joseph A, Sacramento, CA, 17; Lee R, Bro, 15; Clyde, Bro, 12; George Dwight, Bro, 11; James W, Bro, 8; Odessa Alice, Sis, 3;   By Laura B, Muskrat, Gdn.

10152 MUSKRAT, Mack, Maysville, AR, 50; 19151, Archili, W, 35; Jesse, S, 16

5304 MUSKRAT, Nancy, Stilwell, OK, 65

22601 MUSKRAT, Nina P, Afton, OK, 21

17321 MUSKRAT, Susie, Webbers Falls, OK, 29

23201 MUSKRAT, Thomas, Webbers Falls, OK, 14;   By Ester Girty, Gdn.

8122 MUSKRAT, Thomas J, Grove, OK, 46

1717 MUSKRAT, Wilson, Webbers Falls, OK, 61; 1718, Sallie, W, 61

[MYERS, Andrew. See #4015]   *(Note: entry separate from other family groups)*

26542 MYERS, Lula, Collinsville, OK, 21; Elijah S, S, 3

24751 MYERS, Will Ella, Coodys Bluff, OK, 24

THE EASTERN CHEROKEES *vs* THE UNITED STATES

No. 23,214

Supplemental Roll of Eastern Cherokees

JANUARY 5, 1910

List of names to be added to and stricken from the original roll Eastern Cherokees as reported on May 28, 1909, as recommended by Guion Miller, Special Commissioner, in his supplemental report of January 5, 1910, together with certain clerical corrections to be made in the original roll.

SUPPLEMENTAL ROLL of
EASTERN CHEROKEES RESIDING WEST OF MISSISSIPPI RIVER.

Key: Guion Miller Application Number, Name, Address, Relation (to Head), Age in 1906.

ADAIR, Mintie, Nowata, OK, 21
ADAMS, Arthur T, Vinita, OK, 20
24238 ADKINSON, Ora B, Catoosa, OK, 22; Ella M, D, 1
AGENT, Sallie, Oaks, OK, 22

[ALBERTY, Allen. See Roll #30726] *(Note: Application number not given..)*

ALEXANDER, Lewis, Tahlequah, OK, 14   By Ross Daniels, Gdn.

[ALLEN, Clarence. See #21014]

43347 ANDERSON, John F, Eureka, OK, 25
ANDOE, Nellie C, Collinsville, OK, 17
5220 ARCHER, Anna B, Vinita, OK, 28; Ina, D, 8; Otto B, S, 6; Fannie B, D, 4;
Thomas B, Jr, S, 3; Abram, S, 1

BAILEY, Josie, Christie, OK, 21
BARBER, Peggie, Porum, OK, 60
10887 BARNETT, Bertha M, Flint, OK, 2   By Sarah F. Barnett, Mother and Gdn.
33091 BARNEY, Cordelia, Plateau, CA, 23
32271 BARRY, Billie B, Adair, OK, 15; 32272, Stella M, (Prob. Sis), 13   By Kidder S.
Barry, Father
36074 BASSETT, Henry, Cottonwood, CA, 26
21014 BASSETT, Nancy C, Cottonwood, CA, 56; Enos, Carrie, D, 18; Allen, Clarence,
GS, 4
BATT, Akie, Stilwell, OK, 44
BATT, Lizzie, Campbell, OK, 76 [Deceased.]   By Joseph Batt, Son.
1785 BEAN, Susan, Baron, OK, 56
6468 BECK, Daniel S, Needmore, OK, 19; Sut R, Bro, 16; Grace P, Sis, 9;   By
Arthur W. Beck, Brother and Gdn.
13365 BELL, Mattie M, Oolagah, OK, 41; Daniel H, S, 16; James E, Jr, S, 10; Pearl, D,
7; Mark R, S, 5; Irene, D, 3
BENGE, Young or Dooley, Sand Point, ID, 34; Young, Lawrence, S, 5; Arthur,
S, 2
BIGHAM, James M, Lewiston, ID, ?
14396 BIGHAM, Tolithia E, Redding, CA, 46; Pearl, D, 16; Edith, D, 14; Earl, S, 9
BIGHEART, Alice, Bigheart, OK, 34
44118 BISHOP, Fannie, Miles, OK, 36
BLACKBEAR, Nancy, Locust Grove, OK, 20
25814 BLAIR, Thomas W, Cookson, OK, 1   By Jesse T. Blair, Parent and Gdn.
BLOSSOM, Betsy, Locust Grove, OK, 26
8366 BOWERS, Ida, Tallahassee, OK, 45; Paul W, S, 5
BRYSON, Mary J, Stilwell, OK, 15; Williametta, Sis, 14   By Martha Duncan,
Grandmother.
BURKS, Elmer H, Vinita, OK, 22

Key: Guion Miller Application Number, Name, Address, Relation (to Head), Age in 1906.

BURROWS, Annie E, Claremore, OK, 16

BUTCHER, Ollie, Hulbert, OK, 17

11780 BUTLER, Robert E, Muskogee, OK, 40; Willie E, S, 9

BUTTON, Minnie, Watova, OK, 17; Ruth, D, 1

CABE, Kate, Proctor, OK, 24; Taylor, Lizzie, S, 9; Cabe, Marvin, S, 6

CABE, Marvin, S, 6

CAPS, Sersis, Westville, OK, 19

CAREY, Sarah A, Grove, OK, 33

CARR, Mary L, Ramona, OK, 48

CARR, Vida, Checotah, OK, 25; Lillian May, D, 5; Ollie Ponder, D, 4

CHAIR, Mary, Whitmire, OK, 8; Jones, Charlie, ½ Bro, 5   By Lohn(sic) Locust, Stepfather.

CHEWIE, Willie, Campbell, OK, 13   By Nancy Rodgers, Gdn.

CHRISTIE, Stand, Wauhillau, OK, 16; Rider, Charlotte, ½ Sis, 4;   By Sarah Rider, Gdn and Mother.

  900 COCHRAN, Scott, Hulbert, OK, 5   By Nellie David, Grandmother

COFFMAN, Jesse S, Fairland, OK, 4; Sequichie(sic) E, Bro, 3; Earl S, Bro, 1 By Cornelia J. Williams, Parent and Gdn.

COLLIER, Richard, Sallisaw, OK, 27

CORDERY, David S, Manard, OK, 14

44348 COUCH, Jesse T, Alluwee, OK, 37

CRITTENDEN, James, Baptist, OK, 6; Lacie, Lizzie, Sis, 1 By Betsy Suwake, Grandmother

CRITTENDEN, Walter S, Claremore, OK, 39

CRUTCHFIELD, Mary, Muskogee, OK, 21

[DAVID, Lucy and child. See #10194]

DEGE, Phillip S, Muskogee, OK, 22 907 N F Street

31336 DIXON, Francis M, Miami, OK, 25; Ruby Mae, D, 1

DOUTHITT, Cora E, Afton, OK, 16

DOWNING, Mary, Muldrow, OK, 38

EARLEY, Clara A, Checotah, OK, 26

EIBING, Marie H, Galena, KS, 26, 803 Short St.; Georgia S, S, 6; Frank A, S, 2; Gertrude M, D, 1

ELMORE, Mary, Brent, OK, 20

[ENOS, Carrie. See #21014]

ERCHBACH, Mae Ora, San Bernardino, 665 Arrowhead Ave. CA, ?

FARMER, William L, Checotah, OK, 24

SUPPLEMENTAL ROLL of
EASTERN CHEROKEES RESIDING WEST OF MISSISSIPPI RIVER.

Key: Guion Miller Application Number, Name, Address, Relation (to Head), Age in 1906.

[FIELDS, Cora W. See #24140]

FITE, Houston B, Tahlequah, OK, 21
12519 FLYING, Linda A, Oglesby, OK, 10; Jessie J, ?, 8   By Rebecca Minew, Parent
and Gdn.

[FREELAND, Martha C. See #2713]

GENTRY, Kizzie, Tyrone, OK, 25; William F, S, 6; Henry L, S, 3; George D, S,
2
GETTINGDOWN, Betsy, Stilwell, OK, 30; Holmes Simon, AdS, 13
44946 GILBERT, Dennis B, Muskogee, OK, 24
GIRTY, Jacob, Porum, OK, 4   By Nancy Toney, Parent and Gdn.
GOINS, Noble, Vian, OK, 26
24235 GRAVITT, Addie, Catoosa, OK, 17
24236 GRAVITT, Alice, Catoosa, OK, 19
GRAVITT, Esther D, Catoosa, OK, 10   By Ella Gravitt, Gdn.
24234 GRAVITT, Eula, Catoosa, OK, 13   By Ella Gravitt, Gdn.
24237 GRAVITT, Lillie P, Catoosa, OK, 20
24239 GRAVITT, Luther O, Catoosa, OK, 23
GREEN, Jennie M, Stilwell, OK, 20
GRITTS, Daniel, Tahlequah, OK, 19; Charlie, Bro, 17; Cahnundeski, Sis, 15;
Teesuyahkee, Sis, 11   By Sarah Gritts, Parent and Gdn.
GRITTS, Florence, Braggs, OK, 21
GUINN, Bell, Ahniwake, OK, 17

43630 HARLIN, James R, Quapaw, OK, 23
54588 HARLIN, Lewis S, Quapaw, OK, 30
28342 HARRISON, Susan E, Warner, OK, 28; Edward, S, 1
24285 HARTNESS, Josie, Tahlequah, OK, 14   By Octavia Hartness, Parent and Gdn.
HEARTLY, Mary, Vian, OK, 30

[HEFLIN, Ada. See #23243]

HENRY, Benjamin L, Claremore, OK, 18
HENRY, Florence A, Claremore, OK, 16 [Deceased] By Eddie E. Rector, Adm.
20210 HENSON, Bessie, Vinita, OK, 14
HIBBS, Maggie M, Estella, OK, 16; Sarah J, Sis, 14; Leona E, Sis, 11   By
Mary A. Hibbs, Parent and Gdn.
HILDEBRAND, Joe, Estella, OK, 26
HILDEBRAND, Linda, Peggs, OK, 9; Rowe, Alice, Sis, 5   By C. C. Manus,
Gdn.

[HILL, Louisa S. See #16432]

SUPPLEMENTAL ROLL of
EASTERN CHEROKEES RESIDING WEST OF MISSISSIPPI RIVER.

Key: Guion Miller Application Number, Name, Address, Relation (to Head), Age in 1906.

HINES, Frank, Wann, OK, 22

15969 HINMAN, Vinita Frances, Las Animas, CO, D, 4   By Anna B. Hinman, Mother.

HOGNER, Nancy, Stilwell, OK, 31

[HOLMES, Simon. See Roll #30600]   *(Note: Application number not given.)*

28312 HOOVERMALE, William, Pryor Creek, OK, 19   By Mary A. Hoovermale, Parent and Gdn.

HORN, Narcie, Vian, OK, 8   By Bettie McCoy, Parent and Gdn.

24697 HOSEA, Tim, Locust Grove, OK, 25

17052 HOWELL, Juliette Smith, Ft. Gibson, OK, 23

23518 HUGHES, Icie V, Stilwell, OK, 1   By Theodocia Hughes, Parent and Gdn.

ISAACS, Agent, Locust Grove, OK, 16   By Mary Sanders, Parent and Gdn.

ISBELL, Charles T, Vinita, OK, 6; Harold Cleo, Bro, 3; Clifford LeRoy, Bro, 1
By Morris F. Isbell, Parent and Gdn.

24158 ISRAEL, Philip, Braggs, OK, 14; Mary or Nellie, (S?), 12   [Children of #12814 (John Israel)]

JERNIGAN, Elde E, Madill, OK, 4   By Drusilla A. Jernigan, Mother and Gdn.

[JOHNSON, Alice R. See #31367]

1379 JOHNSON, Henry, Tahlequah, OK, 18   By Cicero Johnson, Father and Gdn.

22612 JOHNSON, Henry A, Tahlequah, OK, 15; Joseph F, Bro, 13; Charles P, Bro, 10
By Rebecca A. Johnson, Parent and Gdn.

[JONES, Charlie. See Roll #30564]   *(Note: Application number not given.)*

JORDAN, Fary A, Glydeville, MO, 18

31410 JORDAN, John C, Muskogee, OK, 43; Herbert R, S, 12; Roy C, S, 10

[JOREE. (See) JOEREE and JESSON.]

KEENER, Lizzie, Hulbert, OK, 26

16160½ KEYS, Levi, Porter, OK, 46; Carrie M, D, 16; Herbert G, S, 11; Carl L, S, 9;
Cora E, D, 4

KIDD, Crecie L, Warner, OK, 30

KILLER, David, Marble City, OK, 8   By Sallie Walkingstick, Mother and Gdn.

32023 KIRKSEY, James F, Bower Mills, MO, 44; Charles P, S, 17; George W, S, 16;
William T, S, 14; Jeffy F, S, 12; Fanny B, D, 10; Beula G, D, 5; Finis W, S, 2;
Elton, S, 1

KLEIN, Mary E, Ft. Smith, AR, 22

SUPPLEMENTAL ROLL of
EASTERN CHEROKEES RESIDING WEST OF MISSISSIPPI RIVER.

Key: Guion Miller Application Number, Name, Address, Relation (to Head), Age in 1906.

KNAPP, Clara E, Camas, WA, 21

[KNIPPENBERG, Mollie. See #11011]

KNOWLES, Ethel A, Tahlequah, OK, 16

[LACIE, Lizzie. See Roll #30576]   *(Note: Application number not given.)*

10748 LATTA, Mary F, Porum, OK, 12; Felix, Bro, 10; Samuel, ½ Bro, 3   By Felix Latte, Parent and Gdn.

[LENOIR, Thomas R. See #13206]

17676 LEPHEW, Charles C, Muskogee, OK, 5   By Robert E. Lephew, Parent and Gdn.
12830 LEWIS, Hettie, Chetopa, KS, 27; Grace E, D, 3; Ira A, D, 1

19190 LIZZARD, Dudie, Gritts, OK, 59
       LOCUST, Maggie, Tulsa, OK, 24
24841 LOVE, John Ella, Chelsea, OK, 23; Samuel Drake, S, 2
       LOWERY, Carrie M, Wann, OK, 25
13523 LYNCH, Ellen, Ft. Gibson, OK, 57

11287 McCAFFREE, Bradley D, Ramona, OK, 5; Barton A, Bro, 3; Laura V, Sis, 1
       By Czarina V. McCaffree, Mother and Gdn.

       MANLEY, Minnie W, Claremore, OK, 23; Charles Lawrence, S, 3
11485 MARTIN, Daniel, Sallisaw, OK, 46
       MARTIN, Enos Q, Los Angeles, CA, 34; 1917½ E. 14th St.
43704 MARTIN, Harvey C, Banning, CA, 36
23787 MARTIN, Joysoline, Bluejacket, OK, 6; Mary E, D(sic), 5; Dorothy L, D(sic), 2
       By Florence Martin, Parent and Gdn.
11662 MARTIN, Richard, Braggs, OK, 48; Octavia, D, 13; Sanford M, S, 8
11486 MARTIN, Thomas, Sallisaw, OK, 32; Lora, D, 7; Phronia, D, 3
22644 MARTIN, Walter A, Blunt, OK, 24
25594 MARTIN, William A.H, Braggs, OK, 21
44080 MARTIN, William W, San Bernardino, CA, 48
       MAYES, Mary L, Pryor Creek, OK, 29
       MAYFIELD, William W, Muldrow, OK, 14   By D. M. Patton, Gdn.
 5223 MEEK, William A, Vinita, OK, 26
 7580 MEIGS, James R, Park Hill, OK, 21 [Deceased.]   By Return R. Meigs, Parent and Gdn.

[MERCER, Etta M, See #32250]

Key: Guion Miller Application Number, Name, Address, Relation (to Head), Age in 1906.

44793 MILLER, Beatrice, Braggs, OK, 11;   By A. C. Collier, Gdn.

MILLER, Cornelius B, Needmore, OK, 22
MOATS, Bertha, Hulbert, OK, 15
MOORE, Walter F, Pryor Creek, OK, 23
MULKEY, James D, Warner, OK, 29
MULKEY, Julia, Warner, OK, 35
13261 MURPHY, Lizzie, Marble, OK, 10   By James L. Murphy, Parent and Gdn.
27254 MURPHY, Thomas, Metory, OK, 43, Sallie, D, 16, Looney, S, 13, Jesse, S, 7,
Thomas J, S, 1

NELSON, Roxie D, Oolagah, OK, 28; Robbins, William O, S, 12; Alberty,
Allen, S, 9

OLDFIELD, Fannie, Kansas, OK, 25

PALONE, Nona B, Lenapah, OK, 7   By Lacie R. Palone, Parent and Gdn.
25983 PARIS, Sirena, Braggs, OK, 17
24974 PARKS, Jennie B, Vinita, OK, 6   By Samuel F. Parks, Parent and Gdn.
44023 PARRIS, Mose, Rose, OK, 21
PARTIN, Everett T, Oklahoma City, OK 1415 R. North Broadway, 7   By
William T. Partin, Parent and Gdn.
PAYNE, Valzie E, Lofton, LA, 25

[PENINGTON, Josephine. See #41797]

[PERDUE, Ada E. See Roll #30755]   *(Note: Application number not given.)*

[PERDUE, William H. See #30756]   *(Note: Application number not given.)*

PHILLIPS, Jessie D, Baxter Springs, KS, 25; Volney, D, 5; Archie, S, 1
PHILLIPS, Macajah H, Jr, Nowata, OK, 21
POLSON, Martin, Coffeyville, KS, 9; Mattie, D, 6; Earl S, 5; John W, S, 3;
Charley, S, 1   By Kellie Polson, Mother and Gdn.
PRATHER, Elizabeth, Foyil, OK, 17
PRATHER, George E, Claremore, OK, 19
PRATHER, John E, Claremore, OK, 22 [Deceased] By G. W. Spann, Adm.
PRICE, Esther L, Uvalde, TX, 7; Bunyon M, Bro, 3 By David W. Price, Parent
and Gdn.
PUMPKIN, Betsy, Tahlequah, OK, 12; Sparrowhawk, Maggie, Sis, 7   By
Annie Stopp Standingdeer, Mother

RAMSEY, Rebecca, Tyrone, OK, 27
3649 RAPER, Harley, Durant, OK, 21 [Incompetent.]   By Berry Raper, Father

SUPPLEMENTAL ROLL of
EASTERN CHEROKEES RESIDING WEST OF MISSISSIPPI RIVER.

Key: Guion Miller Application Number, Name, Address, Relation (to Head), Age in 1906.

RAPER, Margaret, Pryor Creek, OK, 10   By Vida Raper, Mother and Gdn.

[RIDER, Charlotte. See Roll #30567]   *(Note: Application number not given.)*

ROACH, Thomas, Muskogee, OK, 27

[ROBBINS, William O. See Roll #30725]   *(Note: Application number not given.)*

ROBINSON, Etta, Tulsa, OK, 31; Perdue, Ada E, D, 14; William H, S, 13
RODGERS, Bettie, Braggs, OK, 16
ROGERS, Charley, Braggs, OK, 18; Cynthia, Sis, 17; Laura, Sis, 16   By
Missouri E. Rogers, Parent and Gdn.
15621 ROGERS, Frederic E, Claremore, OK, 22
15620 ROGERS, Iola, Claremore, OK, 41
ROGERS, Lovely, Campbell, OK, 16   By William Rogers, Father and Gdn.
 9178 ROGERS, Walter S, Claremore, OK, 35; Camille, D, 4; Kenneth S, S, 3

[ROOKER (or RUCKER), Josie. See #30655]

ROSS, Jess, Coffeyville, KS, 26 [Deceased.]   By Maria Ross, Adm.

44945 ROSS, Maud W, Muskogee, OK, 32 438 North 13th St.
ROSS, Sarah, Locust Grove, OK, 27

[ROWE, Alice. See #30631]   *(Note: Application number not given.)*

 4055 RUNYON, Robert C, Ft. Gibson, OK, 3; Thomas J, Bro, 1   By Robert Runyon,
Father

SANDERS, James M, Stilwell, OK, 21
10715 SANDERS, Thomas D, Braggs, OK, 32
SAWNEY, Columbus, Stilwell, OK, 51
SCOBEY, Floyd L, Sapulpa, OK, 6
23468 SCOTT, Elizabeth F, Warner, OK, 18
 9175 SEABOLT, James, Hanson, OK, 22
SEABOLT, Sallie, Muldrow, OK, 32
26697 SIX, John W, Southwest City, MO, 16   By William H. Martin, Stepfather
34330 SMITH, Edwin B, Braggs, OK, 28
11424 SMITH, Elizabeth J, Braggs, OK, 51; Junie, S, 14; Jennie, D, 11

[SMITH, Juliette. See Roll #30634]   *(Note: Application number not given.)*

32096 SMITH, Juliette T, Braggs, OK, 24
32088 SMITH, Mae, Braggs, OK, 18

32097 SMITH, Mannie G, Braggs, OK, 21
19605 SMITH, Roach Young, Keefeton, OK, 14; Annie, Sis, 12; Jennie, Sis, 10
By Frank Smith, Gdn.
SMITH, Samuel, Keefeton, OK, 16
SMITH, Susan, Keefeton, OK, 16
42288 SMITH, Walter, Braggs, OK, 26
40066 SMITH, Wilson N, Braggs, OK, 22
SPANN, Josphine, Claremore, OK, 14

[SPARROWHAWK, Maggie. See Roll #30749] *(Note: Application number not given.)*

SPLITLOG, Myrtle, Grove, OK, 16
SPRINGWATER, Pollie, Sallisaw, OK, 15

[STANDINGDEER, Annie Stop. See #21029]

STARR, Lucinda, Grove, OK, 27
STARR, Saphronia, Stilwell, OK, 43
4727 STEEL, Sarah, Ramona, OK, 23
16967 STEWART, Margaret A, Welch, OK, 31; James Austin, S, 8; John W, S, 6;
Nancy J, D, 4; Land, S, 2
STILL, Edward, Jr, Tahlequah, OK, 21
9762 STILL, Elias, Oktaha, OK, B of #16003 (Martha McDowell), 17 By Jane Still,
Mother
20235 STILWELL, Sarah E, Cushing, OK, 25
5069½ STONE, Foster, Oolagah, OK, 19
24838 STRANGE, Mary B, Chelsea, OK, 28; Mary E, D, 12; John D, S, 8; Janie A, D,
6; Ella, D, 5; Lula, E, D, 2
STROUP, Edward L, Inola, OK, 20
4873 STUDY, Polly, Southwest City, MO, 16
SUNDAY, George, Porum, OK, 27
SUNDAY, Izora, Porum, OK, 21
SUNDAY, James, Porum, OK, 23
SUWAT, Margaret, Honey Creek, OK, 20

43184 TAFT, Asa S, Roland, OK, 17; Nellie H, Sis, 16; Sherman W, Bro, 14; Stanley
B, Bro, 10; Daniel E, Bro, 8 By J. J. Spencer, Gdn.
33484 TAFT, Austin K, Roland, OK, 21
33483 TAFT, Clarence A, Roland, OK, 25
TALBERT, Arna, Newport, WA, 21
TANNER, Nancy, Eucha, OK, 11; Peter, Bro, 10 By Leander Vann,
Grandmother
TAYLOR, Clinton Roger, McKay, OK, 3; Sequoyah Gordon, Bro, 2
By John Taylor, Parent and Gdn.

Key: Guion Miller Application Number, Name, Address, Relation (to Head), Age in 1906.

[TAYLOR, Lizzie. See #11780]

27496 THOMPSON, Laura, Valeda, KS, 9 By William E. Thompson, Parent and Gdn.
THOMPSON, Lois, Taylor, TX, 22
8950½ THORNTON, Polly, Baron, OK, 27; Watt, Edna, D, 7

[TILLEY, Oma. See #27357]

TONEY, Nancy, Porum, OK, 21

[TOOKAH. See #14099]

TOONIGE, (No other name), Adair, OK, [Deceased]; 64 By J. E. Smith, Adm.
18540 TYNER, Amy E, St. Joe, AR, 12; Jesse, Bro, 10 By Nancy Tyner Scott, Gdn.
TYNER, Daniel, N.F.H.C, Vian, OK, 36

VANN, William, Lofton, LA, 22
VICTOR, Delilah C, Tahlequah, OK, 37; Octa Lucile, D, 15; Fred Samuel, S,
13; James Y, S, 10; Sadoe, D, 9; Gladys, D, 7

WAKEFIELD, Iva May, Bishop, CA, 26
34149 WALKABOUT, Henry, Jr, Tahlequah, OK, 23
36158 WALKABOUT, Joseph, Tahlequah, OK, 26
42689 WALKABOUT, Levi, Inola, OK, 20
WATERS, Albert, Long, OK, 31
16194 WATSON, Homer, Vineyard, TX, 8 By Emma Crutchfield, Gdn.
WATT, Charley, Baron, OK, 31

[WATT, Edna. See #8950½]

WATT. Jennie, Baron, OK, 15
8956 WATT, Rosa, Westville, OK, 2 By Nannie Watt, Gdn.
WAYNE, John, Stilwell, OK, 25
WEIR, Brack C, Vinita, OK, 21
11750 WELLS, Effie M, Inola, OK, 32 By Volnie E. Wells, Committee
WESSON, George N, McKay, OK, 6; Virginia, Sis, 4; Wiley A, Bro, 1 By
Catherine Wesson, Mother and Gdn.
WHALEN, Eliza, Tahlequah, OK, 26
1847 WHITMIRE, Roy C, Westville, OK, 6; Reginald H, Bro, 2 By Eli H.
Whitmire, Father and Gdn.
WHITNEY, Mack W, Adair, OK, 21
WITT, Dee, Okoee, OK, 15 By William F. Witt, Gdn.
44280 WITT, William F, Vinita, OK, 37
25984 WOODS, Anna M, Braggs, OK, 24; Amos R, S, 4; Cornelius M. H, S, 1

Key: Guion Miller Application Number, Name, Address, Relation (to Head), Age in 1906.

[WOODS, Laura S. See #7876]

WOODWARD, Viola, Braggs, OK, 32; Jennie, D ?, 1
WRIGHT, Annie, Southwest City, MO, 30

[YOUNG, Amy. See #6689]

YOUNGBLOOD, Annie B, Kilgore, R.F.D. #4   TX, 28

THE FOLLOWING NAMES, ORIGINALLY ENROLLED AS ENTITLED TO PARTICIPATE IN THE FUND, ORDERED BY THE COURT OF CLAIMS TO BE STRICKEN FROM THE ROLL OF MAY 28, 1909.

Key: Guion Miller Application Number, Name, Address, Relation (to Head), Age in 1906.

31260 GOBLE, James, Albertville, AL, 21   [Duplicate]

15704 SMITH, Jessie, Cherokee, NC, 14; Mandy, ?, 11; Martha, ?, 10

 3721 ADAIR, May E, Stilwell, OK, 17; George W, Bro, 15; Samuel W, Bro, 13; Lula E, Sis, 11; Lilly E, Sis, 8   [Duplicates]

41210 CHANDLER, William P, Tahlequah, OK, 35

28252 JORDAN, Felix R, Collinsville, OK, 17   [Duplicate]
36166 JORDAN, Mollie, Collinsville, OK, 15   [Duplicate]

37062 KRIGBAUM, James A, Coweta, OK, 7   [Duplicate]

12530 LOWERY, Susie, Muskogee, OK, 17; Elsie J, Sis, 14; Andrew, Bro, 12; Henry C, Bro, 7   [Duplicates]
12892 LYNCH, Nancy E, Bunch, OK, 1   [Duplicate]

13701 MABRY, Sallie B, Briertown, OK, 47

40048 RYAN, Emmett, Proctor, OK, 10; Calvin, ?, 8; William, ?, 5   [Duplicates]

34463 SCALES, Mattie, Flint, OK, 38; Grover, S, 17; Joseph, S, 15; Lillie, D, 12; Louisa, D, 10; George, S, 7; Ann L, D, 3; Mary E, D, 5/12
11862 SMITH, Lee, Braggs, OK, 17; Arch, Bro, 14; Mattie, Sis, 11   [Duplicates]
31995 STEWART, Celina K, Grove, OK, 60
31998 STEWART, George W, Bluejacket, OK, 24
31996 STEWART, John H, Bluejacket, OK, 34; Max, S, 6
31997 STEWART, William W, Grove, OK, 31
 8233 SWEANEY, John T, Eugene, MO, 32
  175 SWIMMER, Louisa, Rose, OK, 17   [Duplicate]

13564 VICTORY, Samuel, Collinsville, OK 19; Charles, Bro, 17; Susan, Sis, 15; Andrew, Bro, 13; Anna A, Sis, 10; Donney, Sis, 9; Tensy, Sis, 20 [Duplicates]

 3005 WATERS, Polly, Cleveland, TN, 71
 5011 WILLIAMS, Louisa, Tyro, KS, 55   [Duplicate]